Kaplan Publishing are constantly fir~~~~
ways to make a difference to your st~~~~
exciting online resources really do c~~~~
different to students looking for exa~~~~

CW00456340

This book comes with free MyKaplan online resources so that you can study anytime, anywhere. This free online resource is not sold separately and is included in the price of the book.

Having purchased this book, you have access to the following online study materials:

CONTENT	ACCA (including FFA,FAB,FMA)		FIA (excluding FFA,FAB,FMA)	
	Text	Kit	Text	Kit
Eletronic version of the book	✓	✓	✓	✓
Check Your Understanding Test with instant answers	✓			
Material updates	✓	✓	✓	✓
Latest official ACCA exam questions*		✓		
Extra question assistance using the signpost icon**		✓		
Question debriefs using clock icon***		✓		
Consolidation Test including questions and answers	✓			

* Excludes AB, MA, FA, LW, FAB, FMA and FFA; for all other subjects includes a selection of questions, as released by ACCA

** For ACCA SBR, AFM, APM, AAA only

*** Excludes AB, MA, FA, LW, FAB, FMA and FFA

How to access your online resources

Kaplan Financial students will already have a MyKaplan account and these extra resources will be available to you online. You do not need to register again, as this process was completed when you enrolled. If you are having problems accessing online materials, please ask your course administrator.

If you are not studying with Kaplan and did not purchase your book via a Kaplan website, to unlock your extra online resources please go to www.mykaplan.co.uk/addabook (even if you have set up an account and registered books previously). You will then need to enter the ISBN number (on the title page and back cover) and the unique pass key number contained in the scratch panel below to gain access.

You will also be required to enter additional information during this process to set up or confirm your account details.

If you purchased through Kaplan Flexible Learning or via the Kaplan Publishing website you will automatically receive an e-mail invitation to MyKaplan. Please register your details using this email to gain access to your content. If you do not receive the e-mail or book content, please contact Kaplan Publishing.

Your Code and Information

This code can only be used once for the registration of one book online. This registration and your online content will expire when the final sittings for the examinations covered by this book have taken place. Please allow one hour from the time you submit your book details for us to process your request.

Please scratch the film to access your MyKaplan code.

Please be aware that this code is case-sensitive and you will need to include the dashes within the passcode, but not when entering the ISBN. For further technical support, please visit www.MyKaplan.co.uk

ACCA

Applied Skills

Performance Management (PM)

EXAM KIT

British Library Cataloguing-in-Publication Data

A catalogue record for this book is available from the British Library.

Published by:

Kaplan Publishing UK

Unit 2 The Business Centre

Molly Millar's Lane

Wokingham

Berkshire

RG41 2QZ

ISBN: 978-1-78740-102-0

Acknowledgements

These materials are reviewed by the ACCA examining team. The objective of the review is to ensure that the material properly covers the syllabus and study guide outcomes, used by the examining team in setting the exams, in the appropriate breadth and depth. The review does not ensure that every eventuality, combination or application of examinable topics is addressed by the ACCA Approved Content. Nor does the review comprise a detailed technical check of the content as the Approved Content Provider has its own quality assurance processes in place in this respect.

The past ACCA examination questions are the copyright of the Association of Chartered Certified Accountants. The original answers to the questions from June 1994 onwards were produced by the examiners themselves and have been adapted by Kaplan Publishing.

We are grateful to the Chartered Institute of Management Accountants and the Institute of Chartered Accountants in England and Wales for permission to reproduce past examination questions. The answers have been prepared by Kaplan Publishing.

CONTENTS

	Page
Index to questions and answers	P.5
Analysis of past exams	P.11
Exam Technique	P.12
Exam specific information	P.14
Kaplan's recommended revision approach	P.17
Kaplan's detailed revision plan	P.21
Formulae	P.26

Section

1	Objective Test Questions – Section A	1
2	Objective Test Case Study Questions – Section B	69
3	Constructed Response Questions – Section C	109
4	Answers to Objective Test Questions – Section A	177
5	Answers to Objective Test Case Study Questions – Section B	215
6	Answers to Constructed Response Questions – Section C	241
7	Specimen Exam Questions	405
8	Answers to Specimen Exam Questions	423

Key features in this edition

In addition to providing a wide ranging bank of practice questions, we have also included in this edition:

- An analysis of all of the recent examinations.

- Exam-specific information and advice on exam technique.

- Our recommended approach to make your revision for this particular subject as effective as possible.

- This includes step by step guidance on how best to use our Kaplan material (Study text, pocket notes and exam kit) at this stage in your studies.

- Enhanced tutorial answers packed with specific key answer tips, technical tutorial notes and exam technique tips from our experienced tutors.

- Complementary online resources including full tutor debriefs to point you in the right direction when you get stuck

You will find a wealth of other resources to help you with your studies on the following sites:

www.MyKaplan.co.uk

www.**acca**global.com/students/

Quality and accuracy are of the utmost importance to us so if you spot an error in any of our products, please send an email to mykaplanreporting@kaplan.com with full details.

Our Quality Co-ordinator will work with our technical team to verify the error and take action to ensure it is corrected in future editions.

INDEX TO QUESTIONS AND ANSWERS

INTRODUCTION

Following the introduction of the revised exam format, all previous ACCA constructed response (long) exam questions within this kit have been adapted.

The specimen exam is included at the end of the kit.

KEY TO THE INDEX

EXAM ENHANCEMENTS

We have added the following enhancements to the answers in this exam kit:

Key answer tips

All answers include key answer tips to help your understanding of each question.

Tutorial note

Many answers include more tutorial notes to explain some of the technical points in more detail.

Top tutor tips

For selected questions, we 'walk through the answer' giving guidance on how to approach the questions with helpful 'tips from a top tutor', together with technical tutor notes.

These answers are indicated with the 'footsteps' icon in the index.

Within the questions in the exam kit you will see the following icons, shown in the question requirements:

= word processing

= spreadsheet

The icons highlighting the constructed response workspace tool alongside some of the questions are for guidance only – it is important to recognise that each question is different and that the answer space provided by ACCA in the exam is determined by both the technical content of the question as well as the quality assurance processes ACCA undertakes to ensure the student is provided with the most appropriate type of workspace.

ONLINE ENHANCEMENTS

 *Question debrief*

For selected questions, we recommend that they are to be completed in full exam conditions (i.e. properly timed in a closed book environment).

In addition to the examiner's technical answer, enhanced with key answer tips and tutorial notes in this exam kit, online you can find an answer debrief by a top tutor that:

- works through the question in full

- points out how to approach the question

- shows how to ensure that the easy marks are obtained as quickly as possible, and

- emphasises how to tackle exam questions and exam technique.

These questions are indicated with the 'clock' icon in the index.

Online answer debriefs will be available on MyKaplan at:
www.MyKaplan.co.uk

SECTION A – OBJECTIVE TEST QUESTIONS

Page number

	Question	*Answer*

SPECIALIST COST AND MANAGEMENT ACCOUNTING TECHNIQUES

	Question	Answer
Activity-based costing	1	177
Target costing	6	180
Lifecycle costing	8	181
Throughput accounting	11	182
Environmental accounting	14	184

DECISION-MAKING TECHNIQUES

	Question	Answer
Relevant cost analysis	15	185
Cost volume profit analysis	19	187
Limiting factors	25	190
Pricing decisions	28	192
Make-or-buy and other short term decisions	31	194
Dealing with risk and uncertainty in decision-making	33	195

BUDGETING AND CONTROL

	Question	Answer
Budgetary systems	36	196
Types of budget	37	197
Quantitative analysis in budgeting	40	198
Standard costing	42	201
Material mix and yield variances	44	201
Sales mix and quantity variances	48	203
Planning and operational variances	50	205
Performance analysis and behavioural aspects	52	206

PERFORMANCE MEASUREMENT AND CONTROL

	Question	Answer
Performance management information systems	53	206
Sources of management information	54	207
Management reports	55	207
Performance analysis in private sector organisations	56	208
Divisional performance and transfer pricing	60	210
Performance analysis in not-for-profit organisations and the public sector	65	213
External considerations and behavioural aspects	67	213

SECTION B – OBJECTIVE TEST CASE STUDY QUESTIONS

SPECIALIST COST AND MANAGEMENT ACCOUNTING TECHNIQUES

		Page number		
		Question	Answer	Past exam (Adapted)
206	Duff Co	69	215	June 2014 (A)
207	Beckley Hill	71	217	June 2015
208	Bowd	73	218	
209	Helot Co	74	219	Sept 2016
210	Chemical Free Clean Co	76	220	Dec 2015
211	Shoe Co	77	221	June 2016
212	Sweet Treats Bakery	79	221	Dec 2016

DECISION-MAKING TECHNIQUES

213	Sip Co	81	223	
214	Hare Events	83	224	Dec 2016
215	Cardio Co	85	224	Dec 2015
216	Beft Co	88	226	
217	ALG Co	90	227	June 2015
218	Jewel Co	91	229	June 2016
219	Gam Co	93	230	June 2014

BUDGETING AND CONTROL

220	Mylo	94	231	Sept 2016
221	LRA	96	232	June 2015
222	Bokco	98	233	June 2015
223	Corfe Co	100	234	Sept 2016
224	OBC	102	235	Dec 2015
225	Variances – sales	103	237	
226	Romeo Co	104	238	Dec 2016

PERFORMANCE MEASUREMENT AND CONTROL

| 227 | Pind Co | 106 | 239 | |

SECTION C – CONSTRUCTED RESPONSE QUESTIONS

SPECIALIST COST AND MANAGEMENT ACCOUNTING TECHNIQUES

			Page number		
			Question	Answer	Past exam (Adapted)
228	Gadget Co		109	241	*Dec 2010*
229	Brick by Brick		110	244	*June 2010*
230	Jola Publishing Co		111	246	*June 2008*
231	Abkaber plc		113	250	
232	Lifecycle costing		114	253	
233	Manpac		114	255	
234	Wargrin		115	258	*Dec 2008*
235	Edward Co		116	262	*Dec 2007*
236	Yam Co		119	269	*June 2009*
237	FloPro plc		120	272	
238	Environmental Management Accounting		121	274	
239	Chocolates are forever (CAF)		122	275	
240	Mango Leather		122	279	
241	Breakeven		123	281	
242	EC Ltd		124	282	

DECISION MAKING TECHNIQUES

243	B Chemicals		125	283	
244	Cosmetics Co		125	285	*Dec 2010*
245	Cut and Stitch		127	287	*June 2010*
246	CSC Co		128	290	*Sept 2016*
247	Bits and pieces		130	293	*June 2009*
248	Stay Clean		131	296	*Dec 2009*
249	Choice of contracts		132	298	
250	HS Equation		134	299	
251	MKL		135	301	
252	Hammer		136	302	*June 2010*
253	Sniff Co		136	304	*Dec 2007*
254	Furnival		138	308	
255	Man Co		139	310	*June 2016*
256	Recyc		140	312	
257	Ticket agent		141	313	
258	Shifters Haulage		142	316	*Dec 2008*
259	RY Decision Tree		142	320	
260	Amelie		143	321	

BUDGETING AND CONTROL

		Question	Answer	Past exam (Adapted)
		Page number		
261	Static Co	145	322	*Dec 2016*
262	Effective budgeting	146	325	
263	NN	147	326	
264	Zero Based budgeting	147	328	*Dec 2010*
265	Big Cheese Chairs	148	331	*Dec 2009*
266	Henry Company	148	333	*Dec 2008*
267	TR Co	149	336	*Sept/Dec 2017*
268	Perseus Co – revision of basic variances	150	339	
269	Valet Co	151	343	*Jun 2014*
270	The School Uniform Co	152	344	*Mar/Jun 2017*
271	Glove Co	153	349	*June 2016*
272	Safe Soap Co	153	351	*Dec 2014*

PERFORMANCE MEASUREMENT AND CONTROL

		Question	Answer	Past exam (Adapted)
273	B5 cars EIS	154	353	
274	Printing Company	155	355	
275	Rees Investments	155	357	
276	CDE	156	358	
277	The MG organisation	157	361	
278	Jump Performance Appraisal	157	363	*June 2010*
279	Accountancy Teaching Co	158	365	*Dec 2010*
280	Lens Co	160	368	*Dec 2016*
281	CIM	161	371	*Dec 2015*
282	Sports Co	162	373	*Sept/Dec 2017*
283	Rotech	164	376	*June 2014*
284	CTD	165	378	
285	Division A	166	379	
286	Jungle Co	166	381	*Sept 2016*
287	Oliver's Salon	168	384	*June 2009*
288	Ties Only	169	388	*Dec 2007*
289	Jamair	171	393	*Dec 2014*
290	The People's Bank	171	396	*Dec 2017*
291	Public sector organisation	173	399	
292	Woodside Charity	174	400	*Jun 2007*

ANALYSIS OF PAST EXAMS

The table below summarises the key topics that have been tested in the new syllabus examinations to date.

Note that the references are to the number of the question in this edition of the exam kit, but the Specimen exam is produced in its original form at the end of the kit and therefore these questions have retained their original numbering in the exam itself.

	J14	D14	J15	S15/D15	M16/J16	S16	D16	M17/J17	S17/D17
Specialist cost and management accounting techniques									
ABC	✓		✓						
Target costing				✓		✓			
Lifecycle costing					✓				
Throughput accounting		✓					✓		
Decision making techniques					✓		✓		
Key factor analysis									
Linear programming	✓					✓			
Pricing	✓	✓			✓				✓
Relevant costing		✓							
Uncertainty and risk	✓					✓			
Budgeting									
Budgeting			✓			✓	✓		
Forecasting									
Learning curves		✓	✓						
Standard costing and variance analysis									
Standard costing									
Variances				✓	✓		✓	✓	
Mix	✓	✓							
Planning and operational									
Performance measurement and control									
Performance measurement		✓				✓		✓	
ROI/RI	✓			✓			✓		✓
Transfer pricing	✓		✓		✓				
Not for profit organisations				✓					

EXAM TECHNIQUE

GENERAL COMMENTS

- Read the examination questions carefully
- **Divide the time** you spend on questions in proportion to the marks on offer:
    - one suggestion for this examination is to allocate 1.8 minutes to each mark available, so a 20 mark question should be completed in approximately 36 minutes.
    - within that, try to allow time at the end of each question to review your answer and address any obvious issues.

    Whatever happens, always keep your eye on the clock and **do not over run on any part of any question!**
- If you **get completely stuck** with a question:
    - flag the question and
    - **return to it later.**
- Stick to the question and **tailor your answer** to what you are asked.
    - Pay particular attention to the verbs in the question.
    - Try to apply your comments to the scenario where possible.
- If you do not understand what a question is asking, **state your assumptions**.

    Even if you do not answer in precisely the way the examiner hoped, you should be given some credit, if your assumptions are reasonable.
- You should do everything you can to make things easy for the marker.

    The marker will find it easier to identify the points you have made if your **answers are legible and well labelled.**

OBJECTIVE TEST QUESTIONS

- Decide whether you want to attempt these at the start of the exam or at the end.
- No credit for working will be given in these questions, the answers will either be correct (2 marks) or incorrect (0 marks)
- Read the question carefully, as any alternative answer choices will be given based on common mistakes that could be made in attempting the question.
- If a question looks particularly difficult or time consuming, then miss it out first time through (make sure you flag it) and come back to it later.

KAPLAN PUBLISHING

CONSTRUCTED RESPONSE (LONG) QUESTIONS

- **Written elements**:

  Your answer should have:

  - – a clear structure

  - – a brief introduction, a main section and a conclusion.

  Be concise.

  It is better to write a little about a lot of different points than a great deal about one or two points.

  Where possible, try to relate comments to the specific context given rather than your answer looking like it was simply copied out of the textbook.

- **Computations**:

  It is essential to include all your workings in your answers.

COMPUTER-BASED EXAMS – ADDITIONAL TIPS

- Do not attempt a CBE until you have **completed all study material** relating to it.

- On the ACCA website there is a CBE demonstration. It is **ESSENTIAL** that you attempt this before your real CBE. You will become familiar with how to move around the CBE screens and the way that questions are formatted, increasing your confidence and speed in the actual exam.

- Be sure you understand how to use the **software** before you start the exam. If in doubt, ask the assessment centre staff to explain it to you.

- Questions are **displayed on the screen** and answers are entered using keyboard and mouse.

- In addition to the traditional multiple choice question type, CBEs will also contain other types of questions, such as number entry questions, formulae entry questions, multiple correct answers (select two or more), matching labels to targets, stem questions with multiple parts and written questions requiring text entry.

- You need to be sure you **know how to answer questions** of these types before you sit the exam, through practice.

EXAM-SPECIFIC INFORMATION

THE EXAM

FORMAT OF THE EXAM

The exam will be in **THREE sections**, and will be a mix of narrative and computational answers.

All questions are compulsory.

		Number of marks
Section A:	Fifteen objective test questions of 2 marks each	30
Section B:	Three objective test case studies	
	– five questions per case study of 2 marks each	30
Section C:	Two constructed response (long) questions, mainly from the syllabus areas of working capital management, investment appraisal and business finance:	
	Question 1	20
	Question 2	20
		100

There will be an additional ten marks of seeded content which do not contribute to the mark but which are used to aid in standardisation. These ten marks will either be as five extra questions within section A or an extra set of case study questions in section B.

Total time allowed: 3 hours and 20 minutes.

In some countries, a paper –based version of the exam will still be available. In this exam, the section A and B questions will be of multiple choice style only. There will be no seeded questions so the exam will contain 100 marks' worth of questions and will be 3 hours and 15 minutes long.

Note that:

* the Financial Management exam will have both a discursive and computational element. The objective test questions and the objective test case study questions will therefore include a mix of calculation-based and explanation-based questions.

* there is likely to be a discussion element included in the constructed response questions in Section C.

PASS MARK

The pass mark for all ACCA Qualification examination exams is 50%.

SECTION A QUESTIONS

Note that in the paper-based exam, all Section A questions will be multiple choice questions.

The computer-based exam will include different question styles, as described in the previous section on exam technique.

A mixture of these question types is included within this exam kit.

KAPLAN PUBLISHING

The CBE will contain 110 marks of exam content; 100 marks contribute to the student result and 10 marks do not. These 10 marks of exam content are referred to as 'seeded questions' and will either be one OT case (five OT questions based around a single scenario) or 5 single OTs distributed randomly within the exam. Of the exam duration of 3 hours and 20 minutes, 3 hours relate to the 100 marks of exam content which contribute to the student result and 20 minutes relate to the seeded content. Seeded questions are included in the exam for quality assurance and security purposes and ensure that a student's mark is fair and reliable. The paper exam does not include seeded content so has 100 marks of exam content that needs to be completed within 3 hours and 15 minutes. In recognition that paper exams do not have any of the time saving efficiencies which can be incorporated in a computer exam, students are allocated more time for the same 100 marks.

APPROACH TO THIS EXAM

Financial Management is divided into three different sections, requiring the application of different skills to be successful.

Section A

Stick to the timing principle of 1.8 minutes per mark. This means that the 15 OT questions in section A (30 marks) should take 54 minutes.

Work steadily. Rushing leads to careless mistakes and the OT questions are designed to include answers which result from careless mistakes.

If you don't know the answer, eliminate those options you know are incorrect and see if the answer becomes more obvious.

Remember that there is no negative marking for an incorrect answer. After you have eliminated the options that you know to be wrong, if you are still unsure, guess.

Section B

There is likely to be a significant amount of information to read through for each case. You should begin by reading the OT questions that relate to the case, so that when you read through the information for the first time, you know what it is that you are required to do.

Each OT question is worth two marks. Therefore you have 18 minutes (1.8 minutes per mark) to answer the five OT questions relating to each case. It is likely that all of the cases will take the same length of time to answer, although some of the OT questions within a case may be quicker than other OT questions within that same case.

Once you have read through the information, you should first answer any of the OT questions that do not require workings and can be quickly answered. You should then attempt the OT questions that require workings utilising the remaining time for that case.

All of the tips for section A are equally applicable to each section B question.

Section C

The constructed response questions in section C will require a written response rather than being OT questions. Therefore, different techniques need to be used to score well.

Unless you know exactly how to answer the question, spend some time planning your answer. Stick to the question and tailor your answer to what you are asked. Pay particular attention to the verbs in the question e.g. 'Calculate', 'State', 'Explain'.

As stated earlier, if you **get completely stuck** with a question, leave space in your answer and return to it later.

If you do not understand what a question is asking, state your assumptions. Even if you do not answer in precisely the way the examining team hoped, you should be given some credit, provided that your assumptions are reasonable.

You should do everything you can to make things easy for the marker. The marker will find it easier to identify the points you have made if your answers are legible.

Computations: It is essential to include all your workings in your answers. Many computational questions require the use of a standard format. Be sure you know these formats thoroughly before the examination and use the layouts that you see in the answers given in this book and in model answers.

Adopt a logical approach and cross reference workings to the main computation to keep your answers tidy.

All sections

Don't skip parts of the syllabus. The PM exam has 32 different questions so the examination can cover a very broad selection of the syllabus each sitting.

Spend time learning the rules and definitions.

Practice plenty of questions to improve your ability to apply the techniques and perform the calculations.

Spend the last five minutes reading through your answers and making any additions or corrections.

 Always keep your eye on the clock and do not over run on any part of any question!

DETAILED SYLLABUS, STUDY GUIDE AND CBE SPECIMEN EXAM

The detailed syllabus and study guide written by the ACCA, along with the specimen exam, can be found at:

www.accaglobal.com/financial-management

KAPLAN'S RECOMMENDED REVISION APPROACH

QUESTION PRACTICE IS THE KEY TO SUCCESS

Success in professional examinations relies upon you acquiring a firm grasp of the required knowledge at the tuition phase. In order to be able to do the questions, knowledge is essential.

However, the difference between success and failure often hinges on your exam technique on the day and making the most of the revision phase of your studies.

The **Kaplan study text** is the starting point, designed to provide the underpinning knowledge to tackle all questions. However, in the revision phase, pouring over text books is not the answer.

Kaplan Online fixed tests help you consolidate your knowledge and understanding and are a useful tool to check whether you can remember key topic areas.

Kaplan pocket notes are designed to help you quickly revise a topic area, however you then need to practice questions. There is a need to progress to full exam standard questions as soon as possible, and to tie your exam technique and technical knowledge together.

The importance of question practice cannot be over-emphasised.

The recommended approach below is designed by expert tutors in the field, in conjunction with their knowledge of the examiner and their recent real exams.

The approach taken for the fundamental exams is to revise by topic area. However, with the professional stage exams, a multi topic approach is required to answer the scenario based questions.

You need to practice as many questions as possible in the time you have left.

OUR AIM

Our aim is to get you to the stage where you can attempt exam standard questions confidently, to time, in a closed book environment, with no supplementary help (i.e. to simulate the real examination experience).

Practising your exam technique on real past examination questions, in timed conditions, is also vitally important for you to assess your progress and identify areas of weakness that may need more attention in the final run up to the examination.

In order to achieve this we recognise that initially you may feel the need to practice some questions with open book help and exceed the required time.

The approach below shows you which questions you should use to build up to coping with exam standard question practice, and references to the sources of information available should you need to revisit a topic area in more detail.

Remember that in the real examination, all you have to do is:

- attempt all questions required by the exam
- only spend the allotted time on each question, and
- get them at least 50% right!

Try and practice this approach on every question you attempt from now to the real exam.

EXAMINER COMMENTS

We have included the examiners comments to the specific new syllabus examination questions in this kit for you to see the main pitfalls that students fall into with regard to technical content.

However, too many times in the general section of the report, the examiner comments that students had failed due to:

- "not answering the question"

- "a poor understanding of why something is done, not just how it is done"

- "simply writing out numbers from the question. Candidates must understand what the numbers tell them about business performance"

- "a lack of common business sense" and

- "ignoring clues in the question".

Good exam technique is vital.

THE KAPLAN PAPER PERFORMANCE MANAGEMENT (PM) REVISION PLAN

Stage 1: Assess areas of strengths and weaknesses

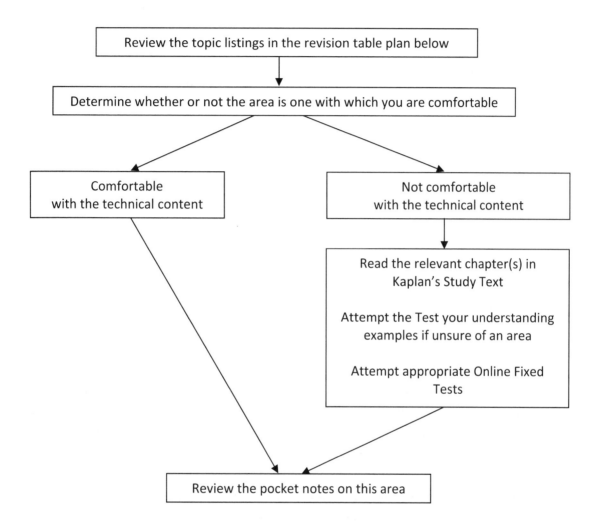

Stage 2: Practice questions

Follow the order of revision of topics as recommended in the revision table plan below and attempt the questions in the order suggested.

Try to avoid referring to text books and notes and the model answer until you have completed your attempt.

Try to answer the question in the allotted time.

Review your attempt with the model answer and assess how much of the answer you achieved in the allocated exam time.

Fill in the self-assessment box below and decide on your best course of action.

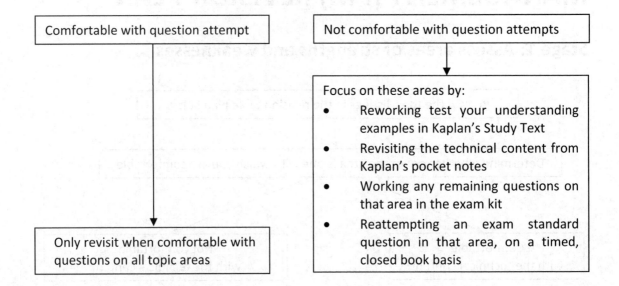

| Comfortable with question attempt | Not comfortable with question attempts |

Focus on these areas by:

- Reworking test your understanding examples in Kaplan's Study Text
- Revisiting the technical content from Kaplan's pocket notes
- Working any remaining questions on that area in the exam kit
- Reattempting an exam standard question in that area, on a timed, closed book basis

Only revisit when comfortable with questions on all topic areas

Note that:

 The "footsteps questions" give guidance on exam techniques and how you should have approached the question.

Stage 3: Final pre-exam revision

We recommend that you **attempt at least one three hour mock examination** containing a set of previously unseen exam standard questions.

It is important that you get a feel for the breadth of coverage of a real exam without advanced knowledge of the topic areas covered – just as you will expect to see on the real exam day.

Ideally this mock should be sat in timed, closed book, real exam conditions and could be:

- a mock examination offered by your tuition provider, and/or
- the specimen exam in the back of this exam kit, and/or
- the last real examination (available shortly afterwards on MyKaplan with "enhanced walk through answers" and a full "tutor debrief").

KAPLAN'S DETAILED REVISION PLAN

Specialist cost and management accounting techniques

Topic	Study Text Chapter	Pocket note Chapter	Questions to attempt	Tutor guidance	Date attempted	Self assessment
— ABC	2	2	1 to 13 inclusive in Section A. Questions 206, 207 and 208 in Section B. Question 228 in Section C.	Activity Based Costing (ABC) is a key costing technique. In Question 228, 'Gadget Co', make sure that you can calculate the cost per unit using both full absorption costing, and an ABC approach. As well as the calculations in this question, be ready to explain the reasons for the development of ABC, its pros and cons and its implications. Successful completion of the recommended questions like this one should reassure you that you would be able to tackle an ABC question in the exam.		
— Target costing	2	2	14 to 20 inclusive in Section A. Questions 209 and 210 in Section B Question 233 in Section C.	This question in section C (Manpac) is an excellent question on target costing and other concepts. It will be good practice after all the numerical questions on Target costing from sections A and B. Exam questions may also ask for a discussion of the implications of target costing or of the use of target costing in the service industry.		

– Lifecycle costing	2	21 to 27 inclusive in Section A. Question 211 in Section B. Question 234 in Section C.	This is a relatively straightforward technique but it is still important to practice at the very least one long question to ensure you have the required knowledge.
– Environmental management accounting	2	36 to 40 in Section A. Question 211 in Section B. Question 238 in Section C.	Question 244 is a good written question on EMA. It is important that you can explain what is meant by EMA and that you understand how it should be used. Make sure that you reference your points back to the scenario.
– Throughput accounting	2	28 to 35 inclusive in Section A. Question 212 in Section B. Questions 236 and 237 in Section C.	Two good Section C questions covering the different calculations and written areas that could be examined on throughput accounting. This is a more difficult costing technique and it is therefore important to complete these questions before the exam.
Decision making techniques			
– Cost volume profit analysis	3	53 to 62 inclusive in Section A. Questions 214 and 215 in Section B. Question 240 in Section C.	A good question ('Mango Leather') covering multi-products breakeven charts. Even if you are not going to be requested to draw a graph in the exam, constructing one in revision will help consolidate your understanding. A complete question with well-split requirements that also refer to an article on the ACCA website – an absolute must.

Linear programming	4	4	Question 69 in Section A. Question 216 in Section B. Question 244 in Section C.	Excellent questions on linear programming. In addition to the six step approach, the examiner is likely to examine some peripheral areas such as shadow prices, slack or linear programming assumptions.
Pricing	5	5	75 to 86 inclusive in Section A. Questions 217, 218 in Section B. Question 267 in Section C.	The section C question, 'TR Co', is a very recent question testing pricing and learning curves. It also mixes calculations with written parts. An excellent question to practice as part of your revision programme.
Relevant costing	6	6	42 to 53 inclusive in Section A. Question 213 in Section B. Question 249 in Section C.	This is a tricky area but a methodical approach to answering questions should help. If you are not sure about a particular number, take a guess and move on. The aim is not to get the question 100% correct but to get through the question in time and to score a pass in the question.
Uncertainty and risk	7	7	92 to 100 inclusive in Section A. Question 219 in Section B. Question 257 in Section C.	The calculations are important and the decision trees techniques must be well rehearsed. Look for other questions to practice in this area as you must also be prepared to discuss the various methods of managing risk. Some of the terms, e.g. minimax regret, make this area appear difficult but the underlying concepts are relatively straightforward.

Budgeting and control

—	Budgeting	8	8	101 to 114 in Section A. Question 220, 221, 222 in Section B. Question 261 in Section C.	Do not overlook this area. Knowledge of the written areas of budgeting can help you to score relatively easy marks in the exam, like most well-prepared candidates do when narrative questions are set. Q261, 'Static Co' is very recent and very important when it comes to testing the examiner's favourite topic of rolling budgets.
—	Learning curves (Quantitative Analysis)	9	9	115 to 123 in Section A. Question 222 in Section B. Question 267 in Section C.	Excellent questions on learning curves and representative of what you should expect in the exam. Be prepared to discuss the reservations with the learning curve.
—	Mix and yield variances	10	10	132 to 139 in Section A. Question 224 in Section B. Question 272 in Section C.	These require a calculation of mix and yield variances and are good preparation for the exam. They are also very recent exam questions. Sales mix and quantity variances should not be omitted either (questions 140 to 145.)
—	Planning and operational variances	10	10	146 to 152 in Section A. Question 221 in Section B. Question 270 in Section C.	This is representative of the type of question that may come up on this area. Question 270 'The School Uniform Company' (March/June 2017) is a must-practice question on revision.

Performance measurement and control

– ROI/RI	12	12	184, 188, 190 and 191 in Section A. Question 280 in Section C.	It is important that you can calculate the ROI and RI but you must also be able to discuss the pros and cons of each of these methods. Some of these questions are challenging but necessary, testing your knowledge of how (ROI) is affected by different transactions which may take place. Question 280 is very recent and should be part of your revision plan.
– Transfer pricing	12	12	192 in Section A. Question 272 in Section C.	For all questions on transfer pricing, you will require an in-depth understanding of the information contained in the scenario.
– Not for profit organisations	13	13	197 and 198 in Section A. Question 221 in Section B. Question 292 in Section C.	Questions on not-for-profit organisations will serve as excellent preparation for any exam question on this area. You should focus on understanding and applying the 'Value For Money' (or 3E) framework.
– Information systems	14	14	155 to 160 Section A. Question 274 in Section C.	Two questions on systems and information but these will serve as excellent preparation for any exam question on this area.

Note that not all of the questions are referred to in the programme above. We have recommended a large number of exam standard questions and successful completion of these should reassure you that you have a good grounding of all of the key topics and are well prepared for the exam.

The remaining questions are available in the kit for extra practice for those who require more questions and focus on some areas.

FORMULAE

Learning curve

$Y = ax^b$

Where y   = cumulative average time per unit to produce x units

a   = the time taken for the first unit of output

x   = the cumulative number of units produced

b   = the index of learning (log LR/log 2)

LR   = the learning rate as a decimal

Demand curve

$P = a - bQ$

$$b = \frac{\text{Change in price}}{\text{Change in quantity}}$$

a = price when Q = 0

MR = a − 2bQ

Section 1

OBJECTIVE TEST QUESTIONS – SECTION A

SPECIALIST COST AND MANAGEMENT ACCOUNTING TECHNIQUES

ACTIVITY BASED COSTING

1   VPS is a large manufacturing business that is introducing an activity based costing system into its business. VPS ships components via its own logistics operation to its central manufacturing centre in Glasgow from a wide variety of locations. It is attempting to identify the correct cost driver for the cost pool called 'component handling'.

   Which of the following would be the correct figure to use?

   A   Average components per unit

   B   Total number of components shipped

   C   Average distance travelled by a component

   D   Total components-distance travelled

   (Handwritten: TOTAL FIGURE & Distance = #COST)

2   A company which makes two products, Alpha and Zeta, uses activity-based costing to absorb its overheads. It has recently identified a new overhead cost pool for inspection costs and has decided that the cost driver is the number of inspections.

   The following information has been provided:

   Total inspection costs $250,000

	Alpha	Zeta
Production volume (units)	2,500	8,000
Machine hours per unit	1	1.5
Units per batch	500	1,000
Inspections per batch	4	1

   The inspection cost per unit for product Alpha is equal to pick from list

   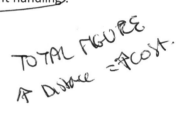

   List options are as follows:

   - $23.81
   - $17.24
   - $71.43
   - $80.00

   (Handwritten working:

   Cost Pool   Cost Dr
   Inspection 250 000   No inspect

   Alpha.   Zeta   Total
   25000   8000
   500   1000
   = 5. x4   8 x 1
   = 20   = 8   28

   OAR = 250 000 / 28 = $8928.57
   Alpha. = 8928.57 x 20 / 2500 = 71.43.)*

3 **Which of the following statements are true regarding ABC and cost drivers?**

(1) A cost driver is any factor that causes a change in the cost of an activity.

(2) For long-term variable overhead costs, the cost driver will be the volume of activity.

(3) Traditional absorption costing tends to under-allocate overhead costs to low-volume products.

A   1 and 3

B   2 and 3

C   1 and 2

(D)   1, 2 and 3

4 **Which of the following statements are true regarding activity-based costing?**

(1) A cost pool is an activity which consumes resources and for which overhead costs are identified and allocated.

(2) The overhead absorption rate (OAR) is calculated in the same way as the absorption costing OAR, and the same OAR will be calculated for each activity.

(A)   1 only

B   2 only

C   Neither 1 nor 2

(D)   Both 1 and 2

5 *This objective test question contains a question type which will only appear in a computer-based exam, but this question provides valuable practice for all students whichever version of the exam they are taking.*

The ABC Company manufactures two products, Product Alpha and Product Beta. Both are produced in a very labour-intensive environment and use similar processes. Alpha and Beta differ by volume. Beta is a high-volume product, while Alpha is a low-volume product. Details of product inputs, outputs and the costs of activities are as follows:

	Direct labour hours/unit	Annual output (units)	Number of purchase orders	Number of set-ups
Alpha	5	1,200	75	40
Beta	5	12,000	85	60
			160	100

A   5×1200 = 6000 } 66000
B   5×12000 = 60 000 }

Fixed overhead costs amount to a total of $420,000 and have been analysed as follows:

	$
Volume-related	100,000
Purchasing related	145,000
Set-up related	175,000

Using a traditional method of overhead absorption based on labour hours, what is the overhead cost per unit for each unit of product Alpha? (2 d.p.)

$ 31.80

$$OAR = \frac{Total\ OAH}{Total\ no.\ DLH}$$

$$= \frac{420\ 000}{66000} = 6.36\ per\ lab.\ hr$$

Alpha = 5 × 6.36 = 31.80

6   The ABC Company manufactures two products, Product Alpha and Product Beta. Both are produced in a very labour-intensive environment and use similar processes. Alpha and Beta differ by volume. Beta is a high-volume product, while Alpha is a low-volume product. Details of product inputs, outputs and the costs of activities are as follows:

	Direct labour hours/unit	Annual output (units)	Number of purchase orders	Number of set-ups
Alpha	5	1,200	75	40
Beta	5	12,000	85	60
			160	100

Fixed overhead costs amount to a total of $420,000 and have been analysed as follows:

	$
Volume-related	100,000
Purchasing related	145,000
Set-up related	175,000

Using a traditional method of overhead absorption based on labour hours, what is the overhead cost per unit for each unit of product Beta?

A $6.36

B $22.75

C $31.82

D $122.55

7   The ABC Company manufactures two products, Product Alpha and Product Beta. Both are produced in a very labour-intensive environment and use similar processes. Alpha and Beta differ by volume. Beta is a high-volume product, while Alpha is a low-volume product. Details of product inputs, outputs and the costs of activities are as follows:

	Direct labour hours/unit	Annual output (units)	Number of purchase orders	Number of set-ups
Alpha	5	1,200	75	40
Beta	5	12,000	85	60
			160	100

Fixed overhead costs amount to a total of $420,000 and have been analysed as follows:

	$
Volume-related	100,000
Purchasing related	145,000
Set-up related	175,000

Using Activity Based Costing as method of overhead absorption, what is the overhead cost per unit for each unit of product Alpha?

A $6.36

B $22.75

C $122.55

D   Cannot be determined without more information

8   A company makes two products using the same type of materials and skilled workers. The following information is available:

	Product A	Product B
Budgeted volume (units)	1,000	2,000
Material per unit ($)	10	20
Labour per unit ($)	5	20

Fixed costs relating to material handling amount to $100,000. The cost driver for these costs is the volume of material purchased.

General fixed costs, absorbed on the basis of labour hours, amount to $180,000.

Using activity-based costing, what is the total fixed overhead amount to be absorbed into each unit of product B (to the nearest whole $)?

A $113

B $120

C $40

D $105

9   *This objective test question contains a question type which will only appear in a computer-based exam, but this question provides valuable practice for all students whichever version of the exam they are taking.*

A company manufactures two products, C and D, for which the following information is available:

	Product C	Product D	Total
Budgeted production (units)	1,000	4,000	5,000
Labour hours per unit/in total	8	10	48,000
Number of production runs required	13	15	28
Number of inspections during production	5	3	8

Total production set up costs $140,000

Total inspection costs $80,000

Other overhead costs $96,000

Other overhead costs are absorbed on the basis of labour hours per unit.

Using activity-based costing, what is the budgeted overhead cost per unit of product D? (2 d.p.)

$ [   ]

10 A company is changing its costing system from traditional absorption costing based on labour hours to Activity Based Costing. It has overheads of $156,000 which are related to taking material deliveries.

The delivery information about each product is below.

Product:	X	Y	Z
Total units required	1,000	2,000	3,000
Delivery size	200	400	1,000

Total labour costs are $360,000 for 45,000 hours. Each unit of each product takes the same number of direct hours.

Assuming that the company uses the number of deliveries as its cost driver, is there an increase or a decrease in unit costs arising from the change from Absorption Costing to Activity Based Costing?

	Increase	Decrease
Product X		
Product Y		
Product Z		

11 A company uses activity-based costing to calculate the unit cost of its products. The figures for Period 3 are as follows: production set-up costs are $84,000. Total production is 40,000 units of each of products A and B, and each run is 2,000 units of A or 5,000 units of B.

What is the set-up cost per unit of B? (2 d.p.)

$ [   ]

12 DRP Ltd has recently introduced an ABC system. It manufactures three products, details of which are set out below:

Product:	D	R	P
Budgeted annual production (units)	100,000	100,000	50,000
Batch size (units)	100	50	25
Machine set-ups per batch	3	4	6
Purchase orders per batch	2	1	1
Processing time per unit (minutes)	2	3	3

Three cost pools have been identified. Their budgeted costs for the year ending 30 June 2003 are as follows:

Machine set-up costs	$150,000
Purchasing of materials	$70,000
Processing	$80,000

What is the budgeted machine set-up cost per unit of product R?

A $6.52

B $0.52

C $18.75

D $1.82

13 *This objective test question contains a question type which will only appear in a computer-based exam, but this question provides valuable practice for all students whichever version of the exam they are taking.*

A company makes products A and B. It is experimenting with Activity Based Costing. Production set-up costs are $12,000; total production will be 20,000 units of each of products A and B. Each run is 1,000 units of A or 5,000 units of B.

What is the set-up cost per unit of A, using ABC?

$ [   ]

TARGET COSTING

14 The following are all steps in the implementation of the target costing process for a product:

(1)   Calculate the target cost.

(2)   Calculate the estimated current cost based on the existing product specification.

(3)   Set the required profit.

(4)   Set the selling price.

(5)   Calculate the target cost gap.

Which of the following represents the correct sequence if target costing were to be used?

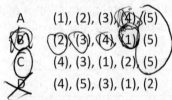

A   (1), (2), (3), (4), (5)

B   (2), (3), (4), (1), (5)

C   (4), (3), (1), (2), (5)

D   (4), (5), (3), (1), (2)

15   In target costing, which of the following would be a legitimate strategy to reduce a cost gap for a product that existed in a competitive industry with demanding shareholders?

A   Increase the selling price

B   Reduce the expectation gap by reducing the selling price

C   Reducing the desired margin on the product

D   Mechanising production in order to reduce average production cost

16   Which of the following strategies would be immediately acceptable methods to reduce an identified cost gap?

A   Reduce the desired margin without discussion with business owners

B   Reduce the predicted selling price

C   Source similar quality materials from another supplier at reduced cost

D   Increase the predicted selling price

17 *This objective test question contains a question type which will only appear in a computer-based exam, but this question provides valuable practice for all students whichever version of the exam they are taking.*

The predicted selling price for a product has been set at $56 per unit. 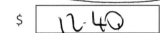 The desired mark-up on cost is 25% and the material cost for the product is estimated to be $16 before allowing for additional materials to allow for shrinkage of 20% (for every 10 kg of material going in only 8 kg comes out). If labour is the only other cost and 2 hours are needed what is the most the business can pay per hour if a cost gap is to be avoided?

The maximum rate per hour is $ 12.40

18 **Which of the following techniques is NOT relevant to target costing?**

    A   Value analysis

    B   Variance analysis

    C   Functional analysis

    D   Activity analysis

19 **The selling price of product Zigma is set to be $250 for each unit and sales for the coming year are expected to be 500 units. If the company requires a return of 15% in the coming year on its investment of $250,000 in product Zigma, the target cost for each unit for the coming year is** pick from list

List options are as follows:
• $145
• $155
• $165
• $175

20 VC Co is a firm of opticians. It provides a range of services to the public, such as eye tests and contact lens consultations, and has a separate dispensary selling glasses and contact lenses. Patients book appointments with an optician in advance.

A standard appointment is 30 minutes long, during which an optician will assess the patient's specific requirements and provide them with the eye care services they need. After the appointment, patients are offered the chance to buy contact lenses or glasses from the dispensary.

Which of the following describes a characteristic of the services provided by an optician at VC Co during a standard appointment?

    A   Tangible

    B   Homogeneous

    C   Non-perishable

    D   Simultaneous

LIFECYCLE COSTING

21 A manufacturing company which produces a range of products has developed a budget for the life-cycle of a new product, P. The information in the following table relates exclusively to product P:

	Lifetime total	Per unit
Design costs	$800,000	
Direct manufacturing costs		$20
Depreciation costs	$500,000	
Decommissioning costs	$20,000	
Machine hours		4
Production and sales units	300,000	

The company's total fixed production overheads are budgeted to be $72 million each year and total machine hours are budgeted to be 96 million hours. The company absorbs overheads on a machine hour basis.

What is the budgeted life-cycle cost per unit for product P?

A $24.40

B $25.73

C $27.40

D $22.73

22 A company has produced the following information for a product it is about to launch:

Units	2,000	5,000	7,000
Variable production cost per unit	$2.30	$1.80	$1.20
Fixed production costs	$3,000	$3,500	$4,000
Variable selling cost per unit	$0.50	$0.40	$0.40
Fixed selling costs	$1,500	$1,600	$1,600
Administrative costs	$700	$700	$700

What is the life-cycle cost per unit?

A $2.81

B $2.32

C $3.22

D $3.07

23 SNT is a Japanese electronics ~~giant~~ specialising in the production of game consoles. SNT is planning to introduce the latest 'next-generation' console and range of games in the summer of 2015. Development of the new console is due to commence on January 1, 2015 and SNT is currently working out at what price the new console should be sold then.

The new console is expected to incur the following costs in the four years it will be developed and commercialised:

	2015	2016	2017	2018	
Consoles manufactured and sold	10,000	12,000	11,100	3,000	36100
R&D costs	$950,000	$0	$0	$0	950 000
Marketing costs	$230,000	$120,000	$20,000	$5,000	375 000
Production cost per console	$450	$430	$290	$290	1460
Warranty costs per console	$30	$30	$40	$45	145
End of life costs	$0	$0	$0	$125,000	125 000

(handwritten: 1451605)

Market research has indicated that customers will be prepared to pay an average price of $420 per console, but SNT's Chief Executive believes this will not be sufficient to make production worthwhile.

Which of the following statements, made by the Chief Executive, are true regarding the costs of the console?

(1) The cost per console, calculated using lifecycle costing principles, is higher than the price customers are prepared to pay.

(2) More attention to R&D costs in 2015 could reduce warranty costs in later years.

A   1 only

B   2 only

C   Neither 1 nor 2

D   Both 1 and 2

24 *This objective test question contains a question type which will only appear in a computer-based exam, but this question provides valuable practice for all students whichever version of the exam they are taking.*

While a drag and drop style question is impossible to fully replicate within a paper based medium, some questions of this style have been included for completeness.

Which of the following are said to be benefits of lifecycle costing?

- It provides the true financial cost of a product ✓
- The length of the lifecycle can be shortened ✗
- Expensive errors can be avoided in that potentially failing products can be avoided ✓
- Lower costs can be achieved earlier by designing out costs ✓
- Better selling prices can be set ✓
- Decline stages of the lifecycle can be avoided ✗

Drag the items selected into the box below:

25 Which of the following statements are true regarding the justification of the use of life cycle costing?

(1) Product life cycles are becoming increasingly short. This means that the initial costs are an increasingly important component in the product's overall costs. ✓

(2) Product costs are increasingly weighted to the start of a product's life cycle, and to properly understand the profitability of a product these costs must be matched to the ultimate revenues. ✓

(3) The high costs of (for example) research, design and marketing in the early stages in a product's life cycle necessitate a high initial selling price. ✗

(4) Traditional capital budgeting techniques do not attempt to minimise the costs or maximise the revenues over the product life cycle.

   A   1, 2 and 4

   B   2 and 3 only

   C   1 and 3 only

   D   1, 2, 3 and 4

26 Which of the following statements is/are true regarding lifecycle costing?

(1) Life cycle costing takes into account <u>all costs</u> incurred in a product life cycle with exception of sunk costs incurred on research and development. ✗

(2) Life cycle costing ensures a profit is generated over the life of the product. ✓

(3) Life cycle costing is most useful for products with an <u>even weighting of costs over their life</u>. ✗

   A   1 and 2

   B   2 only

   C   2 and 3

   D   1, 2 and 3

27 Company B is about to being developing a new product for launch in its existing market. They have forecast sales of 20,000 units and the marketing department suggest a selling price of $43/unit. The company seeks to make a mark-up of 40% product cost. It is estimated that the lifetime costs of the product will be as follows:

(1) Design and development costs $43,000.

(2) Manufacturing costs $15/unit.

(3) Plant decommissioning costs $30,000.

The company estimates that if it were to spend an additional $15,000 on design, manufacturing costs/unit could be reduced.

 not relevant.

What is the life cycle cost?

   A $18.65

   B $22

   C $22.87

   D $24

THROUGHPUT ACCOUNTING

28 Which ONE of the following would serve to increase the Throughput Accounting Ratio?

A An increase in the speed of the fastest machine in the production process

B An unexpected increase in the factory rent

C A 5% wage increase linked to an 8% improvement in productivity

D A 10% sales discount to stimulate demand by 20%

29 A manufacturing company decides which of three mutually exclusive products to make in its factory on the basis of maximising the company's throughput accounting ratio.

Current data for the three products is shown in the following table:

	Product X	Product Y	Product Z
Selling price per unit	$60	$40	$20
Direct material cost per unit	$40	$10	$16
Machine hours per unit	10	20	2.5

Total factory costs (excluding direct materials) are $150,000. The company cannot make enough of any of the products to satisfy external demand entirely as machine hours are restricted.

Which of the following actions would improve the company's existing throughput accounting ratio?

A Increase the selling price of product Z by 10%

B Increase the selling price of product Y by 10%

C Reduce the material cost of product Z by 5%

D Reduce the material cost of product Y by 5%

30 *This objective test question contains a question type which will only appear in a computer-based exam, but this question provides valuable practice for all students whichever version of the exam they are taking.*

Skye Limited has a two process environment, and details of these processes are as follows:

Process P: Each machine produces 6 units an hour and Skye has 8 machines working at 90% capacity.

Process Q: Each machine produces 9 units per hour and Skye has 6 machines working at 85% capacity.

One of Skye products is Cloud. Cloud is not particularly popular but does sell at a selling price of $20 although discounts of 15% apply. Material costs are $5 and direct labour costs are double the material cost. Cloud spends 0.2 hours in process P but 0.3 hours in process Q.

What is Cloud's throughput per hour in its bottleneck process?

$ _____

31 A manufacturing company uses three processes to make its two products, X and Y. The time available on the three processes is reduced because of the need for preventative maintenance and rest breaks.

The table below details the process times per product and daily time available:

Process	Hours available per day	Hours required to make one unit of product X	Hours required to make one unit of product Y
1	22	1.00	0.75
2	22	0.75	1.00
3	18	1.00	0.50

Daily demand for product X and product Y is 10 units and 16 units respectively.

Which of the following will improve throughput?

A   Increasing the efficiency of the maintenance routine for Process 2

B   Increasing the demand for both products

C   Reducing the time taken for rest breaks on Process 3

D   Reducing the time product X requires for Process 1

32 The following statements have been made about throughput accounting:

A   Throughput accounting considers that the only variable costs in the short run are materials and components.

B   Throughput accounting considers that time at a bottleneck resource has value, not elsewhere.

C   Throughput accounting views stock building as a non-value-adding activity, and therefore discourages it.

D   Throughput accounting was designed as a decision-making tool for situations where there is a bottleneck in the production process.

Which ONE of the above statements is not true of throughput accounting?

A   A

B   B

C   C

D   D

33 **Which of the following is a definition of the throughput accounting ratio?**

A   Throughput contribution/hours on bottleneck

B   Conversion costs per hour/throughput per hour

C   Throughput per hour/conversion costs per hour

D   Total conversion costs/total throughput

34 The following information is available for a single product:

Units produced		500
Time taken		200 hours
Maximum time available		200 hours →
Materials purchased	1,000 kg costing	$3,000
Materials used	800 kg	
Labour costs		$2,000
Overheads		$1,500
Sales		$9,000

Handwritten: Sales - all Mat / 9000-3000 / =6000

Handwritten near Labour/Overheads: cost = 3500, cost

The throughput accounting ratio for this product is pick from list

List options are:

0

1.00

1.50

1.70

Handwritten: TPAR $\frac{6000}{3500} = 1.71$

35 A company has recently adopted throughput accounting as a performance measuring tool. Its results for the last month are shown below.

Units produced		1,150
Units sold		800
Materials purchased	900 kg costing	$13,000
Opening material inventory used	450 kg costing	$7,250
Labour costs		$6,900
Overheads		$4,650
Sales price		$35

There was no opening inventory of finished goods or closing inventory of materials.

The throughput accounting ratio for this product is pick from list:

List options are:

0

0.80

1.30

1.50

Handwritten:

Sales - all Mat.

28000 - 13000 = 15000

Conversion costs

(6900 + 4650) = 11550

1.30

ENVIRONMENTAL ACCOUNTING

36   Different management accounting techniques can be used to account for environmental costs.

One of these techniques involves analysing costs under three distinct categories: material, system, and delivery and disposal.

What is this technique known as?

A   Activity-based costing✗

B   Life-cycle costing ✗

C   Input-output analysis

(D)   Flow cost accounting

37   **Which TWO of the following statements about material flow cost accounting (MFCA) are correct?**

- ✓   Manufacturing costs are categorised into material costs, system costs and delivery and disposal costs

- •   MFCA records material inflows and balances this with outflows both in terms of physical quantities and, at the end of the process, in monetary terms too, so that businesses are forced to focus on environmental costs.

- •   In MFCA, output costs are allocated between positive and negative product costs. ✗

- •   The aim of flow cost accounting is to increase the quantity of materials which, as well as having a positive effect on the environment, should have a positive effect on a company's total costs in the long run.

38   **Which of the following statements is/are true regarding the issues faced by businesses in the management of their environmental costs?**

(1)   The costs involved are difficult to define.

(2)   Environmental costs can be categorised as quality related costs.

(3)   Cost control can be an issue, in particular if costs have been identified incorrectly in the first place.

A   1 only

B   2 and 3 only

C   None of them

D   All of them

39   **Which TWO of the following statements about the advantages of using Activity Based Costing for Environmental Management Accounting are correct?**

- •   Higher environmental costs can be reflected in higher prices.

- •   Cost savings achieved through environmental policies can be measured.

- •   It is simple to determine the environmental costs and cost drivers.

- •   It considers all environmental effects of the company's actions.

40 Flow cost accounting is a technique which can be used to account for environmental costs. Inputs and outputs are measured through each individual process of production.

Which of the following is NOT a category used within flow cost accounting?

A   Material flows

B   System flows

C   Delivery and disposal flows

D   Waste flows

41 **Environmental costs are difficult to deal with for an accountant. Which of the following is not a reason for this?**

A   Costs are often hidden

B   Costs are mostly minor

C   Costs are often very long term

D   Accounting systems rarely split off these costs automatically

DECISION-MAKING TECHNIQUES

RELEVANT COST ANALYSIS

42 UU Company has been asked to quote for a special contract. The following information about the material needed has been given:

Material X:

Book value	Scrap value	Replacement cost
$5.00 per kg	$0.50 per kg	$5.50 per kg

The contract requires 10 kgs of Material X. There are 250 kgs of this material in inventory which was purchased in error over two years ago. If Material X is modified, at a cost of $2 per kg, it could then be used as a substitute for material Y which is in regular use and currently costs $6 per kg.

What is the relevant cost of the materials for the special contract?

A $5

B $40

C $50

D $55

43 VV Company has been asked to quote for a special contract. The contract requires 100 hours of labour. However, the labourers, who are each paid $15 per hour, are working at full capacity.

There is a shortage of labour in the market. The labour required to undertake this special contract would have to be taken from another contract, Z, which currently utilises 500 hours of labour and generates $5,000 worth of contribution.

If the labour was taken from contract Z, then the whole of contract Z would have to be delayed, and such delay would invoke a penalty fee of $1,000.

What is the relevant cost of the labour for the special contract?

A $1,000

B $1,500

C $2,500

D $7,500

Labour cost = $1500

Fee $1000

2500

44 An organisation is considering the costs to be incurred in respect of a special order opportunity. The order would require 1,250 kgs of material D, that is readily available and regularly used by the organisation on its normal products.

There are 265 kgs of material D in inventory which cost $795 last week. The current market price is $3.24 per kg. Material D is normally used to make product X. Each unit of X requires 3 kgs of material D, and if material D is costed at $3 per kg, each unit of X yields a contribution of $15.

Historic

What is the relevant cost of material D to be included in the costing of the special order?

A $3,990

B $4,050

C $10,000

D $10,300

1250 × 3.24 = 4050

45 H has in inventory 15,000 kg of M, a raw material which it bought for $3/kg five years ago, for a product line which was discontinued four years ago. M has no use in its existing state but could be sold as scrap for $1.00 per kg. One of the company's current products (HN) requires 4 kg of a raw material, available for $5.00 per kg. M can be modified at a cost of $0.75 per kg so that it may be used as a substitute for this material. However, after modification, 5 kg of M is required for every unit of HN to be produced.

H has now received an invitation to tender for a product which could use M in its present state.

What is the relevant cost per kg of M to be included in the cost estimate for the tender?

A $0.75

B $1.00

C $3.00

D $3.25

46 In order to utilise some spare capacity, K is preparing a quotation for a special order which requires 2,000 kgs of material J.

K has 800 kgs of material J in inventory (original cost $7.00 per kg). Material J is used in the company's main product L. Each unit of L uses 5 kgs of material J and, based on an input value of $7.00 per kg of J, each unit of L yields a contribution of $10.00.

The resale value of material J is $5.50 per kg. The present replacement price of material J is $8.00 per kg. Material J is readily available in the market.

What is the relevant cost of the 2,000 kgs of material J to be included in the quotation?

A $11,000

B $14,000

C $16,000

D $18,000

47 A company is calculating the relevant cost of the material to be used on a particular contract. The contract requires 4,200 kgs of material H and this can be bought for $6.30 per kg. The company bought 10,000 kgs of material H some time ago when it paid $4.50 per kg. Currently 3,700 kgs of this remains in inventory. The inventory of material H could be sold for $3.20 per kg.

The company has no other use for material H other than on this contract, but it could be modified it at a cost of $3.70 per kg and use it as a substitute for material J. Material J is regularly used by the company and can be bought for $7.50 per kg.

What is the relevant cost of the material for the contract?

A $17,210

B $19,800

C $26,460

D $30,900

48 Ace Limited is considering a new project that will require the use of a currently idle machine. The machine has a current book value of $12,000 and a potential disposal value of $10,500 (before $200 disposal costs) and hence has been under depreciated by $1,500 over its life to date. If the machine is to be fit for purpose on the new project it will have to be relocated at a cost of $500 and refitted at a further cost of $800.

What is the relevant cost of using the machine on the new project?

A $9,000

B $10,300

C $11,600

D $13,300

49 Blunt is considering a new project but is unsure how much overhead to include in the calculations to help him decide whether or not to proceed. Existing fixed overheads are absorbed at the rate of $8 per hour worked. Blunt is certain that the project will involve an incremental 500 labour hours.

The project will involve extra machine running costs and these variable overheads cost him $4 per hour. The number of extra machine hours is expected to be 450 hours. The difference between this figure and the 500 labour hours above is expected idle time.

The project will require a little more temporary space that can be rented at a fixed cost of $1,200 for the period of hire. This overhead is not included in the fixed overhead absorption rate above.

What is the overhead to be charged against the project decision?

A $3,000

B $3,200

C $7,000

D $7,200

$4 \times 450 = 1800$
$\underline{1200}$
3000

50 Cleverclogs is short of labour for a new one-off project needing 600 hours of labour and has choices as to where to source this. He could hire new people temporarily from an agency at a cost of $9 per hour. Alternatively he could recruit new temporary staff at a fixed cost of advertising of $1,200 but then only pay $6 per hour for the time. He could also redirect some staff from existing work who are currently paid $7 per hour and who make sandals that generate a contribution of $3 per hour after all variable costs. Sandals are a good selling product and Cleverclogs will lose the production and the related sales whilst staff is working on the new one-off project.

What is the relevant cash flow?

A $1,800

B $3,600

C $4,200

D $4,800

51 Drippy is producing a list of relevant cash flows regarding a decision she has to make. She is considering launching a new type of USB memory stick that guarantees better protection to the host computer.

Drippy manages many existing products and has a standing arrangement with a technology magazine for advertising space entitling her to advertise each month. The contract has just been signed and covers the next twelve months. Payment is made in the month following an advert appearing. Drippy is going to use the magazine to advertise her exciting new USB stick.

Is the cost of the advertising space best described as a:

A   Sunk cost

B   Historic cost

C   Relevant cost

D   Committed cost

52 Which of the following terms would not normally be used to describe a relevant cost for a decision?

A   Incremental ✓

B   Future ✓

C   Material

D   Cash ✓

53 X plc intends to use relevant costs as the basis of the selling price for a special order: the printing of a brochure. The brochure requires a particular type of paper that is not regularly used by X plc although a limited amount is in X plc's inventory which was left over from a previous job. The cost when X plc bought this paper last year was $15 per ream and there are 100 reams in inventory. The brochure requires 250 reams. The current market price of the paper is $26 per ream, and the resale value of the paper in inventory is $10 per ream.

What is the relevant cost of the paper to be used in printing the brochure?

A $2,500

B $4,900

C $5,400

D $6,500

$$250 - 100 = 150 \times 26 = 3900$$

$$100 \times 10 \qquad \underline{1000}$$

$$\underline{4900}$$

COST VOLUME PROFIT ANALYSIS (CVP)

54 A company makes and sells product X and product Y. Twice as many units of product Y are made and sold as that of product X. Each unit of product X makes a contribution of $10 and each unit of product Y makes a contribution of $4. Fixed costs are $90,000.

What is the total number of units which must be made and sold to make a profit of $45,000?

A   7,500

B   22,500

C   15,000

D   16,875

$$\begin{array}{ccc} & X & Y & Tot \\ Cont. & \$10 & \$4 & 18/3 = \$6 \\ & \times 2 & \$8 & \end{array}$$

$$\frac{90000 + 45000}{6}$$

55 Betis Limited is considering changing the way it is structured by asking its employed staff to become freelance. Employees are currently paid a fixed salary of $240,000 per annum, but would instead be paid $200 per working day. On a typical working day, staff can produce 40 units. Other fixed costs are $400,000 pa.

The selling price of a unit is $60 and material costs are $20 per unit.

What will be the effect of the change on the breakeven point of the business and the level of operating risk?

A   The breakeven point reduces by 6,000 units and the operating risk goes down

B   The breakeven point reduces by 4,571 units and the operating risk goes down

C   The breakeven point reduces by 4,571 units and the operating risk goes up

D   The breakeven point reduces by 6,000 units and the operating risk goes up

FC ↓

less op nsk

$$\text{Sell p. } 60$$
$$\text{mat } 20$$
$$(a)\ \text{Con pv. } 40$$
$$lab, \ \frac{5}{35}$$

$$\text{Breakea Part} = \frac{FC}{Cont\ pv.}$$

$$(a) = \frac{240000 + 400000}{40}$$
$$= 16000$$
$$\text{Diff. } \Phi\ (16000 - 11429) = 4571$$

$$(b)\ \frac{400000}{35}$$
$$= 11429$$

56 *This objective test question contains a question type which will only appear in a computer-based exam, but this question provides valuable practice for all students whichever version of the exam they are taking.*

P CO makes two products – P1 and P2 – budgeted details of which are as follows:

	P1	P2
	$	$
Selling price	10.00	8.00
Cost per unit:		
Direct materials	3.50	4.00
Direct labour	1.50	1.00
Variable overhead	0.60	0.40
Fixed overhead	1.20	1.00
Profit per unit	**3.20**	**1.60**

Handwritten: 1.20 × 10000 = 12 000; 1.00 = 12500 (2500) 10000

Budgeted production and sales for the year ended 30 November 2015 are:

Product P1	10,000 units
Product P2	12,500 units

The fixed overhead costs included in P1 relate to apportionment of general overhead costs only. However P2 also includes specific fixed overheads totalling $2,500.

If only product P1 were to be made, how many units (to the nearest unit) would need to be sold in order to achieve a profit of $60,000 each year?

Handwritten answer in box: 18 637

57 *This objective test question contains a question type which will only appear in a computer-based exam, but this question provides valuable practice for all students whichever version of the exam they are taking.*

The CS ratio for a business is 0.4 and its fixed costs are $1,600,000. Budget revenue has been set at 6 times the amount of the fixed costs.

What is the margin of safety % measured in revenue?

Handwritten answer in box: 58.3   %

Handwritten working:

$C/S = 0.4$
$FC = 1600\ 000$
Revenue $= 9600\ 000$

$Breven = \dfrac{FC}{C/S\ rate} = \dfrac{1600\ 000}{0.4}$
$= 4\ 000\ 000$

Margin Safety $= \dfrac{Budgeted\ AL - Breeven}{Budge\ AL}$

$= \dfrac{9600\ 000 - 4000000}{9600\ 000} \times 100\%$

$= 58.3\%$

58 An organisation manufactures and sells a single product, the G. It has produced the following budget for the coming year:

	$000	$000
Sales revenue (20,000 units)		5,000
Manufacturing costs		
Fixed	1,600	
Variable	1,400	
Selling costs		
Fixed	1,200	
Variable	400	
Cost of sales		(4,600)
Profit		400

(handwritten): Sales 5000 (1400) (400) total 3200 000 pu = $160 pu

If inventory levels are negligible, what is the breakeven point in units?

A 13,634

B 13,750

C 17,500

D 28,000

(handwritten): $BE = \frac{FC}{Cost\ pu} = \frac{(1600 + 1200) \times 1000}{160} = 17500$

59 A company manufactures and sells a single product with a variable cost per unit of $36. It has a contribution ratio of 25%. The company has weekly fixed costs of $18,000.

The weekly breakeven point is pick from list units.

List options are as follows:

1,500

1,600

1,800

2,000

(handwritten): $Breakeven = \frac{FC}{contribution\ contr\ pu} = \frac{18000}{12} = 1500$

$Sales = \frac{36}{0.75} = 48$ Ctpu 48 - 36 = 12

60 A company makes a single product with the following data:

	$	$
Selling price		25
Material	5	
Labour	7	
Variable overhead	3	
Fixed overhead	4	
		(19)
Profit per unit		6

(handwritten): $C/s\ Ratio = \frac{10}{25} = 0.4$

Cont. pu = 25 - 5 - 7 - 3 = 10

$Breaker = \frac{4}{10} = 0.4$

$Margin\ safety = \frac{30\,000 - 12000}{30\,000} = 60\%$

$\frac{270\,000 + 120\,000}{10} = 39\,000$

Budgeted output is 30,000 units.

In relation to this data, which of the following statements is correct?

A The margin of safety is 40%

B The contribution to sales ratio is 24%

C The volume of sales needed to make a profit of $270,000 is 45,000 units

D If budgeted sales increase to 40,000 units, budgeted profit will increase by $100,000

(handwritten): 10 000 units more @ 10 p.u = $100 000

61 The management accountant of Caroline plc has calculated the firm's breakeven point from the following data:

Selling price per unit	$20
Variable costs per unit	$8
Fixed overheads for next year	$79,104

It is now expected that the product's selling price and variable cost will increase by 8% and 5.2% respectively.

These changes will cause Caroline's breakeven point for next year to:

A Rise by 9.0%

B Rise by 2.8%

C Fall by 2.8%

D Fall by 9%

62 Edward sells two products with selling prices and contributions as follows:

	Product F	Product G
Selling price	$40	$20
Contribution	$10	$4
Budgeted sales units	150,000	100,000

Edwards's fixed costs are $1,400,000 per year.

What is Edwards's current breakeven revenue to the nearest $?

A $100,000

B $200,000

C $5,600,000

D $5,894,737

63 Edward sells two products with selling prices and contributions as follows:

	Product F	Product G
Selling price	$40	$20
Contribution	$10	$4
Budgeted sales units	150,000	100,000

Edwards's fixed costs are $1,400,000 per year.

Edward now anticipates that more customers will buy the cheaper product G and that budgeted sales will be 150,000 units for each product.

If this happens, what would happen to the breakeven revenue?

A Increase by the extra revenue from G of 50,000 × $20/u or $1,000,000

B Decrease by the extra revenue from G of 50,000 × $20/u or $1,000,000

C Increase by a different amount

D Decrease by a different amount

64 The following breakeven chart has been drawn for a company's single product:

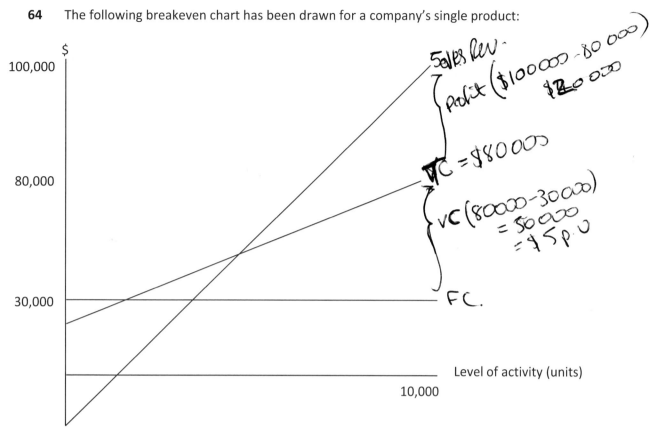

Handwritten notes: Sales Rev. Profit ($100 000 - 80 000) $20 000. TC = $80 000. VC (80000 - 30000) = 50 000 = $5 p.u. FC.

Which of the following statements about the product are correct?

(1) The product's selling price is $10 per unit.

(2) The product's variable cost is $8 per unit.

(3) The product incurs fixed costs of $30,000 per period.

(4) The product earns a profit of $70,000 at a level of activity of 10,000 units.

A (1), (2) and (3) only

B (1) and (3) only

C (1), (3) and (4) only

D (1), (2) and (4) only

65 Hubbard Ltd manufactures and sells a single product that has the following cost and selling price structure:

	$/unit
Selling price	199
Direct material	54
Direct labour	50
Variable overhead	20
Fixed overhead	22
	—
	53
	—

The fixed overhead absorption rate is based on the normal budgeted capacity of 6,200 units per month. The same amount is spent each month on fixed overheads.

Which TWO of the following statements about the performance of Hubbard Ltd next month are correct?

- 1,921 units are required to breakeven next month $\left(1819\right)$
- 3,152 units of sales are required to achieve a profit of $100,000 next month.
- Monthly fixed costs amount to $136,400
- The margin of safety next month is 75%. $\left(71\%\right)$

66

The following breakeven chart has been prepared:

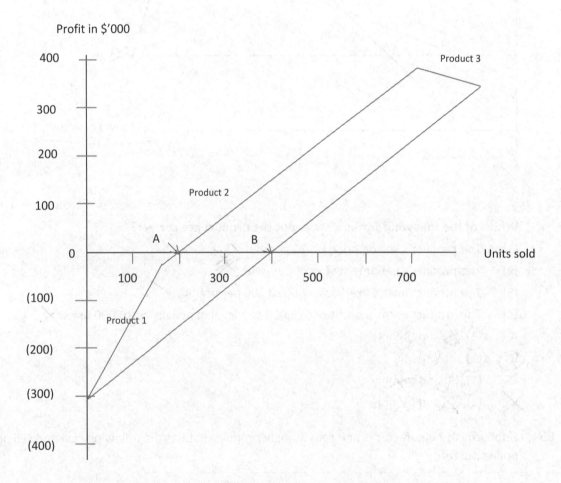

Which TWO of the following statements about the above chart are correct?

- Point A is the breakeven point if the company's products are sold in order of their C/S ratio
- Point B is the breakeven point if the company's products are sold in the budgeted sales mix
- Changing the product mix in favour of Product 3 would improve the overall c/s ratio
- If all three products are produced, then the company can expect sales revenues of $350,000.

LIMITING FACTORS

67 A company has the following production planned for the next four weeks. The figures reflect the full capacity level of operations. Planned output is equal to the maximum demand per product.

	Product A $/unit	Product B $/unit	Product C $/unit	Product D $/unit
Selling price	160	214	100	140
Raw material cost	24	56	22	40
Direct labour cost	66	88	33	22
Variable overhead cost	24	18	24	18
Fixed overhead cost	16	10	8	12
Profit	30	42	13	48
Planned output	300	125	240	400
Direct labour hours per unit	6	8	3	2

The direct labour force is threatening to go on strike for two weeks out of the coming four. This means that only 2,160 hours will be available for production, rather than the usual 4,320 hours.

If the strike goes ahead, which product or products should be produced if profits are to be maximised?

	Should be produced	Should not be produced
Product A	✓	
Product B		✓
Product C		✓
Product D	✓	

68 A jewellery company makes rings (R) and necklaces (N).

The resources available to the company have been analysed and two constraints have been identified:

Labour time $3R + 2N \le 2,400$ hours   Machine time $0.5R + 0.4N \le 410$ hours

The management accountant has used linear programming to determine that R = 500 and N = 400.

Which of the following is/are slack resources?

(1) Labour time available

(2) Machine time available

A   1 only

B   2 only

C   Both 1 and 2

D   Neither 1 nor 2

$3(500) + 2(400) \le 2400$

$2300 \le 2400$

$0.5(500) + 0.4(400) \le 410$

$410 \le 410$

69 Q plc makes two products – Quone and Qutwo – from the same raw material. The selling price and cost details of these products are as shown below:

	Quone $	Qutwo $
Selling price	20.00	18.00
Direct material ($2.00 per kg)	6.00	5.00
Direct labour	4.00	3.00
Variable overhead	2.00	1.50
	12.00	9.50
Contribution per unit	8.00	8.50

The maximum demand for these products is 500 units per week for Quone, and an unlimited number of units per week for Qutwo.

The shadow price of these materials is pick from list**, if material were limited to 2,000 kgs per week?**

List options are:	8.50
$nil	
$2.00 per kg	2.50
$2.66 per kg	
$3.40 per kg	

70 P is considering whether to continue making a component or to buy it from an outside supplier. It uses 12,000 of the components each year.

The internal manufacturing cost comprises:

	$/unit
Direct materials	3.00
Direct labour	4.00
Variable overhead	1.00
Specific fixed cost	2.50
Other fixed costs	2.00
	12.50

If the direct labour were not used to manufacture the component, it would be used to increase the production of another item for which there is unlimited demand. This other item has a contribution of $10.00 per unit but requires $8.00 of labour per unit.

What is the maximum price per component, at which buying is preferable to internal manufacture?

A $8.00

B $10.50

C $12.50

D $15.50

71 The following details relate to three services provided by RST Company:

	Service R	Service S	Service T
	$	$	$
Fee charged to customers	100	150	160
Unit service costs:			
Direct materials	15	30	25
Direct labour	20	35	30
Variable overhead	15	20	22
Fixed overhead	25	50	50

All three services use the same type of direct labour which is paid $25 per hour.

The fixed overheads are general fixed overheads that have been absorbed on the basis of machine hours.

What are the most and least profitable uses of direct labour, a scarce resource?

	Most profitable	*Least profitable*
A	S	R
B	S	T
C	T	R
D	T	S

72 A linear programming model has been formulated for two products, X and Y. The objective function is depicted by the formula C = 5X + 6Y, where C = contribution, X = the number of product X to be produced and Y = the number of product Y to be produced.

Each unit of X uses 2 kg of material Z and each unit of Y uses 3 kg of material Z. The standard cost of material Z is $2 per kg.

The shadow price for material Z has been worked out and found to be $2.80 per kg.

If an extra 20 kg of material Z becomes available at $2 per kg, what will the maximum increase in contribution be?

A   Increase of $96

B   Increase of $56

C   Increase of $16

D   No change

73 A linear programming model has been formulated for two products, A and B, manufactured by J co.

Which TWO of the following statements about linear programming are true?

- J Co can use linear programming if it starts to manufacture another product, C.
- J Co would not need to use linear programming if there was not a demand constraint.
- J Co should ignore fixed costs when making decisions about how to utilise production capacity in the short run, using linear programming.
- Linear programming models can be used when there is an experience curve, once the steady state has been reached.

74 The shadow price of skilled labour for CBV is currently $8 per hour. What does this mean?

- A The cost of obtaining additional skilled labour resources is $8 per hour
- B There is a hidden cost of $8 for each hour of skilled labour actively worked
- C Contribution will be increased by $8 per hour for each extra hour of skilled labour that can be obtained
- D Total costs will be reduced by $8 for each additional hour of skilled labour that can be obtained

PRICING DECISIONS

75 Which of the following statements is true of pricing?

- A Discrimination is always illegal so everyone should pay the same amount
- B Early adopters get a discount for being first in the market
- C Pricing against a similar competitor is important in the Internet age
- D Price to make the most sales in that way you will always get the most profit

76 Which of the following conditions would need to be true for a price skimming policy to be sensible?

- A An existing product where the owners have decided to increase prices to move the product up market
- B Where the product has a long lifecycle
- C Where the product has a short lifecycle
- D Where only modest development costs had been incurred

77 Which TWO of the following circumstances (in relation to the launch of a new product) favour a penetration pricing policy?

- • Demand is relatively inelastic.
- • There are significant economies of scale.
- • The firm wishes to discourage new entrants to the market.
- • The product life cycle is particularly short.

78 Which of the following statements regarding market penetration as a pricing strategy is/are correct?

- (1) It is useful if significant economies of scale can be achieved.
- (2) It is useful if demand for a product is highly elastic.

- A 1 only
- B 2 only
- C Neither 1 nor 2
- D Both 1 and 2

79 Which of the following conditions must be true for a price discrimination policy to be sensible?

  A   Buying power of customers must be similar in both market segments ✗

  (B)   Goods must not be able to move freely between market segments ✓

  C   Goods must be able to move freely between market segments ✗

  D   The demand curves in each market must be the same ✗

80 In a traditional pricing environment which of the following "C" words is not traditionally considered when setting a price?

  A   Cost

  B   Cash flow

  (C)   Competition

  D   Customers

Cost
Cop
Cus

81 A product has a prime cost of $12, variable overheads of $3 per unit and fixed overheads of $6 per unit.

  Which pricing policy gives the highest price?

  A   Prime cost + 80%   21·60

  B   Marginal cost + 60%   24

  (C)   TAC + 20%   25·20

  D   Net margin of 14% on selling price $\frac{21 \times 100}{86} = 24.42$

82 If demand for a product is 5,000 units when the price is $400 and 6,000 units when the price is $380, what are the demand and MR equations?

	Demand	MR
A	P = 300 − 0.02Q	MR = 300 − 0.02Q
B	P = 500 + 0.02Q	MR = 500 + 0.04Q
C	P = 300 + 0.02Q	MR = 300 + 0.02Q
(D)	P = 500 − 0.02Q	MR = 500 − 0.04Q

83 If the demand for a product is 5,000 units when the price is $400 and 6,000 units when price is $380, what is the optimal price to be charged in order to maximise profit if the variable cost of the product is $200?

  A $150

  B $200

  (C) $350

  D $700

$P = a - bQ$ $MR = MC$

$400 = a - b(5000)$

$380 = a - b(6000)$

$P = 500 - 0.02(7500)$ $500 - 0.04Q = 200$

$= 350$ $0.04Q = 300$

$Q = 7500$

84   The following price and demand combinations have been given:

P1 = 400, Q1 = 5,000

P2 = 380, Q2 = 5,500

The variable cost is a constant $80 per unit and fixed costs are $600,000 pa.

What is the demand function?

A   P = 200 – 0.04Q

B   P = 600 – 0.04Q

C   P = 600 + 0.04Q

D   P = 200 – 20Q

85   *This objective test question contains a question type which will only appear in a computer-based exam, but this question provides valuable practice for all students whichever version of the exam they are taking.*

The following price and demand combinations have been given:

P1 = 400, Q1 = 5,000

P2 = 380, Q2 = 5,500

The variable cost is a constant $80 per unit and fixed costs are $600,000 pa. The optimal price is:

$  ~~338~~ 340

86   *This objective test question contains a question type which will only appear in a computer-based exam, but this question provides valuable practice for all students whichever version of the exam they are taking.*

While a drag and drop style question is impossible to fully replicate within a paper based medium, some questions of this style have been included for completeness.

A brand new game is about to be launched. The game is unique and can only be played on the Star2000 gaming console, another one of the businesses products.

Which of the following pricing strategies could be used to price the game? Students are entitled to a small discount.

Drag the correct options into the box below:

- Penetration pricing *High low*
- Price skimming *Hs a A*
- Complimentary product pricing
- Product line pricing
- Price discrimination ✗ *(student discount)*
- Variable production cost + %

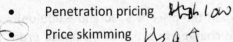

MAKE-OR-BUY AND OTHER SHORT TERM DECISIONS

87 *This objective test question contains a question type which will only appear in a computer-based exam, but this question provides valuable practice for all students whichever version of the exam they are taking.*

In a make or buy decision which FOUR of the following are to be correctly included in the considerations? Select all that apply.

- (i) The amount of re-allocated rent costs caused by using the production space differently.
- (ii) The variable costs of purchase from the new supplier.
- (iii) The amount of the bribe from the potential new supplier. ✗
- (iv) The level of discount available from the new supplier. ·
- (v) The redundancy payments to the supervisor of the product in question.
- (vi) The saved labour costs of the production staff re-directed to other work ~save nothing
- (vii) The materials no longer bought to manufacture the product.

88 *This objective test question contains a question type which will only appear in a computer-based exam, but this question provides valuable practice for all students whichever version of the exam they are taking.*

Appler is considering the relevant cash flows involved in a short-term decision. An important client has asked for the minimum price for the processing of a compound. The compound involves the following:

Material A: Appler needs 500 kg of material for the compound but has 200 kg in stock present. The stock items were bought 3 months ago for $5/kg but have suffered 10% ~not relevant shrinkage since that date. Material A is not regularly used in the business and would have to be disposed of at a cost to Appler of $400 in total. The current purchase price of material A is $6.25/kg.

Material B: Appler needs 800 kg of material B and has this in stock as it is regularly needed. The stock was bought 2 months ago for $4/kg although it can be bought now at $3.75/kg due to its seasonal nature.

Processing energy costs would be $200 and the supervisor says he would allocate $150 of his weekly salary to the job in the company's job costing system. ⎱ not relevant

Based upon the scenario information, what is the total cost of material A and B to be built in to the minimum price calculation?

$ 4475

89 *This objective test question contains a question type which will only appear in a computer-based exam, but this question provides valuable practice for all students whichever version of the exam they are taking.*

Appler is considering the relevant cash flows involved in a short-term decision. An important client has asked for the minimum price for the processing of a compound. The compound involves the following:

Material A: Appler needs 500 kg of material for the compound but has 200 kg in stock present. The stock items were bought 3 months ago for $5/kg but have suffered 10% shrinkage since that date. Material A is not regularly used in the business and would have to be disposed of at a cost to Appler of $400 in total. The current purchase price of material A is $6.25/kg.

Material B: Appler needs 800 kg of material B and has this in stock as it is regularly needed. The stock was bought 2 months ago for $4/kg although it can be bought now at $3.75/kg due to its seasonal nature.

Processing energy costs would be $200 and the supervisor says he would allocate $150 of his weekly salary to the job in the company's job costing system.

Based upon the scenario information, what is the total cost for processing and supervision to be included in the minimum price calculation?

$ [200]

90 *This objective test question contains a question type which will only appear in a computer-based exam, but this question provides valuable practice for all students whichever version of the exam they are taking.*

While a drag and drop style question is impossible to fully replicate within a paper based medium, some questions of this style have been included for completeness.

Ace Limited is considering whether or not to cease production of leather-bound diaries.

Which of the following items are valid factors to consider in this decision?

- The diaries made a loss in the year just passed
- The diaries made a positive contribution in the year just passed
- The market outlook in the long term looks very poor
- The budget for next year shows a loss
- The business also sells pens and many diary buyers will often also buy a pen
- The business was founded to produce and sell diaries

Drag and drop the correct factors in the box below:

91 Jorioz Co makes joint products X and Y. $120,000 joint processing costs are incurred.

At the split-off point, 10,000 units of X and 9,000 units of Y are produced, with selling prices of $1.20 for X and $1.50 for Y.

The units of X could be processed further to make 8,000 units of product Z. The extra costs incurred in this process would be fixed costs of $1,600 and variable costs of $0.50 per unit of input.

The selling price of Z would be $2.25.

A pick from list is the outcome to be expected if product X is further processed.

List options are
$600 loss
$400 gain
$3,900 gain
$1,600 loss

DEALING WITH RISK AND UNCERTAINTY IN DECISION-MAKING

92 *This objective test question contains a question type which will only appear in a computer-based exam, but this question provides valuable practice for all students whichever version of the exam they are taking.*

Shuffles is attempting to decide which size of fork-lift truck to buy to use in its warehouses. There are three grades of truck, the A series, B series and the C series. The uncertainty faced is the expected growth in the on-line market it serves, which could grow at 15%, 30% or even 40% in the next period.

Shuffles has correctly produced the following decision table and has calculated the average daily contribution gained from each combination of truck and growth assumption.

Decision table		Type of truck		
		A series	B series	C series
Growth rate	15%	$2,400	$1,800	$3,600
	30%	$1,400	$1,900	$4,500
	40%	$4,900	$2,800	$3,900

Which truck would the pessimistic buyer purchase? Enter only the letter:

C. series

– Best result
if worst happens
maxi min

93 *This objective test question contains a question type which will only appear in a computer-based exam, but this question provides valuable practice for all students whichever version of the exam they are taking.*

Shuffles is attempting to decide which size of fork-lift truck to buy to use in its warehouses. There are three grades of truck, the A series, B series and the C series. The uncertainty faced is the expected growth in the on-line market it serves, which could grow at 15%, 30% or even 40% in the next period.

Shuffles has correctly produced the following decision table and has calculated the average daily contribution gained from each combination of truck and growth assumption.

Decision table		Type of truck		
		A series	B series	C series
Growth rate	15%	$2,400	$1,800	$3,600
	30%	$1,400	$1,900	$4,500
	40%	$4,900	$2,800	$3,900

Which truck would the optimistic buyer purchase? Enter only the letter:

A series

Best result.

94   *This objective test question contains a question type which will only appear in a computer-based exam, but this question provides valuable practice for all students whichever version of the exam they are taking.*

Shuffles is attempting to decide which size of fork-lift truck to buy to use in its warehouses. There are three grades of truck, the A series, B series and the C series. The uncertainty faced is the expected growth in the on-line market it serves, which could grow at 15%, 30% or even 40% in the next period.

Shuffles has correctly produced the following decision table and has calculated the average daily contribution gained from each combination of truck and growth assumption.

Decision table		Type of truck		
		A series	B series	C series
Growth rate	15%	$2,400	$1,800	$3,600
	30%	$1,400	$1,900	$4,500
	40%	$4,900	$2,800	$3,900

Based upon the scenario information, if the buyer was prone to regretting decisions that have been made which truck would the buyer purchase? Enter only the letter:

C	series

95   *This objective test question contains a question type which will only appear in a computer-based exam, but this question provides valuable practice for all students whichever version of the exam they are taking.*

Shuffles is attempting to decide which size of fork-lift truck to buy to use in its warehouses. There are three grades of truck, the A series, B series and the C series. The uncertainty faced is the expected growth in the on-line market it serves, which could grow at 15%, 30% or even 40% in the next period.

Shuffles has correctly produced the following decision table and has calculated the average daily contribution gained from each combination of truck and growth assumption.

Decision table		Type of truck		
		A series	B series	C series
Growth rate	15%	$2,400	$1,800	$3,600
	30%	$1,400	$1,900	$4,500
	40%	$4,900	$2,800	$3,900

Based upon the scenario information, if the probabilities of the given growth rates are 15%: 0.4, 30%: 0.25 and 40%: 0.35, which truck would the risk-neutral buyer purchase?

C	series

96 Which TWO of the following statements about sensitivity analysis are correct?

- Sensitivity analysis can be used to gain insight into which assumptions or variables in a situation are critical.

- Sensitivity analysis provides information on the basis of which decisions can be made but it does not point to the correct decision directly.

- As well as identifying how far a variable needs to change, sensitivity analysis looks at the probability of such a change

- Sensitivity analysis not only assumes that variables can change independently, it also allows to change more than one variable at a time.

97 Indicate, by clicking in the relevant boxes, whether the following statements about simulation are true or not true:

	True	Not true
Simulation models the behaviour of a system. T		
Simulation models can be used to study alternative solutions to a problem. T		
The equations describing the operating characteristics of the system are known. F		
A simulation model cannot prescribe what should be done about a problem. t		

98 A company has used expected values to evaluate a one-off project. The expected value calculation assumed two possible profit outcomes which were assigned probabilities of 0.4 and 0.6.

Which TWO of the following statements about this approach are correct?

- The expected value profit is the profit which has the highest probability of being achieved.

- The expected value gives no indication of the dispersion of the possible outcomes. ✓

- Expected values are relatively insensitive to assumptions about probability.

- The expected value may not correspond to any of the actual possible outcomes.

99 Tree Co is considering employing a sales manager. Market research has shown that a good sales manager can increase profit by 30%, an average one by 20% and a poor one by 10%. Experience has shown that the company has attracted a good sales manager 35% of the time, an average one 45% of the time and a poor one 20% of the time. The company's normal profits are $180,000 per annum and the sales manager's salary would be $40,000 per annum.

Based on the expected value criterion, which of the following represents the correct advice which Tree Co should be given?

A Do not employ a sales manager as profits would be expected to fall by $1,300

B Employ a sales manager as profits will increase by $38,700

C Employ a sales manager as profits are expected to increase by $100

D Do not employ a sales manager as profits are expected to fall by $39,900

100 A company is considering the development and marketing of a new product. Development costs will be $2m. There is a 75% probability that the development effort will be successful, and a 25% probability that it will be unsuccessful. If development *is* successful and the product *is* marketed, it is estimated that:

	Expected profit	Probability
Product very successful	$6.0m	0.4
Product moderately successful	$1.8m	0.4
Product unsuccessful	($5.0m)	0.2

What is the expected value of the project?

A ($0.41m)

B $2.12m

C $1.59m

D $0.41m

BUDGETING AND CONTROL

BUDGETARY SYSTEMS

101 Which of the following statements are true regarding Activity-Based Budgeting (ABB)?

(1) The costs determined using ABC are used as a basis for preparing budgets.

(2) The aim of ABB is to control the number of units output rather than the costs themselves.

A 1 only

B 2 only

C Neither 1 nor 2

D Both 1 and 2

102 Which of the following statement(s) is/are true regarding budgetary systems in the performance hierarchy?

(1) Developing new products in response the changes in technology is a budgeting activity that would fall within operational planning and control.

(2) Budgetary systems at strategic planning levels look at the business as a whole and define resource requirements.

A 1 only

B 2 only

C Neither 1 nor 2

D Both 1 and 2

103 The purpose of a flexible budget is to:

A Compare actual and budgeted results at virtually any level of production

B Reduce the total time in preparing the annual budget

C Allow management some latitude in meeting goals

D Eliminate cyclical fluctuations in production reports by ignoring variable costs

TYPES OF BUDGET

104 *This objective test question contains a question type which will only appear in a computer-based exam, but this question provides valuable practice for all students whichever version of the exam they are taking.*

While a drag and drop style question is impossible to fully replicate within a paper based medium, some questions of this style have been included for completeness.

Incremental budgeting can sometimes be an appropriate methodology for setting budgets.

Which of the following statements are true?

- Incremental budgets could be appropriate when:
- The business is growing rapidly
- Applied to total sales in an international seasonal business
- Applied to stationary costs
- Applied to production costs
- The business is stable
- For administration costs when the experience of the managers is limited

Drag the correct answers in to the box:

105 **Which of the following statement(s) is/are true regarding feed-forward control budgetary systems?**

(1) Feedforward control systems have an advantage over other types of control in that it establishes how effective planning was.

(2) Feedforward control occurs while an activity is in progress.

A   1 only

B   2 only

C   Neither 1 nor 2

D   Both 1 and 2

106 **An incremental budgeting system is:**

A   a system which budgets only for the extra costs associated with a particular plan

B   a system which budgets for the variable manufacturing costs only

C   a system which prepares budgets only after the manager responsible has justified the continuation of the relevant activity

D   a system which prepares budgets by adjusting the previous year's values by expected changes in volumes of activity and price/inflation effects

107 **Which of the following is an advantage of non-participative budgeting as compared to participative budgeting?**

A   It increases motivation

B   It is less time consuming

C   It increases acceptance

D   The budgets produced are more attainable

108 EFG uses an Activity Based Budgeting system. It manufactures three products, budgeted details of which are set out below:

	Product E	Product F	Product G
Budgeted annual production (units)	75,000	120,000	60,000
Batch size (units)	200	60	30
Machine set-ups per batch	5	3	9
Purchase orders per batch	4	2	2
Processing time per unit (minutes)	3	4	4

Three cost pools have been identified. Their budgeted costs for the year ending 30 September 20X3 are as follows:

Machine set-up costs	$180,000
Purchasing of materials	$95,000
Processing	$110,000

The budgeted machine set-up cost per unit of product F is | pick from list |

List options are:
• $0.1739
• $0.35
• $6.96
• Cannot be determined without any more information

109 **A master budget comprises the:**

A   budgeted income statement and budgeted cash flow only

B   budgeted income statement and budgeted balance sheet only

C   budgeted income statement and budgeted capital expenditure only

D   budgeted income statement, budgeted balance sheet and budgeted cash flow only

110 **Which of the following statement(s) are true regarding different types of budget?**

(1)   A flexible budget can be used to control operational efficiency.

(2)   Incremental budgeting can be defined as a system of budgetary planning and control that measures the additional costs that are incurred when there are unplanned extra units of activity.

(3)   Rolling budgets review and, if necessary, revise the budget for the next quarter to ensure that budgets remain relevant for the remainder of the accounting period.

A   1 and 3 only

B   2 and 3 only

C   3 only

D   1 only

111 X Co uses rolling budgeting, updating its budgets on a quarterly basis. After carrying out the last quarter's update to the cash budget, it projected a forecast cash deficit of $400,000 at the end of the year. Consequently, the planned purchase of new capital equipment has been postponed.

Which of the following types of control is the sales manager's actions an example of?

A   Feedforward control

B   Negative feedback control

C   Positive feedback control

D   Double loop feedback control

112 A definition of zero-based budgeting is set out below, with two blank sections.

"Zero-based budgeting: a method of budgeting which requires each cost element _____, as though the activities to which the budget relates _____."

Which combination of two phrases correctly completes the definition?

	Blank 1	Blank 2
A	to be specifically justified	could be out-sourced to an external supplier
B	to be set at zero	could be out-sourced to an external supplier
C	to be specifically justified	were being undertaken for the first time
D	to be set at zero	were being undertaken for the first time

113 **Which TWO of the following statements regarding zero based budgeting are correct?**

- It is best applied to support expenses rather than to direct costs.
- It can link strategic goals to specific functional areas.
- It carries forward inefficiencies from previous budget periods.
- It is consistent with a top-down budgeting approach.

114 **Which of the following statement(s) regarding the drawbacks of activity-based budgeting is/are true?**

(1) It is not always useful or applicable, as in the short term many overhead costs are not controllable and do not vary directly with changes in the volume of activity for the cost driver.

(2) ABB will not be able to provide useful information for a total quality management programme (TQM).

A   1 only

B   2 only

C   Neither 1 nor 2

D   Both 1 and 2

QUANTITATIVE ANALYSIS IN BUDGETING

115 The following table shows the number of clients who attended a particular accountancy practice over the last four weeks and the total costs incurred during each of the weeks:

Week	Number of clients	Total cost
		$
1	400	36,880
2	440	39,840
3	420	36,800
4	460	40,000

Applying the high low method to the above information, which of the following could be used to forecast total cost ($) from the number of clients expected to attend (where x = the expected number of clients)?

A   7,280 + 74x

B   16,080 + 52x

C   3,200 + 80x

D   40,000/x

116 The management accountant of a business has identified the following information:

Activity level	800 units	1,200 units
Total cost	$16,400	$23,600

The fixed costs of the business step up by 40% at 900 units.

What is the variable cost per unit?

A $8.00

B $18.00

C $19.67

D $20.00

117 The management accountant of a business has identified the following information:

Activity level	800 units	1,200 units
Total cost	$16,400	$23,600

The fixed costs of the business step up by 40% at 900 units.

What is the fixed cost at 1,100 units?

A $6,400

B $7,600

C $10,000

D $14,000

118 *This objective test question contains a question type which will only appear in a computer-based exam, but this question provides valuable practice for all students whichever version of the exam they are taking.*

The budgeted electricity cost for a business is $30,000 based upon production of 1,000 units. However if 1,400 units were to be produced the budgeted cost rises to $31,600.

Using the high/low approach what would be the budgeted electricity cost if 2,100 units were to be produced?

$ [   ]

119 *This objective test question contains a question type which will only appear in a computer-based exam, but this question provides valuable practice for all students whichever version of the exam they are taking.*

The time for the first unit produced was 100 hours. The time for the second unit was 90 hours.

What is the learning rate?

[   ] %

120 *This objective test question contains a question type which will only appear in a computer-based exam, but this question provides valuable practice for all students whichever version of the exam they are taking.*

The time for the first batch of 50 units was 500 hours. The total time for the first 16 batches of 50 units was 5,731 hours.

What is the learning rate?

[   ] %

121 *This objective test question contains a question type which will only appear in a computer-based exam, but this question provides valuable practice for all students whichever version of the exam they are taking.*

The time for the first batch of 50 units was 400 hours but the labour budget is the subject of a learning effect where the learning rate is 90%. The rate of pay for labour is $12 per hour.

The business had received and satisfied an order for 600 units but it has now received a second order for another 800 units.

The value of b is = –0.152

What will be the cost of this second order? (no decimals please)

$ [   ]

122 *This objective test question contains a question type which will only appear in a computer-based exam, but this question provides valuable practice for all students whichever version of the exam they are taking.*

The times taken to produce each of the first four batches of a new product were as follows:

Batch number	Time taken
1	100 minutes
2	70 minutes
3	59 minutes
4	55 minutes

What was the rate of learning closest to? (1 d.p)

	%

123 Kim Co has recently developed a new product. The nature of Caroline's work is repetitive, and it is usual for there to be an 80% learning effect when a new product is developed. The time taken for the first unit was 22 minutes. An 80% learning effect applies.

The fourth unit will take pick from list **minutes**

List options are as follows:
17.6 minutes
14.08 minutes
15.45 minutes
9.98 minutes

STANDARD COSTING

124 **Which of the following best describes a 'basic standard' within the context of budgeting?**

A   A standard which is kept unchanged over a period of time

B   A standard which is based on current price levels

C   A standard set at an ideal level, which makes no allowance for normal losses, waste and machine downtime

D   A standard which assumes an efficient level of operation, but which includes allowances for factors such as normal loss, waste and machine downtime

125 **Which TWO of the following statements about budgets and standards are true?**

- Budgets can be used in situations where output cannot be measured, but standards cannot be used in such situations.

- Budgets can include allowances for inefficiencies in operations, but standards use performance targets which are attainable under the most favourable conditions.

- Budgets are used for planning purposes, standards are used only for control purposes.

- Standards which remain unaltered for long periods of time are referred to as basic standards

126 **An accurate definition of standard costing is a system of budgeting where:**

   A   all activities are examined without reference to history each year

   B   output level and costs are predetermined, actual results then compared with these predetermined costs and variances analysed

   C   actual costs are compared with predetermined costs for the level of activity

   D   costs are assigned to a manager in order that controllable and non-controllable costs are accounted for

127 **Which of the following accounting procedures are used for controlling costs conditional on a given volume of production?**

	Flexible budgeting	Standard costing
A	Yes	Yes
B	Yes	No
C	No	Yes
D	No	No

128 The following are management accounting techniques:

   (i)   Actual versus flexed budget calculations.

   (ii)   Variance analysis.

   (iii)   Trend of costs analysis.

   Which of the above techniques could be used by a company to control costs?

   A   (i) and (ii) only

   B   (i) and (iii) only

   C   (ii) and (iii) only

   D   (i), (ii) and (iii)

129 **When considering setting standards for costing, which of the following would NOT be appropriate?**

   A   The normal level of activity should always be used for absorbing overheads

   B   Average prices for materials should be used, encompassing any discounts that are regularly available

   C   The labour rate used will be the rate at which the labour is paid

   D   Average material usage should be established based on generally-accepted working practices

130 **Which of the following statements is/are true regarding standard costing and total quality management (TQM)?**

   (1)   They focus on assigning responsibility solely to senior managers.

   (2)   They work well in rapidly changing environments.

   A   1 only

   B   2 only

   C   Neither 1 nor 2

   D   Both 1 and 2

131 *This objective test question contains a question type which will only appear in a computer-based exam, but this question provides valuable practice for all students whichever version of the exam they are taking.*

While a drag and drop style question is impossible to fully replicate within a paper based medium, some questions of this style have been included for completeness.

A business is expanding rapidly and buying its material in a variety of countries in a variety of currencies. It has an exclusive supply delivery contract whereby the same logistics expert makes all deliveries in to its warehouses on a cost plus basis. It pays all delivery charges on a per unit basis.

Which of the following are valid explanations of an adverse material price variance measured to include delivery costs as part of the cost per kg delivered?

Drag the correct items into the box below:

- Exchange rate movements
- Extra discounts agreed
- Increased world-wide demand for the material
- Extra supply of the material becoming available from new suppliers
- World oil price rises
- Increases in the dividends paid by the delivery business

MATERIALS MIX AND YIELD VARIANCES

132 *This objective test question contains a question type which will only appear in a computer-based exam, but this question provides valuable practice for all students whichever version of the exam they are taking.*

While a drag and drop style question is impossible to fully replicate within a paper based medium, some questions of this style have been included for completeness.

The following are potential causes of a material usage variance; drag the ones that could properly explain an adverse usage variance and at the same time indicate poor performance of the production manager into the box below.

The business has separate managers for production, material purchase and machine maintenance.

- Selection of a new supplier offering similar quality for lower prices
- Inadequate training of newly recruited staff in the production department
- Movements in the exchange rates causing more expensive materials
- Machine breakdown due to delays in the annual maintenance schedule
- Reduced quality materials bought
- Change in the production process causing extra losses of materials

133 **Which of the following statements is/are true regarding the material mix variance?**

(1) A favourable total mix variance would suggest that a higher proportion of a cheaper material is being used instead of a more expensive one.

(2) A favourable total mix variance will usually result in a favourable material yield variance.

A 1 only

B 1 and 2

C 2 only

D Both statements are false

134 **Which of the following statements is/are true regarding the materials yield variance?**

(1) An adverse total yield variance would suggest that less output has been achieved for a given input, i.e. that the total input in volume is more than expected for the output achieved.

(2) A favourable total mix variance will usually result in an adverse material yield variance.

A (1) only

B (1) and (2)

C (2) only

D Both statements are false

135 JC Ltd mixes three materials to produce a chemical SGR. The following extract from a standard cost card shows the materials to be used in producing 100 kg of chemical SGR:

	kg
Material A	50 @ $10 per kg
Material B	40 @ $5 per kg
Material C	20 @ $9 per kg
	110

During October 23,180 kg of SGR were produced using the following materials:

	kg
Material A	13,200
Material B	7,600
Material C	5,600
	26,400

What is the total material mix variance?

A $1,984 A

B $7,216 A

C $9,200 A

D $16,416 A

136 Product GX consists of a mix of three materials, J, K and L. The standard material cost of a unit of GX is as follows:

		$
Material J	5 kg at $4 per kg	20
Material K	2 kg at $12 per kg	24
Material L	3 kg at $8 per kg	24

During March, 3,000 units of GX were produced, and actual usage was:

Material J	13,200 kg
Material K	6,500 kg
Material L	9,300 kg

What was the materials yield variance for March?

A $6,800 favourable

B $6,800 adverse

C $1,000 favourable

D $1,000 adverse

137 *This objective test question contains a question type which will only appear in a computer-based exam, but this question provides valuable practice for all students whichever version of the exam they are taking.*

Mr. Green makes salads. The standard plate of salad has 30 g of lettuce (L), 50 g of peppers (P) and 80 g of beetroot (B). The standard prices of the three ingredients are $0.2/kg, 0.4/kg and 0.8/kg respectively. The actual prices were $0.22/kg, $0.38/kg and $0.82/kg.

Mr. Green has been experimenting and so in July he changed the mix of vegetables on the plate thus: 1,500 plates contained 62,000 grams of lettuce, 81,000 grams of peppers and 102,000 grams of beetroot.

What is the cost difference between the actual mix and the standard mix to the nearest cent?

$ [   ]

138 Mr. Green makes salads. The standard plate of salad has 30 g of lettuce (L), 50 g of peppers (P) and 80 g of beetroot (B). The standard prices of the three ingredients are $0.2/kg, 0.4/kg and 0.8/kg respectively.

Mr. Green has been experimenting and so in July he changed the mix of vegetables on the plate thus: 1,500 plates contained 62,000 grams of lettuce, 81,000 grams of peppers and 102,000 grams of beetroot.

What is the yield variance (do not round your answer)?

A $2.8125 Fav

B $2.8125 Adv

C $2,812.5 Fav

D $2,812.5 Adv

139 A company has a process in which the standard mix for producing 9 litres of output is as follows:

	$
4.0 litres of D at $9 per litre	36.00
3.5 litres of E at $5 per litre	17.50
2.5 litres of F at $2 per litre	5.00
Total	58.50

A standard loss of 10% of inputs is expected to occur. The actual inputs for the latest period were:

	$
4,300 litres of D at $9.00 per litre	38,700
3,600 litres of E at $5.50 per litre	19,800
2,100 litres of F at $2.20 per litre	4,620
Total	63,120

Actual output for this period was 9,100 litres.

What is the total materials mix variance?

A $2,400 (A)

B $2,400 (F)

C $3,970 (A)

D $3,970 (F)

SALES MIX AND QUANTITY VARIANCES

140 *This objective test question contains a question type which will only appear in a computer-based exam, but this question provides valuable practice for all students whichever version of the exam they are taking.*

Bloom Limited was the subject of the following press story:

"Bloom is proud to announce that it has managed to maintain its market share despite an overall increase in the market size by 10%." However, the sales director when challenged, by this journalist recently admitted having been forced to reduce prices by $1.50 per bunch on average on a budget volume of 12,000 bunches. All is not as rosy as it seems in Bloom's garden!

If the standard variable cost of a bloom bunch of flowers is $20 and the standard contribution gained is $5 what is the adverse sales price variance?

$ [   ]

141 *This objective test question contains a question type which will only appear in a computer-based exam, but this question provides valuable practice for all students whichever version of the exam they are taking.*

Bloom Limited was the subject of the following press story:

"Bloom is proud to announce that it has managed to maintain its market share despite an overall increase in the market size by 10%." However, the sales director when challenged, by this journalist recently admitted having been forced to reduce prices by $1.50 per bunch on average on a budget volume of 12,000 bunches. All is not as rosy as it seems in Bloom's garden!

If the standard variable cost of a bloom bunch of flowers is $20 and the standard contribution gained is $5 what is the favourable sales volume variance?

$ [   ]

142 *This objective test question contains a question type which will only appear in a computer-based exam, but this question provides valuable practice for all students whichever version of the exam they are taking.*

Bloom Limited was the subject of the following press story:

Yellow sells two types of squash balls: the type A and the type B. The standard contribution from these balls is $4 and $5 respectively and the standard profit per ball is $1.50 and $2.40 respectively. The budget was to sell 5 type A balls for every 3 type B balls.

Actual sales were up 20,000 at 240,000 balls with type A balls being 200,000 of that total. Yellow values its stock of balls at standard marginal cost.

What is the value of the adverse sales mix variance?

$ [   ]

143 *This objective test question contains a question type which will only appear in a computer-based exam, but this question provides valuable practice for all students whichever version of the exam they are taking.*

Bloom Limited was the subject of the following press story:

Yellow sells two types of squash ball, the type A and the type B. The standard contribution from these balls is $4 and $5 respectively and the standard profit per ball is $1.50 and $2.40 respectively. The budget was to sell 5 type A balls for every 3 type B balls.

Actual sales were up 20,000 at 240,000 balls with type A balls being 200,000 of that total. Yellow values its stock of balls at standard marginal cost.

What is the value of the favourable sales quantity variance?

$ [   ]

144 Jones' monthly absorption costing variance analysis report includes a sales mix variance, which indicates the effect on profit of actual sales mix differing from the budgeted sales mix. The following data are available.

	Product X		Product Y	
	$	$	$	$
Selling price		12		11
Less Variable cost	6		2	
Fixed cost	2		3	
	—	(8)	—	(5)
Standard net profit per unit		4		6
July sales (units)				
Budget		3,000		6,000
Actual		2,000		8,000

The favourable sales mix variance is pick from list **in July.**

List options include:
$8,000
$5,333
$4,000
$2,667

145 You have been provided with the following information relating to three products:

	Product X	Product Y	Product Z
Demand (units)	1,000	2,000	3,000
Selling price	$15	$20	$30
Profit per unit	$2	$5	$2

Actual sales for the year showed the following results.

	Product X	Product Y	Product Z
Units sold	1,100	2,050	2,800
Sales value	$17,050	$38,950	$86,800
Profit	$3,080	$10,455	$6,160

What is the sales quantity variance?

A $150 adverse

B $50 favourable

C $1,208 adverse

D $1,695 favourable

PLANNING AND OPERATIONAL VARIANCES

146 **Which of the following statements are true regarding material price planning variances?**

(1)   The publication of material price planning variances should always lead to automatic updates of standard costs.

(2)   The causes of material price planning variances do not need to be investigated by managers at any level in the organisation.

A   1 only

B   2 only

C   Neither 1 nor 2

D   Both 1 and 2

147 Leaf limited has had a mixed year. Its market share has improved two percentage points to 20% but the overall market had contracted by 5% in the same period. The budgeted sales were 504,000 units and standard contribution was $12 per unit.

What is the level of actual sales?

A   Two percentage points up on budget at 510,080 units

B   Three percent down overall on budget at 488,880 units

C   Three percent up on budget at 519,120 units

D   Up by a little over five and a half percent to 532,000 units

148 Leaf Limited has had a mixed year. Its market share has improved two percentage points to 20% but the overall market had contracted by 5% in the same period. The budgeted sales were 504,000 units and standard contribution was $12 per unit.

The sales market size variance is:

A $1,680,000 Fav

B $1,680,000 Adv

C $302,400 Adv

D $302,400 Fav

149 A company manufactures a specific clinical machine used in hospitals. The company holds a 2% share of the market and the total market demand has been constant at 250,000 machines for the last few years. The budgeted selling price for each machine is $10,000 and standard contribution is equivalent to 10% of the budgeted selling price.

An initial performance review of the company's actual results showed a sales volume of 5,600 machines had been achieved. The total market demand for the machines, though, had risen to 300,000 units.

What is the market share variance for the clinical machines?

A $200,000 favourable

B $400,000 adverse

C $600,000 favourable

D $1,000,000 adverse

150 PlasBas Co uses recycled plastic to manufacture shopping baskets for local retailers. The standard price of the recycled plastic is $0.50 per kg and standard usage of recycled plastic is 0.2 kg for each basket. The budgeted production was 80,000 baskets.

Due to recent government incentives to encourage recycling, the standard price of recycled plastic was expected to reduce to $0.40 per kg. The actual price paid by the company was $0.42 per kg and 100,000 baskets were manufactured using 20,000 kg of recycled plastic.

What is the materials operational price variance?

A $2,000 favourable

B $1,600 favourable

C $400 adverse

D $320 adverse

151 A profit centre manager claims that the poor performance of her division is entirely due to factors outside her control. She has submitted the following table along with notes from a market expert, which she believes explains the cause of the poor performance:

Category	Budget this year	Actual this year	Actual last year	Market expert notes
Sales volume (units)	500	300	400	The entire market has decreased by 25% compared to last year. The product will be obsolete in four years
Sales revenue	$50,000	$28,500	$40,000	Rivalry in the market saw selling prices fall by 10%
Total material cost	$10,000	$6,500	$8,000	As demand for the raw materials is decreasing, suppliers lowered their prices by 5%

After adjusting for the external factors outside the manager's control, in which category/categories is there evidence of poor performance?

A Material cost only

B Sales volume and sales price

C Sales price and material cost

D Sales price only

152 Which of the following statement(s) is/are true regarding **planning and operational variances?**

(1) Planning and operational variances are calculated when it is necessary to assess a manager on results that are within his/her control.

(2) Revised standards are required because variances may arise partly due to an unrealistic budget, and not solely due to operational factors.

A   1 only

B   2 only

C   Neither 1 nor 2

D   Both 1 and 2

PERFORMANCE ANALYSIS AND BEHAVIOURAL ASPECTS

153 The finance director of Paint Mixers Ltd has produced the table below showing the variance results for the first three months of the year:

	January	February	March
Material price variance	$3,000 A	$2,000 A	$1,000 A
Material mix variance	$2,000 A	$750 A	$100 F
Material yield variance	$4,000 A	$2,000 A	$50F

Which of the following interpretations of the variances analysis exercise above is NOT correct?

A   The purchasing manager should be able to threaten to switch suppliers to get better deals and address the adverse material price variance

B   The materials mix variance is entirely under the control of the production manager

C   The favourable yield variance in March could be the result of operational efficiency

D   The responsibility for the initial poor performance must be borne by both the purchasing manager and the production manager

154 Which of the following statement(s) regarding the use of standard costs in rapidly changing environments is/are true?

(1) Variance analysis results will take into account important criteria such as customer satisfaction or quality of production.

(2) Achieving standards is suitable in most modern manufacturing environments.

A   1 only

B   2 only

C   Neither 1 nor 2

D   Both 1 and 2

PERFORMANCE MEASUREMENT AND CONTROL

PERFORMANCE MANAGEMENT INFORMATION SYSTEMS

155 Which of the following statements regarding planning and control as described in the three tiers of Robert Anthony's decision-making hierarchy is/are true?

(1) Strategic planning is concerned with making decisions about the efficient and effective use of existing resources.

(2) Operational control is about ensuring that specific tasks are carried out efficiently and effectively.

A 1 only

B 2 only

C Neither 1 nor 2

D Both 1 and 2

156 Long-term sales forecasts are an example of accounting information used at which level of control in an organisation?

A Strategic planning

B Management control

C Tactical control

D Operational control

157 Are information systems described below suited or not suited to all levels of management in an organisation?

	Suited to all levels of management	Not suited to all levels of management
A Management Information System producing management accounts showing margins for individual customers	✓	
An Expert System holding specialist tax information	✓	
An Executive Information System giving access to internal and external information in summarised form, with the option to drill down to a greater level of activity		✓

158 A manufacturer and retailer of kitchens introduces an enterprise resource planning system.

Which of the following is NOT likely to be a potential benefit of introducing this system?

A Schedules of labour are prepared for manufacturing

B Inventory records are updated automatically

C Sales are recorded into the financial ledgers

D Critical strategic information can be summarised

159 **Electronic Executive Information Systems (EIS) and Expert Systems (ES) are examples of:**

A   Customer relationship management software

B   Database management systems

C   Computer networking

D   Decision based software

160 You have been presented with a summary report of sales in the last month, with a breakdown of totals per product, and with variances from the corresponding monthly sales plan.

This report is an output from:

A   A transaction processing system

B   A management information system

C   An executive Information system

D   None of the above

SOURCES OF MANAGEMENT INFORMATION

161 **Which of the following statement regarding the use of external information is/are true?**

(1)   External information is usually more reliable than internal information.

(2)   External information can be general and vague, and may not really help an organisation with decision making.

A   1 only

B   2 only

C   Neither 1 nor 2

D   Both 1 and 2

162 **Would the following sources of information be considered internal or external?**

	Internal	External
Interviewing potential customers		✓
Reading business magazines		✓
Listing employee records from the company's payroll system	✓	
Looking through sales records for the last year	✓	

163 **Where would you most likely find information concerning the frequency of machine breakdowns causing lost production?**

A   The fixed asset register

B   The machine maintenance schedule

C   Production output reports

D   The purchase ledger account for the supplier that provides replacement machine parts

164   Which of the following could be described as an expert system?

    A   An ATM dispensing cash provided there is enough money in the account

    B   A stock management system, which highlights stock-outs

    C   A marketing database holding records of past advertising campaigns and the sales generated by those campaigns

    D   A tax calculator which predicts the level of tax payable in different scenarios

165   Which of the following is the most reliable source of information on a country's inflation rate?

    A   Spending on groceries by a family from one point of time to the next

    B   Journalist reports concerning the difficulties local families are having making ends meet

    C   Average house prices measured across the country from one point of time to the next

    D   The government figures for RPI or CPI

166   The qualities of good information contained in reports are more easily remembered using the mnemonic ACCURATE. Which one of the following is not normally associated with a quality of good information?

    A   Adaptable to the needs of the user

    B   Acceptable to the user

    C   Accurate

    D   Understandable by the user

MANAGEMENT REPORTS

167   Strategic reports have many features, which of the following would be most likely true of a strategic report?

    A   Prepared regularly

    B   Normally considered accurate and reliable

    C   Highly summarised showing overall trends

    D   Demonstrates current position

168   Local managers within organisations often use operational reports. Which of the following features of reports would be most true of an operational report?

    A   Summarised information

    B   Mainly external information on local competition

    C   Accurate information on current position

    D   Infrequent

169 A government department generates information which should <u>not be disclosed</u> to anyone who works outside of the department. There are <u>many other government departments</u> working within the same building.

Which of the following would <u>NOT be an effective control</u> procedure for the generation and distribution of the information within the government department?

A   If working from home, departmental employees must use a memory stick to transfer data, as laptop computers are not allowed to leave the department.

B   All departmental employees must enter <u>non-disclosed</u> and <u>regularly</u> updated passwords to access their computers.

C   All authorised employees must swipe an officially <u>issued</u>, personal identity card at the entrance to the department before they can gain access.

D   All hard copies of confidential information must be <u>shredded</u> at the end of each day or locked overnight in a safe if needed again.

170 **Which of the following methods would be <u>LEAST</u> effective in ensuring the security of confidential information?**

A   Monitoring emails

B   Encryption of files

C   Dial back facility

D   Universal passwords

PERFORMANCE ANALYSIS IN PRIVATE SECTOR ORGANISATIONS

171 The following are types of <u>Key Performance Indicators</u>:

(i)   Return on Capital Employed · *financial*

(ii)   Gross profit percentage *financial*

(iii) Acid Test ratio *liquidity*

(iv)   Gearing ratio *risk*

Which of the above KPIs would be used to assess the liquidity of a company?

A   (i) and (ii) only

B   (iii) only

C   (iv) only

D   (iii) and (iv) only

172 **Why would a company want to encourage the use of <u>non-financial performance indicators</u>?**

A   To encourage short-termism

B   To look at the fuller picture of the business

C   To enable results to be easily manipulated to the benefit of the manager

D   To prevent goal congruence

173 Michigan is an insurance company. Recently, there has been concern that too many quotations have been sent to clients either late or containing errors. The department concerned has responded that it is understaffed, and a high proportion of current staff has recently joined the firm. The performance of this department is to be carefully monitored.

Which ONE of the following non-financial performance indicators would NOT be an appropriate measure to monitor and improve the department's performance?

A   Percentage of quotations found to contain errors when checked

B   Percentage of quotations not issued within company policy of three working days

C   Percentage of department's quota of staff actually employed

D   Percentage of budgeted number of quotations actually issued

174 *This objective test question contains a question type which will only appear in a computer-based exam, but this question provides valuable practice for all students whichever version of the exam they are taking.*

Which of the following items would best go into the Customer Perspective within a traditional balanced scorecard? Select all that apply.

- Customer profitability analysis
- Customer retention rates
- Customer satisfaction ratings
- Customer ordering processing times

175 HH plc monitors the % of total sales that derives from products developed in the last year. This would be classified in the pick from list part of the balanced scorecard.

List options are as follows:
Financial perspective
Customer perspective
Internal perspective
Learning perspective

176 **Which of the following is the best measure of quality to be included within a building block model in a rapidly growing clothing business?**

A   Number of returns in the month

B   Number of faulty goods returned as a percentage of number of orders received in the month

C   Average customer satisfaction rating where customers were asked a range of questions including quality, delivery and customer service

D   Number of faulty goods returned as a percentage of deliveries made in the month

177 This objective test question contains a question type which will only appear in a computer-based exam, but this question provides valuable practice for all students whichever version of the exam they are taking.

While a drag and drop style question is impossible to fully replicate within a paper based medium, some questions of this style have been included for completeness.

Drag the six dimensions of performance contained within the Building Block model into the box below:

- Customers
- Competitiveness
- Learning
- Innovation
- Financial
- Profitability
- Resource utilisation
- Flexibility
- Equity
- Controllability
- Quality

C
I
F
R
F
Q

[Handwritten in box:]
Competitiveness
Innovation
Resource utilisation
Flexibility
Financial
Quality

178 The following extracts relate to Company X and Company Y for 20X1:

	Co X	Co Y
	$000	$000
Revenue	20,000	26,000
Cost of sales	(15,400)	(21,050)
Gross profit	4,600	4,950
Expenses	(2,460)	(2,770)
Operating profit	2,140	2,180

What is the operating profit margin for both companies for 20X1?

	Co X	Co Y
A	10.7%	8.38%
B	8.38%	10.7%
C	23%	19%
D	12%	10%

[Handwritten:]
Co X 2140/20 000 × 100
Co Y 2180/26 000 × 100

179 Companies A and B are both involved in retailing. Relevant information for the year ended 30 September 20X1 was as follows:

	A	B
	$000	$000
Sales revenue	50,000	200,000
Profit	10,000	10,000
Capital employed	50,000	50,000

(handwritten annotations:) Profit Marg. A 20% B 5%. A higher Profit margin. ROCE 20%. 20%. Same-generally Some profit. Asset turnover 1000, 4. B Major asset turn. Asset more efficient.

Which of the following statements is true?

A   The profit margin of both companies is the same

B   Company B is generating more profit from every $1 of asset employed than Company A

C   Company B is using its assets more efficiently

D   Company B is controlling its costs better than Company A

180 In an investment centre, a divisional manager has autonomy over negotiating all selling prices, has local functions set up for payables, inventory and cash management, and uses a full debt factoring service.

Which of the following should the divisional manager be held accountable for?

	Accountable	Not accountable
The generation of revenues	✓	
Transfer prices	✓	✗
Management of working capital	✓	
Apportioned head office costs		✓

181 **Which TWO of the following matters would the manager of an investment centre have the power to make decisions over?**

- Granting credit to customers
- Settling inter-departmental disputes
- The apportionment of head office costs
- Inventory carrying decisions.

182 The trading account of Calypso for the year ended 30 June 20X0 is set out below:

	$	$
Sales		430,000
Opening inventories	50,000	
Purchases	312,500	
	362,500	
Closing inventories	(38,000)	
Cost of sales		(324,500)
Gross profit		105,500

The following amounts have been extracted from the company's statement of financial position at 30 June 20X0.

	$
Trade receivables	60,000
Prepayments	4,000
Cash in hand	6,000
Bank overdraft	8,000
Trade payables	40,000
Accruals	3,000
Declared dividends	5,000

Calculate the inventories days (using average inventories) and the current ratio for Calypso Ltd for the period.

	Inventory days	Current ratio
A	33 days	1.25:1
B	49 days	1.25:1
C	49 days	1.93:1
D	33 days	1.93:1

DIVISIONAL PERFORMANCE AND TRANSFER PRICING

183 **Which TWO of the following statements about transfer pricing are correct?**

- Internal transfers can sometimes occur even if the supplying division is operating at full capacity supplying external customers.

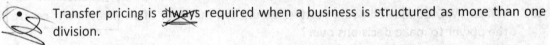

- Transfer pricing is always required when a business is structured as more than one division.

- The minimum transfer price is equal to the variable costs plus any lost contribution of the selling division.

- External sales should be preferred over internal transfers, as there will be more control over quality and delivery.

184 Dust Co has two divisions, A and B. Each division is currently considering the following separate projects:

	Division A	Division B
Capital required for the project	$32.6 million	$22.2 million
Sales generated by the project	$14.4 million	$8.8 million
Operating profit margin	30%	24%
Cost of capital	10%	10%
Current return on investment of division	15%	9%

If residual income is used as the basis for the investment decision, what decision is each division likely to make?

	Would choose to invest in the project	Would choose not to invest in the project
Division A	✓	
Division B		✓

185 *This objective test question contains a question type which will only appear in a computer-based exam, but this question provides valuable practice for all students whichever version of the exam they are taking.*

JB Ltd is a divisionalised organisation comprising a number of divisions, including divisions A and B. Division A makes a single product, which it sells on the external market at a price of $12 per unit. The variable cost of the product is $8 per unit and the fixed cost is $3 per unit. Market demand for the product considerably exceeds Division A's maximum production capacity of 10,000 units per month.

Division B would like to obtain 500 units of the product from Division A. If Division A does transfer some of its production internally rather than sell externally, then the saving in packaging costs would be $1.50 per unit. What transfer price per unit should Division A quote in order to maximise group profit?

$  10.50

186 Oxco has two divisions, A and B. Division A makes a component for air conditioning units which it can only sell to Division B. It has no other outlet for sales.

Current information relating to Division A is as follows:

Marginal cost per unit	$100
Transfer price of the component	$165
Total production and sales of the component each year	2,200 units
Specific fixed costs of Division A per year	$10,000

Cold Co has offered to sell the component to Division B for $140 per unit. If Division B accepts this offer, Division A will be shut.

If Division B accepts Cold Co's offer, what will be the impact on profits per year for the group as a whole?

A   Increase of $65,000

B   Decrease of $78,000

C   Decrease of $88,000

D   Increase of $55,000

187 *This objective test question contains a question type which will only appear in a computer-based exam, but this question provides valuable practice for all students whichever version of the exam they are taking.*

Summary financial statements are given below for JE, the division of a large divisionalised company:

Balance sheet		Income statement	
	$000		$000
Non-current assets	2,400	Revenue	7,300
Current assets	1,000	Operating costs	(6,800)
Total assets	3,400	Operating profit	500
		Interest paid	(320)
Divisional equity	1,500	Profit before tax	180
Long-term borrowings	900		
Current liabilities	1,000		
Total equity and liabilities	3,400		

The cost of capital for the division is estimated at 11% each year. The annual rate of interest on the long-term loans is 9%. All decisions concerning the division's capital structure are taken by central management.

What is the divisional return on capital employed (ROCE) for the year ended 31 December? (1 d.p.)

 **20.8** %

188 Summary financial statements are given below for JE, the division of a large divisionalised company:

Balance sheet	$000	Income statement	$000
Non-current assets	2,400	Revenue	7,300
Current assets	1,000	Operating costs	(6,800)
Total assets	3,400	Operating profit	500
		Interest paid	(320)
Divisional equity	1,500	Profit before tax	180
Long-term borrowings	900		
Current liabilities	1,000		
Total equity and liabilities	3,400		

The cost of capital for the division is estimated at 11% each year. The annual rate of interest on the long-term loans is 9%. All decisions concerning the division's capital structure are taken by central management.

What is the divisional residual income (RI) for the year ended 31 December?

- A −$84
- B $180
- C $236
- D $284

189 *This objective test question contains a question type which will only appear in a computer-based exam, but this question provides valuable practice for all students whichever version of the exam they are taking.*

Pro is a division of Mo and is an investment centre. The head office controls finance, HR and IT expenditure but all other decisions are devolved to the local centres.

The statement of financial position for Pro shows net value of all assets and liabilities to be $4,500m. It carries no debt itself although the group has debt liabilities.

The management accounts for income read as follows:

	$m
Revenue	3,500
Cost of sales	1,800
Local administration	250
IT costs	50
Distribution	80
Central administration	30
Interest charges	90
Net profit	1,200

Ignore taxation.

If the cost of capital is 12%, what is the division's residual income?

1200+90+30+50

7A-7L

$RI = EBIT - (CE \times ndu\ CofC.)$

$= 1370 - (4500 \times 12.1)$

$= 830$

$ \quad 830m.

190 *This objective test question contains a question type which will only appear in a computer-based exam, but this question provides valuable practice for all students whichever version of the exam they are taking.*

Pro is a division of Mo and is an investment centre. The head office controls finance, HR and IT expenditure but all other decisions are devolved to the local centres.

The statement of financial position for Pro shows net value of all assets and liabilities to be $4,500m at the start of the year and $4,890m at the end. It carries no debt itself although the group has debt liabilities.

The management accounts for income read as follows:

	$m
Revenue	3,500
Cost of sales	1,800
Local administration	250
IT costs	50
Distribution	80
Central administration	30
Interest charges	90
Net profit	1,200

Ignore taxation.

1200+90+30+50

$ROI = \dfrac{EBIT}{CE.}$ 4890-4500

$= \dfrac{1370}{4500} \times 100$

$= 30.4.$

What is the divisional ROI to the nearest % point? (1 d.p.)

30.4 %

191 *This objective test question contains a question type which will only appear in a computer-based exam, but this question provides valuable practice for all students whichever version of the exam they are taking.*

At the end of 20X1, an investment centre has net assets of $1m and annual operating profits of $190,000. However, the bookkeeper forgot to account for the following:

A machine with a net book value of $40,000 was sold at the start of the year for $50,000, and replaced with a machine costing $250,000. Both the purchase and sale are cash transactions. No depreciation is charged in the year of purchase or disposal. The investment centre calculates return on investment (ROI) based on closing net assets.

Assuming no other changes to profit or net assets, what is the return on investment (ROI) for the year? (1 d.p.)

19.8	%

192 Perrin Co has two divisions, A and B.

Division A has limited skilled labour and is operating at full capacity making product Y. It has been asked to supply a different product, X, to division B. Division B currently sources this product externally for $700 per unit.

The same grade of materials and labour is used in both products. The cost cards for each product are shown below:

Product	Y	X
	($)/unit	($)/unit
Selling price	600	–
Direct materials ($50 per kg)	200	150
Direct labour ($20 per hour)	80	120
Apportioned fixed overheads ($15 per hour)	60	90

Using an opportunity cost approach to transfer pricing, what is the minimum transfer price?

A $270
B $750
C $590
D $840

193 Division B of a company makes units which are then transferred to other divisions. The division has no spare capacity.

Which of the following statement(s) regarding the minimum transfer price that will encourage the divisional manager of B to transfer units to other divisions is/are true?

(1)   Any price above variable cost will generate a positive contribution, and will therefore be accepted.

(2)   The division will need to give up a unit sold externally in order to make a transfer; this is only worthwhile if the income of a transfer is greater than the net income of an external sale.

A   1 only
B   2 only
C   Neither 1 nor 2
D   Both 1 and 2

194 *This objective test question contains a question type which will only appear in a computer-based exam, but this question provides valuable practice for all students whichever version of the exam they are taking.*

TM plc makes components which it sells internally to its subsidiary RM Ltd, as well as to its own external market.

The external market price is $24.00 per unit, which yields a contribution of 40% of sales. For external sales, variable costs include $1.50 per unit for distribution costs, which are not incurred on internal sales.

TM plc has sufficient capacity to meet all of the internal and external sales. The objective is to maximise group profit.

At what unit price should the component be transferred to RM Ltd?

Internally = 60% of sales.
= 24 × 60% = 14.4.
14.4 − 1.50 = 12.90.

$ 14 12.90

PERFORMANCE ANALYSIS IN NON-FOR-PROFIT ORGANISATIONS AND THE PUBLIC SECTOR

195 Def Co provides accounting services to government. On average, each staff member works six chargeable hours per day, with the rest of their working day being spent on non-chargeable administrative work. One of the company's main objectives is to produce a high level of quality and customer satisfaction.

Def Co has set its targets for the next year as follows:

(1) Cutting departmental expenditure by 5%.

(2) Increasing the number of chargeable hours handled by advisers to 6.2 per day.

(3) Obtaining a score of 4.7 or above on customer satisfaction surveys.

Which of the above targets assesses economy, efficiency and effectiveness at Def Co?

	Economy	Efficiency	Effectiveness
Target (1)	✓		
Target (2)		✓	
Target (3)			✓

196 A government is looking at assessing hospitals by reference to a range of both financial and non-financial factors, one of which is survival rates for heart by-pass operations and another is 'cost per successfully treated patient'.

Which of the three E's in the 'Value For Money' framework is not measured here? ↗ effect

A Economy

B Effectiveness ✗

C Efficiency

D Externality − NOT . VFM

197 Which of the following statements, regarding the existence of multiple objectives in not-for-profit organisations, is/are correct?

(1) They ensure goal congruence between stakeholders. ✗

(2) Compromise between objectives can be problematic. ✓

A 1 only

B 2 only

C Both 1 and 2

D Neither 1 nor 2

198 A government is trying to assess schools by using a range of financial and non-financial factors. One of the chosen methods is the percentage of students passing five exams or more.

Which of the three Es in the value for money framework is being measured here?

A Economy

B Efficiency

C Effectiveness

D Expertise

199 Which of the following statements regarding measurement of performance in not-for-profit organisations is/are true?

(1) Output does not usually have a market value, and it is therefore more difficult to measure effectiveness. ✗

(2) Control over the performance can only be satisfactorily achieved by assessments of 'value for money'. ✓

A 1 only

B 2 only

C Neither 1 nor 2

D Both 1 and 2

200 Which of the following statement(s) about measuring effectiveness in not-for-profit organisations is/are true?

(1) Effectiveness targets cannot usually be expressed financially, and therefore non-financial targets must be used. ✓

(2) The effective level of achievement could be measured by comparing actual performance against target. ✓

A 1 only

B 2 only

C Neither 1 nor 2

D Both 1 and 2

EXTERNAL CONSIDERATIONS AND BEHAVIOURAL ASPECTS

201 The senior manager is suspicious of a local manager's accounts and thinks that the profit performance may have been overstated.

Which of the following would be a plausible explanation of an overstatement of profit?

A   Delaying payments to payables

B   Shortening the useful economic life of a non-current asset

C   Overstatement of a prepayment

D   Overstatement of an accrual

202   Which of the following statements regarding standard setting is correct?

A   Imposed standards are more likely to be achieved

B   Managers across the organisation should be targeted using the same standards

C   Standards should be set at an ideal level with no built in stretch

D   Participation in standard setting is more motivating than where standards are imposed

203 *This objective test question contains a question type which will only appear in a computer-based exam, but this question provides valuable practice for all students whichever version of the exam they are taking.*

When setting performance measures, external factors should be taken into account. Which of the following statements regarding external factors is true? Select all that apply.

A   Stakeholders will have different objectives and companies may deal with this by having a range of performance measures to assess the achievement of these objectives

B   A downturn in the industry or in the economy as a whole could have a negative impact on performance

C   It is only important for companies to take account of internal stakeholders when setting performance targets

D   Company performance could be affected if a competitor reduces its prices or launches a successful advertising campaign

204 When setting performance measurement targets it should be considered that there is the possibility that managers will take a short term view of the company and may even be tempted to manipulate results in order to achieve their targets.

Which of the following would assist in overcoming the problems of short-termism and manipulation of results?

A   Rewards should be linked to a wider variety of performance measures including some nonfinancial measures

B   Managers should only be rewarded for the results achieved in their own departments

C   Any capital investment decision should be judged using the payback method of investment appraisal

D   Setting targets involving the overall performance of the company will be more motivating for managers

205 Stakeholders will have different objectives and companies may deal with this by having a range of performance measures to assess the achievement of these objectives.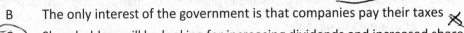

Which of the following statements is true in relation to stakeholders?

A   The aim of all performance measures should be to increase short term profit

B   The only interest of the government is that companies pay their taxes

C   Shareholders will be looking for increasing dividends and increased share price

D   Only internal stakeholders need to be considered by companies

Section 2

OBJECTIVE TEST CASE STUDY QUESTIONS – SECTION B

SPECIALIST COST AND MANAGEMENT ACCOUNTING TECHNIQUES

206 DUFF CO (JUNE 2014, ADAPTED)

Duff Co manufactures three products, X, Y and Z and uses cost-plus pricing. Each product uses the same materials and the same type of direct labour, but in different quantities. For many years, the company has been using full absorption costing and absorbing overheads on the basis of direct labour hours. Budgeted production and sales volumes for X, Y and Z for the next year are 20,000 units, 16,000 units and 22,000 units respectively.

The budgeted direct costs of the three products are:

	X	Y	Z
	$ per unit	$ per unit	$ per unit
Direct materials	25	22	28
Direct labour ($12 per hour)	30	36	24
Batch size (units per set-up)	500	800	400
Number of purchase orders per batch	4	5	4
Machine hours per unit	1.5	1.25	1.4

In the next year, Duff Co also expects to incur indirect production costs of $1,377,400, and the company has calculated the Overhead Absorption Rate (OAR) to be $9.70 per direct labour hour.

The indirect production costs of $1,377,400 are analysed as follows:

Cost pools	$	Cost drivers
Machine set up costs	280,000	Number of batches
Material ordering costs	316,000	Number of purchase orders
Machine running costs	420,000	Number of machine hours
General facility costs	361,400	Number of machine hours

1   What is the full production cost per unit of product Z, using Duff's Co current method of absorption costing?

- (A) $71.40 per unit
- B $79.25 per unit
- C $93.10 per unit
- D   Cannot be determined without more information

2 What is the overhead cost per unit for product X, using activity-based costing?

    A $19.25 per unit

    B $24.64 per unit

    C $26.21 per unit

    D $72.21 per unit

3 Using activity-based costing, total overheads allocated to Product Z amount to $576, 583. What is the budgeted full cost production per unit using activity-based costing, for Product Z?

    A $65.40 per unit

    B $78.21 per unit

    C $79.64 per unit

    D $83.2 per unit

[Handwritten working: $\frac{576583}{22000}$ = 26·21; Direct mat 28, Direct LAB 24, OH p.u 26·21, 78·21]

4 Which of the following statements about ABC in Duff Co are correct?

    (1)   ABC can be applied to all overhead costs, not just production overheads.

    (2)   ABC provides a more accurate cost per unit of X, Y or Z, and as a result pricing should be improved.

    (3)   ABC recognises that overhead costs are not all related to production and sales volume of X, Y and Z.

    (4)   ABC will be of limited benefit if Duff Co's overhead costs are primarily volume related, or if the overheads represent a small proportion of the overall cost.

    A   (1) and (2)

    B   (1) and (4)

    C   (1), (2) and (3)

    D   (1), (2), (3) and (4)

5 Using ABC, the production cost of product X is very similar to the cost calculated using traditional absorption costing, but the cost for product Y is almost $10 less.

Demand for products X and Y is relatively elastic. *[Handwritten: Demand ↑ price ↓]*

Which statements regarding products X and Y are true?

    (1)   If the company decides to adopt ABC, the price of product X will change.

    (2)   If the company decides to adopt ABC, sales volumes of X are likely to remain unchanged.

    (3)   If the company decides to adopt ABC, the price of product Y will go down.

    (4)   A reduced selling price is unlikely to give rise to increased sales volumes.

    A   (1) and (2)

    B   (2) and (3)

    C   (2) and (4)

    D   (1), (2), (3) and (4)

207 BECKLEY HILL (JUNE 2015)

Beckley Hill (BH) is a private hospital carrying out two types of procedures on patients. Each type of procedure incurs the following direct costs:

	Procedure A	Procedure B
Surgical time and materials	$1,200	$2,640
Anaesthesia time and materials	$800	$1,620

BH currently calculates the overhead cost per procedure by taking the total overhead cost and simply dividing it by the number of procedures, then rounding the cost to the nearest 2 decimal places. Using this method, the total cost is $2,475.85 for Procedure A and $4,735.85 for Procedure B.

Recently, another local hospital has implemented activity-based costing (ABC). This has led the finance director at BH to consider whether this alternative costing technique would bring any benefits to BH. He has obtained an analysis of BH's total overheads for the last year and some additional data, all of which is shown below:

Cost	Cost driver	Costs in $
Administrative costs	Administrative time per procedure	1,870,160
Nursing costs	Length of patient stay	6,215,616
Catering costs	Number of meals	966,976
General facility costs	Length of patient stay	8,553,600
Total overhead costs		**17,606,352**

	Procedure A	Procedure B
Number of procedures	14,600	22,400
Administrative time per procedure (hours)	1	1.5
Length of patient stay per procedure (hours)	24	48
Average no. of meals required per patient	1	4

1   Using the traditional costing system, what is the overhead cost per procedure?

   A $237.93 per procedure

   B $713.78 per procedure

   C $475.85 per procedure

   D $951.70 per procedure

2   Recently, another local hospital has implemented activity-based costing (ABC). This has led the finance director at BH to consider whether this alternative costing technique would bring any benefits to BH. He has obtained an analysis of BH's total overheads for the last year and some additional data, all of which is shown below:

Cost	Cost driver	Costs in $
Administrative costs	Administrative time per procedure	1,870,160
Nursing costs	Length of patient stay	6,215,616
Catering costs	Number of meals	966,976
General facility costs	Length of patient stay	8,553,600
Total overhead costs		**17,606,352**

	Procedure A	Procedure B
Number of procedures	14,600	22,400
Administrative time per procedure (hours)	1	1.5
Length of patient stay per procedure (hours)	24	48
Average no. of meals required per patient	1	4

Under ABC, what is the administration cost per hour?

A $38.80 per hour

B $50.54 per hour

C $58.20 per hour

D $77.60 per hour

3 **Under ABC, what is the nursing cost per hour?**

A $4.30 per admin hour

B $4.30 per patient hour

C $4.36 per admin hour

D $4.36 per patient hour

4 When using ABC, the full cost for Procedure A is approximately $2,297 and $4,853 for Procedure B.

Which of the following statements is/are true?

(1) Using ABC, the allocation of overhead costs would more fairly represent the use of resources driving the overheads. ✓

(2) The cost of Procedure A goes up using ABC and the cost of Procedure B goes down because the largest proportion of the overhead costs is the nursing and general facility costs.

A (1) only

B (2) only

C Both (1) and (2)

D Neither (1) nor (2)

5 When using ABC, the full cost for Procedure A is approximately $2,297 and $4,853 for Procedure B. BH has decided that an ABC system is too time consuming and costly to implement.

Which of the following statements is/are true?

(1) Whilst the comparative costs of Procedures A and B are different under ABC, they are not different enough to justify the implementation of an ABC system. ✓

(2) A similar allocation of overheads can be achieved simply by using 'patient hours' as a basis to absorb the costs. ✓

A (1) only

B (2) only

C Both (1) and (2)

D Neither (1) nor (2)

208 BOWD

This objective test case question contains question types which will only appear in a computer-based exam, but this question provides valuable practice for all students whichever version of the exam they are taking.

Bowd Co manufactures two products, Dest and Else. A few years ago, Bowd Co changed from absorbing overheads on a unitary basis (total overheads/total units produced) which gave an overhead per unit of $106.21, to the current system of absorbing overheads on a labour hour basis.

Bowd Co is now considering changing to Activity Based Costing (ABC) as the method used to absorb overheads into production.

The following information is available:

	Direct labour hours per unit	Annual Output	Number of orders	Number of set ups
Dest	4	1,500	200	65
Else	3	2,000	275	60

The fixed overhead costs of $371,750 have been analysed:

	$
Purchasing related	142,500
Set up related	31,250
Other	198,000

1   Which TWO of the following statements about ABC are correct?

- ABC can only be used to analyse the past, not to make decisions about the future.

- The benefits of ABC will always outweigh the costs of implementing the system.

- ABC can be used within both service and manufacturing industries.

- ABC is of less benefit if the majority of the costs suffered by an organisation are variable costs.

2   The following statements have been made about ABC and cost drivers.

(1)   In addition to estimating more accurately the true cost of production, ABC will also give a better indication of where cost savings can be made.

(2)   Traditional absorption costing tends to under-allocate overhead costs to low-volume products.

Which of the above statements is/are true?

A   (1) only

B   (2) only

C   (1) and (2)

D   Neither (1) nor (2)

3   Using ABC, what is the overhead cost per unit, to two decimal places, for each unit of Else?

$_____

4 If Bowd changed to ABC, the overhead cost per unit of Dest would be $116.83.

What is the purchase order cost per unit included in the $116.83?

$_____

5 **For Dest, if ABC is used, what is the decrease in overhead cost per unit compared to the current, labour-hours based absorption system?**

A $17.77

B $7.09

C $10.62

D $23.89

209 HELOT CO (SEPTEMBER 2016)

Helot Co develops and sells computer games. It is well known for launching innovative and interactive role-playing games and its new releases are always eagerly anticipated by the gaming community. Customers value the technical excellence of the games and the durability of the product and packaging.

Helot Co has previously used a traditional absorption costing system and full cost plus pricing to cost and price its products. It has recently recruited a new finance director who believes the company would benefit from using target costing. He is keen to try this method on a new game concept called Spartan, which has been recently approved.

After discussion with the board, the finance director undertook some market research to find out customers' opinions on the new game concept and to assess potential new games offered by competitors. The results were used to establish a target selling price of $45 for Spartan and an estimated total sales volume of 350,000 units. Helot Co wants to achieve a target profit margin of 35%.

The finance director has also begun collecting cost data for the new game and has projected the following:

Production costs per unit	$
Direct material	3.00
Direct labour	2.50
Direct machining	5.05
Set-up	0.45
Inspection and testing	4.30
Total non-production costs	**$000**
Design (salaries and technology)	2,500
Marketing consultants	1,700
Distribution	1,400

1   **Which of the following statements would the finance director have used to explain to Helot Co's board what the benefits were of adopting a target costing approach so early in the game's life-cycle?**

    (1)   Costs will be split into material, system, and delivery and disposal categories for improved cost reduction analysis.

    (2)   Customer requirements for quality, cost and timescales are more likely to be included in decisions on product development.

    (3)   Its key concept is based on how to turn material into sales as quickly as possible in order to maximise net cash.

    (4)   The company will focus on designing out costs prior to production, rather than cost control during live production.

    A   (1), (2) and (4)

    B   (2), (3) and (4)

    C   (1) and (3)

    D   (2) and (4) only

2   **What is the forecast cost gap for the new game?**

    A $2.05

    B $0.00

    C $13.70

    D $29.25

3   The board of Helot Co has asked the finance director to explain what activities can be undertaken to close a cost gap on its computer games.

    Which of the following would be appropriate ways for Helot Co to close a cost gap?

	Appropriate ways to close a cost gap	Not an appropriate ways to close a cost gap
Buy cheaper, lower grade plastic for the game discs and cases.		
Using standard components wherever possible in production.		
Employ more trainee game designers on lower salaries.		
Use the company's own online gaming websites for marketing.		

4   The direct labour cost per unit has been based on an expected learning rate of 90% but now the finance director has realised that a 95% learning rate should be applied.

    Which of the following statements is true?

    A   The target cost will decrease and the cost gap will increase

    B   The target cost will increase and the cost gap will decrease

    C   The target cost will remain the same and the cost gap will increase

    D   The target cost will remain the same and the cost gap will decrease

5   Helot Co is thinking about expanding its business and introducing a new computer repair service for customers. The board has asked if target costing could be applied to this service.

Which of the following statements regarding services and the use of target costing within the service sector is true?

A   The purchase of a service transfers ownership to the customer

B   Labour resource usage is high in services relative to material requirements

C   A standard service cannot be produced and so target costing cannot be used

D   Service characteristics include uniformity, perishability and intangibility

210   CHEMICAL FREE CLEAN CO (DECEMBER 2015)

The Chemical Free Clean Co (C Co) provides a range of environmentally-friendly cleaning services to business customers, often providing a specific service to meet a client's needs. Its customers range from large offices and factories to specialist care wards at hospitals, where specialist cleaning equipment must be used and regulations adhered to.

C Co offers both regular cleaning contracts and contracts for one-off jobs. For example, its latest client was a chain of restaurants which employed them to provide an extensive clean of all their business premises after an outbreak of food poisoning.

The cleaning market is very competitive, although there are only a small number of companies providing a chemical free service. C Co has always used cost-plus pricing to determine the prices which it charges to its customers but recently, the cost of the cleaning products C Co uses has increased. This has meant that C Co has had to increase its prices, resulting in the loss of several regular customers to competing service providers.

The finance director at C Co has heard about target costing and is considering whether it could be useful at C Co.

1   **What would be, in the right sequence, the main steps involved in deriving a target cost for C Co?**

A   Define the service, set a target price, derive the operating profit and calculate a target cost.

B   Set a target price, derive the total operating profit, calculate a target cost per hour and define the service.

C   Define the service, derive the operating profit, set a target price and calculate a target cost.

D   Define the service, derive a target price, calculate a target cost and set the operating profit.

2   **Which TWO of the following statements correctly explain the difficulties faced if target costing is used in a service industry?**

- The service can be defined too easily and lacks the necessary complexity.

- The service is used at the same time it is produced.

- The service is standardised too easily.

- Unused labour capacity cannot be stored for use the next day.

3   Which of the following statements is/are true?

(1)   C Co may not be able to get hold of any comparative data available for the one-off jobs, and therefore setting the target cost will be difficult.

(2)   Some of the work available is very specialist. It may be difficult to establish the market price for a service like this, thus making it difficult to derive a target cost.

A   (1) only

B   (2) only

C   (1) and (2)

D   Neither (1) nor (2)

4   Which of the following statements is/are true?

- Target costing is useful in competitive markets where a company is dominant in their market, like C Co is.

- Target costing is useful in C Co's competitive market in which price increases does lead to loss of customers.

- C Co can ignore the market price for cleaning services and simply pass on cost increases as it has done.

- Target costing would help C Co to focus on the market price of similar services provided by competitors, where this information is available.

5   Which of the following statements is/are true?

(1)   If after calculating a target cost C Co finds that a cost gap exists, it will then be forced to examine its internal processes and costs more closely.

(2)   If C Co cannot achieve any reduction in the cost of the cleaning products it uses, it should consider whether it can source cheaper non-chemical products from alternative suppliers.

A   (1) only

B   (2) only

C   (1) and (2)

D   Neither (1) nor (2)

211 SHOE CO (JUNE 2016)

This objective test case question contains question types which will only appear in a computer-based exam, but this question provides valuable practice for all students whichever version of the exam they are taking.

Shoe Co, a shoe manufacturer, has developed a new product called the 'Smart Shoe' for children, which has a built-in tracking device. The shoes are expected to have a life cycle of two years, at which point Shoe Co hopes to introduce a new type of Smart Shoe with even more advanced technology. Shoe Co plans to use life cycle costing to work out the total production cost of the Smart Shoe and the total estimated profit for the two-year period. Shoe Co has spent $5.6m developing the Smart Shoe.

The time spent on this development meant that the company missed out on the opportunity of earning an estimated $800,000 contribution from the sale of another product.

The company has applied for and been granted a ten-year patent for the technology, although it must be renewed each year at a cost of $200,000. The costs of the patent application were $500,000, which included $20,000 for the salary costs of Shoe Co's lawyer, who is a permanent employee of the company and was responsible for preparing the application.

The following information relating to the Smart Shoe is also available for the next two years:

Total 'Smart Shoe' Revenue $34.3m

	Year 1	Year 2
Sales volumes (units)	280,000	420,000
Material costs per unit	$16	$14
Labour costs per unit	$8	$7
Total fixed production overheads	$3.8 m	
Selling and distribution costs	$1.5m	

Shoe Co is negotiating with marketing companies with regard to its advertising campaign on another product, 'Smart Boots'. Shoe Co is uncertain as to what the total marketing costs will be each year. However, the following information is available as regards the probabilities of the range of costs which are likely to be incurred:

Year 1		Year 2	
Expected cost ($m)	Probability	Expected cost ($m)	Probability
2.2	0.2	1.8	0.3
2.6	0.5	2.1	0.4
2.9	0.3	2.3	0.3

1 **Which TWO of the following statements about lifecycle costing are true?**

- Lifecycle costing should not be used by Shoe Co, because the material costs per unit differ between the two years of the life of the product.

- Lifecycle costing should not be used by Shoe Co, because the lifecycle of the 'Smart Shoe' is short and the development costs too high.

- Lifecycle costing should be used by Shoe Co because it will provide the true financial cost of producing the shoes.

- A higher price should be charged by Shoe Co from the start, as the product will be unique.

2 **What is the total expected profit for Shoe Co on the 'Smart Shoe' for the two-year period?** $_____

3 Further research has shown that there will be environmental costs at the end of production of $250,000. Shoe Co is considering how to account for these costs.

Which TWO of the following statements about Environmental Management Accounting are true?

- Cost savings in environmental costs are easily identified.

- Environmental management accounting considers financial costs only.

- ABC can be used to analyse environmental costs.

- Flow cost accounting is a recognised method of accounting for environmental costs.

4 **What is the total expected marketing cost for the two years on the 'Smart Boots' range?**

    A $2.61 m

    B $2.07 m

    C $4.68 m

    D $5.21m

5 **Which ONE of the following statements is true, if a decision is made using expected values?**

    A   The risk is minimised for a set level of return

    B   The risk is minimised irrespective of the level of return

    C   The return is maximised for a given level of risk

    D   The return is maximised irrespective of the level of risk

212 SWEET TREATS BAKERY (DECEMBER 2016)

Sweet Treats Bakery makes three types of cake: brownies, muffins and cupcakes. The costs, revenues and demand for each of the three cakes are as follows:

	Brownies	Muffins	Cupcakes
Batch size (units)	40	30	20
Selling price ($ per unit)	1.50	1.40	2.00
Material cost ($ per unit)	0.25	0.15	0.25
Labour cost ($ per unit)	0.40	0.45	0.50
Overheads ($ per unit)	0.15	0.20	0.30
Minimum daily demand (units)	30	20	10
Maximum daily demand (units)	140	90	100

The minimum daily demand is required for a long-term contract with a local café and must be met.

The cakes are made in batches using three sequential processes: weighing, mixing and baking. The products must be produced in their batch sizes but are sold as individual units. Each batch of cakes requires the following amount of time for each process:

	Brownies	Muffins	Cupcakes
Weighing (minutes)	15	15	20
Mixing (minutes)	20	16	12
Baking (minutes)	120	110	120

The baking stage of the process is done in three ovens which can each be used for eight hours a day, a total of 1,440 available minutes. Ovens have a capacity of one batch per bake, regardless of product type.

Sweet Treats Bakery uses throughput accounting and considers all costs, other than material, to be 'factory costs' which do not vary with production.

1   On Monday, in addition to the baking ovens, Sweet Treats Bakery has the following process resources available:

Process	Minutes available
Weighing	240
Mixing	180

Which of the three processes, if any, is a bottleneck activity?

A   Weighing

B   Mixing

C   Baking

D   There is no bottleneck

2   On Wednesday, the mixing process is identified as the bottleneck process. On this day, only 120 minutes in the mixing process are available.

Assuming that Sweet Treats Bakery wants to maximise profit, what is the optimal production plan for Wednesday?

A   80 brownies, 30 muffins and 100 cupcakes

B   0 brownies, 90 muffins and 100 cupcakes

C   120 brownies, 0 muffins and 100 cupcakes

D   40 brownies, 60 muffins and 100 cupcakes

3   Sweet Treats Bakery has done a detailed review of its products, costs and processes and has identified potential actions to improve its throughput accounting ratio (TPAR).

Which of the following statements will improve the throughput accounting ratio (TPAR)?

	Will improve the TPAR	Will not improve the TPAR
The café customer will be given a loyalty discount		
A bulk discount on flour and sugar is available from suppliers		
There is additional demand for the cupcakes in the market.		
The rent of the premises has been reduced for the next year.		

4   On Friday, due to a local food festival at the weekend, Sweet Treats Bakery is considering increasing its production of cupcakes. These cupcakes can be sold at the festival at the existing selling price.

The company has unlimited capacity for weighing and mixing on Friday but its existing three ovens are already fully utilised. Therefore in order to supply cupcakes to the festival, Sweet Treats Bakery will need to hire another identical oven at a cost of $45 for the day.

How much will profit increase by if the company hires the new oven and produces as many cupcakes as possible?

A $55.00

B $140.00

C $95.00

D $31.00

5   In a previous week, the weighing process was the bottleneck and the resulting throughput accounting ratio (TPAR) for the bakery was 1.45.

Which of the following statements about the TPAR for the previous week is/are true?

(1)   The bakery's operating costs exceeded the total throughput contribution generated from its three products.

(2)   Less idle time in the mixing department would have improved the TPAR.

(3)   Improved efficiency during the weighing process would have improved the TPAR.

A   (3) only

B   (2) only

C   (1) and (2)

D   (1) and (3)

DECISION-MAKING TECHNIQUES

213   SIP CO

This objective test case question contains question types which will only appear in a computer-based exam, but this question provides valuable practice for all students whichever version of the exam they are taking.

Sip Co specialises in refurbishing the inside of yachts and has been asked to quote, on a relevant cost basis, for the refurbishment of a yacht called Bow. The refurbishment will start in one week's time. Sip Co has spent $100 obtaining the following information about the refurbishment:

Materials

The material required will be:

- 20 m of upholstery fabric

- 10 m of teak wood for the flooring.

The cheapest source for the upholstery fabric would be from an overseas supplier at a cost of $85/m. Sip Co buys most of its fabric from overseas and pays $400 per month to a shipping company as a retainer and then $7.50/m for each metre transported.

Sip Co has 5m of teak wood in inventory which cost $100/m and could be sold at a 5% discount on original cost. This teak is left from a previous job and is stained dark mahogany. The colour of the stain required for Bow, tan, is lighter and the costs of sanding and staining the teak are:

- sanding $14/m

- staining $4.50/m

- reset of staining machine, arising after each staining job is completed $80.

To ensure the colour of the teak is consistent, all the teak for one job is stained at the same time, and the staining cost is the same irrespective of the age of the teak. The cost of purchasing new teak is $110/m. New teak can be stained the correct colour for Bow with no preparation.

Non-current assets

A new galley will be required. This can be purchased for $4,500 and the fitting costs will be $2,000. Alternatively, the existing galley can be refurbished. The materials for refurbishment will cost $4,000, and 40 hours of semi-skilled labour will be employed specifically for the refurbishment at a cost of $15/hr. The fitting costs of the refurbished galley will be 10% less than a new galley.

Labour

100 hours of skilled and 56 hours of unskilled labour will be required for the upholstery and flooring work. Skilled labour is paid the market rate of $25/hour and is currently fully employed on another job, where they earn a contribution of $6/hour. Alternatively new skilled labour could be employed, but the new workers will require training at a cost of $14/hour for the first 10 hours they are working.

Unskilled workers are currently paid $12/hour and each of the 5 workers is guaranteed a minimum wage of $420 per week. Each unskilled employee has enough work allocated to them for the next three weeks to earn $372 per week. The work to be done by the unskilled labour on Bow must be completed within the first week of the project starting and overtime is paid at time and half.

Other costs

It is factory policy to add $2,200 per week to a project, for the duration of the project. This is to cover:

Factory rates	$500
Plant and equipment depreciation	$700
Interest on long term loan to purchase plant and equipment	$400
Profit element	$600

1   **What are the figures to be included in the quote for the upholstery fabric and galley?**

   $_____ upholstery fabric

   $_____ galley

2   **What figure should be included in the quote for the teak wood?**

   A $1,220

   B $1,140

   C $1,225

   D $1,145

3   **What cost should be included in the quote for the skilled and unskilled labour?**

   $_____ skilled labour $_____ unskilled labour

4   **Which option correctly classifies these costs?**

	Committed	Notional
Factory rates		
Depreciation		
Interest		

5   **Which TWO of the following statements are true?**

- The $100 spent obtaining the cost information should be included in the quote.

- Sip Co should consider the effect of the refurbishment on the tax the company will pay, and include the tax effect in the quote as a relevant cost.

- Opportunity costs arise when a scarce resource, which has an alternative use in the business, is used in a project.

- Relevant costing techniques should be used in cost volume profit analysis.

214 HARE EVENTS (DECEMBER 2016)

Hare Events is a company which specialises in organising sporting events in major cities across Teeland. It has approached the local council of Edglas, a large city in the north of Teeland, to request permission to host a running festival which will include both a full marathon and a half marathon race.

Based on the prices it charges for entry to similar events in other locations, Hare Events has decided on an entry fee of $55 for the full marathon and $30 for the half marathon. It expects that the maximum entries will be 20,000 for the full marathon and 14,000 for the half marathon.

Hare Events has done a full assessment of the likely costs involved. Each runner will receive a race pack on completion of the race which will include a medal, t-shirt, water and chocolate. Water stations will need to be available at every five kilometre (km) point along the race route, stocked with sufficient supplies of water, sports drinks and gels. These costs are considered to be variable as they depend on the number of race entries.

Hare Events will also incur the following fixed costs. It will need to pay a fixed fee to the Edglas council for permits, road closures and support from the local police and medical services. A full risk assessment needs to be undertaken for insurance purposes. A marketing campaign is planned via advertising on running websites, in fitness magazines and at other events Hare Events is organising in Teeland, and the company which Hare Events usually employs to do the race photography has been approached.

The details of these costs are shown below:

	Full marathon	Half marathon
	$	$
Race packs	15.80	10.80
Water stations	2.40	1.20
		$
Council fees		300,000
Risk assessment and insurance		50,000
Marketing		30,000
Photography		5,000

1   **If Hare Events decides to host only the full marathon race, what is the margin of safety?**

A   35.0%

B   47.7%

C   52.3%

D   65.0%

2 Assuming that the race entries are sold in a constant sales mix based on the expected race entry numbers, what is the sales revenue Hare Events needs to achieve in order to break even (to the nearest $000)?

A $385,000

B $575,000

C $592,000

D $597,000

3 Hare Events wishes to achieve a minimum total profit of $500,000 from the running festival.

What are the number of entries Hare Events will have to sell for each race in order to achieve this level of profit, assuming a constant sales mix based on the expected race entry numbers applies?

Work to the nearest whole number.

A   Full marathon: 17,915 entries and half marathon: 12,540 entries

B   Full marathon: 14,562 entries and half marathon: 18,688 entries

C   Full marathon: 20,000 entries and half marathon: 8,278 entries

D   Full marathon: 9,500 entries and half marathon: 6,650 entries

4 Hare Events is also considering including a 10 km race during the running festival. It expects the race will have an entry fee of $20 per competitor and variable costs of $8 per competitor. Fixed costs associated with this race will be $48,000.

If the selling price per competitor, the variable cost per competitor and the total fixed costs for this 10 km race all increase by 10%, what will happen to the breakeven volume and the breakeven revenue?

	Will change	Will not change
Breakeven volume		√
Breakeven revenue	√	

5 Which of the following statements relating to cost volume profit analysis are true?

(1) Production levels and sales levels are assumed to be the same so there is no inventory movement.

(2) The contribution to sales ratio (C/S ratio) can be used to indicate the relative profitability of different products.

(3) CVP analysis assumes that fixed costs will change if output either falls or increases significantly.

(4) Sales prices are recognised to vary at different levels of activity especially if higher volume of sales is needed.

A   (1), (2) and (3)

B   (2), (3) and (4)

C   (1) and (2) only

D   (3) and (4) only

215 CARDIO CO (DECEMBER 2015)

Cardio Co manufactures four types of fitness equipment: elliptical trainers (E), treadmills (T), cross trainers (C) and rowing machines (R). Cardio Co is considering ceasing to produce elliptical trainers at the end of 2015.

The budgeted sales prices and volumes for the next year (2016) are as follows:

	T	C	R	
Selling price	$1,600	$1,800	$1,400	
Units	420	400	380	
Total sales revenue	$672,000	$720,000	$532,000	**$1,924,000**

The standard cost card for each product is shown below.

	T	C	R
Material	$430	$500	$360
Labour	$220	$240	$190
Variable overheads	$110	$120	$95

Labour costs are 60% fixed and 40% variable. General fixed overheads excluding any fixed labour costs are expected to be $55,000 for the next year.

The following multi-product breakeven chart for Cardio Co has correctly been drawn:

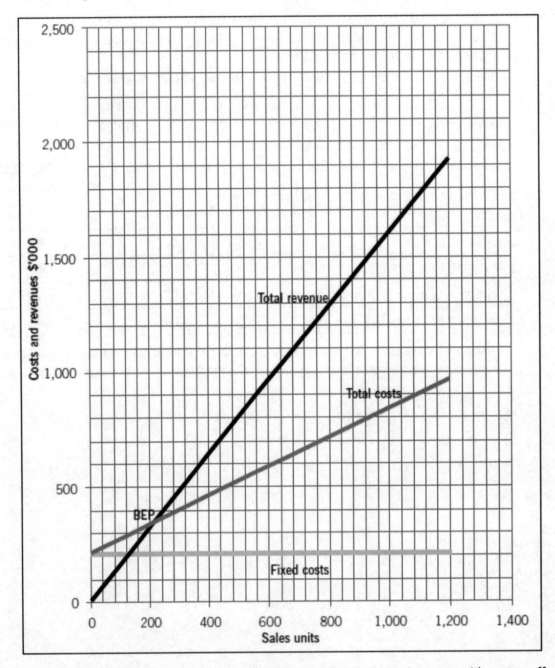

Cardio Co has recently received a request from a customer, Heart Co, to provide a one-off order of fitness machines (T, C and R), in excess of normal budgeted production for 2016. The order would need to be completed within two weeks.

1 **Which of the following are valid factors to consider in the decision to cease the production of elliptical trainers at the end of 2015?**

(1) The elliptical trainers made a loss in 2015.

(2) The elliptical trainers made a positive contribution in the year just passed.

(3) The elliptical trainer market outlook in the long term looks very poor.

(4) Cardio Co also sells treadmills and many elliptical trainers buyers will also buy treadmills.

(5) The business was founded to produce and sell elliptical trainers.

A Only (3) and (4)

B (1), (3), (4), (5)

C (2), (3), and (4)

D None of the above

2 **Which of the following statements about relevant costing are true?**

(1) Fixed costs are always general in nature and therefore never relevant.

(2) Notional costs are always relevant, as they make the estimate more realistic.

(3) An opportunity cost represents the cost of the best alternative foregone.

(4) Avoidable costs would be saved if an activity did not happen, and therefore are relevant.

A (2) and (4)

B (3) and (4)

C (2), (3), and (4)

D (1), (2) and (4)

3 **What is the margin of safety in $ revenue for Cardio Co in 2016?**

A $1,172,060

B $1,577,053

C $1,924,000

D $1,993,632

4 **What would happen to the breakeven point if the products were sold in order of the most profitable products first?**

A The breakeven point would be reached earlier.

B The breakeven point would be reached later.

C The breakeven point would be reached at the same time as in the graph above.

D The breakeven point would never be reached.

5 **Which statement correctly describes the treatment of general fixed overheads when preparing the Heart Co quotation?**

A The overheads should be excluded because they are a sunk cost.

B The overheads should be excluded because they are not incremental costs.

C The overheads should be included because they relate to production costs.

D The overheads should be included because all expenses should be recovered.

216   BEFT CO

This objective test case question contains question types which will only appear in a computer-based exam, but this question provides valuable practice for all students whichever version of the exam they are taking.

Beft Co makes house signs. Three different styles of sign are made and the following unitary information is available:

	Square	Oval	Clover Leaf
	$	$	$
Materials:			
− Metal @$1/kg	4.00	5.00	6.00
− Paint @ $4/L	2.00	3.00	4.00
Labour:			
− Manufacturing @$4/hr	8.00	14.00	10.00
− Painting @$6/hr	3.00	9.00	12.00
Variable overheads	7.00	10.50	20.00
Fixed overheads	13.00	12.00	15.00
Profit	2.00	3.00	1.00
Selling price	39.00	56.50	68.00
Maximum monthly demand	4,000	4,500	1,800

Painting labour is limited to 7,250 hours for the next month while some of the workers are away on a training course.

1   **Which TWO of the following statements about limiting factor analysis are true?**

- The learning effect of labour cannot be incorporated within limiting factor analysis.

- The shadow price is calculated by considering the extra profit that can be earned from one more unit of a scarce resource.

- Linear programming cannot incorporate joint products into its analysis.

- Linear programming is a technique for making decisions under uncertainty.

2   **What is the production plan that would maximise profit for the next month?**

	Square	Oval	Clover Leaf
A	4,000	3,500	−
B	−	4,500	250
C	4,000	1,100	1,800
D	1,000	4,500	−

3 Beft Co does not want to disappoint any customers next week and is considering sub-contracting out some painting, even if it results in a short term loss. The cost of contracting out (which includes material costs and labour costs for painting) would be:

	Square	Oval	Clover Leaf
$	7.00	15.00	22.00

A major customer, Z Co, who orders 500 of each type of plate each week insists that their plates are painted in-house and not sub-contracted.

How many oval plates should be sent to the sub-contractors for painting? _____ Oval plates

4 Beft Co has been advised that the training has been extended for the painters into a second week. Beft has also been told that during that 2nd week, both the metal and the paint supplier will be limiting their supplies to 36,000 kg of metal and 4,500L or paint.

Beft Co has decided to concentrate its activities on the square and oval plates and temporarily shut down the clover leaf production line. Their customers have been informed and Z Co has withdrawn its business, giving 1 weeks' notice.

Which TWO of the following statements are true?

(1) Labour will have a shadow price of zero.

(2) The objective function will be to maximise 15 S + 15 O, where S is the number of square plates produced and O is the number of Oval plates produced.

(3) If solved graphically, the optimal solution will be where the constraints for metal and paint intersect.

(4) Paint will have a positive shadow price.

A (1) and (2)

B (1) and (3)

C (3) and (4)

D (2) and (4)

5 Beft Co is considering permanently ceasing production of the clover leaf plaques.

Which TWO of the following factors should be considered in this decision?

(1) The head office costs apportioned to the clover leaf plaques.

(2) The decommissioning costs for the clover leaf plaque.

(3) The budget for clover leaf plaques shows a loss for next year.

(4) The impact on reputation of reducing the range of plaques produced by Beft Co.

A (1) and (2)

B (1) and (3)

C (2) and (4)

D (3) and (4)

217   ALG CO (JUNE 2015)

ALG Co is launching a new, innovative product onto the market and is trying to decide on the right launch price for the product.

The product's expected life is three years. Given the high level of costs which have been incurred in developing the product, ALG Co wants to ensure that it sets its price at the right level and has therefore consulted a market research company to help it do this.

The research, which relates to similar but not identical products launched by other companies, has revealed that at a price of $60, annual demand would be expected to be 250,000 units. However, for every $2 increase in selling price, demand would be expected to fall by 2,000 units and for every $2 decrease in selling price, demand would be expected to increase by 2,000 units.

A forecast of the annual production costs which would be incurred by ALG Co in relation to the new product are as follows:

Annual production units	200,000	250,000	300,000	350,000
	$	$	$	$
Direct materials	2,400,000	3,000,000	3,600,000	4,200,000
Direct labour	1,200,000	1,500,000	1,800,000	2,100,000
Overheads	1,400,000	1,550,000	1,700,000	1,850,000

Using the high-low method, the variable overhead cost has correctly been calculated at $3 per unit.

1   What is the total variable cost per unit?

A $6

B $12

C $18

D $21

2   What are total fixed overheads?

A $800,000

B $1,000,000

C $1,850,000

D $6,500,000

3   If total marginal cost (MC) is $21, what is the optimum (profit maximising) selling price for the new product?

A $150

B $165.50

C $289

D $310

4 The sales director is unconvinced that the sales price calculated above is the right one to charge on the initial launch of the product. He believes that a high price should be charged at launch so that those customers prepared to pay a higher price for the product can be 'skimmed off' first.

Which TWO of the following statements are true?

(1) Market skimming is a strategy which initially charges high prices for the product in order to take advantage of those buyers who want to buy it as soon as possible, and are prepared to pay high prices in order to do so.

(2) The strategy could be a suitable one for ALG Co as its product is new and different.

(3) Where products have a long life cycle, this skimming strategy is more likely to be used.

(4) There is no barrier to entry in the case of ALG Co.

A (1) and (2)

B (1) and (3)

C (3) and (4)

D (2) and (4)

5 ALG's product is truly unique can only be used in conjunction with another one of the business' products.

Which of the following pricing strategies could be used to price the game? Students are entitled to a small discount.

(1) Price skimming.

(2) Complimentary product pricing.

(3) Penetration pricing.

(4) Price discrimination.

A (1) and (2)

B (1), (2) and (3)

C (1), (2) and (4)

D (2), (3) and (4)

218 JEWEL CO (JUNE 2016)

This objective test case question contains question types which will only appear in a computer-based exam, but this question provides valuable practice for all students whichever version of the exam they are taking.

Jewel Co is setting up an online business importing and selling jewellery headphones. The cost of each set of headphones varies depending on the number purchased, although they can only be purchased in batches of 1,000 units. It also has to pay import taxes which vary according to the quantity purchased.

Jewel Co has already carried out some market research and identified that sales quantities are expected to vary depending on the price charged. Consequently, the following data has been established for the first month:

Number of batches imported and sold	Average cost per unit, including import taxes	Total fixed costs per month	Expected selling price per unit
	$	$	$
1	10.00	10,000	20
2	8.80	10,000	18
3	7.80	12,000	16
4	6.40	12,000	13
5	6.40	14,000	12

Most of Jewel Co's total fixed costs are set-up costs.

1   **How many batches should Jewel Co import and sell? _____ batches**

2   **Which of the following statements regarding Jewel Co's fixed costs are correct?**

   (1)   Jewel Co's fixed costs are stepped.

   (2)   Increasing batch sizes from 1,000 units to 2,000 units would dramatically reduce setup costs and increase profits.

   A   (1) only

   B   (2) only

   C   Both (1) and (2)

   D   Neither (1) nor (2)

3   The following statements have been made about the tabular method used to establish an optimum price:

   (1)   With the tabular method, there must be a consistent relationship between price (P) and demand (Q), as well as a close relationship between demand (Q) and marginal costs (MC).

   (2)   The tabular method is only suitable for companies operating in a monopoly.

   Which of the following statements regarding Jewel Co's fixed costs are correct?

   A   (1) only

   B   (2) only

   C   Both (1) and (2)

   D   Neither (1) nor (2)

4   Jewel Co is also producing luxury earphones and has entered two different new markets. In the USA, it is initially charging low prices so as to gain rapid market share while demand is relatively inelastic. In Europe, it is initially charging high prices so as to earn maximum profits while demand is relatively inelastic.

   Which price strategy is Jewel Co using in each market?

   A   Penetration pricing in the USA and price skimming in Europe

   B   Price discrimination in the USA and penetration pricing in Europe

   C   Price skimming in the USA and penetration pricing in Europe

   D   Price skimming in the USA and price discrimination in Europe

5 Market research has revealed that the maximum demand for Jewel Co's earphones in the USA is 72,000 units per year, and that demand will reduce by 8,000 units for every $5 that the selling price is increased. Based on this information, Jewel Co has calculated that the profit-maximising level of sales for its earphones, for the coming year, is 32,000 units.

Calculate the unit price at which these earphones will be sold: $_____

219 GAM CO (JUNE 2014)

Gam Co sells electronic equipment and is about to launch a new product onto the market. It needs to prepare its budget for the coming year and is trying to decide whether to launch the product at a price of $30, or $35 per unit. The following information has been obtained from market research:

Price per unit $30		Price per unit $35	
Probability	Sales volume	Probability	Sales volume
0.4	120,000	0.3	108,000
0.5	110,000	0.3	100,000
0.1	140,000	0.4	194,000

The six possible profit outcomes which could arise for Gam Co in the coming year have been correctly tabulated as follows:

Price per unit $30		Price per unit $35	
Sales volume	Profit	Sales volume	Profit
120,000	$930,000	108,000	$1,172,000
110,000	$740,000	100,000	$880,000
140,000	$1,310,000	194,000	$742,000

1 **What is the expected value of profit for the $30 price option?**

   A $117,000

   B $291,000

   C $873,000

   D $1,310,000

2 **What is the expected value of profit for the $35 price option?**

   A $117,000

   B $140,000

   C $912,400

   D $1,172,000

3 **Which is the correct definition of the maximin decision rule?**

   A   Under this rule, the decision-maker is an optimist who selects the alternative which maximises the maximum pay-off achievable.

   B   Under this rule, the decision-maker selects the alternative which maximises the minimum payoff achievable.

   C   Under this rule, the decision-maker selects the alternative which minimises the maximum regret.

   D   Under this rule, the decision-maker selects the alternative which minimises the minimum profit.

4   **Which price should be chosen by management if they use the maximin rule to decide which price should be charged?**

  A $30

  B $35

  C   Any price between $30 and $35

  D   Either $30 or $35, as it makes no difference to the profit

5   **Which price should be chosen by management if they use the maximax rule to decide which price should be charged?**

  A $30

  B $35

  C   Any price between $30 and $35

  D   Either $30 or $35, as it makes no difference to the profit

BUDGETING AND CONTROL

220   MYLO (SEPTEMBER 2016)

Mylo runs a cafeteria situated on the ground floor of a large corporate office block. Each of the five floors of the building are occupied and there are in total 1,240 employees.

Mylo sells lunches and snacks in the cafeteria. The lunch menu is freshly prepared each morning and Mylo has to decide how many meals to make each day. As the office block is located in the city centre, there are several other places situated around the building where staff can buy their lunch, so the level of demand for lunches in the cafeteria is uncertain.

Mylo has analysed daily sales over the previous six months and established four possible demand levels and their associated probabilities. He has produced the following payoff table to show the daily profits which could be earned from the lunch sales in the cafeteria:

Demand level	Probability	Supply level			
		450	620	775	960
		$	$	$	$
450	0.15	1,170	980	810	740
620	0.30	1,170	1,612	1,395	1,290
775	0.40	1,170	1,612	2,015	1,785
960	0.15	1,170	1,612	2,015	2,496

1   **If Mylo adopts a maximin approach to decision-making, which daily supply level will he choose?**

  A   450 lunches

  B   620 lunches

  C   775 lunches

  D   960 lunches

2   **If Mylo adopts a minimax regret approach to decision-making, which daily supply level will he choose?**

  A   450 lunches

  B   620 lunches

  C   775 lunches

  D   960 lunches

3 **Which of the following statements is/are true if Mylo chooses to use expected values to assist in his decision-making regarding the number of lunches to be provided?**

(1) Mylo would be considered to be taking a defensive and conservative approach to his decision.

(2) Expected values will ignore any variability which could occur across the range of possible outcomes.

(3) Expected values will not take into account the likelihood of the different outcomes occurring.

(4) Expected values can be applied by Mylo as he is evaluating a decision which occurs many times over.

A (1), (2) and (3)

B (2) and (4)

C (1) and (3)

D (4) only

4 The human resources department has offered to undertake some research to help Mylo to predict the number of employees who will require lunch in the cafeteria each day. This information will allow Mylo to prepare an accurate number of lunches each day.

What is the maximum amount which Mylo would be willing to pay for this information (to the nearest whole $)?

A $191

B $359

C $478

D $175

5 Mylo is now considering investing in a speciality coffee machine. He has estimated the following daily results for the new machine:

	$
Sales (650 units)	1,300
Variable costs	(845)
Contribution	455
Incremental fixed costs	(70)
Profit	385

Which of the following statements are true regarding the sensitivity of this investment?

(1)   The investment is more sensitive to a change in sales volume than sales price.

(2)   If variable costs increase by 44% the investment will make a loss.

(3)   The investment's sensitivity to incremental fixed costs is 550%.

(4)   The margin of safety is 84.6%.

A   (1), (2) and (3)

B   (2) and (4)

C   (1), (3) and (4)

D   (3) and (4)

221   LRA (JUNE 2015)

Lesting Regional Authority (LRA) is responsible for the provision of a wide range of services in the Lesting region, which is based in the south of the country 'Alaia'. These services include, amongst other things, responsibility for residents' welfare, schools, housing, hospitals, roads and waste management. Over recent months the Lesting region experienced the hottest temperatures on record, resulting in several forest fires, which caused damage to several schools and some local roads. Unfortunately, these hot temperatures were then followed by flooding, which left a number of residents without homes and saw higher than usual numbers of admissions to hospitals due to the outbreak of disease. These hospitals were full and some patients were treated in tents. Residents have been complaining for some years that a new hospital is needed in the area.

Prior to these events, the LRA was proudly leading the way in a new approach to waste management, with the introduction of its new 'Waste Recycling Scheme.' Two years ago, it began phase 1 of the scheme and half of its residents were issued with different coloured waste bins for different types of waste. The final phase was due to begin in one month's time. The cost of providing the new waste bins is significant but LRA's focus has always been on the long-term savings both to the environment and in terms of reduced waste disposal costs.

The LRA is about to begin preparing its budget for the coming financial year, which starts in one month's time. Over recent years, zero-based budgeting (ZBB) has been introduced at a number of regional authorities in Alaia and, given the demand on resources which LRA faces this year, it is considering whether now would be a good time to introduce it.

1   **What are the main steps involved in preparing a zero-based budget?**

A   Identifying previous inefficiencies, using adaptative management processes and avoiding wasteful expenditure in planning.

B   Recognising different cost behaviour patterns, planning on a rolling basis and ignoring wasteful expenditure.

C   Analysing the cost of each activity, identifying alternative methods and assessing the consequences of performing the activity at different levels.

D   Updating the budget continually, setting performance standards and controlling performance monthly with the use of variance analysis.

2   **Which TWO of the following statements are true?**

(1)   Now is a good time to introduce ZBB in LRA.

(2)   The introduction of ZBB in any organisation is relatively straightforward.

(3)   The introduction of ZBB in LRA would be lengthy and costly.

(4)   A conflict situation may arise if ZBB is introduced in LRA.

A   (1) and (2)

B   (1) and (3)

C   (3) and (4)

D   (2) and (4)

3   **Which of the following correctly describes a 'decision package' within the context of zero-based budgeting?**

A   A method of budgeting that requires each cost element to be specifically justified, as though the activities to which the budget relates were being undertaken for the first time.

B   The decision or choice between making a product in-house or outsourcing and buying in.

C   A method of budgeting based on an activity framework and utilising cost driver data in the budget-setting and variance feedback processes.

D   A list of costs that will not result in an outflow of cash either now or in the future or result in a 'real' cash expenditure.

4   **Which ONE of the following statements is true?**

A   If any of the activities or operations at LRA are wasteful, ZBB will not be able to identify these and remove them.

B   With the implementation of ZBB, managers may become less motivated as they have had a key role in putting the budget together.

C   ZBB would discourage a more questioning attitude and lead managers to just the status quo.

D   Overall, ZBB at LRA will lead to a more efficient allocation of resources.

5   **Which of the following describe difficulties in assessing performance in not-for-profit organisations?**

(i)   Benefits and costs are not always easy to quantify.

(ii)   These organisations often have multiple stakeholders and therefore multiple objectives.

(iii)   These organisations often have unlimited funds and are therefore not motivated to measure performance.

A   (i) only

B   (i) and (ii)

C   (ii) only

D   (ii) and (iii)

222 BOKCO (JUNE 2015)

Bokco is a manufacturing company. It has a small permanent workforce, but it is also reliant on temporary workers, whom it hires on three-month contracts whenever production requirements increase. All buying of materials is the responsibility of the company's purchasing department. and the company's policy is to hold low levels of raw materials in order to minimise inventory holding costs.

Budgeting is done on spreadsheets and detailed variance reports are produced each month for sales, material costs and labour costs. Departmental managers are then paid a monthly bonus depending on the performance of their department.

BokCo is operating in a fast changing environment and its Finance Manager thinks the original standard costs are unrealistic. He is considering revising the budget by analysing existing variances into a planning and operational element would help to improve performance.

One month ago, Bokco began production of a new product. The standard cost card for one unit was drawn up to include a cost of $84 for labour, based on seven hours of labour at $12 per hour.

Actual output of the product during the first month of production was 460 units and the actual time taken to manufacture the product totalled 1,860 hours at a total cost of $26,040.

After being presented with some initial variance calculations, the production manager has realised that the standard time per unit of seven hours was the time taken to produce the first unit and that a learning rate of 90% should have been anticipated for the first 1,000 units of production.

The production manager has consequently been criticised by other departmental managers who have said that, 'He has no idea of all the problems this (i.e. the failure to anticipate the learning effect) has caused.'

Bokco uses cost plus pricing to set the selling prices for its products once an initial cost card has been drawn up. Prices are then reviewed on a quarterly basis.

1   **Which TWO of the following sentences about using spreadsheets in budgeting are true?**

(1)   Spreadsheets enable managers to consider many different budget options and also carry out sensitivity analysis on the budget figures.

(2)   Minor errors in the spreadsheet cannot affect the validity of the data.

(3)   Spreadsheets are able to take qualitative factors into account.

(4)   The possibility of experimentation with data is so great that it is possible to lose sight of the original intention of the spreadsheet.

A   (1) and (2)

B   (1) and (4)

C   (2) and (3)

D   (3) and (4)

2   **Which TWO of the following sentences about the manipulation issues involved in revising budgets are true?**

(1)   The establishment of ex-post budgets is very difficult. Managers whose performance is reported to be poor using such a budget are unlikely to accept them as performance measures because of the subjectivity in setting such budgets. ✓

(2)   Frequent demands for budget revisions may result in bias. ✓

(3)   The operational variances do not give a fair reflection of the actual results achieved in the actual conditions that existed. ✗

(4)   The analysis does not help in the standard-setting learning process. ✗

A   (1) and (2)

B   (1) and (3)

C   (2) and (3)

D   (3) and (4)

3   **What is the labour efficiency planning variance AFTER taking account of the learning effect?**

Note: The learning index for a 90% learning curve is −0.1520.

$$y = ax^b$$

A $1,360 F

B $1, 360 A

C $7,104 A

D $23,424 F

4   **What is the labour efficiency operational variance AFTER taking account of the learning effect?**

Note: The learning index for a 90% learning curve is –0.1520.

A $1,360 F

B $1, 360 A

C $7,104 A

D $23,424 F

5   **Which ONE of the following statements about the production manager's failure to anticipate the learning effect is true?**

A   There will be no unnecessary extra labour costs. ✗

B   The selling price of the company's products would have been set too low. high.

C   An adverse material price variance would have arisen.

D   The sales manager's bonus would have still be guaranteed, in spite of the production manager's failure to anticipate the learning effect. ✗

223 CORFE CO (SEPTEMBER 2016)

Corfe Co is a business which manufactures computer laptop batteries and it has developed a new battery which has a longer usage time than batteries currently available in laptops. The selling price of the battery is forecast to be $45.

The maximum production capacity of Corfe Co is 262,500 units. The company's management accountant is currently preparing an annual flexible budget and has collected the following information so far:

Production (units)	185,000	200,000	225,000
	$	$	$
Material costs	740,000	800,000	900,000
Labour costs	1,017,500	1,100,000	1,237,500
Fixed costs	750,000	750,000	750,000

In addition to the above costs, the management accountant estimates that for each increment of 50,000 units produced, one supervisor will need to be employed. A supervisor's annual salary is $35,000.

The production manager does not understand why the flexible budgets have been produced as he has always used a fixed budget previously.

1   Assuming the budgeted figures are correct, what would the flexed total production cost be if production is 80% of maximum capacity?

   A $2,735,000

   B $2,770,000

   C $2,885,000

   D $2,920,000

2   The management accountant has said that a machine maintenance cost was not included in the flexible budget but needs to be taken into account.

   The new battery will be manufactured on a machine currently owned by Corfe Co which was previously used for a product which has now been discontinued. The management accountant estimates that every 1,000 units will take 14 hours to produce. The annual machine hours and maintenance costs for the machine for the last four years have been as follows:

	Machine time (hours)	Maintenance costs ($000)
Year 1	5,000	850
Year 2	4,400	735
Year 3	4,850	815
Year 4	1,800	450

   What is the estimated maintenance cost if production of the battery is 80% of maximum capacity (to the nearest $000)?

   A $575,000

   B $593,000

   C $500,000

   D $735,000

3 In the first month of production of the new battery, actual sales were 18,000 units and the sales revenue achieved was $702,000. The budgeted sales units were 17,300.

Based on this information, which of the following statements is true?

A   When the budget is flexed, the sales variance will include both the sales volume and sales price variances.

B   When the budget is flexed, the sales variance will only include the sales volume variance.

C   When the budget is flexed, the sales variance will only include the sales price variance.

D   When the budget is flexed, the sales variance will include the sales mix and quantity variances and the sales price variance.

4 **Which of the following statements relating to the preparation of a flexible budget for the new battery are true?**

(1)   The budget could be time-consuming to produce as splitting out semi-variable costs may not be straightforward.

(2)   The range of output over which assumptions about how costs will behave could be difficult to determine.

(3)   The flexible budget will give managers more opportunity to include budgetary slack than a fixed budget.

(4)   The budget will encourage all activities and their value to the organisation to be reviewed and assessed.

A   (1) and (2)

B   (1), (2) and (3)

C   (1) and (4)

D   (2), (3) and (4)

5 The management accountant intends to use a spreadsheet for the flexible budget in order to analyse performance of the new battery.

Which of the following statements are benefits regarding the use of spreadsheets for budgeting?

(1)   The user can change input variables and a new version of the budget can be quickly produced.

(2)   Errors in a formula can be easily traced and data can be difficult to corrupt in a spreadsheet.

(3)   A spreadsheet can take account of qualitative factors to allow decisions to be fully evaluated.

(4)   Managers can carry out sensitivity analysis more easily on a budget model which is held in a spreadsheet.

A   (1), (3) and (4)

B   (1), (2) and (4)

C   (1) and (4)

D   (2) and (3)

224 OBC (DECEMBER 2015)

The Organic Bread Company (OBC) makes a range of breads for sale direct to the public. The production process begins with workers weighing out ingredients on electronic scales and then placing them in a machine for mixing. A worker then manually removes the mix from the machine and shapes it into loaves by hand, after which the bread is then placed into the oven for baking. All baked loaves are then inspected by OBC's quality inspector before they are packaged up and made ready for sale. Any loaves which fail the inspection are donated to a local food bank. The standard cost card for OBC's 'Mixed Bloomer', one of its most popular loaves, is as follows:

White flour	450 grams at $1.80 per kg	$0.81
Wholegrain flour	150 grams at $2.20 per kg	$0.33
Yeast	10 grams at $20 per kg	$0.20
Total	610 grams	$1.34

Budgeted production of Mixed Bloomers was 1,000 units for the quarter, although actual production was only 950 units. The total actual quantities used and their actual costs were:

	kgs	$ per kg
White flour	408.50	1.90
Wholegrain flour	152.0	2.10
Yeast	10.0	20.00
Total	570.5	

1 What is the total material usage variance for OBC for the last quarter?

A $3.3 F

B $20.9 F

C $20.9 A

D $34.20 F

2 What is the total material mix variance for OBC for the last quarter?

A $3.3 F

B $16.51 F

C $16.51 A

D $19.77 F

3 What is the total material yield variance for OBC for the last quarter?

A $3.3 F

B $16.51 F

C $16.51 A

D $19.81 F

4   Which ONE of the following statements below is false?

(1)   An adverse material mix variance may arise because the mix may not be removed completely out of the machine, leaving some mix behind.

(2)   An adverse material yield variance may arise because Since the loaves are made by hand, they may be made slightly too large, meaning that fewer loaves can be baked.

A   (1) only

B   (2) only

C   Both (1) and (2)

D   Neither (1) nor (2)

5   Which of the following statements below is true?

(1)   Errors or changes in the mix may cause some loaves to be sub-standard and therefore rejected by the quality inspector.

(2)   The loaves might be baked at the wrong temperature and therefore be rejected by the quality inspector.

A   (1) only

B   (2) only

C   Both (1) and (2)

D   Neither (1) nor (2)

225 VARIANCES – SALES

This objective test case question contains question types which will only appear in a computer-based exam, but this question provides valuable practice for all students whichever version of the exam they are taking.

Fort Co. produces and sells three models of family car: The basic model (the Drastic), an upgraded model (the Bomber) and a deluxe model (the Cracker). All of the cars are priced to achieve a 6% mark up on standard cost. For the month of June, Fort Co budgeted to sell 30,000 units of the Drastic and so have 10% market share of the budgeted sales at a price of $10,600 each. Fort Co. actually achieved a 15% share of the market, though the market had actually contracted by 5%.

The following information is available for July.

	Drastic	Bomber	Cracker
Sales units:			
– Budgeted	27,000	15,000	18,000
– Actual	26,000	16,000	14,000
Budgeted sales price	**$10,600**	**$13,250**	**$16,960**

1   Which option correctly fills the gaps in the paragraph?

"The difference between the sales quantity and __volume__ variances is that the standard __mix__ is considered in the former. The difference between standard and actual is __ignored__."

A   volume, mix, ignored

B   price, mix, calculated

C   volume, quantity, ignored

D   price, quantity, calculated

2 Calculate the market share and size variance for the Drastic:

Share $_____ Favourable   Size $_____ Adverse

3 What is the sales mix variance? $_____ _____

4 What is the sales quantity variance? $_____ _____

5 Which TWO of the following statements are true?

(1) The sales mix variance would not give useful information to the management of Fort Co if the Cracker was a van.

(2) The sales mix variance will not be affected if the labour efficiency on the Drastic production line increases, all other factors remaining the same.

(3) The market share variance is a planning variance, not an operational variance.

(4) If the mix variance was calculated as a physical quantity, the answer would always be zero.

A (1) and (2)

B (2) and (3)

C (3) and (4)

D (1) and (4)

226 ROMEO CO (DECEMBER 2016)

Romeo Co is a business which makes and sells fresh pizza from a number of mobile food vans based at several key locations in the city centre. It offers a variety of toppings and dough bases for the pizzas and has a good reputation for providing a speedy service combined with hot, fresh and tasty food to customers.

Each van employs a chef who is responsible for making the pizzas to Romeo Co's recipes and two sales staff who serve the customers. All purchasing is done centrally to enable Romeo Co to negotiate bulk discounts and build relationships with suppliers.

Romeo Co operates a standard costing and variances system and the standard cost card for Romeo Co's basic tomato pizza is as follows:

Ingredient	Weight	Price
	(kg)	($ per kg)
Dough	0.20	7.60
Tomato sauce	0.08	2.50
Cheese	0.12	20.00
Herbs	0.02	8.40
	———	
	0.42	
	———	

In Month 3, Romeo Co produced and sold 90 basic tomato pizzas and actual results were as follows:

Ingredient	Kgs bought and used	Actual cost per kg
Dough	18.9	6.50
Tomato sauce	6.6	2.45
Cheese	14.5	21.00
Herbs	2.0	8.10
	42	

In Month 4, Romeo Co produced and sold 110 basic tomato pizzas. Actual results were as follows:

Ingredient	Kgs bought and used	Actual cost per kg
Dough	21.3	6.60
Tomato sauce	7.5	2.45
Cheese	14.2	20.00
Herbs	2.0	8.50
	45	

In Month 6, 100 basic tomato pizzas were made using a total of 42 kg of ingredients. A new chef at Romeo Co used the expected amount of dough and herbs but used less cheese and more tomato sauce per pizza than the standard. It was noticed that the sales of the basic tomato pizza had declined in the second half of the month.

1   **What was the total material price variance for Month 3?**

   A $7.22 adverse

   B $7.22 favourable

   C $40.50 favourable

   D $40.50 adverse

2   **What was the total materials mix variance for Month 3?**

   A $81.02 adverse

   B $41.92 adverse

   C $42.88 adverse

   D $38.14 adverse

3   **What was the materials yield variance for month 4?**

   Note: Calculate all workings to 2 decimal places.

   A $12.21 favourable

   B $11.63 favourable

   C $21.95 adverse

   D $9.75 adverse

4   In Month 5, Romeo Co reported a favourable materials mix variance for the basic tomato pizza.

Which of the following statements would explain why this variance has occurred?

A   The proportion of the relatively expensive ingredients used in production was less than the standard.

B   The prices paid for the ingredients used in the mix were lower than the standard prices.

C   Each pizza used less of all the ingredients in actual production than expected.

D   More pizzas were produced than expected given the level of ingredients input.

5   **Based on the above information about Month 6, which of the following statements are correct?**

(1)   The actual cost per pizza in Month 6 was lower than the standard cost per pizza.

(2)   The sales staff should lose their Month 6 bonus because of the reduced sales.

(3)   The value of the ingredients usage variance and the mix variance are the same.

(4)   The new chef will be responsible for the material price, mix and yield variances.

A   (3) and (4)

B   (1) and (2)

C   (1) and (3)

D   (2) and (4)

PERFORMANCE MEASUREMENT AND CONTROL

227   PIND CO

This objective test case question contains question types which will only appear in a computer-based exam, but this question provides valuable practice for all students whichever version of the exam they are taking.

The following information is available for Pind Co, a manufacturing company. You are provided with an extract from the Income Statement:

	$
Operating profit	42,000
Interest charges	(16,000)
	———
PBT	26,000
Taxation	(5,460)
	———
	20,540

Pind Co has an operating profit margin of 15%. You are provided with an extract from its Statement of Financial Position:

	$
Equity and reserves	
Total equity and reserves	420,000
Non-current liabilities	
Loan	150,000
5% Preference shares	40,000
Current liabilities	
Payable	50,000

[handwritten: $\dfrac{Debt}{equity} = \dfrac{150+40}{420+150+40} = \dfrac{190}{610}$]

1 What are the gearing ratio and interest cover for Pind Co?

	25%	31%	2.625	1.625
Gearing ratio		✓		
Interest cover			✓	

[handwritten: gearing = $\dfrac{Debt}{equity}$ = $\dfrac{500}{...}$]

[handwritten: Interest cover = $\dfrac{Op.\ profit}{Int.\ cost.}$ = $\dfrac{42000}{16000}$]

2 Which TWO of the following statements are correct?

(1) A reduction in the tax rate will improve the interest cover ratio. *[handwritten: ✓]*

(2) If the level of long term debt in Pind Co is reduced, the interest cover and dividend cover ratios will improve. *[handwritten: ✓]*

(3) If the level of long term debt in Pind Co is reduced, the asset turnover ratio will improve. *[handwritten: ✗]*

(4) Financial gearing is a measure of (risk) but interest cover is a measure of profitability. *[handwritten: ✗]*

A (1) and (2)

B (2) and (3)

C (3) and (4)

D (1) and (4)

Pind Co has a current ratio of 1.5 and a quick ratio of 0.9.

[handwritten: $\dfrac{CA - Inventory}{CL}$ >1 Desirable]

3 If cash in the bank is used to pay some of the payable, what will be the effect on the current and quick ratios? *[handwritten: ↓ Pay, Somewore; $\dfrac{CA}{CL}$]*

	Current ratio	Quick ratio
A	Increase ✓	Increase
B	Increase ✓	Decrease ✓
C	Decrease ✗	Increase
D	Decrease ✗	Decrease

4 If Pind Co has a receivables to cash ratio of 2 : 2.5, what are the receivable days (to the nearest whole day)? _____26_____ days

[handwritten:
Receivable : Cash
2 : 2.5
45000
Quick Ratio 0.9
Payable 50 000
45000 = 2:2.5
20000 : 25000.
Cash = 0.9 = $\dfrac{CA}{50000}$ + Receivables.
= 45000.
$\dfrac{Receivable}{Turnover} \times 365$
$\dfrac{20000}{42000 \times 15\%} \times 365$
$= 26$]*

5   **Which of the following statements are true?**

(1)   If the turnover of Pind Co increased by 20%, the asset turnover would increase by 20%.

(2)   If Pind Co has a different depreciation policy to its competitors, the asset turnover ratio will not be comparable.

A   (1) only

B   (2) only

C   Both (1) and (2)

D   Neither (1) nor (2)

Section 3

CONSTRUCTED RESPONSE QUESTIONS – SECTION C

SPECIALIST COST AND MANAGEMENT ACCOUNTING TECHNIQUES

228 GADGET CO (DECEMBER 2010)

The Gadget Co produces three products, A, B and C, all made from the same material. Until now, it has used traditional absorption costing to allocate overheads to its products. The company is now considering an activity based costing system in the hope that it will improve profitability. Information for the three products for the last year is as follows:

	A	B	C
Production and sales volumes (units)	15,000	12,000	18,000
Selling price per unit	$7.50	$12	$13
Raw material usage (kg) per unit	2	3	4
Direct labour hours per unit	0.1	0.15	0.2
Machine hours per unit	0.5	0.7	0.9
Number of production runs per annum	16	12	8
Number of purchase orders per annum	24	28	42
Number of deliveries to retailers per annum	48	30	62

The price for raw materials remained constant throughout the year at $1.20 per kg. Similarly, the direct labour cost for the whole workforce was $14.80 per hour. The annual overhead costs were as follows:

	$
Machine set up costs	26,550
Machine running costs	66,400
Procurement costs	48,000
Delivery costs	54,320

Required:

(a) Calculate the full cost per unit for products A, B and C under traditional absorption costing, using direct labour hours as the basis for apportionment. ▦   **(5 marks)**

(b) Calculate the full cost per unit of each product using activity based costing. ▦

(9 marks)

(c) Using your calculation from (a) and (b) above, explain how activity based costing may help The Gadget Co improve the profitability of each product. ▭   **(6 marks)**

(Total: 20 marks)

229 BRICK BY BRICK (JUNE 2010)

Brick by Brick (BBB) is a building business that provides a range of building services to the public. Recently they have been asked to quote for garage conversions (GC) and extensions to properties (EX) and have found that they are winning fewer GC contracts than expected.

BBB has a policy to price all jobs at budgeted total cost plus 50%. Overheads are currently absorbed on a labour hour basis. BBB thinks that a switch to activity based costing (ABC) to absorb overheads would reduce the cost associated to GC and hence make them more competitive.

You are provided with the following data:

Overhead category	Annual overheads $	Activity driver	Total number of activities per year
Supervisors	90,000	Site visits	500
Planners	70,000	Planning documents	250
Property related	240,000	Labour hours	40,000
	———		
Total	400,000		
	———		

A typical GC costs $3,500 in materials and takes 300 labour hours to complete. A GC requires only one site visit by a supervisor and needs only one planning document to be raised. The typical EX costs $8,000 in materials and takes 500 hours to complete. An EX requires six site visits and five planning documents. In all cases labour is paid $15 per hour.

Required:

(a) Calculate the cost and quoted price of a GC and of an EX using labour hours to absorb the overheads. ▦   (5 marks)

(b) Calculate the cost and the quoted price of a GC and of an EX using ABC to absorb the overheads. ▦   (5 marks)

(c) Assuming that the cost of a GC falls by nearly 7% and the price of an EX rises by about 2% as a result of the change to ABC, suggest possible pricing strategies for the two products that BBB sells and suggest two reasons other than high prices for the current poor sales of the GC. ▭   (6 marks)

(d) One BBB manager has suggested that only marginal cost should be included in budget cost calculations as this would avoid the need for arbitrary overhead allocations to products. Briefly discuss this point of view and comment on the implication for the amount of mark-up that would be applied to budget costs when producing quotes for jobs. ▭   (4 marks)

(Total: 20 marks)

230 JOLA PUBLISHING CO (JUNE 2008)

Jola Publishing Co publishes two forms of book.

The company publishes a children's book (CB), which is sold in large quantities to government controlled schools. The book is produced in only four large production runs but goes through frequent government inspections and quality assurance checks.

The paper used is strong, designed to resist the damage that can be caused by the young children it is produced for. The book has only a few words and relies on pictures to convey meaning.

The second book is a comprehensive technical journal (TJ). It is produced in monthly production runs, 12 times a year. The paper used is of relatively poor quality and is not subject to any governmental controls and consequently only a small number of inspections are carried out. The TJ uses far more machine hours than the CB in its production.

The directors are concerned about the performance of the two books and are wondering what the impact would be of a switch to an activity based costing (ABC) approach to accounting for overheads. They currently use absorption costing, based on machine hours for all overhead calculations. They have accurately produced an analysis for the accounting year just completed as follows:

	CB	TJ
	$ per unit	$ per unit
Direct production costs:		
Paper	0.75	0.08
Printing ink	1.45	4.47
Machine costs	1.15	1.95
Overheads	2.30	3.95
Total cost	5.65	10.45
Selling price	9.05	13.85
Margin	3.40	3.40

The main overheads involved are:

Overhead	% of total overhead	Activity driver
Property costs	75.0%	Machine hours
Quality control	23.0%	Number of inspections
Production set up costs	2.0%	Number of set ups

If the overheads above were re-allocated under ABC principles then the results would be that the overhead allocation to CB would be $0.05 higher and the overhead allocated to TJ would be $0.30 lower than previously.

Required:

(a) **Explain why the overhead allocations have changed in the way indicated above.** 🖳

(7 marks)

The directors are keen to introduce ABC for the coming year and have provided the following cost and selling price data:

(1)   The paper used costs $2 per kg for a CB but the TJ paper costs only $1 per kg. The CB uses 400g of paper for each book, four times as much as the TJ uses.

(2)   Printing ink costs $30 per litre. The CB uses one third of the printing ink of the larger TJ. The TJ uses 150 ml of printing ink per book.

(3)   The CB needs six minutes of machine time to produce each book, whereas the TJ needs 10 minutes per book. The machines cost $12 per hour to run.

(4)   The sales prices are to be $9.30 for the CB and $14.00 for the TJ.

As mentioned above there are three main overheads, the data for these are:

Overhead	Annual cost for the coming year ($)
Property costs	2,160,000
Quality control	668,000
Production set up costs	52,000
	————
Total	2,880,000
	————

The CB will be inspected on 180 occasions next year, whereas the TJ will be inspected just 20 times.

Jola Publishing will produce its annual output of 1,000,000 CBs in four production runs and approximately 10,000 TJs per month in each of 12 production runs.

Required:

(b)   **Calculate the cost per unit and the margin for the CB and the TJ using machine hours to absorb the overheads.** ⊞   **(5 marks)**

(c)   **Calculate the cost per unit and the margin for the CB and the TJ using activity based costing principles to absorb the overheads.** ⊞   **(8 marks)**

(Total: 20 marks)

Note: The original question, as written by the examiner also had the following requirement for 4 marks:

Briefly explain the implementation problems often experienced when ABC is first introduced.

---

231 ABKABER PLC

Abkaber plc assembles three types of motorcycle at the same factory: the 50cc Sunshine; the 250cc Roadster and the 1000cc Fireball. It sells the motorcycles throughout the world. In response to market pressures Abkaber plc has invested heavily in new manufacturing technology in recent years and, as a result, has significantly reduced the size of its workforce.

Historically, the company has allocated all overhead costs using total direct labour hours, but is now considering introducing Activity Based Costing (ABC). Abkaber plc's accountant has produced the following analysis.

	Annual output (units)	Annual direct labour hours	Selling price ($ per unit)	Raw material cost ($ per unit)
Sunshine	2,000	200,000	4,000	400
Roadster	1,600	220,000	6,000	600
Fireball	400	80,000 *500,000*	8,000	900

The three cost drivers that generate overheads are:

- Deliveries to retailers – the number of deliveries of motorcycles to retail showrooms.

- Set-ups – the number of times the assembly line process is re-set to accommodate a production run of a different type of motorcycle.

- Purchase orders – the number of purchase orders.

The annual cost driver volumes relating to each activity and for each type of motorcycle are as follows:

	Number of deliveries to retailers	Number of set-ups	Number of purchase orders
Sunshine	100	35	400
Roadster	80	40	300
Fireball	70	25	100

The annual overhead costs relating to these activities are as follows:

	$
Deliveries to retailers	2,400,000
Set-up costs	6,000,000
Purchase orders	3,600,000

All direct labour is paid at $5 per hour. The company holds no inventories.

At a board meeting there was some concern over the introduction of activity based costing.

The finance director argued: 'I very much doubt whether selling the Fireball is viable but I am not convinced that activity based costing would tell us any more than the use of labour hours in assessing the viability of each product.'

The marketing director argued: 'I am in the process of negotiating a major new contract with a motorcycle rental company for the Sunshine model. For such a big order they will not pay our normal prices but we need to at least cover our incremental costs. I am not convinced that activity based costing would achieve this as it merely averages costs for our entire production'.

The managing director argued: 'I believe that activity based costing would be an improvement but it still has its problems. For instance if we carry out an activity many times surely we get better at it and costs fall rather than remain constant. Similarly, some costs are fixed and do not vary either with labour hours or any other cost driver.'

The chairman argued: 'I cannot see the problem. The overall profit for the company is the same no matter which method of allocating overheads we use. It seems to make no difference to me.'

Required:

(a) Calculate the total profit on each of Abkaber plc's three types of product using each of the following methods to attribute overheads:

    (i) the existing method based upon labour hours

    (ii) activity based costing. ▦   **(12 marks)**

(b) Explain the implications of activity based costing for Abkaber plc, and is so doing evaluate the issues raised by each of the directors.   **(8 marks)**

                                                 (Total: 20 marks)

232 LIFECYCLE COSTING

'Companies operating in an advanced manufacturing environment are finding that about 90% of a product's life cycle cost is determined by decisions made early in the cycle. Management accounting systems should therefore be developed that aid the planning and control of product life-cycle costs and monitor spending at the early stages of the life cycle.'

Required:

Having regard to the above statement:

(a) explain the nature of the product life cycle concept and its impact on businesses operating in an advanced manufacturing environment.   **(7 marks)**

(b) explain life cycle costing and state what distinguishes it from more traditional management accounting practices.   **(9 marks)**

(c) explain briefly the concept of activity based management and TWO benefits that its adoption could bring for a business.   **(4 marks)**

                                                 (Total: 20 marks)

233 MANPAC

SY Company, a manufacturer of computer games, has developed a new game called the MANPAC. This is an interactive 3D game and is the first of its kind to be introduced to the market. SY Company is due to launch the MANPAC in time for the peak selling season.

Traditionally SY Company has priced its games based on standard manufacturing cost plus selling and administration cost plus a profit margin. However, the management team of SY Company has recently attended a computer games conference where everyone was talking about life cycle costing, target costing and market-based pricing approaches. The team has returned from the conference and would like more details on the topics they heard about and how they could have been applied to the MANPAC.

Required:

As management accountant of SY Company:

(a) Discuss how the following techniques could have been applied to MANPAC:

- life cycle costing

- target costing. 🖳 (8 marks)

(b) Evaluate the market-based pricing strategies that should have been considered for the launch of the MANPAC and recommend a strategy that should have been chosen. 🖳 (6 marks)

(c) Explain briefly each stage in the product life cycle of the MANPAC and consider ONE issue that the management team will need to consider at each stage. 🖳 (6 marks)

(Total: 20 marks)

234 WARGRIN (DECEMBER 2008)

Wargrin designs, develops and sells many PC games. Games have a short lifecycle lasting around three years only. Performance of the games is measured by reference to the profits made in each of the expected three years of popularity. Wargrin accepts a net profit of 35% of turnover as reasonable. A rate of contribution (sales price less variable cost) of 75% is also considered acceptable.

Wargrin has a large centralised development department which carries out all the design work before it passes the completed game to the sales and distribution department to market and distribute the product.

Wargrin has developed a brand new game called Stealth and this has the following budgeted performance figures.

The selling price of Stealth will be a constant $30 per game. Analysis of the costs show that at a volume of 10,000 units a total cost of $130,000 is expected. However at a volume of 14,000 units a total cost of $150,000 is expected. If volumes exceed 15,000 units the fixed costs will increase by 50%.

Stealth's budgeted volumes are as follows:

	Year 1	Year 2	Year 3
Sales volume	8,000 units	16,000 units	4,000 units

In addition, marketing costs for Stealth will be $60,000 in year one and $40,000 in year two. Design and development costs are all incurred before the game is launched and has cost $300,000 for Stealth. These costs are written off to the income statement as incurred (i.e. before year 1 above).

Required:

(a) Explain the principles behind lifecycle costing and briefly state why Wargrin in particular should consider these lifecycle principles. 🖳 (4 marks)

(b) Produce the budgeted results for the game 'Stealth' and briefly assess the game's expected performance, taking into account the whole lifecycle of the game. ▦ (9 marks)

(c) Explain why incremental budgeting is a common method of budgeting and outline the main problems with such an approach. 🖳 (7 marks)

(Total: 20 marks)

> **Note:** The original question, as written by the examiner, also had the following requirement for 6 marks:
>
> **Discuss the extent to which a meaningful standard cost can be set for games produced by Wargrin. You should consider each of the cost classifications mentioned above.**

235 EDWARD CO (DECEMBER 2007) *Walk in the footsteps of a top tutor*

Edward Limited assembles and sells many types of radio. It is considering extending its product range to include digital radios. These radios produce a better sound quality than traditional radios and have a large number of potential additional features not possible with the previous technologies (station scanning, more choice, one touch tuning, station identification text and song identification text etc).

A radio is produced by assembly workers assembling a variety of components. Production overheads are currently absorbed into product costs on an assembly labour hour basis.

Edward Limited is considering a target costing approach for its new digital radio product.

Required:

(a) Briefly describe the target costing process that Edward Limited should undertake.
(3 marks)

(b) Explain the benefits to Edward Limited of adopting a target costing approach at such an early stage in the product development process.
(4 marks)

A selling price of $44 has been set in order to compete with a similar radio on the market that has comparable features to Edward Limited's intended product. The board have agreed that the acceptable margin (after allowing for all production costs) should be 20%.

Cost information for the new radio is as follows:

Component 1 (Circuit board) – these are bought in and cost $4.10 each. They are bought in batches of 4,000 and additional delivery costs are $2,400 per batch.

Component 2 (Wiring) – in an ideal situation 25 cm of wiring is needed for each completed radio. However, there is some waste involved in the process as wire is occasionally cut to the wrong length or is damaged in the assembly process. Edward Limited estimates that 2% of the purchased wire is lost in the assembly process. Wire costs $0.50 per metre to buy.

Other material – other materials cost $8.10 per radio.

Assembly labour – these are skilled people who are difficult to recruit and retain. Edward Limited has more staff of this type than needed but is prepared to carry this extra cost in return for the security it gives the business. It takes 30 minutes to assemble a radio and the assembly workers are paid $12.60 per hour. It is estimated that 10% of hours paid to the assembly workers is for idle time.

Production overheads – recent historic cost analysis has revealed the following production overhead data:

	Total production overhead ($)	Total assembly labour hours
Month 1	620,000	19,000
Month 2	700,000	23,000

Fixed production overheads are absorbed on an assembly hour basis based on normal annual activity levels. In a typical year 240,000 assembly hours will be worked by Edward Limited.

Required:

(c) Calculate the expected cost per unit for the radio and identify any cost gap that might exist.
(13 marks)

(Total: 20 marks)

Note: The original question also had the following requirement for 5 marks:

Assuming a cost gap was identified in the process, outline possible steps Edward Limited could take to reduce this gap.

Walk in the footsteps of a top tutor

For tips on approaching the question, work through the boxed notes in order.

Once each requirement has been completed review the answer detail. Use this approach to reading and answering the question when tackling other questions.

(2) New product

(1) Start by reading each requirement and allocating time (1.8 mins per mark). Now read back through the question. Make notes or annotate the question whilst reading.

Edward Limited assembles and sells many types of radio. It is considering extending its product range to include digital radios. These radios produce a better sound quality than traditional radios and have a large number of potential additional features not possible with the previous technologies (station scanning, more choice, one touch tuning, station identification text and song identification text etc).

A radio is produced by assembly workers assembling a variety of components. Production overheads are currently absorbed into product costs on an assembly labour hour basis.

Edward Limited is considering a target costing approach for its new digital radio product.

(3) Traditional absorption costing

(4) New costing approach being considered

Required:

(a) Briefly describe the target costing process that Edward Limited should undertake. 🖥 **(3 marks)**

(b) Explain the benefits to Edward Limited of adopting a target costing approach at such an early stage in the product development process. 🖥 **(4 marks)**

(5) Now answer parts (a) – (b). See separate notes at end of question.

A selling price of $44 has been set in order to compete with a similar radio on the market that has comparable features to Edward Limited's intended product. The board have agreed that the acceptable margin (after allowing for all production costs) should be 20%.

> (7) This is the target selling price and margin. Calculate target cost using this info.

> (8) Include this cost.

Cost information for the new radio is as follows:

Component 1 (Circuit board) – these are bought in and cost $4.10 each. They a bought in batches of 4,000 and additional delivery costs are $2,400 per batch.

> (9) Spread this cost over the number of batches

Component 2 (Wiring) – in an ideal situation 25 cm of wiring is needed for ea completed radio. However, there is some waste involved in the process as wir occasionally cut to the wrong length or is damaged in the assembly process. Edward Limited estimates that 2% of the purchased wire is lost in the assembly process. Wire costs $0.50 per metre to buy.

Other material – other materials cost $8.10 per radio.

> (11) Include these costs.

> (10) Adjust usage for loss.

Assembly labour – these are skilled people who are difficult to recruit and reta... Edward Limited has more staff of this type than needed but is prepared to carry this extra cost in return for the security it gives the business. It takes 30 minutes to assemble a radio and the assembly workers are paid $12.60 per hour. It is estimated that 10% of hours paid to the assembly workers is for idle time.

> (12) Adjust hours for idle time.

Production overheads – recent historic cost analysis has revealed the following production overhead data:

	Total production Overhead ($)	Total assembly labour hours
Month 1	620,000	19,000
Month 2	700,000	23,000

> (13) A mix of fixed and variable costs. Use hi-low to separate.

(6) Now read this requirement and allocate time. Read back through the remainder of the question, making notes or annotating the question in the same way as before.

Fixed production overheads are absorbed on an assembly hour basis based on normal annual activity levels. In a typical year 240,000 assembly hours will be worked by Edward Limited.

(14) Use to calculate the OAR.

(15) Now answer part (c). Set up a summary of costs with separate workings where required

Required:

(c) **Calculate the expected cost per unit for the radio and identify any cost gap that might exist.** ⊞

(13 marks)

(Total: 20 marks)

Notes

- This is only a short scenario and so it should not take long to read and annotate the question. That should leave plenty of time to plan and write up the answer to requirements (a) – (c).

- Requirement (a) is worth 3 marks. Aim for 3 – 4 concise points. Brainstorm the key points first. Headings could be used for each key stage of the target costing process.

- Requirement (b) is worth 4 marks so aim to brainstorm 4 benefits first. A succinct explanation is all that is required and therefore 7 minutes should enough time to plan and write up the answer. Separate each of the benefits using individual paragraphs or headings. Make sure the actual requirement is answered, i.e. do not talk about general benefits of target costing.

236 YAM CO (JUNE 2009)

 Question debrief

Yam Co is involved in the processing of sheet metal into products A, B and C using three processes, pressing, stretching and rolling. Like many businesses Yam faces tough price competition in what is a mature world market.

The factory has 50 production lines each of which contain the three processes: Raw material for the sheet metal is first pressed then stretched and finally rolled. The processing capacity varies for each process and the factory manager has provided the following data:

	Processing time per metre in hours		
	Product A	*Product B*	*Product C*
Pressing	0.50	0.50	0.40
Stretching	0.25	0.40	0.25
Rolling	0.40	0.25	0.25

The factory operates for 18 hours each day for five days per week. It is closed for only two weeks of the year for holidays when maintenance is carried out. On average one hour of labour is needed for each of the 225,000 hours of factory time. Labour is paid $10 per hour.

The raw materials cost per metre is $3.00 for product A, $2.50 for product B and $1.80 for product C. Other factory costs (excluding labour and raw materials) are $18,000,000 per year. Selling prices per metre are $70 for product A, $60 for product B and $27 for product C.

Yam carries very little inventory.

Required:

(a) Identify the bottleneck process and briefly explain why this process is described as a 'bottleneck'. **(3 marks)**

(b) Calculate the throughput accounting ratio (TPAR) for each product assuming that the bottleneck process is fully utilised. **(8 marks)**

(c) Assuming that the TPAR of product C is less than 1:

   (i) Explain how Yam could improve the TPAR of product C. **(4 marks)**

   (ii) Briefly discuss whether this supports the suggestion to cease the production of product C and briefly outline three other factors that Yam should consider before a cessation decision is taken. **(5 marks)**

   (Total: 20 marks)

Calculate your allowed time, allocate the time to the separate parts..............

---

237 FLOPRO PLC

(a) Flopro plc makes and sells two products A and B, each of which passes through the same automated production operations. The following estimated information is available for period 1:

   (i) *Product unit data:*

	A	B
Direct material cost ($)	2	40
Variable production overhead cost ($)	28	4
Overall hours per product unit (hours)	0.25	0.15

   (ii) Production/sales of products A and B are 120,000 units and 45,000 units with selling prices per unit $60 and $70 respectively.

   (iii) Maximum demand for each product is 20% above the estimated sales levels.

   (iv) Total fixed production overhead cost is $1,470,000. This is absorbed at an average rate per hour based on the estimated production levels.

Required:

Using net profit as the decision measure, show why the management of Flopro plc argues that it is indifferent on financial grounds as to the mix of products A and B which should be produced and sold. **(5 marks)**

(b) One of the production operations has a maximum capacity of 3,075 hours which has been identified as a bottleneck which limits the overall production/sales of products A and B. The bottleneck hours required per product unit for products A and B are 0.02 and 0.015 respectively.

Flopro plc has decided to determine the profit maximising mix of products A and B based on the Throughput Accounting principle of maximising the throughput return per production hour of the bottleneck resources. This may be measured as throughput return per production hour = (selling price – material cost)/bottleneck hours per unit.

Required:

(i) **Calculate the mix (units) of products A and B which will maximise net profit and the value of that net profit.** ⊞ **(8 marks)**

(ii) **Calculate the throughput ratio for product B which is calculated as: throughput return per hour of bottleneck resource for product B/overall total cost per hour of bottleneck resource.** ⊞ **(3 marks)**

(iii) **Comment on the interpretation of throughput accounting ratios and their use as a control device. You should refer to the ratio for product B in your answer.** 💻 **(4 marks)**

(Total: 20 marks)

238 ENVIRONMENTAL MANAGEMENT ACCOUNTING

FXT is a pharmaceutical company trying to decide whether to continue with the production of one of its drugs. On economic grounds, the decision to continue manufacture is marginal; However, in the light or recent high–profile corporate scandals linked to environmental disasters, FTX is particularly anxious to make an informed decision based mainly on the environmental effects of continued production.

Following up on a review of its operations and various reports from its Operations Director, FXT's management accountant has identified the company's main environmental costs as follows:

(1) Waste disposal

(2) Water consumption

(3) Energy consumption

(4) Transport and travel.

Required:

(a) **Explain how the costs listed above arise and what control measures could be implemented by FXT in order to manage them.** 💻 **(10 marks)**

(b) **Briefly describe four management accounting techniques for the identification and allocation of environmental costs.** 💻 **(10 marks)**

(Total: 20 marks)

239 CHOCOLATES ARE FOREVER (CAF)

As the exams are tested as CBE, candidates will not have to draw a graph. However, it is good practice to attempt a question such as this as part of a robust revision programme. In the exam, graphs will be part of the question scenario and candidates may be asked to provide further calculation or analysis.

CAF Ltd produces a single large item of confectionary, Product S, that is sold for $12 per unit. You have been provided with the following information about the 'S' for the forthcoming year:

Sales   6,000 units

Variable costs $7 per unit

CAF's overheads are budgeted to amount to $20,000. CAF's Financial Director has asked you to prepare some documents for a presentation to the Board of Directors.

Required:

(a)   **Calculate, and briefly explain the significance of, CAF'S breakeven point and margin of safety, expressed as a percentage.** 🖾   **(4 marks)**

(b)   **Based on CAF's information above, construct and explain the purpose of the three following charts:**

(1)   **A breakeven chart**

(2)   **A contribution graph**

(3)   **A profit – volume chart.**   **(12 marks)**

(c)   **Briefly outline the limitations of breakeven analysis.** 💻   **(4 marks)**

(Total: 20 marks)

240 MANGO LEATHER

As the exams are tested as CBE, candidates will not have to draw a graph. However, it is good practice to attempt a question such as this as part of a robust revision programme. In the exam, graphs will be part of the question scenario and candidates may be asked to provide further calculation or analysis.

Mango has been in the clothing market for the last 3 years and operates in an industry which is very competitive and volatile. Mango's management accountant has heard that break even analysis could be used to assess the risks of the business and helps decision making.

The following information on Mango and its product portfolio is also available – figures are per annum:

Products	Production/sales volume	Selling price (per unit)	Variable cost(excluding material cost) per unit	Material (leather) per unit
		$	$	(Meters)
Bags	1,000	400	150	1
Belts	2,000	125	50	0.25
Shoes	1,500	150	65	0.5
Jackets	3,500	300	125	1.5

Leather is regularly used in the production of all the products above. The company has recently discovered that there is likely to be a shortage of leather on the market for the coming year. Leather used in production is bought from a supplier on a JIT basis for $60 per meter. For now, enough material can be sourced from the supplier to satisfy the production requirement. Fixed cost per annum is $580,000.

Required:

(a)   **Calculate the break even sales revenue.** ▦   **(3 marks)**

(b)   **Draw a profit volume chart by clearly showing all the workings to arrive at the graph.**   **(8 marks)**

(c)   **Explain how the unavailability of leather and the rise in its price affect the profitability and breakeven point of Mango. No calculation is required.** 🖥

                                                                         (5 marks)

(d)   **Explain how breakeven analysis could be used in decision making, and outline the limitations of the technique.** 🖥   **(4 marks)**

                                                                      (Total: 20 marks)

241   BREAKEVEN

C Ltd has presented you with its break-even chart:

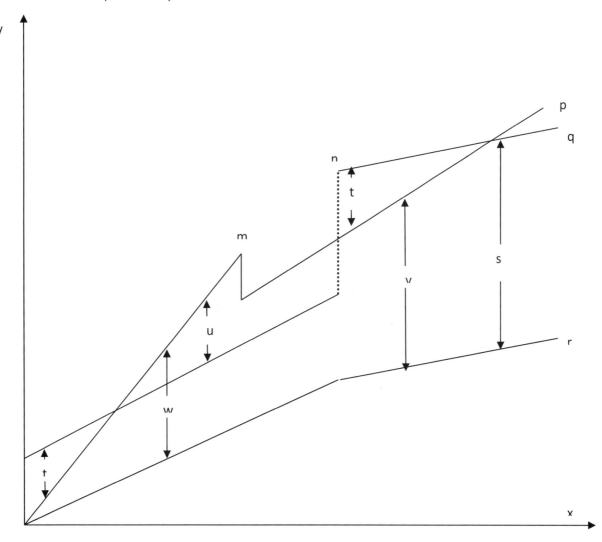

Required:

(a)   Identify the components of the breakeven chart labelled *p ,q ,r, s, t, u, v w, x* and *y*. 💻
(10 marks)

(b)   Suggest what events are represented at the values of *x* that are labelled *m* and *n* on the chart. 💻
(5 marks)

(c)   Briefly comment on the usefulness of breakeven analysis to senior management of a small company. 💻
(5 marks)

(Total: 20 marks)

242   EC LTD

As the exams are tested as CBE, candidates will not have to draw a graph. However, it is good practice to attempt a question such as this as part of a robust revision programme. In the exam, graphs will be part of the question scenario and candidates may be asked to provide further calculation or analysis.

EC Ltd produces and sells the following two products throughout the year in a constant mix:

	Product X	Product Y
Variable cost per $ of sales	$0.45	$0.60
Fixed costs	$1,212,000 per period	

The management of EC has stated that total sales revenue will reach a maximum of $4,000,000, and is generated by the two products in the following proportions:

	Product X	Product Y
Variable cost per $ of sales	70%	30%

Required:

(a)   Calculate the breakeven sales revenue required per period, based on the sales mix assumed above. ▦
(4 marks)

(b)   Prepare a profit-volume chart of the above situation for the maximum sales revenue. Show on the same chart the effect of a change in the sales mix to product X 50%, product Y 50%, and clearly indicate on the chart the breakeven point for each situation.
(12 marks)

(c)   Of the fixed costs, $455,000 are attributable to Product X. Calculate the sales revenue required on Product X in order to recover the attributable fixed costs and provide a net contribution of $700,000 towards general fixed costs and profit. ▦
(4 marks)

(Total: 20 marks)

DECISION MAKING TECHNIQUES

243   B CHEMICALS

As the exams are tested as CBE, candidates will not have to draw a graph. However, it is good practice to attempt a question such as this as part of a robust revision programme. In the exam, graphs will be part of the question scenario and candidates may be asked to provide further calculation or analysis.

B Chemicals refines crude oil into petrol. The refining process uses two types of crude oil – heavy and light. A mixture of these oils is blended into either Super or Regular petrol.

In the refining process one gallon (g) of Super is made from 0.7g of heavy crude and 0.5g of light crude. One gallon of Regular is made from 0.5g of heavy crude and 0.7g of light crude oil. (There is a refining loss of 0.2g in each case.)

At present, 5,000g of heavy crude and 6,000g of light crude oil are available for refining each day. Market conditions suggest that at least two-thirds of the petrol refined should be Super. The company makes contribution of $0.25 per gallon of Super and $0.10 per gallon of Regular.

Required:

(a)   State the objective function and three constraints, one for heavy crude, one for light crude and one for market conditions. 🖥️   **(6 marks)**

(b)   Graph the constraints and shade the feasible region.   **(8 marks)**

(c)   Deduce the optimal policy and the contribution generated, and comment briefly on your answer. 🖥️   **(6 marks)**

(Total: 20 marks)

244   COSMETICS CO (DECEMBER 2010, AMENDED)

The Cosmetic Co is a company producing a variety of cosmetic creams and lotions. The creams and lotions are sold to a variety of retailers at a price of $23.20 for each jar of face cream and $16.80 for each bottle of body lotion. Each of the products has a variety of ingredients, with the key ones being silk powder, silk amino acids and aloe vera. Six months ago, silk worms were attacked by disease causing a huge reduction in the availability of silk powder and silk amino acids. The Cosmetic Co had to dramatically reduce production and make part of its workforce, which it had trained over a number of years, redundant.

The company now wants to increase production again by ensuring that it uses the limited ingredients available to maximise profits by selling the optimum mix of creams and lotions. Due to the redundancies made earlier in the year, supply of skilled labour is now limited in the short-term to 160 hours (9,600 minutes) per week, although unskilled labour is unlimited. The purchasing manager is confident that they can obtain 5,000 grams of silk powder and 1,600 grams of silk amino acids per week. All other ingredients are unlimited.

The following information is available for the two products:

	Cream	Lotion
Materials required: silk powder (at $2.20 per gram)	3 grams	2 grams
– silk amino acids (at $0.80 per gram)	1 gram	0.5 grams
– aloe vera (at $1.40 per gram)	4 grams	2 grams
Labour required: skilled ($12 per hour)	4 minutes	5 minutes
– unskilled (at $8 per hour)	3 minutes	1.5 minutes

Each jar of cream sold generates a contribution of $9 per unit, whilst each bottle of lotion generates a contribution of $8 per unit. The maximum demand for lotions is 2,000 bottles per week, although demand for creams is unlimited. Fixed costs total $1,800 per week. The company does not keep inventory although if a product is partially complete at the end of one week, its production will be completed in the following week.

The following graph has been accurately drawn:

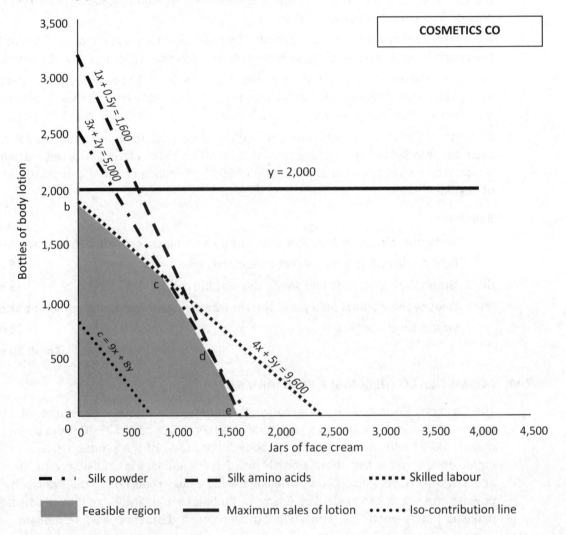

Required:

(a) Calculate the optimum number of each product that the Cosmetics Co should make per week, assuming that it wishes to maximise contribution. Calculate the total contribution per week for the new production plan. All workings MUST be rounded to 2 decimal places. ▦ **(14 marks)**

(b) Calculate the shadow price for silk powder and the slack for silk amino acids. All workings MUST be rounded to 2 decimal places. ▦ **(6 marks)**

(Total: 20 marks)

245 CUT AND STITCH (JUNE 2010)

Cut and Stitch (CS) make two types of suits using skilled tailors (labour) and a delicate and unique fabric (material). Both the tailors and the fabric are in short supply and so the accountant at CS has correctly produced a linear programming model to help decide the optimal production mix.

The model is as follows:

Variables:

Let W = the number of work suits produced

Let L = the number of lounge suits produced

Constraints

Tailors' time: $7W + 5L \leq 3{,}500$ (hours) – this is line T on the diagram

Fabric: $2W + 2L \leq 1{,}200$ (metres) – this is line F on the diagram

Production of work suits: $W \leq 400$ – this is line P on the diagram

Objective is to maximise contribution subject to:

$C = 48W + 40L$

On the diagram provided the accountant has correctly identified OABCD as the feasible region and point B as the optimal point.

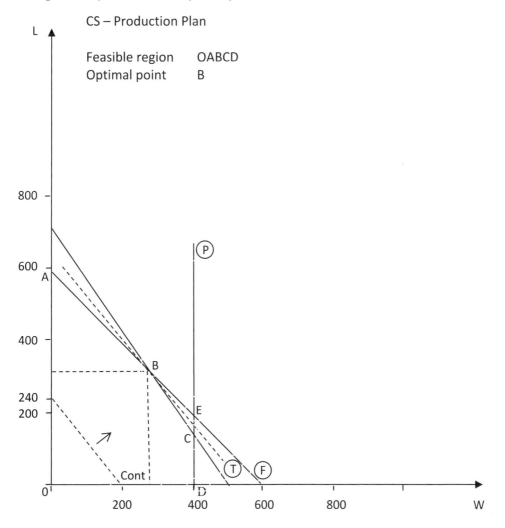

Required:

(a) Find by appropriate calculation the optimal production mix and related maximum contribution that could be earned by CS. ⊞ **(4 marks)**

(b) Calculate the shadow prices of the fabric per metre and the tailor time per hour. ⊞ **(6 marks)**

The tailors have offered to work an extra 500 hours provided that they are paid three times their normal rate of $1.50 per hour at $4.50 per hour.

Required:

(c) Briefly discuss whether CS should accept the offer of overtime at three times the normal rate. 🖥 **(6 marks)**

(d) Calculate the new optimum production plan if maximum demand for W falls to 200 units. ⊞ **(4 marks)**

(Total: 20 marks)

246 CSC CO (SEPTEMBER 2016)

CSC Co is a health food company producing and selling three types of high-energy products: cakes, shakes and cookies, to gyms and health food shops. Shakes are the newest of the three products and were first launched three months ago. Each of the three products has two special ingredients, sourced from a remote part the world. The first of these, Singa, is a super-energising rare type of caffeine. The second, Betta, is derived from an unusual plant believed to have miraculous health benefits.

CSC Co's projected manufacture costs and selling prices for the three products are as follows:

	Cakes	Cookies	Shakes
Per unit	$	$	$
Selling price	5.40	4.90	6.00
Costs:			
Ingredients: Singa ($1.20 per gram)	0.30	0.60	1.20
Ingredients: Betta ($1.50 per gram)	0.75	0.30	1.50
Other ingredients	0.25	0.45	0.90
Labour ($10 per hour)	1.00	1.20	0.80
Variable overheads	0.50	0.60	0.40
Contribution	2.60	1.75	1.20

For each of the three products, the expected demand for the next month is 11,200 cakes, 9,800 cookies and 2,500 shakes.

The total fixed costs for the next month are $3,000.

CSC Co has just found out that the supply of Betta is going to be limited to 12,000 grams next month. Prior to this, CSC Co had signed a contract with a leading chain of gyms, Encompass Health, to supply it with 5,000 shakes each month, at a discounted price of $5.80 per shake, starting immediately. The order for the 5,000 shakes is not included in the expected demand levels above.

Required:

(a) Assuming that CSC Co keeps to its agreement with Encompass Health, calculate the shortage of Betta, the resulting optimum production plan and the total profit for next month. ⊞ **(6 marks)**

One month later, the supply of Betta is still limited and CSC Co is considering whether it should breach its contract with Encompass Health so that it can optimise its profits.

Required:

(b) Discuss whether CSC Co should breach the agreement with Encompass Health. 🖥

Note: No further calculations are required. **(4 marks)**

Several months later, the demand for both cakes and cookies has increased significantly to 20,000 and 15,000 units per month respectively. However, CSC Co has lost the contract with Encompass Health and, after suffering from further shortages of supply of Betta, Singa and of its labour force, CSC Co has decided to stop making shakes at all. CSC Co now needs to use linear programming to work out the optimum production plan for cakes and cookies for the coming month. The variable 'x' is being used to represent cakes and the variable 'y' to represent cookies.

The following constraints have been formulated and a graph representing the new production problem has been drawn:

Singa: $0.25x + 0.5y \leq 12{,}000$

Betta: $0.5x + 0.2y \leq 12{,}500$

Labour: $0.1x + 0.12y \leq 3{,}000$

$x \leq 20{,}000$

$y \leq 15{,}000$

$x, y \geq 0$

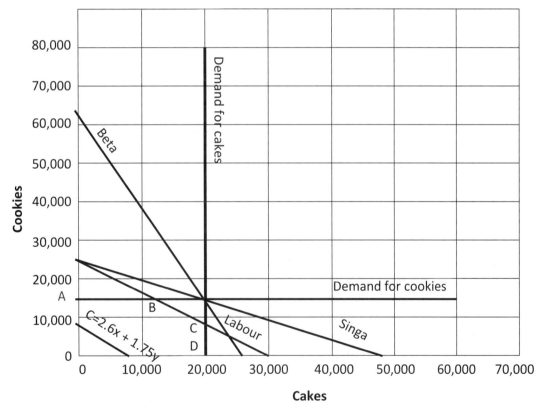

Required:

(c)   (i)   Explain what the line labelled 'C = 2.6x + 1.75y' on the graph is and what the area represented by the points 0ABCD means.   (4 marks)

       (ii)   Explain how the optimum production plan will be found using the line labelled 'C = 2.6x + 1.75y' and identify the optimum point from the graph. 🖥   (2 marks)

       (iii)   Explain what a slack value is and identify, from the graph, where slack will occur as a result of the optimum production plan. 🖥   (4 marks)

      Note: No calculations are needed for part (c).

(Total: 20 marks)

247 BITS AND PIECES (JUNE 2009)

> 🕐 *Question debrief*

Bits and Pieces (B&P) operates a retail store selling spares and accessories for the car market. The store has previously only opened for six days per week for the 50 working weeks in the year, but B&P is now considering also opening on Sundays.

The sales of the business on Monday through to Saturday averages at $10,000 per day with average gross profit of 70% earned.

B&P expects that the gross profit % earned on a Sunday will be 20 percentage points lower than the average earned on the other days in the week. This is because they plan to offer substantial discounts and promotions on a Sunday to attract customers. Given the price reduction, Sunday sales revenues are expected to be 60% more than the average daily sales revenues for the other days. These Sunday sales estimates are for new customers only, with no allowance being made for those customers that may transfer from other days.

B&P buys all its goods from one supplier. This supplier gives a 5% discount on all purchases if annual spend exceeds $1,000,000.

It has been agreed to pay time and a half to sales assistants that work on Sundays. The normal hourly rate is $20 per hour. In total five sales assistants will be needed for the six hours that the store will be open on a Sunday. They will also be able to take a half-day off (four hours) during the week. Staffing levels will be allowed to reduce slightly during the week to avoid extra costs being incurred.

The staff will have to be supervised by a manager, currently employed by the company and paid an annual salary of $80,000. If he works on a Sunday he will take the equivalent time off during the week when the assistant manager is available to cover for him at no extra cost to B&P. He will also be paid a bonus of 1% of the extra sales generated on the Sunday project.

The store will have to be lit at a cost of $30 per hour and heated at a cost of $45 per hour. The heating will come on two hours before the store opens in the 25 'winter' weeks to make sure it is warm enough for customers to come in at opening time. The store is not heated in the other weeks.

The rent of the store amounts to $420,000 annum.

Required:

(a) Calculate whether the Sunday opening incremental revenue exceeds the incremental costs over a year (ignore inventory movements) and on this basis reach a conclusion as to whether Sunday opening is financially justifiable. ▦ **(12 marks)**

(b) Discuss whether the manager's pay deal (time off and bonus) is likely to motivate him. 💻 **(4 marks)**

(c) Briefly discuss whether offering substantial price discounts and promotions on Sunday is a good suggestion. 💻 **(4 marks)**

(Total: 20 marks)

 Calculate your allowed time, allocate the time to the separate parts…………….

248 STAY CLEAN (DECEMBER 2009)

Stay Clean manufactures and sells a small range of kitchen equipment. Specifically the product range contains a dishwasher (DW), a washing machine (WM) and a tumble dryer (TD). The TD is of a rather old design and has for some time generated negative contribution. It is widely expected that in one year's time the market for this design of TD will cease, as people switch to a washing machine that can also dry clothes after the washing cycle has completed.

Stay Clean is trying to decide whether or not to cease the production of TD now *or* in 12 months' time when the new combined washing machine/drier will be ready. To help with this decision the following information has been provided:

(1) The normal selling prices, annual sales volumes and total variable costs for the three products are as follows:

	DW	WM	TD
Selling price per unit	$200	$350	$80
Material cost per unit	$70	$100	$50
Labour cost per unit	$50	$80	$40
Contribution per unit	$80	$170	–$10
Annual sales	5,000 units	6,000 units	1,200 units

(2) It is thought that some of the customers that buy a TD also buy a DW and a WM. It is estimated that 5% of the sales of WM and DW will be lost if the TD ceases to be produced.

(3) All the direct labour force currently working on the TD will be made redundant immediately if TD is ceased now. This would cost $6,000 in redundancy payments. If Stay Clean waited for 12 months the existing labour force would be retained and retrained at a cost of $3,500 to enable them to produce the new washing/drying product. Recruitment and training costs of labour in 12 months' time would be $1,200 in the event that redundancy takes place now.

(4) Stay Clean operates a just in time (JIT) policy and so all material cost would be saved on the TD for 12 months if TD production ceased now. Equally, the material costs relating to the lost sales on the WM and the DW would also be saved. However, the material supplier has a volume based discount scheme in place as follows:

Total annual expenditure ($)	Discount
0 – 600,000	0%
600,001 – 800,000	1%
800,001 – 9 00,000	2%
900,001 – 960,000	3%
960,001 and above	5%

Stay Clean uses this supplier for all its materials for all the products it manufactures. The figures given above in the cost per unit table for material cost per unit are net of any discount Stay Clean already qualifies for.

(5) The space in the factory currently used for the TD will be sublet for 12 months on a short-term lease contract if production of TD stops now. The income from that contract will be $12,000.

(6) The supervisor (currently classed as an overhead) supervises the production of all three products spending approximately 20% of his time on the TD production. He would continue to be fully employed if the TD ceases to be produced now.

Required:

(a) **Calculate whether or not it is worthwhile ceasing to produce the TD now rather than waiting 12 months (ignore any adjustment to allow for the time value of money).** ▦ **(13 marks)**

(b) **Explain two pricing strategies that could be used to improve the financial position of the business in the next 12 months assuming that the TD continues to be made in that period.** 💻 **(4 marks)**

(c) **Briefly describe three issues that Stay Clean should consider if it decides to outsource the manufacture of one of its future products.** 💻 **(3 marks)**

(Total: 20 marks)

249 CHOICE OF CONTRACTS

A company in the civil engineering industry with headquarters located 22 miles from London undertakes contracts anywhere in the United Kingdom.

The company has had its tender for a job in north-east England accepted at $288,000 and work is due to begin in March 20X3. However, the company has also been asked to undertake a contract on the south coast of England. The price offered for this contract is $352,000. Both of the contracts cannot be taken simultaneously because of constraints on staff site management personnel and on plant available. An escape clause enables the company to withdraw from the contract in the north-east, provided notice is given before the end of November and an agreed penalty of $28,000 is paid.

The following estimates have been submitted by the company's quantity surveyor:

Cost estimates

	North-east $	South-coast $
Materials:		
In inventory at original cost, Material X	21,600	
In inventory at original cost, Material Y		24,800
Firm orders placed at original cost, Material X	30,400	
Not yet ordered – current cost, Material X	60,000	
Not yet ordered – current cost, Material Z		71,200
Labour – hired locally	86,000	110,000
Site management	34,000	34,000
Staff accommodation and travel for site management	6,800	5,600
Plant on site – depreciation	9,600	12,800
Interest on capital, 8%	5,120	6,400
Total local contract costs	253,520	264,800
Headquarters costs allocated at rate of 5% on total contract costs	12,676	3,240
	266,196	278,040

	North-east $	South-coast $
Contract price	288,000	352,000
Estimated profit	21,804	73,960

(1)   X, Y and Z are three building materials. Material X is not in common use and would not realise much money if re-sold; however, it could be used on other contracts but only as a substitute for another material currently quoted at 10% less than the original cost of X. The price of Y, a material in common use, has doubled since it was purchased; its net realisable value if re-sold would be its new price less 15% to cover disposal costs. Alternatively it could be kept for use on other contracts in the following financial year.

(2)   With the construction industry not yet recovered from the recent recession, the company is confident that manual labour, both skilled and unskilled, could be hired locally on a sub-contracting basis to meet the needs of each of the contracts.

(3)   The plant which would be needed for the south coast contract has been owned for some years and $12,800 is the year's depreciation on a straight-line basis. If the north-east contract is undertaken, less plant will be required but the surplus plant will be hired out for the period of the contract at a rental of $6,000.

(4)   It is the company's policy to charge all contracts with notional interest at 8% on estimated working capital involved in contracts. Progress payments would be receivable from the contractee.

(5)   Salaries and general costs of operating the small headquarters amount to about $108,000 each year. There are usually ten contracts being supervised at the same time.

(6)   Each of the two contracts is expected to last from March 20X3 to February 20X4 which, coincidentally, is the company's financial year.

(7)   Site management is treated as a fixed cost.

Required:

As the management accountant to the company present comparative statements to show the net benefit to the company of undertaking the more advantageous of the two contracts.

Explain the reasoning behind the inclusion in (or omission from) your comparative financial statements, of each item given in the cost estimates and the notes relating thereto. 🖳 (Total: 20 marks)

250 HS EQUATION

HS manufactures components for use in computers. The business operates in a highly competitive market where there are a large number of manufacturers of similar components. HS is considering its pricing strategy for the next 12 weeks for one of its components. The Managing Director seeks your advice to determine the selling price that will maximise the profit to be made during this period.

You have been given the following data:

Market demand

The current selling price of the component is $1,350 and at this price the average weekly demand over the last four weeks has been 8,000 components. An analysis of the market shows that, for every $50 increase in selling price, the demand reduces by 1,000 components per week. Equally, for every $50 reduction in selling price, the demand increases by 1,000 components per week.

Costs

The direct material cost of each component is $270. This price is part of a fixed price contract with the material suppliers and the contract does not expire for another year.

Production labour and conversion costs, together with other overhead costs and the corresponding output volumes, have been collected for the last four weeks and they are as follows:

Week	Output volume (units)	$000
1	9,400	7,000
2	7,600	5,688
3	8,500	6,334
4	7,300	5,446

No significant changes in cost behaviour are expected over the next 12 weeks.

Required:

(a) Calculate the optimum (profit-maximising) selling price of the component for the period. ▦ (14 marks)

(b) Identify and explain three reasons why it may be inappropriate for HS to use this theoretical pricing model in practice. 🖳 (6 marks)

(Total: 20 marks)

251 MKL

Product 'M' is currently being tested by MKL and is to be launched in ten weeks' time. The 'M' is an innovative product which the company believes will change the entire market. The company has decided to use a market skimming approach to pricing this product during its introduction stage.

[handwritten: → Set High & ▼]

[handwritten margin: Continue review]

MKL continually reviews its product range and enhances its existing products by developing new models to satisfy the demands of its customers. The company intends to always have products at each stage of the product life cycle to ensure the company's continued presence in the market.

MKL is currently reviewing its two existing flagship products, Product K and Product L. You have been given the following information:

- *[handwritten margin: Maturity 10 weeks]* Product K was introduced to the market some time ago and is now about to enter the maturity stage of its life cycle. The maturity stage is expected to last for ten weeks. Each unit has a variable cost of $38 and takes 1 standard hour to produce. The Managing Director is unsure which of four possible prices the company should charge during the next ten weeks. The following table shows the results of some market research into the level of weekly demand at alternative prices:

| Selling price per unit | $100 | $85 | $80 | $75 |
| Weekly demand (units) | 600 | 800 | 1,200 | 1,400 |

[handwritten: High-low / below]

- *[handwritten margin: Growth 20 weeks]* Product L was introduced to the market two months ago using a penetration pricing policy and is now about to enter its growth stage. This stage is expected to last for 20 weeks. Each unit has a variable cost of $45 and takes 1.25 standard hours to produce. Market research has indicated that there is a linear relationship between its selling price and the number of units demanded, of the form $P = a - bx$. At a selling price of $100 per unit demand is expected to be 1,000 units per week. For every $10 increase in selling price the weekly demand will reduce by 200 units and for every $10 decrease in selling price the weekly demand will increase by 200 units.

The company currently has a production facility which has a capacity of 2,000 standard hours per week. This facility is being expanded but the extra capacity will not be available for ten weeks.

Required:

(a) Calculate which of the four selling prices should be charged for product K, in order to maximise its contribution during its maturity stage. ⊞ (5 marks)

(b) Following on from your answer above in (a), calculate the selling price of product L during its growth stage. ⊞ (8 marks)

(c) Compare and contrast penetration and skimming pricing strategies during the introduction stage, using product M to illustrate your answer. 💻 (7 marks)

(Total: 20 marks)

252 HAMMER (JUNE 2010)

Hammer is a large garden equipment supplier with retail stores throughout Toolland. Many of the products it sells are bought in from outside suppliers but some are currently manufactured by Hammer's own manufacturing division 'Nail'.

The prices (a transfer price) that Nail charges to the retail stores are set by head office and have been the subject of some discussion. The current policy is for Nail to calculate the total variable cost of production and delivery and add 30% for profit. Nail argues that all costs should be taken into consideration, offering to reduce the mark-up on costs to 10% in this case. The retail stores are unhappy with the current pricing policy arguing that it results in prices that are often higher than comparable products available on the market.

Nail has provided the following information to enable a price comparison to be made of the two possible pricing policies for one of its products.

Garden shears

Steel: the shears have 0.4 kg of high quality steel in the final product. The manufacturing process loses 5% of all steel put in. Steel costs $4,000 per tonne (1 tonne = 1,000 kg).

Other materials: Other materials are bought in and have a list price of $3 per kg although Hammer secures a 10% volume discount on all purchases. The shears require 0.1 kg of these materials.

The labour time to produce shears is 0.25 hours per unit and labour costs $10 per hour.

Variable overheads are absorbed at the rate of 150% of labour rates and fixed overheads are 80% of the variable overheads.

Delivery is made by an outsourced distributor that charges Nail $0.50 per garden shear for delivery.

Required:

(a) Calculate the price that Nail would charge for the garden shears under the existing policy of variable cost plus 30%. ⊞ **(6 marks)**

(b) Calculate the increase or decrease in price if the pricing policy switched to total cost plus 10%. ⊞ **(4 marks)**

(c) Discuss whether or not including fixed costs in a transfer price is a sensible policy. 💻 **(4 marks)**

(d) Discuss whether the retail stores should be allowed to buy in from outside suppliers if the prices are cheaper than those charged by Nail. 💻 **(6 marks)**

(Total: 20 marks)

253 SNIFF CO (DECEMBER 2007)

Sniff Limited manufactures and sells its standard perfume by blending a secret formula of aromatic oils with diluted alcohol. The oils are produced by another company following a lengthy process and are very expensive. The standard perfume is highly branded and successfully sold at a price of $39.98 per 100 millilitres (ml).

Sniff Limited is considering processing some of the perfume further by adding a hormone to appeal to members of the opposite sex. The hormone to be added will be different for the male and female perfumes. Adding hormones to perfumes is not universally accepted as a good idea as some people have health concerns. On the other hand, market research carried out suggests that a premium could be charged for perfume that can 'promise' the attraction of a suitor. The market research has cost $3,000.

Data has been prepared for the costs and revenues expected for the following month (a test month) assuming that a part of the company's output will be further processed by adding the hormones.

The output selected for further processing is 1,000 litres, about a tenth of the company's normal monthly output. Of this, 99% is made up of diluted alcohol which costs $20 per litre. The rest is a blend of aromatic oils costing $18,000 per litre. The labour required to produce 1,000 litres of the basic perfume before any further processing is 2,000 hours at a cost of $15 per hour.

Of the output selected for further processing, 200 litres (20%) will be for male customers and 2 litres of hormone costing $7,750 per litre will then be added. The remaining 800 litres (80%) will be for female customers and 8 litres of hormone will be added, costing $12,000 per litre. In both cases the adding of the hormone adds to the overall volume of the product as there is no resulting processing loss.

Sniff Limited has sufficient existing machinery to carry out the test processing.

The new processes will be supervised by one of the more experienced supervisors currently employed by Sniff Limited. His current annual salary is $35,000 and it is expected that he will spend 10% of his time working on the hormone adding process during the test month. This will be split evenly between the male and female versions of the product.

Extra labour will be required to further process the perfume, with an extra 500 hours for the male version and 700 extra hours for the female version of the hormone-added product. Labour is currently fully employed, making the standard product. New labour with the required skills will not be available at short notice.

Sniff Limited allocates fixed overhead at the rate of $25 per labour hour to all products for the purposes of reporting profits.

The sales prices that could be achieved as a one-off monthly promotion are:

- Male version: $75.00 per 100 ml

- Female version: $59.50 per 100 ml.

Required:

(a)   Outline the financial and other factors that Sniff Limited should consider when making a further processing decision. 🖥

   Note: no calculations are required.   (5 marks)

(b)   Evaluate whether Sniff Limited should experiment with the hormone adding process using the data provided. Provide a separate assessment and conclusion for the male and the female versions of the product. ⊞   (15 marks)

(Total: 20 marks)

Note: The original question as written by the examiner had the following additional requirements:

(c)   Calculate the selling price per 100 ml for the female version of the product that would ensure further processing would break even in the test month.   (2 marks)

(d)   Sniff Limited is considering outsourcing the production of the standard perfume. Outline the main factors it should consider before making such a decision.
                                                                              (4 marks)

---

254 FURNIVAL

Furnival has a distillation plant that produces three joint products, P, Q and R, in the proportions 10:5:5. After the split-off point the products can be sold for industrial use or they can be taken to the mixing plant for blending and refining. The latter procedure is normally followed.

For a typical week, in which all the output is processed in the mixing plant, the following income statement can be prepared:

	Product P	Product Q	Product R
Sales volume (gallons)	1,000	500	500
Price per gallon ($)	12.50	20	10
Sales revenue ($)	12,500	10,000	5,000
Joint process cost ($)			
(apportioned using output volume)	5,000	2,500	2,500
Mixing plant cost ($):			
Process costs	3,000	3,000	3,000
Other separable costs	2,000	500	500
Total costs ($)	10,000	6,000	6,000
Profit/(loss) ($)	2,500	4,000	(1,000)

The joint process costs are 25% fixed and 75% variable, whereas the mixing plant costs are 10% fixed and 90% variable and all the 'other separable costs' are variable.

If the products had been sold at the split-off point the selling price per gallon would have been:

Product P	Product Q	Product R
$5.00	$6.00	$1.50

There are only 45 hours available per week in the mixing plant. Typically 30 hours are taken up with the processing of Product P, Q and R (10 hours for each product line) and 15 hours are used for other work that generates (on average) a profit of $200 per hour after being charged with a proportionate share of the plant's costs (including fixed costs). The manager of the mixing plant considers that he could sell all the plant's processing time externally at a price that would provide this rate of profit.

It has been suggested:

(i)   that, since Product R regularly makes a loss, it should be sold off at the split-off point

(ii)   that it might be possible advantageously to change the mix of products achieved in the distillation plant. It is possible to change the output proportions to 7:8:5 at a cost of $1 for each additional gallon of Q produced by the distillation plant.

Required:

Compare the costs and benefits for each of the above proposals. Recommend, for each proposal, whether it should or should not be implemented.   **(Total: 20 marks)**

255 MAN CO (JUNE 2016)

A manufacturing company, Man Co, has two divisions: Division L and Division M. Both divisions make a single standardised product. Division L makes component L, which is supplied to both Division M and external customers. Division M makes product M using one unit of component L and other materials. It then sells the completed product M to external customers. To date, Division M has always bought component L from Division L.

The following information is available:

	Component L	Product M
	$	$
Selling price	40	96
Direct materials:		
Component L		(40)
Other	(12)	(17)
Direct labour	(6)	(9)
Variable overheads	(2)	(3)
Selling and distribution costs	(4)	(1)
	——	——
Contribution per unit before fixed costs	16	26
	——	——
Annual fixed costs	$500,000	$200,000
Annual external demand (units)	160,000	120,000
Capacity of plant	300,000	130,000

Division L charges the same price for component L to both Division M and external customers. However, it does not incur the selling and distribution costs when transferring internally.

Division M has just been approached by a new supplier who has offered to supply it with component L for $37 per unit. Prior to this offer, the cheapest price which Division M could have bought component L for from outside the group was $42 per unit.

It is head office policy to let the divisions operate autonomously without interference at all.

Required:

(a) Calculate the incremental profit/(loss) per component for the group if Division M accepts the new supplier's offer and recommend how many components Division L should sell to Division M if group profits are to be maximised. ▦   **(3 marks)**

(b) Using the quantities calculated in (a) and the current transfer price, calculate the total annual profits of each division and the group as a whole. ▦   **(6 marks)**

(c) Discuss the problems which will arise if the transfer price remains unchanged and advise the divisions on a suitable alternative transfer price for component L. 🖥   **(6 marks)**

(Total: 15 marks)

256 RECYC

Recyc plc is a company which reprocesses factory waste in order to extract good quality aluminium. Information concerning its operations is as follows:

(1)   Recyc plc places an advance order each year for chemical X for use in the aluminium extraction process. It will enter into an advance contract for the coming year for chemical X at one of three levels – high, medium or low, which correspond to the requirements of a high, medium or low level of waste available for reprocessing.

(2)   The level of waste available will not be known when the advance order for chemical X is entered into. A set of probabilities have been estimated by management as to the likelihood of the quantity of waste being at a high, medium or low level.

(3)   Where the advance order entered into for chemical X is lower than that required for the level of waste for processing actually received, a discount from the original demand price is allowed by the supplier for the total quantity of chemical X actually required.

(4)   Where the advance order entered into for chemical X is in excess of that required to satisfy the actual level of waste for reprocessing, a penalty payment in excess of the original demand price is payable for the total quantity of chemical X actually required.

A summary of the information relating to the above points is as follows:

			Chemical X costs per kg		
Level of reprocessing	Waste available 000 kg	Probability	Advance order $	Conversion discount $	Conversion premium $
High	50,000	0.30	1.00		
Medium	38,000	0.50	1.20		
Low	30,000	0.20	1.40		
Chemical X: order conversion:					
Low to medium				0.10	
Medium to high				0.10	
Low to high				0.15	
Medium to low					0.25
High to medium					0.25
High to low					0.60

Aluminium is sold at $0.65 per kg. Variable costs (excluding chemical X costs) are 70% of sales revenue. Aluminium extracted from the waste is 15% of the waste input. Chemical X is added to the reprocessing at the rate of 1 kg per 100 kg of waste.

Required:

(a)   **Prepare a summary which shows the budgeted contribution earned by Recyc plc for the coming year for each of nine possible outcomes.**   **(14 marks)**

(b)   **State the contribution for the coming year which corresponds to the use of (i) maximax, and (ii) maximin decision criteria, and comment on the risk preference of management which is indicated by each. 🖳**   **(6 marks)**

(Total: 20 marks)

257   TICKET AGENT   *Walk in the footsteps of a top tutor*

A ticket agent has an arrangement with a concert hall that holds concerts on 60 nights a year whereby he receives discounts as follows per concert:

For purchase of:	He receives a discount of:
200 tickets	20%
300 tickets	25%
400 tickets	30%
500 tickets or more	40%

Purchases must be in full hundreds. The average price per ticket is $30.

He must decide in advance each year the number of tickets he will purchase. If he has any tickets unsold by the afternoon of the concert he must return them to the box office. If the box office sells any of these he receives 60% of their price.

His sales records over a few years show that for a concert with extremely popular artistes he can be confident of selling 500 tickets, for one with lesser known artistes 350 tickets, and for one with relatively unknown artistes 200 tickets.

His records show that 10% of the tickets he returns are sold by the box office. (**Note:** these are in addition to any sales made by the ticket agent).

His administration costs incurred in selling tickets are the same per concert irrespective of the popularity of the artistes.

Sales records show that the frequency of concerts will be:

With popular artistes	45%
With lesser known artistes	30%
With unknown artistes	25%
	————
	100%
	————

Required:

(a)   Calculate:

- the expected demand for tickets per concert

- the level of his purchases of tickets per concert that will give him the largest profit over a long period of time and the profit per concert that this level of purchases of tickets will yield. ▦   **(11 marks)**

(b)   Calculate the number of tickets the agent should buy, based on the following criteria:

- Maximin

- Maximax

- Minimax regret. ▦   **(5 marks)**

(c)   Advise the ticket agent. 💻   **(4 marks)**

(Total: 20 marks)

258 SHIFTERS HAULAGE (DECEMBER 2008)

Shifters Haulage (SH) is considering changing some of the vans it uses to transport crates for customers. The new vans come in three sizes; small, medium and large. SH is unsure about which type to buy. The capacity is 100 crates for the small van, 150 for the medium van and 200 for the large van.

Demand for crates varies and can be either 120 or 190 crates per period, with the probability of the higher demand figure being 0.6.

The sale price per crate is $10 and the variable cost $4 per crate for all van sizes subject to the fact that if the capacity of the van is greater than the demand for crates in a period then the variable cost will be lower by 10% to allow for the fact that the vans will be partly empty when transporting crates.

SH is concerned that if the demand for crates exceeds the capacity of the vans then customers will have to be turned away. SH estimates that in this case goodwill of $100 would be charged against profits per period to allow for lost future sales regardless of the number of customers that are turned away.

Depreciation charged would be $200 per period for the small, $300 for the medium and $400 for the large van.

SH has in the past been very aggressive in its decision-making, pressing ahead with rapid growth strategies. However, its managers have recently grown more cautious as the business has become more competitive.

Required:

(a) Explain the principles behind the maximax, maximin and expected value criteria that are sometimes used to make decisions in uncertain situations. (5 marks)

(b) Prepare a profits table showing the SIX possible profit figures per period. (9 marks)

(c) Using your profit table from (b) above discuss which type of van SH should buy taking into consideration the possible risk attitudes of the managers. (6 marks)

(Total: 20 marks)

Note: The original question, as written by the examiner, also had the following requirement for six marks:

Describe THREE methods other than those mentioned in (a) above, which businesses can use to analyse and assess the risk that exists in its decision-making.

---

259 RY DECISION TREE

As the exams are tested as CBE, candidates will not have to draw a decision tree. However, it is good practice to attempt a question such as this as part of a robust revision programme. In the exam, a decision tree will be part of the question scenario and candidates may be asked to provide further calculations or analysis.

RY Ltd, a transatlantic airline company, has recently launched a low-cost airline company providing flights within Europe. The market is highly competitive and two other low-cost airlines, B Ltd and G Ltd, together hold 98% of the market.

RY Ltd commissioned some market research to help with the pricing decision for one route, London to Paris, which it is thinking of offering. The research identified three possible market states and the likely number of passengers that would be attracted at three price levels on this route.

Ticket price		£80	£90	£100
Market	*Probability*	*Passenger seats*	*Passenger seats*	*Passenger seats*
Pessimistic	0.2	80	60	30
Most likely	0.6	100	90	80
Optimistic	0.2	150	150	120

Airport charges are incurred for each customer and these are expected to be either £5 or £6 per customer depending on the negotiations with the airports involved. The probabilities for the airport charges are 0.6 for an airport charge of £5 per passenger and 0.4 for an airport charge of £6 per customer.

The fixed costs of a flight from London to Paris are £4,422.

Required:

(a) **Draw a decision tree to illustrate the pricing decision faced by RY Ltd.** (8 marks)

(b) **Using the decision tree or otherwise, establish the optimum price that RY Ltd should charge in order to maximise profit.** 🖥 (6 marks)

(c) **If RY Ltd knew that there would be a pessimistic market, which price should it charge in order to maximise profit?** 🖥 (6 marks)

(Total: 20 marks)

260 AMELIE

Amelie is setting up in business importing French cheeses. She could open up a small shop, a large outlet, or no shop at all if she decides to sell online only (which she won't be able to do for another few years at least.) There will be a 5 year lease on a few shops currently available in the centre of town, and Amelie wants to make the correct decision.

Amelie is also thinking about hiring a consultant to conduct a market research study. If the study is conducted, the results could indicate that the cheese market is either favourable or unfavourable.

Amelie believes there is a 50-50 chance that the market will be favourable, and expects her profits to be as follows if she opens her shop:

	Favourable market	*Unfavourable market*
Large shop	$60,000	($40,000) loss
Small shop	$30,000	($10,000) loss

The consultant has quoted a charge of $5,000 for the marketing research. He has also hinted that there is a 0.6 probability that the survey will indicate that the cheese market would be favourable.

There is a 0.9 probability that the cheese market will be favourable given a favourable outcome from the study. The consultant warned Amelie that there is only a probability of 0.12 of a favourable market if the marketing research results are not favourable. Amelie has accurately drawn the following decision tree:

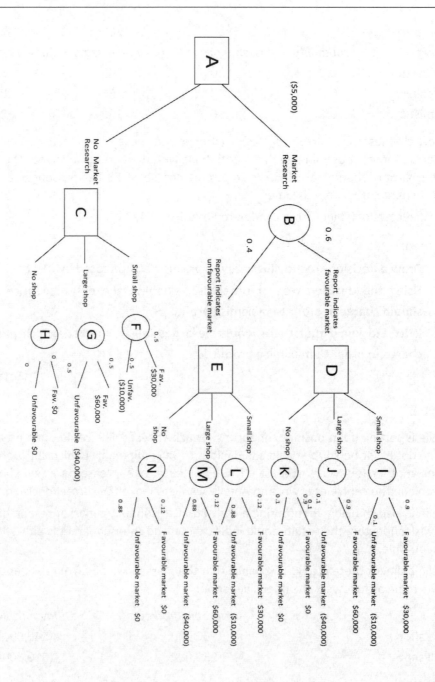

Required:

(a) Explain why Amelie should hire the market research consultant. 🖥️ (7 marks)

(b) After discussing the competence of the consultant with another business owner, Amelie now believes that she'd rather contact another market research company which guarantees perfect information concerning the cheese market profitability.

Calculate the value of this perfect information. 🖥️ 🎞️ (3 marks)

(Total: 10 marks)

BUDGETING AND CONTROL

261   STATIC CO (DECEMBER 2016)

Static Co is a multinational consumer goods company. Traditionally, the company has used a fixed annual budgeting process in which it sets quarterly sales revenue targets for each of its product lines. Historically, however, if a product line fails to reach its sales revenue target in any of the first three quarters, the company's sales director (SD) and finance director (FD) simply go back and reduce the sales revenue targets for the quarter just ended, to make it look like the target was reached. They then increase the target for the final quarter to include any shortfall in sales from earlier quarters.

During the last financial year ended 31 August 20X6, this practice meant that managers had to heavily discount many of their product lines in the final quarter in order to boost sales volumes and meet the increased targets. Even with the discounts, however, they still did not quite reach the targets. On the basis of the sales targets set at the beginning of that year, the company had also invested $6m in a new production line in January 20X6. However, to date, this new production line still has not been used. As a result of both these factors, Static Co saw a dramatic fall in return on investment from 16% to 8% in the year.

Consequently, the managing director (MD), the FD and the SD have all been dismissed. Two key members of the accounts department are also on sick leave due to stress and are not expected to return for some weeks. A new MD, who is inexperienced in this industry, has been appointed and is in the process of recruiting a new SD and a new FD. He has said:

'These mistakes could have been largely avoided if the company had been using rolling budgets, instead of manipulating fixed budgets. From now on, we will be using rolling budgets, updating our budgets on a quarterly basis, with immediate effect.'

The original fixed budget for the year ended 31 August 20X7, for which the first quarter (Q1) has just ended, is shown below:

Budget Y/E 31 August 20X7	Q1	Q2	Q3	Q4	Total
	$000	$000	$000	$000	$000
Revenue	13,425	13,694	13,967	14,247	55,333
Cost of sales	(8,055)	(8,216)	(8,380)	(8,548)	(33,199)
Gross profit	5,370	5,478	5,587	5,699	22,134
Distribution costs	(671)	(685)	(698)	(712)	(2,766)
Administration costs	(2,000)	(2,000)	(2,000)	(2,000)	(8,000)
Operating profit	2,699	2,793	2,889	2,987	11,368

The budget was based on the following assumptions:

(1)   Sales volumes would grow by a fixed compound percentage each quarter.

(2)   Gross profit margin would remain stable each quarter.

(3)   Distribution costs would remain a fixed percentage of revenue each quarter.

(4)   Administration costs would be fixed each quarter.

The actual results for the first quarter (Q1) have just been produced and are as follows:

Actual results	Q1
	$000
Revenue	14,096
Cost of sales	(8,740)
	———
Gross profit	5,356
Distribution costs	(705)
Administration costs	(2,020)
	———
Operating profit	2,631
	———

The new MD believes that the difference between the actual and the budgeted sales figures for Q1 is a result of incorrect forecasting of prices, however, he is confident that the four assumptions the fixed budget was based on were correct and that the rolling budget should still be prepared using these assumptions.

Required:

(a) **Prepare Static Co's rolling budget for the next four quarters.** ▦ **(8 marks)**

(b) **Discuss the problems which have occurred at Static Co due to the previous budgeting process and the improvements which might now be seen through the use of realistic rolling budgets.** 💻 **(6 marks)**

(c) **Discuss the problems which may be encountered when Static Co tries to implement the new budgeting system.** 💻 **(6 marks)**

(Total: 20 marks)

262 EFFECTIVE BUDGETING

Statement 1: The availability of computers and sophisticated financial software has made budgeting a routine, almost automatic, process.

Statement 2: Effective budgeting is much more than just number-crunching.

Required:

(a) **Explain what is meant by 'effective budgeting' in Statement 2 and what features contribute to effective budgeting.** 💻 **(3 marks)**

(b) **Reconcile the apparent contradiction between *Statements 1* and *2*.** **(3 marks)**

(c) **Critically discuss the relative merits of periodic budgeting and continuous budgeting.** 💻 **(8 marks)**

(d) **Discuss the consequences of budget bias (budgetary slack) for cost control.** 💻 **(6 marks)**

(Total: 20 marks)

263 NN

NN Ltd manufactures and markets a range of electronic office equipment. The company currently has a turnover of $40 million per annum. The company has a functional structure and currently operates an incremental budgeting system. The company has a budget committee that is comprised entirely of members of the senior management team. No other personnel are involved in the budget-setting process.

Each member of the senior management team has enjoyed an annual bonus of between 10% and 20% of their annual salary for each of the past five years. The annual bonuses are calculated by comparing the actual costs attributed to a particular function with budgeted costs for that function during the twelve month period ended 31 December in each year.

A new Finance Director, who previously held a senior management position in a 'not for profit' health organisation, has recently been appointed. Whilst employed by the health service organisation, the new Finance Director had been the manager responsible for the implementation of a zero-based budgeting system which proved highly successful.

Required:

(a) Identify and discuss the factors to be considered when implementing a system of zero-based budgeting within NN Ltd. Include, as part of your discussion, a definition of the existing incremental budgeting system and a zero-based budgeting system. 🖳 **(5 marks)**

(b) Identify and discuss the behavioural problems that the management of NN Ltd might encounter in implementing a system of zero-based budgeting, recommending how best to address such problems in order that they are overcome. 🖳 **(10 marks)**

(c) Explain how the implementation of a zero-based budgeting system in NN Ltd may differ from the implementation of such a system in a 'not for profit' health organisation. 🖳 **(5 marks)**

(Total: 20 marks)

264 ZERO BASED BUDGETING (DECEMBER 2010)

Some commentators argue that: 'With continuing pressure to control costs and maintain efficiency, the time has come for all public sector organisations to embrace zero-based budgeting. There is no longer a place for incremental budgeting in any organisation, particularly public sector ones, where zero-based budgeting is far more suitable anyway.'

Required:

(a) Discuss the particular difficulties encountered when budgeting in public sector organisations compared with budgeting in private sector organisations, drawing comparisons between the two types of organisations. 🖳 **(5 marks)**

(b) Explain the terms 'incremental budgeting' and 'zero-based budgeting'. 🖳 **(4 marks)**

(c) State the main stages involved in preparing zero-based budgets. 🖳 **(3 marks)**

(d) Discuss the view that 'there is no longer a place for incremental budgeting in any organisation, particularly public sector ones,' highlighting any drawbacks of zero-based budgeting that need to be considered. 🖳 **(8 marks)**

(Total: 20 marks)

265 BIG CHEESE CHAIRS (DECEMBER 2009)

Big Cheese Chairs (BCC) manufactures and sells executive leather chairs. They are considering a new design of massaging chair to launch into the competitive market in which they operate.

They have carried out an investigation in the market and using a target costing system have targeted a competitive selling price of $120 for the chair. BCC wants a margin on selling price of 20% (ignoring any overheads).

The frame and massage mechanism will be bought in for $51 per chair and BCC will upholster it in leather and assemble it ready for despatch.

Leather costs $10 per metre and two metres are needed for a complete chair although 20% of all leather is wasted in the upholstery process.

The upholstery and assembly process will be subject to a learning effect as the workers get used to the new design. BCC estimates that the first chair will take two hours to prepare but this will be subject to a learning rate (LR) of 95%. The learning improvement will stop once 128 chairs have been made and the time for the 128th chair will be the time for all subsequent chairs. The cost of labour is $15 per hour.

The learning formula is shown on the formula sheet and at the 95% learning rate the value of b is −0.074000581.

Required:

(a) Calculate the average cost for the first 128 chairs made and identify any cost gap that may be present at that stage. ▦ **(8 marks)**

(b) Assuming that a cost gap for the chair exists suggest four ways in which it could be closed. 🖥 **(6 marks)**

The production manager denies any claims that a cost gap exists and has stated that the cost of the 128th chair will be low enough to yield the required margin.

(c) Calculate the cost of the 128th chair made and state whether the target cost is being achieved on the 128th chair. ▦ **(6 marks)**

(Total: 20 marks)

266 HENRY COMPANY (DECEMBER 2008)

Henry Company (HC) provides skilled labour to the building trade. They have recently been asked by a builder to bid for a kitchen fitting contract for a new development of 600 identical apartments. HC has not worked for this builder before. Cost information for the new contract is as follows:

Labour for the contract is available. HC expects that the first kitchen will take 24 man-hours to fit but thereafter the time taken will be subject to a 95% learning rate. After 200 kitchens are fitted the learning rate will stop and the time taken for the 200th kitchen will be the time taken for all the remaining kitchens. Labour costs $15 per hour.

Overheads are absorbed on a labour hour basis. HC has collected overhead information for the last four months and this is shown below:

	Hours worked	Overhead cost $
Month 1	9,300	115,000
Month 2	9,200	113,600
Month 3	9,400	116,000
Month 4	9,600	116,800

HC normally works around 120,000 labour hours in a year.

HC uses the high low method to analyse overheads.

The learning curve equation is $y = ax^b$, where $b = \log r/\log 2 = -0.074$

Required:

(a) Describe FIVE factors, other than the cost of labour and overheads mentioned above, that HC should take into consideration in calculating its bid. 🖥 **(5 marks)**

(b) Calculate the total cost including all overheads for HC that it can use as a basis of the bid for the new apartment contract. ⊞ **(13 marks)**

(c) If the second kitchen alone is expected to take 21.6 man-hours to fit demonstrate how the learning rate of 95% has been calculated. ⊞ **(2 marks)**

(Total: 20 marks)

267 TR CO (SEPTEMBER/DECEMBER 2017)

TR Co is a pharmaceutical company which researches, develops and manufactures a wide range of drugs. One of these drugs, 'Parapain', is a pain relief drug used for the treatment of headaches and until last month TR Co had a patent on Parapain which prevented other companies from manufacturing it. The patent has now expired and several competitors have already entered the market with similar versions of Parapain, which are made using the same active ingredients.

TR Co is reviewing its pricing policy in light of the changing market. It has carried out some market research in an attempt to establish an optimum price for Parapain. The research has established that for every $2 decrease in price, demand would be expected to increase by 5,000 batches, with maximum demand for Parapain being one million batches.

Each batch of Parapain is currently made using the following materials:

Material Z:	500 grams at $0.10 per gram
Material Y:	300 grams at $0.50 per gram

Each batch of Parapain requires 20 minutes of machine time to make and the variable running costs for machine time are $6 per hour. The fixed production overhead cost is expected to be $2 per batch for the period, based on a budgeted production level of 250,000 batches.

The skilled workers who have been working on Parapain until now are being moved onto the production of TR Co's new and unique anti-malaria drug which cost millions of dollars to develop. TR Co has obtained a patent for this revolutionary drug and it is expected to save millions of lives. No other similar drug exists and, whilst demand levels are unknown, the launch of the drug is eagerly anticipated all over the world.

Agency staff, who are completely new to the production of Parapain and cost $18 per hour, will be brought in to produce Parapain for the foreseeable future. Experience has shown there will be a significant learning curve involved in making Parapain as it is extremely difficult to handle. The first batch of Parapain made using one of the agency workers took 5 hours to make. However, it is believed that an 80% learning curve exists, in relation to production of the drug, and this will continue until the first 1,000 batches have been completed.

TR Co's management has said that any pricing decisions about Parapain should be based on the time it takes to make the 1,000th batch of the drug.

Note: The learning co-efficient, b = –0.321928

Required

(a) Calculate the optimum (profit-maximising) selling price for Parapain and the resulting annual profit which TR Co will make from charging this price. ⊞

Note: if P = a − bQ, then MR = a − 2bQ (12 marks)

(b) Discuss and recommend whether market penetration or market skimming would be the most suitable pricing strategy for TR Co when launching the new anti-malaria drug. 🖥 (8 marks)

(Total: 20 marks)

268 PERSEUS CO – REVISION OF BASIC VARIANCES

The Perseus Co a medium sized company, produces a single product in its one overseas factory. For control purposes, a standard costing system was recently introduced.

The standards set for the month of May were as follows:

Production and sales	16,000 units
Selling price (per unit)	$140
Materials:	
Material 007	6 kilos per unit at $12.25 per kilo
Material XL90	3 kilos per unit at $3.20 per kilo
Labour	4.5 hours per unit at $8.40 per hour
Overheads (all fixed)	$86,400 per month.

(They are not absorbed into the product costs)

The actual data for the month of May is as follows:

Produced 15,400 units which were sold at $138.25 each

Materials: Used 98,560 kilos of material 007 at a total cost of $1,256,640 and used 42,350 kilos of material XL90 at a total cost of $132,979.

Labour: Paid an actual rate of $8.65 per hour to the labour force. The total amount paid out, amounted to $612,766.

Overheads (all fixed): $96,840

Required:

(a) Prepare a standard costing profit statement, and a profit statement based on actual figures for the month of May. ⊞ (6 marks)

(b) Prepare a statement of the variances which reconciles the actual with the standard profit or loss figure. (Mix and yield variances are not required.) (9 marks)

(c) Explain briefly the possible reasons for inter-relationships between material variances and labour variances. 🖥 (3 marks)

(d) State TWO possible causes of an adverse labour rate variance. 🖥 (2 marks)

(Total: 20 marks)

269 VALET CO (JUNE 2014)

Valet Co is a car valeting (cleaning) company. It operates in the country of Strappia, which has been badly affected by the global financial crisis. Petrol and food prices have increased substantially in the last year and the average disposable household income has decreased by 30%. Recent studies have shown that the average car owner keeps their car for five years before replacing it, rather than three years as was previously the case. Figures over recent years also show that car sales in Strappia are declining whilst business for car repairs is on the increase.

Valet Co offers two types of valet – a full valet and a mini valet. A full valet is an extensive clean of the vehicle, inside and out; a mini valet is a more basic clean of the vehicle. Until recently, four similar businesses operated in Valet Co's local area, but one of these closed down three months ago after a serious fire on its premises.

Valet Co charges customers $50 for each full valet and $30 for each mini valet and this price never changes. Their budget and actual figures for the last year were as follows:

	Budget		Actual	
Number of valets				
Full valets	3,600		4,000	
Mini valets	2,000		3,980	
	$	$	$	$
Revenue		240,000		319,400
Variable costs				
Staff wages	(114,000)		(122,000)	
Cleaning materials	(6,200)		(12,400)	
Energy costs	(6,520)		(9,200)	
	_____		_____	
		(126,720)		(143,600)
		_____		_____
Contribution		113,280		175,800
Fixed costs				
Rent, rates and depreciation		(36,800)		(36,800)
		_____		_____
Operating profit		76,480		139,000
		_____		_____

The budgeted contribution to sales ratios for the two types of valet are 44.6% for full valets and 55% for mini valets.

Required:

(a) Using the data provided for full valets and mini valets, calculate:

   (i)   The total sales mix contribution variance   **(4 marks)**

   (ii) The total sales quantity contribution variance. ▦   **(4 marks)**

(b) Briefly describe the sales mix contribution variance and the sales quantity contribution variance. 🖥   **(2 marks)**

(c) Discuss the SALES performance of the business for the period, taking into account your calculations from part (a) AND the information provided in the scenario. 🖥

                                                                                                      (10 marks)

                                                                                                      (Total: 20 marks)

270 THE SCHOOL UNIFORM COMPANY (MARCH/JUNE 2017)

The School Uniform Company (SU Co) manufactures school uniforms. One of its largest contracts is with the Girls' Private School Trust (GPST), which has 35 schools across the country, all with the same school uniform.

After a recent review of the uniform at the GPST schools, the school's spring/summer dress has been re-designed to incorporate a dropped waistband. Each new dress now requires 2.2 metres of material, which is 10% more material than the previous style of dress required. However, a new material has also been chosen by the GPST which costs only $2.85 per metre which is 5% cheaper than the material used on the previous dresses. In February, the total amount of material used and purchased at this price was 54,560 metres.

The design of the new dresses has meant that a complicated new sewing technique needed to be used. Consequently, all staff required training before they could begin production. The manager of the sewing department expected each of the new dresses to take 10 minutes to make as compared to 8 minutes per dress for the old style. SU Co has 24 staff, each of whom works 160 hours per month and is paid a wage of $12 per hour. All staff worked all of their contracted hours in February on production of the GPST dresses and there was no idle time. No labour rate variance arose in February.

Activity levels for February were as follows:

Budgeted production and sales (units): 30,000

Actual production and sales (units): 24,000

The production manager at SU Co is responsible for all purchasing and production issues which occur.

SU Co uses standard costing and usually, every time a design change takes place, the standard cost card is updated prior to production commencing.

However, the company accountant responsible for updating the standards has been off sick for the last two months. Consequently, the standard cost card for the new dress has not yet been updated.

Required:

(a)   **Calculate the material variances in as much detail as the information allows for the month of February.** ⊞   (7 marks)

(b)   **Calculate the labour efficiency variances in as much detail as the information allows for the month of February.** ⊞   (5 marks)

(c)   **Assess the performance of the production manager for the month of February.**
                                                                                                                                   (8 marks)

                                                                                                                            (Total: 20 marks)

271 GLOVE CO (JUNE 2016)

Glove Co makes high quality, hand-made gloves which it sells for an average of $180 per pair. The standard cost of labour for each pair is $42 and the standard labour time for each pair is three hours. In the last quarter, Glove Co had budgeted production of 12,000 pairs, although actual production was 12,600 pairs in order to meet demand. 37,000 hours were used to complete the work and there was no idle time. The total labour cost for the quarter was $531,930.

At the beginning of the last quarter, the design of the gloves was changed slightly. The new design required workers to sew the company's logo on to the back of every glove made and the estimated time to do this was 15 minutes for each pair. However, no-one told the accountant responsible for updating standard costs that the standard time per pair of gloves needed to be changed. Similarly, although all workers were given a 2% pay rise at the beginning of the last quarter, the accountant was not told about this either. Consequently, the standard was not updated to reflect these changes.

When overtime is required, workers are paid 25% more than their usual hourly rate.

Required:

(a) Calculate the total labour rate and total labour efficiency variances for the last quarter. ▦ **(2 marks)**

(b) Analyse the above total variances into component parts for planning and operational variances in as much detail as the information allows. ▦ **(6 marks)**

(c) Assess the performance of the production manager for the last quarter. ▭ **(7 marks)**

(Total: 15 marks)

272 SAFE SOAP CO (DECEMBER 2014)

The Safe Soap Co makes environmentally-friendly soap using three basic ingredients. The standard cost card for one batch of soap for the month of September was as follows:

Material	Kilograms	Price per kilogram ($)
Lye	0.25	10
Coconut oil	0.6	4
Shea butter	0.5	3

The budget for production and sales in September was 120,000 batches. Actual production and sales were 136,000 batches. The actual ingredients used were as follows:

Material	Kilograms
Lye	34,080
Coconut oil	83,232
Shea butter	64,200

Required:

(a) Calculate the total material mix variance and the total material yield variance for September. ▦ **(8 marks)**

(b) In October the materials mix and yield variances were as follows:

Mix: $6,000 adverse

Yield: $10,000 favourable

The production manager is pleased with the results overall, stating:

'At the beginning of September I made some changes to the mix of ingredients used for the soaps. As I expected, the mix variance is adverse in both months because we haven't yet updated our standard cost card but, in both months, the favourable yield variance more than makes up for this. Overall, I think we can be satisfied that the changes made to the product mix are producing good results and now we are able to produce more batches and meet the growing demand for our product.'

The sales manager, however, holds a different view and says:

'I'm not happy with this change in the ingredients mix. I've had to explain to the board why the sales volume variance for October was $22,000 adverse. I've tried to explain that the quality of the soap has declined slightly and some of my customers have realised this and simply aren't happy but no-one seems to be listening. Some customers are even demanding that the price of the soap be reduced and threatening to go elsewhere if the problem isn't sorted out.'

Required:

(i) **Briefly explain what the adverse materials mix and favourable materials yield variances indicate about production at Safe Soap Co in October.** 🖳

Note: You are NOT required to discuss revision of standards or operational and planning variances. (4 marks)

(ii) **Discuss whether the sales manager could be justified in claiming that the change in the materials mix has caused an adverse sales volume variance in October.** 🖳 (3 marks)

(c) **Critically discuss the types of standard used in standard costing and their effect on employee motivation.** 🖳 (5 marks)

(Total: 20 marks)

PERFORMANCE MEASUREMENT AND CONTROL

273 B5 CARS EIS

B5 Cars manufactures motor vehicles for sale to the general public and companies. Several other motor vehicle manufacturers operate within the industry, which is highly competitive; there is a trade association which collects a wide range of information.

B5 Cars has five manufacturing plants and 53 sales outlets in the country in which it operates. Information for the company's executive information system (EIS) is obtained both from internal sources such as the production plants, and also external sources such as customers. Internally-generated information is sent to head office over a wide area network.

Due to the overall escalating cost of the company's EIS, the board has decided to collect only internally-produced information. This decision has been taken against the advice of the chief information officer.

Required:

(a) **Suggest and explain reasons why the company's EIS could be becoming expensive to operate.** 🖳 (6 marks)

(b) **Evaluate the decision of the board to concentrate on internally-produced information. Clearly describe the information sources that will be lost and explain the effects on the company's information systems and its products.** 🖳 (14 marks)

(Total: 20 marks)

274   PRINTING COMPANY

During 1990 a printing company designed and installed a Management Information System that met the business needs of a commercial environment which was characterised at that time by:

- a unitary structure with one profit centre
- central direction from senior managers
- 100% internal resourcing of ancillary services
- the employment exclusively of permanent full-time employees
- customers holding large stocks who accepted long delivery times
- most of the work concerned with long print runs for established large publishing houses.

A radical change in the business environment has resulted in the following outcomes:

- the development of a divisionalised structure with four profit centres that utilise each others services
- empowerment of team leaders and devolved decision making
- considerable outsourcing of activities
- a significant proportion of the employees work part-time and/or on temporary contracts
- customers now commonly operate JIT systems requiring immediate replenishment of stocks
- the typical customer requires specialist low volume but complex high value printing.

Required:

Recommend the significant changes in the Management Information Systems that would probably be required to meet the needs of this new situation. Explain the reasons for your recommendations. 🖳   **(Total: 20 marks)**

Note: your answer does not require a consideration of technical matters.

275   REES INVESTMENTS

Rees Investments invests money on behalf of its customers. The company guarantees its customers a favourable interest rate in return for long-term investments. Mark Rees started the company five years ago and he was originally the only investment analyst, making all the investment decisions.

The company was initially very successful, due to a combination of Rees' expertise and a favourable world economic climate. Specialising in investing in the emerging markets of Asia and Africa, Rees Investments achieved excellent returns on their investments; This allowed them to meet guarantees given to clients as well as funding the expansion of the company itself.

The company has grown and it currently employs 60 staff of whom 12 are investment analysts. However, investment returns have declined and the company is now having problems providing its guaranteed return to investors. Consequently, Mark Rees is reviewing investment procedures and exploring options for returning the company to the profitability it enjoyed in its early years.

Required:

(a) Explain the difference between a structured, a semi-structured and an unstructured decision. Would you consider the investment decisions made by Mark Rees and his fellow analysts to be structured, semi-structured or unstructured? 🖥 **(5 marks)**

(b) One of the options Mark Rees is considering is the use of a decision support system to help his investment analysts make appropriate investment decisions.

Briefly describe what is meant by a decision support system and comment on its possible contribution to the investment decisions made by analysts at Rees Investments. 🖥 **(7 marks)**

(c) Mark Rees is also considering the development of an expert system.

Required:

Briefly describe what is meant by an expert system and comment on its possible contribution to the investment decisions made by analysts at Rees Investments. 🖥

(8 marks)

(Total: 20 marks)

276 CDE

CDE is a manufacturer of almost 100 hundred different automotive components that are sold in both large and small quantities on a just-in-time (JIT) basis to the major vehicle assemblers. Business is highly competitive and price sensitive. The company is listed on the stock exchange but CDE's share performance has not matched that of its main competitors.

CDE's management accounting system uses a manufacturing resource planning (MRP II) system to control production scheduling, inventory movements and inventory control, and labour and machine utilisation. The accounting department carries out a detailed annual budgeting exercise, determines standard costs for labour and materials, and allocates production overhead on the basis of machine utilisation. Strict accounting controls over labour and material costs are managed by the detailed recording of operator and machine timesheets and raw material movements, and by calculating and investigating all significant variances.

While the information from the MRP II system is useful to management, there is an absence of integrated data about customer requirements and suppliers. Some information is contained within spreadsheets and databases held by the Sales and Purchasing departments respectively. One result of this lack of integration is that inventories are higher than they should be in a JIT environment.

The managers of CDE (representing functional areas of sales, production, purchasing, finance and administration) believe that, while costs are strictly controlled, the cost of the accounting department is excessive and significant savings need to be made, even at the expense of data accuracy. Managers believe that there may not be optimum use of the production capacity to generate profits and cash flow and improve shareholder value. CDE's management wants to carry out sensitivity and other analyses of strategic alternatives, but this is difficult when the existing management accounting system is focused on control rather than on decision support.

Required:

(a) **(i)** Outline the different types of information system available to manufacturing firms like CDE.

(ii) Recommend with reasons the information system that would be appropriate to CDE's needs. 🖥 **(8 marks)**

(b) Given the business environment that CDE faces, and the desire of management to reduce the cost of accounting:

(i) Evaluate the relevance of the current management accounting system; and

(ii) recommend how the system should be improved. 🖥 **(12 marks)**

(Total: 20 marks)

277 THE MG ORGANISATION

The Information Systems strategy within the MG organisation has been developed over a number of years. However, the basic approach has always remained unchanged. An IT budget is agreed by the board each year. The budget is normally 5% to 10% higher than the previous year's to allow for increases in prices and upgrades to computer systems.

Systems are upgraded in accordance with user requirements. Most users see IT systems as tools for recording day-to-day transactions and providing access to accounting and other information as necessary. There is no Enterprise Resource Planning System (ERPS) or Executive Information System (EIS).

The board tends to rely on reports from junior managers to control the business. While these reports generally provide the information requested by the board, they are focused at a tactical level and do not contribute to strategy formulation or implementation.

Required:

(a) Advise the board on how an ERPS and EIS could provide benefits over and above those provided by transaction processing systems. 🖥 **(12 marks)**

(b) Recommend to the board how it should go about improving its budgetary allocations for IT and how it should evaluate the benefits of ERPS and EIS. 🖥

(8 marks)

(Total: 20 marks)

278 JUMP PERFORMANCE APPRAISAL (JUNE 2010)

Jump has a network of sports clubs which is managed by local managers reporting to the main board. The local managers have a lot of autonomy and are able to vary employment contracts with staff and offer discounts for membership fees and personal training sessions. They also control their own maintenance budget but do not have control over large amounts of capital expenditure.

A local manager's performance and bonus is assessed relative to three targets. For every one of these three targets that is reached in an individual quarter, $400 is added to the manager's bonus, which is paid at the end of the year. The maximum bonus per year is therefore based on 12 targets (three targets in each of the four quarters of the year). Accordingly the maximum bonus that could be earned is 12 × $400 = $4,800, which represents 40% of the basic salary of a local manager. Jump has a 31 March year end.

The performance data for one of the sports clubs for the last four quarters is as follows:

	Qtr to 30 June 2009	Qtr to 30 Sept 2009	Qtr to 31 Dec 2009	Qtr to 31 March 2010
Number of members	3,000	3,200	3,300	3,400
Member visits	20,000	24,000	26,000	24,000
Personal training sessions booked	310	325	310	339
Staff days	450	480	470	480
Staff lateness days	20	28	28	20
Days in quarter	90	90	90	90

Agreed targets are:

(1)   Staff must be on time over 95% of the time (no penalty is made when staff are absent from work).

(2)   On average 60% of members must use the clubs' facilities regularly by visiting at least 12 times per quarter 3. On average 10% of members must book a personal training session each quarter.

Required:

(a)   **Calculate the amount of bonus that the manager should expect to be paid for the latest financial year.** ▦   **(6 marks)**

(b)   **Discuss to what extent the targets set are controllable by the local manager (you are required to make a case for both sides of the argument).** 🖥   **(9 marks)**

(c)   **Describe two methods as to how a manager with access to the accounting and other records could unethically manipulate the situation so as to gain a greater bonus.** 🖥   **(5 marks)**

(Total: 20 marks)

279   ACCOUNTANCY TEACHING CO (DECEMBER 2010)

The Accountancy Teaching Co (AT Co) is a company specialising in the provision of accountancy tuition courses in the private sector. It makes up its accounts to 30 November each year. In the year ending 30 November 2009, it held 60% of market share. However, over the last twelve months, the accountancy tuition market in general has faced a 20% decline in demand for accountancy training leading to smaller class sizes on courses. In 2009 and before, AT Co suffered from an ongoing problem with staff retention, which had a knock-on effect on the quality of service provided to students. Following the completion of developments that have been ongoing for some time, in 2010 the company was able to offer a far-improved service to students. The developments included:

*   A new dedicated 24 hour student helpline

*   An interactive website providing instant support to students

*   A new training programme for staff

*   An electronic student enrolment system

*   An electronic marking system for the marking of students' progress tests. The costs of marking electronically were expected to be $4 million less in 2010 than marking on paper. Marking expenditure is always included in cost of sales.

Extracts from the management accounts for 2009 and 2010 are shown below:

	2009		2010	
	$000	$000	$000	$000
Turnover		72,025		66,028
Cost of sales		(52,078)		(42,056)
Gross profit		19,947		23,972
Indirect expenses:				
Marketing	3,291		4,678	
Property	6,702		6,690	
Staff training	1,287		3,396	
Interactive website running costs	–		3,270	
Student helpline running costs	–		2,872	
Enrolment costs	5,032		960	
Total indirect expenses		(16,312)		(21,866)
Net operating profit		3,635		2,106

On 1 December 2009, management asked all 'freelance lecturers' to reduce their fees by at least 10% with immediate effect ('freelance lecturers' are not employees of the company but are used to teach students when there are not enough of AT Co's own lecturers to meet tuition needs). All employees were also told that they would not receive a pay rise for at least one year. Total lecture staff costs (including freelance lecturers) were $41.663 million in 2009 and were included in cost of sales, as is always the case. Freelance lecturer costs represented 35% of these total lecture staff costs. In 2010 freelance lecture costs were $12.394 million. No reduction was made to course prices in the year and the mix of trainees studying for the different qualifications remained the same. The same type and number of courses were run in both 2009 and 2010 and the percentage of these courses that was run by freelance lecturers as opposed to employed staff also remained the same.

Due to the nature of the business, non-financial performance indicators are also used to assess performance, as detailed below.

	2009	2010
Percentage of students transferring to AT Co from another training provider	8%	20%
Number of late enrolments due to staff error	297	106
Percentage of students passing exams first time	48%	66%
Labour turnover	32%	10%
Number of student complaints	315	84
Average no. of employees	1,080	1,081

Required:

Assess the performance of the business in 2010 using both financial performance indicators calculated from the above information AND the non-financial performance indicators provided. 🖳

Note: Clearly state any assumptions and show all workings clearly. Your answer should be structured around the following main headings: turnover; cost of sales; gross profit; indirect expenses; net operating profit. However, in discussing each of these areas you should also refer to the non-financial performance indicators, where relevant.

(Total: 20 marks)

280 LENS CO (DECEMBER 2016)

Lens Co manufactures lenses for use by a wide range of commercial customers. The company has two divisions: the Photographic Division (P) and the Optometry Division (O). Each of the divisions is run by a divisional manager who has overall responsibility for all aspects of running their division and the divisions are currently treated as investment centres. Each manager, however, has an authorisation limit of $15,000 per item for capital expenditure and any items costing more than this must first be approved by Head Office.

During the year, Head Office made a decision to sell a large amount of the equipment in Division P and replace it with more technologically advanced equipment. It also decided to close one of Division O's factories in a country deemed to be politically unstable, with the intention of opening a new factory elsewhere in the following year.

Both divisions trade with overseas customers, choosing to provide these customers with 60 days' credit to encourage sales. Due to differences in exchange rates between the time of invoicing the customers and receiving the payment 60 days later, exchange gains and losses often occur.

The cost of capital for Lens Co is 12% per annum.

The following data relates to the year ended 30 November 20X6:

	Division P $000	Division O $000
Revenue	14,000	18,800
Gain on sale of equipment	400	–
	14,400	18,800
Direct labour	(2,400)	(3,500)
Direct materials	(4,800)	(6,500)
Divisional overheads*	(3,800)	(5,200)
Trading profit	3,400	3,600
Exchange gain/(loss)	(200)	460
Exceptional costs for factory closure	–	(1,800)
Allocated Head Office costs	(680)	(1,040)
Net divisional profit	2,520	1,220
* Depreciation on uncontrollable assets included in divisional overheads	320	460

	Division P	Division O
	$000	$000
Non-current assets controlled by the division	15,400	20,700
Non-current assets controlled by Head Office	3,600	5,200
Inventories	1,800	3,900
Trade receivables	6,200	8,900
Overdraft	500	–
Trade payables	5,100	7,200

To date, managers have always been paid a bonus based on the return on investment (ROI) achieved by their division. However, the company is considering whether residual income would be a better method.

Required:

(a) Calculate the return on investment (ROI) for each division for the year ended 30 November 20X6, ensuring that the basis of the calculation makes it a suitable measure for assessing the DIVISIONAL MANAGERS' performance. ▦　　　**(6 marks)**

(b) Explain why you have included or excluded certain items in calculating the ROIs in part (a), stating any assumptions you have made. 🖥　　　**(8 marks)**

(c) Briefly discuss whether it is appropriate to treat each of the divisions of Lens Co as investment centres. 🖥　　　**(2 marks)**

(d) Discuss the problems involved in using ROI to measure the managers' performance. 🖥
　　　(4 marks)

　　　(Total: 20 marks)

281 CIM (DECEMBER 2015)

Cardale Industrial Metal Co (CIM Co) is a large supplier of industrial metals. The company is split into two divisions: Division F and Division N. Each division operates separately as an investment centre, with each one having full control over its non-current assets. In addition, both divisions are responsible for their own current assets, controlling their own levels of inventory and cash and having full responsibility for the credit terms granted to customers and the collection of receivables balances. Similarly, each division has full responsibility for its current liabilities and deals directly with its own suppliers.

Each divisional manager is paid a salary of $120,000 per annum plus an annual performance-related bonus, based on the return on investment (ROI) achieved by their division for the year. Each divisional manager is expected to achieve a minimum ROI for their division of 10% per annum. If a manager only meets the 10% target, they are not awarded a bonus. However, for each whole percentage point above 10% which the division achieves for the year, a bonus equivalent to 2% of annual salary is paid, subject to a maximum bonus equivalent to 30% of annual salary.

The following figures relate to the year ended 31 August 2015:

	Division F	Division N
	$000	$000
Sales	14,500	8,700
Controllable profit	2,645	1,970
Less: apportionment of Head Office costs	(1,265)	(684)
Net profit	1,380	1,286
Non-current assets	9,760	14,980
Inventory, cash and trade receivables	2,480	3,260
Trade payables	2,960	1,400

During the year ending 31 August 2015, Division N invested $6.8m in new equipment including a technologically advanced cutting machine, which is expected to increase productivity by 8% per annum. Division F has made no investment during the year, although its computer system is badly in need of updating. Division F's manager has said that he has already had to delay payments to suppliers (i.e. accounts payables) because of limited cash and the computer system 'will just have to wait', although the cash balance at Division F is still better than that of Division N.

Required:

(a)   For each division, for the year ended 31 August 2015:

    (i)   calculate the appropriate closing return on investment (ROI) on which the payment of management bonuses will be based. Briefly justify the figures used in your calculations. Note: There are 3 marks available for calculations and 2 marks available for discussion. 🖥 **(5 marks)**

    (ii)   Based on your calculations in part (i), calculate each manager's bonus for the year ended 31 August 2015. ▦ **(3 marks)**

(b)   Discuss whether ROI is providing a fair basis for calculating the managers' bonuses and the problems arising from its use at CIM Co for the year ended 31 August 2015. 🖥 **(7 marks)**

(c)   Briefly discuss the strengths and weaknesses of ROI and RI as methods of assessing the performance of divisions. Explain two further methods of assessment of divisional performance that could be used in addition to ROI or RI. 🖥 **(5 marks)**

(Total: 20 marks)

282   SPORTS CO (SEPTEMBER/DECEMBER 2017)

Sports Co is a large manufacturing company specialising in the manufacture of a wide range of sports clothing and equipment. The company has two divisions: Clothing (division C) and Equipment (division E). Each division operates with little intervention from Head Office and divisional managers have autonomy to make decisions about long-term investments.

Sports Co measures the performance of its divisions using return on investment (ROI), calculated using controllable profit and average divisional net assets. The target ROI for each of the divisions is 18%. If the divisions meet or exceed this target the divisional managers receive a bonus.

Last year, an investment which was expected to meet the target ROI was rejected by one of the divisional managers because it would have reduced the division's overall ROI.

Consequently, Sports Co is considering the introduction of a new performance measure, residual income (RI), in order to discourage this dysfunctional behaviour in the future. Like ROI, this would be calculated using controllable profit and average divisional net assets.

The draft operating statement for the year, prepared by the company's trainee accountant, is shown below:

	Division C	Division E
	$'000	$'000
Sales revenue	3,800	8,400
Less variable costs	(1,400)	(3,030)
Contribution	**2,400**	**5,370**
Less fixed costs	(945)	(1,420)
Net profit	**1,455**	**3,950**
Opening divisional controllable net assets	13,000	24,000
Closing divisional controllable net assets	9,000	30,000

Notes:

(1)   Included in the fixed costs are depreciation costs of $165,000 and $460,000 for divisions C and E respectively. 30% of the depreciation costs in each division relates to assets controlled but not owned by Head Office. Division E invested $2m in plant and machinery at the beginning of the year, which is included in the net assets figures above, and uses the reducing balance method to depreciate assets. Division C, which uses the straight-line method, made no significant additions to non-current assets. It is the policy of both divisions to charge a full year's depreciation in the year of acquisition.

(2)   Head Office recharges all of its costs to the two divisions. These have been included in the fixed costs and amount to $620,000 for division C and $700,000 for division E.

(3)   Sports Co has a cost of capital of 12%.

Required:

(a)   (i)   Calculate the return on investment (ROI) for each of the two divisions of Sports Co. ▦   (6 marks)

       (ii)   **Discuss the performance of the two divisions for the year, including the main reasons why their ROI results differ from each other. Explain the impact the difference in ROI could have on the behaviour of the manager of the worst performing division.** 🖥   **(6 marks)**

(b)   (i)   **Calculate the residual income (RI) for each of the two divisions of Sports Co and briefly comment on the results of this performance measure.** ▦
                                                                                      (4 marks)

       (ii)   **Explain the advantages and disadvantages of using residual income (RI) to measure divisional performance.** 🖥   **(4 marks)**

                                                                          (Total: 20 marks)

283 ROTECH (JUNE 2014)

The Rotech group comprises two companies, W Co and C Co.

W Co is a trading company with two divisions: The Design division, which designs wind turbines and supplies the designs to customers under licences and the Gearbox division, which manufactures gearboxes for the car industry.

C Co manufactures components for gearboxes. It sells the components globally and also supplies W Co with components for its Gearbox manufacturing division. The financial results for the two companies for the year ended 31 May 2014 are as follows:

	W Co		C Co
	Design Division	Gearbox Division	
	$000	$000	$000
External sales	14,300	25,535	8,010
Sales to Gearbox division			7,550

			15,560

Cost of sales	(4,900)	(16,200)*	(5,280)
Administration costs	(3,400)	(4,200)	(2,600)
Distribution costs	–	(1,260)	(670)
	------	------	------
Operating profit	6,000	3,875	7,010
	------	------	------
Capital employed	23,540	32,320	82,975

* Includes cost of components purchased from C Co.

Required:

(a)   **Discuss the performance of C Co and each division of W Co, calculating and using the following three performance measures:**

   (i)   Return on capital employed (ROCE)

   (ii)   Asset turnover

   (iii) Operating profit margin. ⊞

   Note: There are 4.5 marks available for calculations and 5.5 marks available for discussion.   **(10 marks)**

(b)   C Co is currently working to full capacity. The Rotech group's policy is that group companies and divisions must always make internal sales first before selling outside the group. Similarly, purchases must be made from within the group wherever possible. However, the group divisions and companies are allowed to negotiate their own transfer prices without interference from Head Office.

   C Co has always charged the same price to the Gearbox division as it does to its external customers. However, after being offered a 5% lower price for similar components from an external supplier, the manager of the Gearbox division feels strongly that the transfer price is too high and should be reduced. C Co currently satisfies 60% of the external demand for its components. Its variable costs represent 40% of revenue.

   Required:

   Advise, using suitable calculations, the total transfer price or prices at which the components should be supplied to the Gearbox division from C Co. ⊞ ⌨

                                                                                    (10 marks)

                                                                              (Total: 20 marks)

284 CTD

CTD has two divisions – FD and TM. FD is an iron foundry division which produces mouldings that have a limited external market and are also transferred to TM division. TM division uses the mouldings to produce a piece of agricultural equipment called the 'TX' which is sold externally. Each TX requires one moulding. Both divisions produce only one type of product.

The performance of each Divisional Manager is evaluated individually on the basis of the residual income (RI) of his or her division. The company's average annual 12% cost of capital is used to calculate the finance charges. If their own target residual income is achieved, each Divisional Manager is awarded a bonus equal to 5% of his or her residual income. All bonuses are paid out of Head Office profits.

The following budgeted information is available for the forthcoming year:

	TM division TX per unit	FD division Moulding per unit
External selling price ($)	500	80
Variable production cost ($)	*366	40
Fixed production overheads ($)	60	20
Gross profit ($)	74	20
Variable selling and distribution cost ($)	25	**4
Fixed administration overhead ($)	25	4
Net profit ($)	24	12
Normal capacity (units)	15,000	20,000
Maximum production capacity (units)	15,000	25,000
Sales to external customers (units)	15,000	5,000
Capital employed	$1,500,000	$750,000
Target RI	$105,000	$85,000

* The variable production cost of TX includes the cost of an FD moulding.

** External sales only of the mouldings incur a variable selling and distribution cost of $4 per unit.

FD division currently transfers 15,000 mouldings to TM division at a transfer price equal to the total production cost plus 10%.

Fixed costs are absorbed on the basis of normal capacity.

Required:

(a) Calculate the bonus each Divisional Manager would receive under the current transfer pricing policy and discuss any implications that the current performance evaluation system may have for each division and for the company as a whole. ▦

(14 marks)

(b) Both Divisional Managers want to achieve their respective residual income targets. Based on the budgeted figures, calculate:

(i) the maximum transfer price per unit that the Divisional Manager of TM division would pay ▦

(ii) the minimum transfer price per unit that the Divisional Manager of FD division would accept. ▦ **(6 marks)**

(Total: 20 marks)

285 DIVISION A

Division A, which is a part of the ACF Group, manufactures only one type of product, a Bit, which it sells to external customers and also to division C, another member of the group. ACF Group's policy is that divisions have the freedom to set transfer prices and choose their suppliers.

The ACF Group uses residual income (RI) to assess divisional performance and each year it sets each division a target RI. The group's cost of capital is 12% a year.

Division A

Budgeted information for the coming year is:

Maximum capacity	150,000 Bits
External sales	110,000 Bits
External selling price	$35 per Bit
Variable cost	$22 per Bit
Fixed costs	$1,080,000
Capital employed	$3,200,000
Target residual income	$180,000

Division C

Division C has found two other companies willing to supply Bits:

X could supply at $28 per Bit, but only for annual orders in excess of 50,000 Bits. Z could supply at $33 per Bit for any quantity ordered.

Required:

(a) Division C provisionally requests a quotation for 60,000 Bits from division A for the coming year.

   (i) Calculate the transfer price per Bit that division A should quote in order to meet its residual income target. ▦ **(6 marks)**

   (ii) Calculate the two prices division A would have to quote to division C, if it became group policy to quote transfer prices based on opportunity costs. ▦ **(4 marks)**

(b) Evaluate and discuss the impact of the group's current and proposed policies on the profits of divisions A and C, and on group profit. Illustrate your answer with calculations. 💻 **(10 marks)**

(Total: 20 marks)

286 JUNGLE CO (SEPTEMBER 2016)

Jungle Co is a very successful multinational retail company. It has been selling a large range of household and electronic goods for some years. One year ago, it began using new suppliers from the country of Slabak, where labour is very cheap, for many of its household goods. In 20X4, Jungle Co also became a major provider of 'cloud computing' services, investing heavily in cloud technology. These services provide customers with a way of storing and accessing data and programs over the internet rather than on their computers' hard drives.

All Jungle Co customers have the option to sign up for the company's 'Gold' membership service, which provides next day delivery on all orders, in return for an annual service fee of $40. In September 20X5, Jungle Co formed its own logistics company and took over the delivery of all of its parcels, instead of using the services of international delivery companies.

Over the last year, there has been worldwide growth in the electronic goods market of 20%. Average growth rates and gross profit margins for cloud computing service providers have been 50% and 80% respectively in the last year. Jungle Co's prices have remained stable year on year for all sectors of its business, with price competitiveness being crucial to its continuing success as the leading global electronic retailer.

The following information is available for Jungle Co for the last two financial years:

	Notes	31 August 20X6 $000	31 August 20X5 $000	
Revenue	1	94,660	82,320	↑15%.
Cost of sales	2	(54,531)	(51,708)	
Gross profit		40,129	30,612	
Administration expenses	3	(2,760)	(1,720)	
Distribution expenses		(13,420)	(13,180)	↑1.8%.
Other operating expenses		(140)	(110)	
Net profit		23,809	15,602	

Notes

1   Breakdown of revenue

	31 August 20X6 $000	31 August 20X5 $000	
Household goods	38,990	41,160	↓5%
Electronic goods	41,870	32,640	↑28%
Cloud computing services	12,400	6,520	↑90%.
Gold membership fees	1,400	2,000	↓30%
	94,660	82,320	↑15%.

2   Breakdown of cost of sales

	31 August 20X6 $000	31 August 20X5 $000
Household goods	23,394	28,812
Electronic goods	26,797	21,216
Cloud computing services	4,240	1,580
Gold membership fees	100	100
	54,531	51,708

3   Administration expenses

Included in these costs are the costs of running the customer service department ($860,000 in 20X5; $1,900,000 in 20X6.) This department deals with customer complaints.

4   Non-financial data

	31 August 20X6	31 August 20X5
Percentage of orders delivered on time	74%	92%
No. of customer complaints	1,400,000	320,000
No. of customers	7,100,000	6,500,000
Percentage of late 'Gold' member deliveries	14.00%	2.00%

Required:

Discuss the financial and non-financial performance of Jungle Co for the year ending 31 August 20X6. Note: There are 7 marks available for calculations and 13 marks available for discussion. 💻   **(Total: 20 marks)**

287   OLIVER'S SALON (JUNE 2009)

 Question debrief

Oliver is the owner and manager of Oliver's Salon which is a quality hairdresser that experiences high levels of competition. The salon traditionally provided a range of hair services to female clients only, including cuts, colouring and straightening.

A year ago, at the start of his 2009 financial year, Oliver decided to expand his operations to include the hairdressing needs of male clients. Male hairdressing prices are lower, the work simpler (mainly haircuts only) and so the time taken per male client is much less.

The prices for the female clients were not increased during the whole of 2008 and 2009 and the mix of services provided for female clients in the two years was the same.

The latest financial results are as follows:

	2008		2009	
	$	$	$	$
Sales		200,000		238,500
Less cost of sales:				
Hairdressing staff costs	65,000		91,000	
Hair products – female	29,000		27,000	
Hair products – male			8,000	
		94,000		126,000
Gross profit		106,000		112,500
Rent	10,000		10,000	
Administration salaries	9,000		9,500	
Electricity	7,000		8,000	
Advertising	2,000		5,000	
Total expenses		28,000		32,500
Profit		78,000		80,000

Oliver is disappointed with his financial results. He thinks the salon is much busier than a year ago and was expecting more profit. He has noted the following extra information:

1   Some female clients complained about the change in atmosphere following the introduction of male services, which created tension in the salon.

2   Two new staff were recruited at the start of 2009. The first was a junior hairdresser to support the specialist hairdressers for the female clients. She was appointed on a salary of $9,000 per annum. The second new staff member was a specialist hairdresser for the male clients. There were no increases in pay for existing staff at the start of 2009 after a big rise at the start of 2008 which was designed to cover two years' worth of increases.

Oliver introduced some non-financial measures of success two years ago.

	2008	2009
Number of complaints	12	46
Number of male client visits	0	3,425
Number of female client visits	8,000	6,800
Number of specialist hairdressers for female clients	4	5
Number of specialist hairdressers for male clients	0	1

Required:

(a)   **Calculate the average price for hair services per male and female client for each of the years 2008 and 2009.**   **(3 marks)**

(b)   **Assess the financial performance of the Salon using the data above.** 🖥   **(11 marks)**

(c)   **Analyse and comment on the non-financial performance of Oliver's business, under the headings of quality and resource utilisation.** 🖥   **(6 marks)**

(Total: 20 marks)

> 🕐 *Calculate your allowed time, allocate the time to the separate parts...............*

288   TIES ONLY (DECEMBER 2007)

Ties Only Limited is a new business, selling high quality imported men's ties via the internet. The managers, who also own the company, are young and inexperienced but they are prepared to take risks. They are confident that importing quality ties and selling via a website will be successful and that the business will grow quickly. This is despite the well recognised fact that selling clothing is a very competitive business.

They were prepared for a loss-making start and decided to pay themselves modest salaries (included in administration expenses in table 1 below) and pay no dividends for the foreseeable future.

The owners are so convinced that growth will quickly follow that they have invested enough money in website server development to ensure that the server can handle the very high levels of predicted growth. All website development costs were written off as incurred in the internal management accounts that are shown below in table 1.

Significant expenditure on marketing was incurred in the first two quarters to launch both the website and new products. It is not expected that marketing expenditure will continue to be as high in the future.

Customers can buy a variety of styles, patterns and colours of ties at different prices.

The business's trading results for the first two quarters of trade are shown in the table below:

	Quarter 1		*Quarter 2*	
	$	$	$	$
Sales		420,000		680,000
Less: Cost of sales		(201,600)		(340,680)
Gross profit		218,400		339,320
Less: Expenses				
Website development	120,000		90,000	
Administration	100,500		150,640	
Distribution	20,763		33,320	
Launch marketing	60,000		40,800	
Other variable expenses	50,000		80,000	
Total expenses		(351,263)		(394,760)
Loss for quarter		(132,863)		(55,440)

Required:

(a) Assess the financial performance of the business during its first two quarters using only the data in table 1 above. **(8 marks)**

(b) Briefly consider whether the losses made by the business in the first two quarters are a true reflection of the current and likely future performance of the business. **(4 marks)**

The owners are well aware of the importance of non-financial indicators of success and therefore have identified a small number of measures to focus on. These are measured monthly and then combined to produce a quarterly management report.

The data for the first two quarters management reports is shown below:

Table 2	*Quarter 1*	*Quarter 2*
Website hits*	690,789	863,492
Number of ties sold	27,631	38,857
On time delivery	95%	89%
Sales returns	12%	18%
System downtime	2%	4%

* A website hit is automatically counted each time a visitor to the website opens the home page of Ties Only Limited.

The industry average conversion rate for website hits to number of ties sold is 3.2%. The industry average sales return rate for internet-based clothing sales is 13%.

Required:

(c) Comment on each of the non-financial data in table 2 above taking into account, where appropriate, the industry averages provided, providing your assessment of the performance of the business. **(8 marks)**

(Total: 20 marks)

Note: The original question as written by the examiner gave 12 marks to part (a) and 11 marks to part (b). The suggested answers are thus more extensive than now required.

289 JAMAIR (DECEMBER 2014)

Jamair was founded in September 2007 and is one of a growing number of low-cost airlines in the country of Shania. Jamair's strategy is to operate as a low-cost, high efficiency airline, and it does this by:

- Operating mostly in secondary cities to reduce landing costs.

- Using only one type of aircraft in order to reduce maintenance and operational costs. These planes are leased rather than bought outright.

- Having only one category of seat class.

- Having no pre-allocated seats or in-flight entertainment.

- Focusing on e-commerce with customers both booking tickets and checking in for flights online.

The airline was given an 'on time arrival' ranking of seventh best by the country's aviation authority, who rank all 50 of the country's airlines based on the number of flights which arrive on time at their destinations. 48 Jamair flights were cancelled in 2013 compared to 35 in 2012. This increase was due to an increase in the staff absentee rate at Jamair from 3 days per staff member per year to 4.5 days.

The average 'ground turnaround time' for airlines in Shania is 50 minutes, meaning that, on average, planes are on the ground for cleaning, refuelling, etc for 50 minutes before departing again. Customer satisfaction surveys have shown that 85% of customers are happy with the standard of cleanliness on Jamair's planes.

The number of passengers carried by the airline has grown from 300,000 passengers on a total of 3,428 flights in 2007 to 920,000 passengers on 7,650 flights in 2013. The overall growth of the airline has been helped by the limited route licensing policy of the Shanian government, which has given Jamair almost monopoly status on some of its routes. However, the government is now set to change this policy with almost immediate effect, and it has become more important than ever to monitor performance effectively.

Required:

(a) Explain the arguments for using the profit measure as the all-encompassing measure of the performance of a business. 🖳 **(5 marks)**

(b) Describe each of the four perspectives of the balanced scorecard. 🖳 **(6 marks)**

(c) For each perspective of the balanced scorecard, identify one goal together with a corresponding performance measure which could be used by Jamair to measure the company's performance. The goals and measures should be specifically relevant to Jamair. For each pair of goals and measures, explain why you have chosen them. 🖳 **(9 marks)**

(Total: 20 marks)

290 THE PEOPLE'S BANK (MARCH/JUNE 2017)

The People's Bank is a bank based in the country of Nawkrei. It has a total of 65 branches across the country and also offers online banking (access to services via computer) and telephone banking (access to customer service agents over the telephone) to its customers. Recently, The People's Bank also began offering its customers a range of mobile banking services, which can be accessed from customers' smartphones and tablet computers. Its customer-base is made up of both private individuals and business customers.

The range of services it offers includes:

- Current accounts
- Savings accounts
- Credit cards
- Business and personal loans
- Mortgages (loans for property purchases)

The People's Bank's vision is to be 'the bank that gives back to its customers' and their purpose is 'to help the people and businesses of Nawkrei to live better lives and achieve their ambitions'. In order to achieve this, the bank's values are stated as:

(1) Putting customers' needs first, which involves anticipating and understanding customers' needs and making products and services accessible to as many customers as possible. The People' Bank has recently invested heavily in IT security to prevent fraud and also invested to make more services accessible to disabled and visually impaired customers (2) Making business simple, which involves identifying opportunities to simplify activities and communicating clearly and openly

(3) Making a difference to the communities they serve, which involves primarily helping the disadvantaged and new homeowners but also supporting small and medium-sized businesses (SMEs) and acting fairly and responsibly at all times

Extracts from The People's Bank's balanced scorecard are shown below:

Performance measure	20X6 Actual	20X6 Target
Financial perspective		
Return on capital employed (ROCE)	11%	12%
Interest income	$7.5m	$7m
Net interest margin (margin achieved on interest income)	2.4%	2.5%
Amount of new lending to SMEs	$135m	$150m
Customer perspective		
Number of first-time homebuyers given a mortgage by The People's Bank	86,000	80,000
Number of complaints (per 1,000 customers)	1.5	2
Number of talking cashpoints installed for the visually impaired	120	100
Number of wheelchair ramps installed in branches	55	50
Internal processes		
Number of business processes within The People's Bank re-engineered and simplified	110	100
Number of new services made available through 'mobile banking'	2	5
Incidences of fraud on customers' accounts or credit cards (per 1,000 customers)	3	10
Total carbon dioxide emissions (tonnes)	430,000	400,000
Learning and growth		
Number of colleagues trained to provide advice to SMEs	1,300	1,500
Number of hours (paid for by The People's Bank) used to support community projects	1,020,000	1,000,000
Number of trainee positions taken up by candidates from Nawkrei's most disadvantaged areas	1,990	2,000
Number of community organisations supported (either through funding or by volunteers from The People's Bank)	7,250	7,000

Required:

(a) Explain why the balanced scorecard approach to performance measurement is more useful to measure performance for The People's Bank than a traditional approach using solely financial performance measures. 🖥️ **(4 marks)**

(b) Using all of the information provided, including The People's Bank's vision and values, discuss the performance of The People's Bank in 20X6. Note: Use each of the four headings of the balanced scorecard to structure your discussion. 🖥️

(16 marks)

(Total: 20 marks)

291 PUBLIC SECTOR ORGANISATION

A public sector organisation is extending its budgetary control and responsibility accounting system to all departments. One such department concerned with public health and welfare is called 'Homecare'. The department consists of staff who visit elderly 'clients' in their homes to support them with their basic medical and welfare needs.

A monthly cost control report is to be sent to the department manager, a copy of which is also passed to a Director who controls a number of departments. In the system, which is still being refined, the budget was set by the Director and the manager had not been consulted over the budget or the use of the monthly control report.

Shown below is the first month's cost control report for the Homecare department:

Cost Control Report – Homecare Department

Month ending May 20X0

	Budget	Actual	(Overspend)/underspend
Visits	10,000	12,000	(2,000)
	$	$	$
Department expenses:			
Supervisory salary	2,000	2,125	(125)
Wages (Permanent staff)	2,700	2,400	300
Wages (Casual staff)	1,500	2,500	(1,000)
Office equipment depreciation	500	750	(250)
Repairs to equipment	200	20	180
Travel expenses	1,500	1,800	(300)
Consumables	4,000	6,000	(2,000)
Administration and telephone	1,000	1,200	(200)
Allocated administrative costs	2,000	3,000	(1,000)
	15,400	19,795	(4,395)

In addition to the manager and permanent members of staff, appropriately qualified casual staff are appointed on a week to week basis to cope with fluctuations in demand. Staff use their own transport, and travel expenses are reimbursed. There is a central administration overhead charge over all departments. Consumables consist of materials which are used by staff to care for clients. Administration and telephone are costs of keeping in touch with the staff who often operate from their own homes.

As a result of the report, the Director sent a memo to the manager of the Homecare department pointing out that the department must spend within its funding allocation and that any spending more than 5% above budget on any item would not be tolerated. The Director requested an immediate explanation for the serious overspend.

You work as the assistant to the Directorate Management Accountant. On seeing the way the budget system was developing, he made a note of points he would wish to discuss and develop further, but was called away before these could be completed.

Required:

Develop and explain the issues concerning the budgetary control and responsibility accounting system which are likely to be raised by the management accountant. You should refer to the way the budget was prepared, the implications of a 20% increase in the number of visits, the extent of controllability of costs, the implications of the funding allocation, social aspects and any other points you think appropriate. You may include numerical illustrations and comment on specific costs, but you are not required to reproduce the cost control report. 📖 (Total: 20 marks)

292 WOODSIDE CHARITY (JUNE 2007)

Woodside is a local charity dedicated to helping homeless people in a large city. The charity owns and manages a shelter that provides free overnight accommodation for up to 30 people, offers free meals each and every night of the year to homeless people who are unable to buy food, and runs a free advice centre to help homeless people find suitable housing and gain financial aid. Woodside depends entirely on public donations to finance its activities and had a fundraising target for the last year of $700,000. The budget for the last year was based on the following forecast activity levels and expected costs.

Free meals provision:	18,250 meals at $5 per meal
Overnight shelter:	10,000 bed-nights at $30 per night *($5 FC)*
Advice centre:	3,000 sessions at $20 per session *($5 FC)*
Campaigning and advertising:	$150,000

The budgeted surplus (budgeted fundraising target less budgeted costs) was expected to be used to meet any unexpected costs. Included in the above figures are fixed costs of $5 per night for providing shelter and $5 per advice session representing fixed costs expected to be incurred by administration and maintaining the shelter. The number of free meals provided and the number of beds occupied each night depends on both the weather and the season of the year. The Woodside charity has three full-time staff and a large number of voluntary helpers.

The actual costs for the last year were as follows:

Free meals provision:	20,000 meals at a variable cost of $104,000
Overnight shelter:	8,760 bed-nights at a variable cost of $223,380
Advice centre:	3,500 sessions at a variable cost of $61,600
Campaigning and advertising:	$165,000

The actual costs of the overnight shelter and the advice centre exclude the fixed costs of administration and maintenance, which were $83,000.

The actual costs for the last year were as follows:

Free meals provision: 20,000 meals at a variable cost of $104,000

Overnight shelter: 8,760 bed-nights at a variable cost of $223,380

Advice centre: 3,500 sessions at a variable cost of $61,600

Campaigning and advertising: $165,000

The actual costs of the overnight shelter and the advice centre exclude the fixed costs of administration and maintenance, which were $83,000.

The actual amount of funds raised in the last year was $620,000.

Required:

(a)   **Prepare an operating statement, reconciling budgeted surplus and actual shortfall and discuss the charity's performance over the last year.**   (13 marks)

(b)   **Discuss problems that may arise in the financial management and control of a not-for-profit organisation such as the Woodside charity.**   (7 marks)

(Total: 20 marks)

Section 4

ANSWERS TO OBJECTIVE TEST QUESTIONS – SECTION A

SPECIALIST COST AND MANAGEMENT ACCOUNTING TECHNIQUES

ACTIVITY BASED COSTING

1   D

A total figure is needed and assuming distance travelled increases the costs of handling, then the correct answer is D.

2   C

Alpha batches (2,500/500) = 5; therefore inspections required for Alpha (5 × 4) = 20

Zeta batches (8,000/1,000) = 8; therefore inspections required for Zeta (8 × 1) = 8

OAR = $250,000/28 = $8,928.57

Alpha cost/unit = (20 × $8,928.57)/2,500 units = $71.43

3   D

Statement (1) provides a definition of a cost driver. Cost drivers for long-term variable overhead costs will be the volume of a particular activity to which the cost driver relates, so Statement (2) is correct.

Statement (3) is also correct. In traditional absorption costing, standard high-volume products receive a higher amount of overhead costs than with ABC. ABC allows for the unusually high costs of support activities for low-volume products (such as relatively higher set-up costs, order processing costs and so on).

4   A

Statement (2) is not correct. Although the OAR is calculated in the same way as the absorption costing OAR, a separate OAR will be calculated for each activity.

5 **$31.82**

$$\text{Overhead absorption rate} = \frac{\text{Total overhead cost}}{\text{Total number of direct labour hours}}$$

$$\text{Overhead absorption rate} = \frac{\$420,000}{66,000 \text{ Direct labour hours}}$$

Overhead absorption rate = $6.36 per labour hour. Alpha uses 5 direct labour hours per unit so will have an overhead cost per unit of 5 hours × $6.36 per hour = $31.82.

6 **C**

The overhead cost per unit for each unit of product Beta will be the same as product Alpha, as both products use the same number of labour hours (5 hours).

7 **C**

	Volume related	Purchasing related	Set-up related
Costs	$100,000	$145,000	$175,000
Consumption of activities (cost drivers)	66,000 labour hours	160 purchase orders	100 set-ups
Cost per unit of cost driver	$1.5151 per labour hour	$906.25 per purchase order	$1,750 per set-up
Costs per product			
Product Alpha:	6,000 labour hours cost: $9,090.91	75 purchase orders cost: $67,968.75	40 set-ups cost: $70,000
Product Beta:	60,000 labour hours cost: $90,909.09	85 purchase orders cost: $77,031.25	60 set-up cost: $105,000

Total overhead cost for Alpha = $9,090.91 + $67,968.75 + $70,000 = $147,060. Spread over 1,200 units, this represents a cost per unit of $122.55 approx

8 **B**

Total material budget ((1,000 units × $10) + (2,000 units × $20)) = $50,000 Fixed costs related to material handling = $100,000

OAR = $2/$ of material

Product B = $2 × $20 = $40

Total labour budget ((1,000 units × $5) + (2,000 units × $20) = $45,000 General fixed costs = $180,000

OAR = $4/$ of labour

Product B = $4 × $20 = $80

Total fixed overhead cost per unit of Product B ($40 + $80) = $120.

9   **$46.25**

Set-up costs per production run = $140,000/28 = $5,000

Cost per inspection = $80,000/8 = $10,000

Other overhead costs per labour hour = $96,000/48,000 = $2

Overheads costs of product D:

Set-up costs (15 × $5,000) $75,000

Inspection costs (3 × $10,000) $30,000

Other overheads (40,000 × $2) $80,000

So total overhead costs pf product D: $185,000 and overhead cost per unit = 185,000/ 4,000 = $46.25

10   **INCREASE, INCREASE, DECREASE**

	Increase	Decrease
Product X	√	
Product Y	√	
Product Z		√

Absorption costing

Since the time per unit is the same for each product, the overheads per unit will also be the same.

$156,000 ÷ 6,000 units = $26

Activity based costing

Number of deliveries for X (1,000/200)	5
Number of deliveries for Y (2,000/400)	5
Number of deliveries for Z (3,000/1,000)	3
Total	**13**

Cost per delivery = $156,000/13 = $12,000

Cost per unit of X = ($12,000/1,000 units) × 5 deliveries = $60

Increase = $60 – $26 = $34.

Cost per unit of Y = ($12,000/2,000 units) × 5 deliveries = $30

Increase = $30 – $26 = $4.

Cost per unit of Z = ($12,000/3,000 units) × 3 deliveries = $12

Decrease = $26 – $12 = $14.

11 $0.60

Cost driver = number of set-ups

Cost pool = $84,000

Total set-ups= 20 (for A) + 8 (for B) = 28

Rate =$84,000/28 = 5 $3,000 per set-up

Cost for B = $3,000 × 8 set-ups = $24,000

Per unit = $24,000/40,000 = $0.60.

12   B

Total set-ups = Budget production/batch size × set-ups per batch

D (100,000/100 × 3)	3,000
R (100,000/50 × 4)	8,000
P (50,000/25 × 6)	12,000
	23,000

Cost per set-up = $150,000/23,000 = $6.52

Therefore cost per unit of R = $6.52 × 8,000 set-ups/100,000 units = $0.52.

13 $0.50

Cost driver = number of set-ups   Cost pool = $12,000

Total set-ups = 20 (for A) + 4 (for B) = 24   Rate = $12,000/24 = $500 per set-up

Cost for A = $500 × 20 set-ups = $10,000   Per unit=$10,000/20,000 = $0.50

TARGET COSTING

Tutorial note

A technical article 'Target Costing and Lifecycle Costing' has been published on the ACCA website – make sure you read it as part of your revision.

14   C

15   D

Answer A is not correct: increasing the selling price is not possible, the industry is competitive so product will not sell effectively at higher prices.

Answer B ('Reduce the expectation gap by reducing the selling price') is not target costing.

Answer C ('Reducing the desired margin on the product') is not possible either: shareholders are demanding and would expect a good return.

16   C

To reduce the acceptable margin would normally require agreement from the owners and altering selling prices in any direction is not valid as the start point of target costing is to find a competing product's price, this cannot be changed.

17   The maximum rate per hour is **$12.40**

	$
Selling price	56.00
Profit (56 × 25/125)	11.20
Target cost	**44.80**
Material cost (16 × 10/8)	20.00
Labour – 2 hours	24.80
Labour rate per hour = 24.80/2	$12.40

18   B

Variance analysis is not relevant to target costing as it is a technique used for cost control at the production phase of the product life cycle. It is a feedback control tool by nature and target costing is feedforward.

Value analysis can be used to identify where small cost reductions can be applied to close a cost gap once production commences.

Functional analysis can be used at the product design stage. It ensures that a cost gap is reached or to ensure that the product design is one which includes only features which customers want.

Activity analysis identifies and describes activities in an organisation and evaluates their impact on operations to assess where improvements can be made.

19   D

Sales revenue 500 units @ $250	$125,000
Return on investment required 15% × $250,000	$37,500
Total cost allowed	$87.500
Target cost per unit	$175

20   D

It is simultaneous as there is no delay between the service being provided by the optician and consumed by the patient.

LIFECYCLE COSTING

21   C

OAR for fixed production overheads ($72 million/96 million hours) = $0.75 per hour

Total manufacturing costs (300,000 units × $20) = $6,000,000

Total design, depreciation and decommissioning costs = $1,320,000

Total fixed production overheads (300,000 units × 4 hours × $0.75) = $900,000

Total life-cycle costs = $8,220,000 and life-cycle cost per unit ($8,220,000/300,000 units) = $27.40

22   C

Variable production costs ($2.30 × 2,000) + ($1.80 × 5,000) + ($1.20 × 7,000) = $22,000

Variable selling costs ($0.50 × 2,000) + ($0.40 × 5,000) + ($0.40 × 7,000) = $5,800

Fixed production costs = $10,500; Fixed selling costs = $4,700

Administrative costs = $2,100

Total costs = $45,100

Cost per unit = $45,100/14,000 units = $3.22

23   D

24   Benefits are:

- It provides a true financial cost of a product
- Expensive errors can be avoided in that potentially failing products can be avoided
- Lower costs can be achieved earlier by designing out costs
- Better selling prices can be set.

Note: Shortening the length of a lifecycle is not desirable and decline (for most products) inevitable.

25   A

(i)   This is true, justifying the time and effort of life cycle costing.

(ii)   As above.

(iii)   This is not true: life cycle costing is not about setting selling prices, it is about linking total revenues to total costs. Even if it were about setting a selling price, the early sales may well be at a loss since it is TOTAL revenues and costs that are considered. Furthermore, the pre-launch costs are sunk at launch and are therefore irrelevant when setting a selling price.

(iv)   This is true. The deliberate attempt to maximise profitability is the key to life cycle costing.

26   B

27   A

The original life cycle cost per unit = ($43,000 + (20,000 × $15) + $30,000)/20,000 = $18.65

THROUGHPUT ACCOUNTING

28   C

Overall the cost per unit should reduce, and so the measure for throughput should improve.

A is wrong as the TPAR measures return based on the slowest machine not the fastest. B is wrong since rent has increased so the TPAR will worsen from its current level. D is wrong since we cannot meet demand even at the moment so reducing prices will reduce throughput per unit without any extra sales level benefit.

29   A

As all three products are mutually exclusive, the company would choose to make X as it has the highest throughput return per hour of $2.

Of the four possible options, only increasing the selling price of product Z by 10% would give a higher throughput return per hour of $2.40.

30   The first step is to identify the bottleneck.

Process P output is 6 × 8 × 0.9 = 43.2 per hour. Process Q output is 9 × 6 × 0.85 = 45.9 per hour. In the absence of other information, then process P is slower, and so is the bottleneck.

Cloud:

Throughput:	$
Selling price ($20 × 0.85)	17.00
Material cost	5.00
Throughput per unit	12.00
Time in process P (hrs)	0.2
TP per hour	60.00

31   A

Tutorial note

This question tested candidates' knowledge of throughput accounting, and specifically how throughput can be improved. It is also a good example of a question where it's important not to rush – all of the possible answers could improve throughput, depending on what our bottleneck (limiting factor) is – Process 1,2 or 3. If none of the processes are limited, then increasing demand would improve throughput.

Throughput is determined by the bottleneck resource. Process 2 is the bottleneck as it has insufficient time to meet demand.

The only option to improve Process 2 is to improve the efficiency of the maintenance routine. All the other three options either increase the time available on non-bottleneck resources or increase demand for an increase in supply which cannot be achieved.

32   D

All of these points are true, except D.

Throughput accounting was designed as a performance measurement tool, not a decision-making tool.

One of its advantages is that it will be used by managers to make decisions that have outcomes that are goal congruent with corporate aims. However, it was designed as a performance measurement tool.

33   C

Answer C is the same as total throughput/total conversion costs, which is an alternative, correct, definition (which gives the same value).

Answers B and D are the same: they are the correct ratio inverted.

Answer A is often referred to as the return per hour.

34   D

The throughput accounting ratio is defined as throughput/total factory costs (these can both be calculated per hour, but that is, more work for the same answer).

Throughput = sales – all material costs = $9,000 – $3,000 = $6,000

(Note that we use materials purchased instead of materials used.)

Total factory costs 5 all other production costs = $2,000 + $1,500 = $3,500

TA ratio = $6,000/$3,500 = 1.7.

35   C

The throughput accounting ratio is defined as throughput/total factory costs.

Throughput accounting aims to discourage inventory building, so the ratios do not take account of inventory movements.

Throughput = sales – all material costs = $35 × 800 – $13,000 = $15,000

(Note that we use materials purchased instead of materials used.)

Total factory costs= all other production costs= $6,900 + $4,650 = $11,550

TA ratio = $15,000/$11,550 = 1.3.

ENVIRONMENTAL ACCOUNTING

Tutorial note

A technical article 'Environmental Management Accounting' has been published on the ACCA website – make sure you read it as part of your revision.

36   D

Under a system of flow cost accounting material flows are divided into three categories – material, system, and delivery and disposal.

37   The first and third statements are true.

Manufacturing costs are categorised into material costs, system costs and delivery and disposal costs. After dividing material flows into three categories (material, system and delivery and disposal costs), MFCA calculates the values and costs of each of these three flows. Output costs are allocated between positive products (good finished output) and negative product costs (costs of waste and emissions.)

The second statement is not correct: this is a definition of the input/output analysis method of accounting for environmental costs.

The fourth statement is not correct: The aim of flow cost accounting is to reduce the quantity of materials which, as well as having a positive effect on the environment, should have a positive effect on a business' total costs in the long run.

38   **D**

39   Only the first two statements are true.

40   **D**

Waste flows are not a category used within flow cost accounting, however, the other three categories are.

41   **D**

DECISION-MAKING TECHNIQUES

RELEVANT COST ANALYSIS

42   **B**

The book value is an historic cost and therefore not relevant. There is no intention to replace material X. There are two options for material X, scrap at a value of 50p per kg or use as a replacement for material Y, which would save $4 per kg ($6 – $2). The latter is the preferable option so the relevant cost is $4 per kg for 10 kgs = $40.

43   **C**

Labour is in short supply so there is an opportunity cost. The contribution from Contract Z will still be earned but will be delayed. The relevant cost is therefore the wages earned plus the penalty fee.

($15 × 100) + ($1,000) = $2,500

44   **B**

The material is in regular use by the organisation and so would be replaced if it is used on the special order. The material is readily available at a price of $3.24 per kg.

Therefore the relevant cost of the material is 1,250 kgs × $3.24 = $4,050.

45   D

Replacement material cost saved (4 kg @ $5.00)	$20.00
Less further processing cost ($0.75 × 5 kg)	$3.75
Value of M in current use, for each unit made	$16.25

Therefore opportunity cost of using M on the job being tendered for is $16.25/5 kg = $3.25 per kg.

46   C

Since material J is in regular use and is readily available in the market, its relevant cost is the replacement price of $8/kg.

So 2,000 kgs × $8/kg = $16,000

47   A

3,700 kg × $3.80 + 500 kg × $6.30 = $17,210

Tutorial note

The company needs 4,200 kg. It has 3,700 kg in inventory. It will therefore need to buy 500 kg and these can be bought for $6.30 per kg. The tricky bit is the value to the company of the 3,700 kg in inventory. The $4.50 original purchase price is of course a sunk cost and cannot be relevant. The inventory can be sold for $3.20 per kg, so this is its very minimum value.

The inventory is worth $3.20 per kg unless the company has an even better alternative – and there is a better alternative. The company can take the inventory and, by spending $3.70 per kg on it, can turn it into something worth $7.50 per kg. If something will be worth $7.50 if we spend $3.70 on it, then it is at present worth $3.80. This then is the value of the inventory to the company and to fulfil the contract the company will use 3,700 kg of inventory with a value of $3.80 per kg.

48   C

The relevant cash flow is:

Lost disposal proceeds (net)	$10,300
Additional costs of set up	$1,300
Total	$11,600

49   A

The relevant cash flow is:

Extra variable overheads: 450 hours × $4/hr	$1,800
Rent	$1,200
Total	$3,000

Fixed costs are not incremental and idle time would normally mean that the machines are not in use are so are not an incurred cost.

50   D

The options are:

Agency 600 × $9/hr =	$5,400
Internal transfer 600 × (7 + 3) =	$6,000
Hire new $1,200 + (600 × $6/hr)	$4,800

Cleverclogs would select the lower of the costs and so this is the relevant cash flow.

51   D

It could be argued that it is also a sunk cost but the better and more exact description is that it is a committed cost as the cash has not yet been actually paid over.

52   C

53   B

The book value is not relevant as it is a sunk cost. The relevant cost of the paper in inventory is the resale value as that is its next best use. The remaining material required must be bought at the replacement cost of $26.

100 reams @ $10	$1,000
150 reams @ $26	$3,900
	———
	$4,900
	———

COST VOLUME PROFIT ANALYSIS

54   B

Two units of Y and one unit of X would give total contribution of $18. Weighted average contribution per unit = $18/3 units = $6

Sales units to achieve target profit = ($90,000 + $45,000)/$6 = 22,500

55   B

Current breakeven point is: $640,000/40 =	16,000 units
New breakeven point is: $400,000/35 =	11,429 units
Change in level of breakeven is 16,000 – 11,429 =	4,571 units
Current contribution is: $60 – $20 =	$40
New contribution is $60 – $20 – $5 =	$35

Operating risk reduces with less fixed costs in a business.

56   18,637 units

Number of units required to make target profit = fixed costs + target profit/contribution per unit of P1.

Fixed costs = ($1.2 × 10,000) + ($1 × 12,500) – $2,500 = $22,000.

Contribution per unit of P = $3.20 + $1.20 = $4.40.

($22,000 + $60,000)/$4.40 = 18,637 units rounded up.

57 58.3%

The breakeven revenue is FC/CS = $1,600,000/0.4 =	$4,000,000
Budget revenue is FC × 6 = $1,600,000 × 6 =	$9,600,000
Margin of safety is = (9,600,000 − 4,000,000)/9,600,000 =	58.3%

58 C

Contribution: $5,000,000 − ($1,400,000 + $400,000) =	$3,200,000
For 20,000 units, that is a contribution of	$160 per unit
Fixed costs amount to $1,600,000 + $1,200,000 =	$2,800,000
BEP units = FC/Unit contribution i.e. $2,800,000/$160 =	17,500

59 A

Selling price per unit ($36/0.75) =	$48
Contribution per unit $48 − $36 =	$12
Fixed costs	$18,000
Therefore, breakeven point (units) is $18,000/$12 =	1,500

60 D

If budgeted sales increase to 40,000 units, then budgeted profit will increase by $100,000. This is because 10,000 more units will be sold at a contribution per unit of $10. The fixed costs would not be expected to change.

61 D

	Now	Revised
	$	$
Selling price	20	21,600
Variable cost	8	8,416
	12	13,184

Breakeven volume $79,104/$12 = 6,592

$79,104/$13,184 = 6,000

Decrease in breakeven volume = 592/6,592 × 100% = 9%

62 D

The breakeven revenue (BER) = Fixed costs/average CS ratio

BER = $1,400,000/0.2375 (W1) = $5,894,737

(W1)

	Product F $	Product G $	Total $
Budget revenue	6,000,000	2,000,000	8,000,000
Contribution	1,500,000	400,000	1,900,000
C/S	0.25	0.2	
Average C/S			0.2375

63   C

Because the C/S ratio of product G is lower than F the change in mix would reduce the average C/S ratio. As a consequence the BER would increase by an amount but not by the amount of extra sales of product G. This is not relevant.

64   B

Statement (i) is correct. The line which passes through the origin indicates the sales revenue at various levels of activity. At an activity level of 10,000 units, the sales revenue is $100,000, therefore the selling price is $10 per unit.

Statement (ii) is incorrect. The sloping line which intercepts the vertical axis at $30,000 shows the total cost at various levels of activity. The total cost for 10,000 units is $80,000, from which we subtract the $30,000 fixed costs.

Statement (iii) is correct. The fixed cost is the cost incurred at zero activity, and is shown as a horizontal line at $30,000.

Statement (iv) is incorrect. The profit for 10,000 units is the difference between the sales value $100,000 and the total cost of $80,000, which amounts to $20,000.

65   The second and third statements '3,152 units of sales are required to achieve a profit of $100,000 next month' and 'Monthly fixed costs amount to $136,400' are correct.

Fixed overheads every month amount to $22 fixed overhead per unit × 6,200 units = $136,400

The key to calculating the breakeven point is to determine the contribution per unit.

Contribution per unit = sales price – variable costs

Contribution per unit = $199 – $54 – $50 – $20

Contribution per unit = $75

Breakeven point in units = (Fixed costs/contribution per unit)

Breakeven point in units = $136,400/$75

Breakeven point in units = 1,819 units (and so the first statement is not correct.)

To achieve a profit of $100,000 next month:

Units of sales required = (Fixed costs + target profit)/unit contribution

Units of sales required = ($136,400 + $100,000)/$75

Units of sales required = 3,152

$$\text{Margin of safety expressed as a \%} = \frac{\text{Budgeted sales} - \text{breakeven sales}}{\text{Budgeted sales}} \times 100$$

Margin of safety = (6,200 units – 1,819 units)/6,200 units = 71% (and so the fourth statement is not correct.)

66   The first two statements are correct: point A is the breakeven point if the company's products are sold in order of their C/S ratio, and point B is the breakeven point if the company's products are sold in the budgeted sales mix.

Statement 3 is not correct. Changing the product mix in favour of Product 3, that has a negative contribution and reduces the cumulative profit, would impact negatively on the overall c/s ratio.

Statement 4 is not correct: if all three products are produced, then the company can expect a sales profit (not revenue) of $350,000.

LIMITING FACTORS

67 SHOULD BE PRODUCED, SHOULD NOT BE PRODUCED, SHOULD NOT BE PRODUCED, SHOULD BE PRODUCED

	Should be produced	Should not be produced
Product A	√	
Product B		√
Product C		√
Product D	√	

Product	A	B	C	D
Selling price per unit	$160	$214	$100	$140
Raw material costs	$24	$56	$22	$40
Direct labour cost at $11 per hour	$66	$88	$33	$22
Variable overhead cost	$24	$18	$24	$18
Contribution per unit	$46	$52	$21	$60
Direct labour hours per unit	6	8	3	2
Contribution per labour hour	$7.67	$6.50	$7	$30
Rank	2	4	3	1
Normal monthly hours (total units × hours per unit)	1,800	1,000	720	800

If the strike goes ahead, only 2,160 labour hours will be available. Therefore make all of Product D, then 1,360 hours' worth of Product A (2,160 – 800 hrs).

68 A

If the values for R and N are substituted into the constraints:

Labour required = (3 × 500) + (2 × 400) = 2,300 hours which is less than what is available so there is slack.

Machine time required = (0.5 × 500) + (0.4 × 400) = 410 hours which is exactly what is available and so there is no slack.

69 D

The company maximises contribution by producing Qutwo. Contribution per unit of material is:

$\dfrac{\$8.50}{2.5\text{kg}}$ = $3.40 and this is the shadow price.

70   D

	$
Direct material	3.00
Direct labour (W1)	9.00
Variable overhead	1.00
Specific fixed cost	2.50
	――――
	15.50

(W1)   Relevant cost = Contribution Forgone + Direct labour = $10/2 + $4 = $9

71   D

	R	S	T
	$	$	$
Contribution per unit			
$(100 − 15 − 20 − 15)	50		
$(150 − 30 − 35 − 20)		65	
$(160 − 25 − 30 − 22)			83
Direct labour cost per unit	20	35	30
Contribution per $1 of direct labour	2.50	1.85	2.77
Profitability ranking	2nd	3rd	1st

72   B

By definition, a shadow price is the amount by which contribution will increase if an extra kg of material becomes available. 20 × $2.80 = $56.

Tutorial note

In this question, the shadow price is $2.80 per unit, and therefore if 20 kgs of additional material Z becomes available, the increase in contribution would be $56 (20 × $2.80). The answer is therefore B. In the first distractor A, the cost of the material (20 kg × $2) has also been added to the $56. This is because a common mistake made is to add the cost of the material in too.

Similarly, in distractor C, the $40 has been deducted from the $56 leaving a figure of $16. This is because candidates often fail to realise that the shadow price is the amount over and above the normal cost that one would be prepared to pay for an extra unit of scarce material if it becomes available. Therefore, this would lead candidates to think that contribution would only increase by $0.80 ($2.80 − $2) for each extra kg of material Z that becomes available resulting in a total increase in contribution of only $16.

73   The first statement is not true: linear programming is only suitable when there are two products.

The second statement is not true: : there needs to be more than one limiting factor, but it is not essential for one of these two to be the level of demand.

The third statement is correct: fixed costs do not change and do not need to be considered.

The fourth statement is correct: a steady state being reached means that variable costs are constant.

74   **C**

A shadow price for a scarce resource is its opportunity cost. It is the amount of contribution that would be lost if one unit less of that resource were available. It is similarly the amount of additional contribution that would be earned if one unit more of that resource were available. (This is on the assumption that the scarce resource is available at its normal variable cost.)

PRICING DECISIONS

75   **C**

Not all discrimination is illegal (e.g. the cost of rail travel at peak times). Early adopters normally pay more and maximising sales volume normally means a lower profit.

76   **C**

77   The second and third options are valid. If demand is inelastic or the product life cycle is short, a price skimming approach would be more appropriate.

78   **D**

Penetration pricing involves setting a low price when a product is first launched in order to obtain strong demand.

It is particularly useful if significant economies of scale can be achieved from a high volume of output and if demand is highly elastic and so would respond well to low prices.

79   **B**

80   **B**

81   **C**

Prime cost + 80% = 12 × (1.8) = $21.6

MC + 60% = 15 × (1.6) = $24.00

TAC + 20% = 21 × (1.2) = $25.20

Net margin would mean 21 × 100/86 = $24.40

82   D

P = a + bQ and b = –20/1,000 or –0.02

By substitution:

400 = a – 0.02 (5,000)

a = 500

So demand equation is:

P = 500 – 0.02Q

MR = 500 – 0.04Q

83   C

MR = 500 – 0.04Q (as above)

MC = 200

Set MR = MC in order to profit maximise thus:

500 – 0.04Q = 200

–0.04 Q = – 300

Q = 7,500

Substitute Q = 7,500 in to the demand equation thus:

P = 500 – 0.02 (7,500)

P = 350

84   B

The demand formula is P = a + bQ, with   b = change of price/change of demand quantity

b = –20/500 = –0.04

By substitution:

400 = a –0.04 (5,000)

400 = a – 200

a = 600

Hence: P = 600 – 0.04Q

85 $340

P = 600 – 0.04Q

MR = 600 – 0.08Q

MC = 80

For profit maximisation MR = MC

600 – 0.08Q = 80

Q = –520/–0.08 = 6,500

Again by substitution:

P = 600 – 0.04 (6,500) so P = 340

86   The correct options are price skimming, complimentary product pricing and price discrimination. Without brand loyalty or a long shelf life then a strategy of penetration is unlikely to work. Additionally the uniqueness of the product prevents low prices.

MAKE-OR-BUY AND OTHER SHORT-TERM DECISIONS

87   The correct items are:

- The variable costs of purchase from the new supplier
- The level of discount available from the new supplier
- The redundancy payments to the supervisor of the product in question
- The materials no longer bought to manufacture the product

88   **$4,475**

Material A:

Stock – saved disposal costs =	($400)
Bought 300 kg @ $6.25/kg =	1,875
Net cost	$1,475

Material B
Regularly used so replacement cost needed

800 kg @ $3.75/kg	$3,000
Total	$4,475

89   **$200**

The supervisor is a sunk cost.

90   The correct factors to include are:

- The market outlook in the long term looks very poor
- The business also sells pens and many diary buyers will often also buy a pen

The following were NOT to be included:

- The diaries made a loss in the year just passed is a sunk event
- The diaries made a positive contribution in the year just passed is a sunk event
- The budget for next year shows a loss includes fixed costs and these are not relevant
- The business was founded to produce and sell diaries – things change!

91   Before further processing, the sales value of X (10,000 units × $1.20) = $12,000

After further processing:
Sales value of Z (8,000 units × $2.25) = $18,000
Further processing costs ((10,000 units of X × $0.50) + $1,600) = $6,600
This gives a net return of $11,400 which is **$600 less** than the sales value of X.

DEALING WITH RISK AND UNCERTAINTY IN DECISION-MAKING

92 A pessimistic buyer would seek to achieve the best results if the worst happens. He would adopt the maximin approach, which involves selecting the alternative that maximises the minimum payoff achievable. The minimum payoffs for each truck are as follows:

Truck A – Minimum $1,400

Truck B – Minimum $1,800

Truck C – Minimum $3,600

Therefore, the 'C' series truck would be chosen.

93 'A' series

This maximises the average daily contribution if the growth rate is forty per cent.

94 'C'

Regret table		Type of truck		
		A Series	B Series	C Series
		$	$	$
Growth rate	15%	1,200	1,800	0
	30%	3,100	2,600	0
	40%	0	2,100	1,000
Max Regret		3,100	2,600	1,000

95 'C'

Expected value calculations:

A Series: ($2,400 × 0.4) + ($1,400 × 0.25) + ($4,900 × 0.35) = $3,025

B Series: ($1,800 × 0.4) + ($1,900 × 0.25) + ($2,800 × 0.35) = $2,175

C Series: ($3,600 × 0.4) + ($4,500 × 0.25) + ($3,900 × 0.35) = $3,930

96 The first two statements are correct.

Statement 3 is not correct. Sensitivity analysis only identifies how far a variable needs to change, it does not look at the probability of such a change.

Statement 4 is not correct. Sensitivity analysis assumes that changes to variables can be made independently: for example, material prices will change independently of other variables; but it is simulation that allows more than one variable to be changed at a time.

97 **TRUE, TRUE, NOT TRUE, TRUE**

	True	Not true
Simulation models the behaviour of a system.	√	
Simulation models can be used to study alternative solutions to a problem.	√	
The equations describing the operating characteristics of the system are known.		√
A simulation model cannot prescribe what should be done about a problem.	√	

98   The second and fourth options are correct.

The expected value does not give an indication of the dispersion of the possible outcomes; a standard deviation would need to be calculated, so option 2 is correct.

The expected value is an amalgamation of several possible outcomes and their associated probabilities so it may not correspond to any of the actual possible outcomes, so option 4 is correct.

99   A

New profit figures before salary paid:

Good manager: $180,000 × 1.3 = $234,000 Average manager: $180,000 × 1.2 = $216,000 Poor: $180,000 × 1.1 = $198,000

EV of profits = (0.35 × $234,000) + (0.45 × $216,000) + (0.2 × $198,000) = $81,900 + $97,200 + $39,600 = $218,700

Deduct salary cost and EV with manager = $178,700

Therefore do not employ manager as profits will fall by $1,300.

100   A

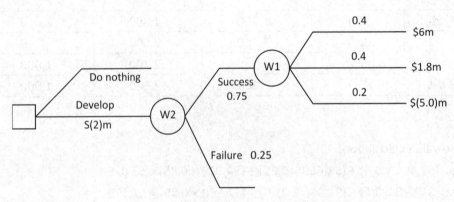

(W1) EV	=	($6m × 0.4) + ($1.8m × 0.4) − ($5m × 0.2)
	=	$2.12m
(W2) EV	=	($2.12m × 0.75) + ($Nil × 0.25)
	=	$1.59m
Net benefit:		$1.59m − $2m = ($0.41m)

BUDGETING AND CONTROL

BUDGETARY SYSTEMS

101   A

(2) is wrong – activities drive costs and the aim is to control the causes (drivers) of costs, rather than the costs themselves. This, in turn, will ensure that the costs are better managed, and better understood.

102   B

(1) is wrong – it would fall under strategic planning.

103   A

TYPES OF BUDGET

104 Incremental budgets are appropriate when applied to stationary costs, the business is stable and for administration costs when the experience of managers is limited.

105 **C**

(1) is wrong, it that would be feedback control. (2) is also wrong, feed-forward control occurs before the activity starts.

106 **D**

An incremental budget starts with the current period's budget and 'builds' on this to produce the budget for the next period.

107 **B**

108

	E	F	G	Total
Budgeted number of batches to be produced:		75,000/200	120,000/60	60,000/30
		= 375	= 2,000	= 2,000
Machine set-ups per batch:		5	3	9
Total machine set-ups		1,875	6,000	18,000	25,875

Budgeted cost per set-up: $180,000/25,875 = $6.96 per set-up

Therefore the budgeted machine set-up cost per unit of F produced is:

($6.96 × 3)/60 = $0.35 per unit or $6.96 × 6,000/120,000 = **$0.35 per unit**

109 **D**

110 **D**

A flexible budget controls operational efficiency by producing a realistic budget cost allowance for the actual level of activity achieved. This allows a more meaningful control comparison with the actual results. Statement (i) is therefore correct.

Incremental budgeting uses the current period's results as a base and adjusts this to allow for any known changes, including the cost increases caused by extra planned units of activity. Statement (ii) is therefore incorrect.

In a rolling budget system an extra quarter is added to the end of the budget when the most recent quarter has expired. The remaining budget might be updated at this point. Statement (iii) is therefore incorrect.

111 **A**

This is an example of feed-forward control, as the manager is using a forecast to assist in making a future decision.

112 **C**

113 ZBB is useful for support expenses as they are discretionary and it can be used to link strategic goals to specific functional areas, so statements 1 and 2 are correct.

114 A

(2) is not correct. ABB can provide useful information for a total quality management programme (TQM) by relating the cost of an activity to the level of service provided and asking the user departments if they feel they are getting a cost-effective service.

QUANTITATIVE ANALYSIS IN BUDGETING

115 B

460 – 400 = 60 clients

$40,000 – $36,880 = $3,120

VC per unit = $3,120/60 = $52

Therefore FC = $40,000 – (460 × $52) = $16,080

Key answer tips

Workings for the following two questions:

One: $16,400 = (800 × VC) + FC

Multiply this by 1.5, we get $24,600 = (1,200 × VC) + 1.5 FC

Two: $23,600 = (1,200 × VC) + 1.4F

Subtracting the last two equations we get $1,000 = 0.1 FC so $10,000 = FC

At the 1,100 unit level the fixed cost would be $14,000

By substitution:

One: $16,400 = 800 × VC + $10,000

6,400 = 800 × VC

6,400/800 = VC

VC = $8.

---

116 A

$23,600 = 1.4FC + 1,200VC   and $16,400 = FC + 800VC

($23,600 – 1,200VC) = 1.4FC + 1,200VC   and $16,400 – 800VC = FC

($23,600 – 1,200VC) = FC

――――――――――

        1.4

By substitution:

$16,400 – 800VC   = ($23,600 – 1,200VC)/1.4

$22,960 – 1,120VC   = $23,600 – 1,200VC

$1,200VC – 1,120VC   = $23,600 – $22,960

80VC   = $640

VC per unit   = $8

117 D

This question uses the same data as Q96 – therefore, initially calculate variable cost per unit as above to be $8.00 per unit, then substitute this value into the equation for the higher level of activity as follows:

$23,600 = 1.4FC + (1,200 × $8VC)

$23,600 = 1.4FC + $9,600

$23,600 – $9,600 – 1.4FC

$14,000 = 1.4FC (i.e. after increasing fixed costs by 40% upon exceeding 900 units)

Note: therefore fixed costs at lower level of activity = $14,000/1.4 = $10,000 (not required).

118 $34,400

A high low method analysis will first of all split out the budgeted VC and FC:

	Units	$ Cost
High	1,400	31,600
Low	1,000	30,000
Increment	400	1,600

VC per unit is $1,600/400 = $4/u

Substitution in high:

TC = FC + VC

TC = FC + (1,400 × 4)

31,600 = FC + 5,600

FC = $26,000

For 2,100 units, Fixed costs	= $26,000
VC (2,100 × 4)	= $8,400
Total	= $34,400

119 95%

Units	Total time	Average time/unit
1	100	100
2	190	95

Learning rate is based on the improvement in the average 95/100 = 95%

120 92%

Batches	Total time	Average time/unit
1	500	500
2		$500 × r$
4		$500 × r^2$
8		$500 × r^3$
16	5,731	$500 × r^4$

$5,731 = 16 × 500 \, r^4$

$5,731/(16 × 500) = r^4$

$r = 0.92$ or 92%

121 $41,509

Key answer tips

We must work in batches here, where 1 batch = 50 units

Time for the first order:

$Y = ax^b$

$Y = 400 \times 12^{-0.152}$

$Y = 274.17285$ hours

Total time = 3,290.07 hours

Time for first 1,400 units (28 batches)

$Y = ax^b$

$Y = 400 \times 28^{-0.152}$

$Y = 241.04158$ hours

Total time = 6,749.16 hours

Time for second order = 6,749.16 – 3,290.07 = 3,459.09 hours

Cost of second order = 3,459.09 × $12/hr = $41,509.08

122   84.3%

$100r^2 = (100 + 70 + 59 + 55)/4$, giving r = 84.3%

Tutorial note

We could also explain this answer as follows: by the time we have produced two units, we have an average per unit of (100 minutes + 70 minutes)/2 units = 85%. If we were to stop there, the rate of learning would be 85%.

By the time we have got to 4 units, we have an average of (100 minutes + 70 minutes + 59 minutes + 55 minutes)/4 units = 71 minutes. These 71 minutes represent (71/85) = 83.53% of the previous average of 85 minutes.

The overall rate of learning is an average of these two rates of learning, so we have (85% + 83.53%)/2 = 84.265, say 84.3%.

123   Using the learning curve model $Y = ax^b$

b = log 0.8/log 2 = –0.3219

	Cumulative average minutes	*Total minutes*
For the 3rd unit	$Y = 22 \times 3^{-0.3219} = 15.45$	× 3 = 46.34
For the 4th unit	$Y = 22 \times 4^{-0.3219} = 14.08$	× 4 = 56.32

Therefore the time for the 4th unit is 56.32 – 46.34 = 9.98 minutes.

STANDARD COSTING

124 A

Option B is a current standard, option C is an idea standard and option D is an attainable standard.

125 The first and fourth statements are true.

The second statement is not correct. Standards can include allowances for inefficiencies in operations, through the use of attainable standards.

The third statement is not correct either, standards and budgets are both used for planning and control purposes.

126 C

127 A

Flexible budgeting is a reporting system wherein the planned level of activity is adjusted to the actual level of activity before the budget to actual comparison report is prepared. It may be appropriately employed for any item which is affected by the level of activity. In standard costing, product costs are predetermined and set up as a goal to be attained. Actual performance is compared to the standard. A primary objective of a standard costing system is to control costs.

128 D

129 C

The standard labour rate should be the expected rate/hour, but allowing for standard levels of idle time. For example, if the work force is paid $9 per hour but idle time of 10% is expected, the standard labour rate will be $10 per hour, not $9.

130 C

131 The correct items are: exchange rate movements, increased demand for the material, world oil price rises.

Extra discounts would reduce prices and give a favourable variance. Dividends do not normally count as a cost to a business, and extra supply would normally reduce prices not increase them.

MATERIALS MIX AND YIELD VARIANCES

132 The correct answers are 'Inadequate training of newly recruited staff in the production department' and 'Change in the production process causing extra losses of materials'.

133 A

A favourable material mix variance is more likely to lead to an adverse material yield variance.

134 B

135 C

	Material A	Material B	Material C	Total
	kg	kg	kg	kg
Actual input	13,200	7,600	5,600	26,400
Actual input in std proportions				⇓
50:40:20	12,000	9,600	4,800	⇐ 26,400
Difference in quantity	1,200 A	2,000 F	800 A	
× Std price	× 10	× 5	× 9	
Mix variance	$12,000 A	$10,000 F	$7,200 A	$9,200 A

Key answer tips

An alternative calculation of the mix variance above can be done, using the standard average price per kilogram, as presented below.

$$\text{Std weighted average price per kg} = \frac{(50 \times 10) + (40 \times 5) + (20 \times 9)}{50 + 40 + 20\text{kg}} = \$8/\text{kg}$$

	Material A	Material B	Material C	Total
	kg	kg	kg	kg
Actual input	13,200	7,600	5,600	26,400
Actual input in std proportions				⇓
50:40:20	12,000	9,600	4,800	⇐ 26,400
Difference in quantity	1,200	(2,000)	800	
× Difference in price				
(weighted average std price –				
Ind. material std price)				
× (8 – 10)				
× (8 – 5) × 3	x – 2			
× (8 – 9)			x – 1	
Mix variance	$2,400 A	$6,000 A	$800 A	$9,200 A

136 A

3,000 units should use 10 kg each (3,000 × 10) = 30,000 kg 3,000 units did use = 29,000 kg

Difference = 1,000 kg favourable

Valued at $6.80 per kg ($68/10 kg)

Variance = $6,800 favourable

---

137   **$11.41**

	Actual mix	Std mix	SP × Act mix	SP × Std mix
Lettuce	62,000	45,937.5	12.400	9.1875
Peppers	81,000	76,562.5	32.400	30.6250
Beetroot	102,000	122,500.0	81.600	98.0000
	245,000	245,000.0	126.400	137.78125
Difference				11.41250

138   **B**

Actual yield	1,500.00
Standard yield	1,531.25
Difference	31.25
Standard cost of a plate	0.09
Yield variance = 31.25 × 0.09 =	2.8125 A
Standard yield is 245,000 × 1/160 =	1,531.25

Standard cost of a plate is:

	Quantity (g)	Price ($)	Cost ($)
Lettuce	30	0.0002	0.006
Peppers	50	0.0004	0.020
Beetroot	80	0.0008	0.064
Standard cost:			0.09

139   **A**

Actual usage in standard proportions	$
D = 4,000 litres at $9 per litre	= 36,000
E = 3,500 litres at $5 per litre	= 17,500
F = 2,500 litres at $2 per litre	= 5,000
10,000 litres	58,500
Actual usage in actual proportions	
D = 4,300 litres at $9 per litre	38,700
E = 3,600 litres at $5 per litre	18,000
F = 2,100 litres at $2 per litre	4,200
	60,900

Mix variance is 58,500 – 60,900 = $2,400 Adverse

SALES MIX AND QUANTITY VARIANCES

140   The sales price variance is $19,800 Adv

AQ × AP = 13,200 × 23.50 =	310,200
AQ × SP = 13,200 × 25.00 =	330,000
Price variance =	19,800 Adv

141 The sales volume variance is $6,000 Fav

AQ × SC = 13,200 × 5 =	66,000
BQ × SC = 12,000 × 5 =	60,000
Volume variance =	6,000 Fav

142 **$50,000**

	Actual mix	Standard mix	Standard contribution from actual mix $	Standard contribution from standard mix $
Type A	200,000	150,000	800,000	600,000
Type B	40,000	90,000	200,000	450,000
	240,000	240,000	1,000,000	1,050,000
Difference in contribution				50,000 Adv

Since Yellow uses MC then the variance should be calculated at standard contribution.

143 **$87,500**

Total actual sales	240,000
Total budget sales	220,000
Difference	20,000
Average standard contribution	$4.375
((5 × 4) + (3 × 5))/8 = 4.375	
Favourable variance is	$87,500

144

> **Tutorial note**
>
> A sales mix variance indicates the effect on profit of changing the mix of actual sales from the standard mix. Looking a July's budgeted sales levels, we can see that the standard mix of sales is one 'X' for two 'Y's, It means that we expect that every time an 'X' is sold, two units of 'Y' will be sold at the same time. The least profitable unit, 'X', represents a third of the budgeted sales volume.
>
> The actual sales mix is 1'X' for four 'Y's, and is different from the budgeted sales mix. The least profitable unit, 'X', represents a fifth of sales volume. To calculate Jones' sales mix variance, we can use the 'Toolbox' method detailed in your ACCA Study Text.

	Actual Quantities, Actual Mix AQAM	Actual Quantities, Standard Mix AQSM	Difference	At standard profit	Variance
Product X	2,000 units	3,333 units	−1,333	$4	($5,332) A
Product Y	8,000 units	6,667 units	1,333	$6	$7,998 F
	10,000 units	**10,000 units**	**0**		**$2,667 F**

145 A

The sales quantity variance is the difference between the actual sales volume in the standard mix and budgeted sales, valued at the standard profit per unit:

	X	Y	Z	Total
Budgeted sales units, in standard mix	1,000 units (1/6 of total)	2,000 units (1/3 of total)	1,000 units (1/2 of total)	6,000 units
Actual sales volume, in standard mix 1/6; 1/3;1/2	991.67	1,983.33	2,975	5,950
Difference in units	8.33 ADV	16.67 ADV	25 ADV	
Standard profit per unit, as per question	$2	$5	$2	
Variance	$16.67 ADV	$83.34 ADV	$50 ADV	**$150 ADV**

PLANNING AND OPERATIONAL VARIANCES

146 C

Statement 1 is not true: the publication of material price planning variances should not always lead to automatic updates of standard costs. There must be a good reason for deciding that the original standard cost is unrealistic.

Statement 2 is not true either. Although planning variances are not usually the responsibility of operational managers, these variances do need to be investigated by senior management when they are substantial, so that lessons may be learned for the future.

147 D

	Budget units	Actual units	Change
Sales	504,000	532,000	Up 5.55%
Market share	18%	20%	Up 2%
Market size	2,800,000	2,660,000	Down 5%

148 C

	Budget units	Revised units	Actual units	Change
Sales	504,000	478,800	532,000	Up 5.55%
Market share	18%	18%	20%	Up 2%
Market size	2,800,000		2,660,000	Down 5%

Market size variance is (478,800 – 504,000) × $12 = $302,400 Adv

149 B

Market share variance compares revised sales volume to actual sales volume.

Revised sales volume (300,000 units × 2%) = 6,000 units Actual sales volume = 5,600 units

Difference = 400 units adverse

Valued at standard contribution of $1,000

Variance = $400,000 adverse

150 C

An operational variance compares revised price to actual price.

20,000 kg should cost $0.40 per kg at the revised price (20,000 kg × $0.40) = $8,000

20,000 kg did cost $0.42 per kg (20,000 kg × $0.42) = $8,400

Variance = $400 adverse

151 A

The material price when flexed is higher than budget whilst the external environment shows that prices are reducing. This indicates that although suppliers lowered their prices, the manager has still overspent which indicates poor performance.

When sales volumes and prices are flexed, it can be seen that the manager has performed better.

152 D

PERFORMANCE ANALYSIS AND BEHAVIOURAL ASPECTS

153 D

The production manager controls both the mix and the production process and must alone bear responsibility for this initial poor performance.

154 C

PERFORMANCE MEASUREMENT AND CONTROL

PERFORMANCE MANAGEMENT INFORMATION SYSTEMS

155 B

156 A

157 SUITED, SUITED, NOT SUITED

	Suited to all levels of management	Not suited to all levels of management
A Management Information System producing management accounts showing margins for individual customers	√	
An Expert System holding specialist tax information	√	
An Executive Information System giving access to internal and external information in summarised form, with the option to drill down to a greater level of activity		√

EIS systems are usually suited to Senior Executives and strategic planning.

158 D

The tracking and summarising of critical strategic information is done by an Executive Information System (EIS).

The other three options are all likely to be potential benefits which would result from the introduction of an ERPS.

159 D

160 B

SOURCES OF MANAGEMENT INFORMATION

161 B

(i) is not correct: Internal information is produced by the company itself, so managers are aware of limitations in its quality or reliability.

162 EXTERNAL, EXTERNAL, INTERNAL, INTERNAL

	Internal	External
Interviewing potential customers		√
Reading business magazines		√
Listing employee records from the company's payroll system	√	
Looking through sales records for the last year	√	

163 C

164 D

165 D

166 B

MANAGEMENT REPORTS

167 C

168 C

169 A

A memory stick is much more likely to get mislaid and compromise security than a password protected laptop. It is likely that memory sticks could get lost or that information is left on home computers.

In the context of the scenario all the other options are good practice.

170 D

A universal password would apply to everyone and therefore there would be no way to trace the person responsible for printing/transferring or amending the information.

The other three options are common methods for securing the confidentiality of information.

PERFORMANCE ANALYSIS IN PRIVATE SECTOR ORGANISATIONS

171 B

(i) and (ii) are financial indicators, and (iv) is a risk indicator.

172 B

173 D

Measuring the budgeted number of quotations actually issued would be monitoring the output and activity of the department but it would not be helpful in improving the department's performance in terms of the accuracy or speed of quotations in the scenario described.

174 'Customer satisfaction ratings' and 'customer retention rates'

'Customer profitability analysis ' results belong to the financial quadrant. 'Customer ordering processing times' belongs to the 'Internal business process' quadrant.

175 D

176 D

'Number of returns in the month' is an absolute measure and not appropriate to measure 'quality'. 'Number of faulty goods returned as a percentage of number of orders received in the month' is not a bad measure, but orders may not have been delivered; 'Average customer satisfaction rating where customers were asked a range of questions including quality, delivery and customer service' seems to lack focus as a measure.

177 The correct items are competitiveness, Innovation, Profitability, Resource utilisation, Flexibility and Quality.

178 A

Co X $(2,140/20,000) \times 100 = 10.7\%$
Co Y $(2,180/26,000) \times 100 = 8.38\%$

179 C

Company B has a higher asset turnover and is therefore using its assets more efficiently than A. The two companies have the same ROCE and are therefore generating the same profit from every \$1 of asset employed. The profit of the two companies is the same but company A has a higher profit margin and is therefore controlling its costs better than company B. The calculations are:

	Co A	Co B
ROCE	20% $(10,000/50,000 \times 100)$	20% $(10,000/50,000 \times 100)$
Profit margin	20% $(10,000/50,000 \times 100)$	5% $(10,000/200,000 \times 100)$
Asset turnover	1 $(50,000/50,000)$	4 $(50,000/200,000)$

180 ACCOUNTABLE, ACCOUNTABLE, ACCOUNTABLE, NOT ACCOUNTABLE

	Accountable	Not accountable
The generation of revenues	√	
Transfer prices.	√	
Management of working capital.	√	
Apportioned head office costs.		√

The manager will be accountable for the generation of revenues, transfer prices and management of working capital as they have control over these areas. The manager will not be accountable for the apportioned head office costs as they have no control over those.

181 The first and fourth options are correct. The investment centre manager would have power to make decisions over granting credit to customers and the level of inventory carried. This affects the investment centre's level of working capital, and hence is the responsibility of the investment centre manager.

The second option is not correct: inter-departmental dispute resolution is carried out by head office and should not be the responsibility of the investment centre manager.

The third option is not correct: The manager will not be accountable for the apportioned head office costs as they have no control over those.

182 C

Inventory days = 44,000/324,500 × 365 days = 49 days

Average inventories/COS × 365

Average inventories = (50,000 + 38,000)/2 = 44,000

Current ratio = 108,000/56,000 = 1.93:1

Current assets: Current liabilities

Current assets = Trade receivables 60,000 + Prepayments 4,000 + Cash in hand 6,000 + Closing inventories 38,000 = 108,000

Current liabilities = Bank overdraft 8,000 + Trade payables 40,000 + Accruals 3,000 + Declared dividends 5,000 = 56,000

183 The first statement is true. Even if the supplying division is operating at full capacity supplying external customers, internals transfers can be made if it is in the company's best interests. This would be the case, for example, if the external market price of obtaining those items is higher than the variable costs plus the lost contribution of items which cannot be made internally if the transfer goes ahead.

The second statement is not correct. Transfer pricing is only required when some divisions provide goods or services to other divisions, which is often but not always the case in multidivisional businesses.

The third statement is true. The minimum transfer price is equal to the variable costs plus any lost contribution of the selling division.

The fourth statement is not true. When there is an external market for the transferred goods, internal transfers should be preferred because the company will have better control over any output quality from an internal division as well as the ability to control scheduling of production and deliveries.

DIVISIONAL PERFORMANCE AND TRANSFER PRICING

184 WOULD CHOOSE TO INVEST, WOULD NOT CHOOSE TO INVEST

	Would choose to invest in the project	Would choose not to invest in the project
Division A	√	
Division B		√

Division A: Profit = $14.4 m × 30% = $4.32 m

Imputed interest charge = $32.6 m × 10% = $3.26 m

Residual income = $1.06 m

Division B: Profit = $8.8 m × 24% = $2.112 m

Imputed interest charge = $22.2 m × 10% = $2.22 m

Residual income = $(0.108) m

185 $10.50

Tutorial note

Division A can sell all of its output on the outside market at $12 per unit. Any internal transfer will be at the expense of external sales. However, the external sales also include a packaging cost of $1.50 per unit which is not incurred on an internal transfer and this saving can be passed on to the buying division. Therefore, the correct transfer price from a decision-making point of view is $12 (the market price) – $1.50 (the saving in packaging cost) = $10.50.

186 B

Increase in variable costs from buying in (2,200 units × $40 ($140 – $100)) = $88,000

Less the specific fixed costs saved if A is shut down = ($10,000)

Decrease in profit = $78,000

187 D

$$\text{ROCE} = \frac{\text{Profit before interest and tax}}{\text{Capital employed}} = \frac{500}{2,400} = 20.8\%$$

Capital employed is equity + long-term debt   = 1,500 + 900 = 2,400

or

Total assets less current liabilities   = 3,400 – 1,000 = 2,400

188 C

	$000
Profit	500
Imputed interest 11% × 2,400	(264)
	———
Residual income	236
	———

189 **$830 m**

Controllable profit is 1,200 + 90 + 30 + 50 =	$1,370m
Assets at start of year are	$4,500m
Notional interest charges at 12% (4,500 × 0.12)	$540m
Residual Income	$830m

190 **30.4%**

ROI = 30%; ROI = 1,370/4,500 = 30.4%

191 **19.8%**

Tutorial note

We need to look at how the transactions given affect profits and net assets. With each transaction in turn:

Firstly, a machine with NBV of $40k was sold for $50k. This will reduce non-current assets by $40k and, as we are told this was a cash transaction, increase cash by $50k – increasing net assets by $10k. As a profit has been made on disposal, it will also increase profits by $10k. Secondly, another machine was purchased for $250k. This will increase non-current assets by $250k, but as this was also a cash transaction, decrease cash by $250k, so no net effect. As no depreciation is charged on either machine there is no further effect. The net effect is therefore +10k to both profit and net assets, so the ROI is ($200k/$1,010k) × 100%=19.8%.

Revised annual profit = $190,000 + $10,000 profit on the sale of the asset = $200,000

Revised net assets = $1,000,000 − $40,000 NBV + $50,000 cash − $250,000 cash + $250,000 asset = $1,010,000 ROI = ($200,000/$1,010,000) × 100 = 19.8%

Tutorial note

Do not make the mistake of omitting the profit on disposal from profits – ($190k/$1,010k) = 18.8% (Answer A), or omitting the profit on disposal and increasing net assets by the $250k machine purchase but not subtracting the cash – ($190/$1,260k) = 15.1%. (Answer C). Answer D was obtained with the correct profit figure but the incorrect net assets of $1,260k – ($200/$1,260) = 15.9%.

192 B

Using the opportunity cost approach to transfer pricing, the minimum price charged by the transferring division must be the marginal (variable) cost of producing X + the contribution that is lost from selling however many units of Y could have been made for each X.

'Division A has limited skilled labour' means that skilled labour is a scarce resource. If Division A now has to make X instead of Y, it will lose the contribution it currently makes on Product Y. This contribution is equal to $600 selling price – $200 Material costs – $80 labour costs = $320.

It takes 4 hours to make a Y and 6 hours to make an X. So, every time we (in Division A) make an X, we will not make 1.5Ys because of the shortage of skilled labour. So we lose 1.5 Y × Contribution per unit $320 = $480.

We add to this lost contribution a marginal cost of making an X of $150 (material) + $170 (labour).

Total transfer price = $480 + $150 + $120 = $750

Tutorial note

There is an alternative to approaching this question. You could calculate the contribution per labour hour for Y and then multiplying this by the number of hours X uses. It is the contribution per labour hour that is relevant, because of the fact that it is labour that is in short supply.

Product	Y in $
Selling Price per unit	600
Less Direct Materials (4 kgs)	200
Less Direct Labour (4 hours)	80
Contribution per unit	320
Contribution per labour hour for Y	80

Therefore, if Division A is to be no worse off by selling Product X to Division B instead of Product Y externally, the contribution per labour hour from selling X must also be $80. The opportunity cost is therefore $80 per labour hour.

Since it uses 6 labour hours to make one unit, one unit must generate a contribution (i.e. opportunity cost in this context) of 6 × $80 i.e. $480. To arrive at a minimum transfer price, the marginal cost of producing X must be added. Total variable cost per unit of X = $150 + $270. Therefore, the minimum transfer price is $750.

193 B

194 $12.90

We must set a price high enough for TM to cover its costs, but not so high that RM cannot make a profit.

For TM, an item sold externally has VC of 60% × $24.00 = $14.40. Of this, $1.50 will not be incurred on an internal transfer so it is not relevant here, VC on internal transfer = $14.40 – $1.50= $12.90. We do not know RM's cost structure, so we leave the price at $12.90; this will ensure that RM is not discouraged from taking an internal transfer when it is profitable to do so.

PERFORMANCE ANALYSIS IN NON-FOR-PROFIT ORGANISATIONS AND THE PUBLIC SECTOR

195 ECONOMY, EFFICIENCY, EFFECTIVENESS

	Economy	Efficiency	Effectiveness
Target (1)	√		
Target (2)		√	
Target (3)			√

196 A

Reducing mortality rates is likely to be a stated objective of the hospital and as such is a measure of output, or effectiveness. Cost per patient is a measure of output related to input i.e. efficiency.

197 B

Multiple objectives often conflict and therefore do not ensure goal congruence between stakeholders, therefore Statement 1 is incorrect. This then can lead to the need for compromise between objectives which can be problematic, therefore Statement 2 is correct.

198 C

Exam success will be a given objective of a school, so it is a measure of effectiveness.

199 B

(1) is not correct: Output does not usually have a market value, and it is therefore more difficult to measure efficiency.

200 D

EXTERNAL CONSIDERATIONS AND BEHAVIOURAL ASPECTS

201 C

Delaying payments to payables affects cash, not profit. Shortening the useful economic life of a non-current asset would reduce profit, and overstatement of an accrual also reduces profit.

202 D

There is nothing to suggest that imposed standards are more likely to be achieved. Where managers are allowed to participate in the setting of standards, they are usually more motivated and this can lead to more acceptance of these standards.

Managers should be targeted on factors which they can control, and be set targets which are specific to their business area.

It is recognised that ideal standard do not generally motivate, therefore standards are generally set at an achievable level with some stretch built in.

203 **A, B and D**

It is important to take account of all stakeholders when setting performance targets.

204 **A**

Managers should also have targets which are based on the overall performance of the company and not solely based on their own responsibility centre to aid goal congruence.

Capital investment decisions may be reviewed centrally and judged on the basis of net present value (NPV).

Setting targets involving the overall performance of the company may not be motivating if poorly performing managers are rewarded in the same way as managers who are performing well.

205 **C**

It is important that performance measures are set to encourage the long term growth of the company. A focus on short term profit could result in risky and dysfunctional behaviour.

The government is also interested in many other aspects including price stability, economic growth and compliance with laws.

Companies have a range of stakeholders, all of which can affect the company and should be considered. Some of these stakeholders are external such as the government, the general public and pressure groups.

Section 5

ANSWERS TO OBJECTIVE TEST CASE STUDY QUESTIONS – SECTION B

SPECIALIST COST AND MANAGEMENT ACCOUNTING TECHNIQUES

206   DUFF CO (JUNE 2014, ADAPTED)

1   **A**

Product	Z
Direct materials	$28.00
Direct labour	$24.00
Overhead ($9.70 × 2 DL hours)	$19.40
Full cost per unit	$71.40

2   **B**

Full budgeted production cost per unit using activity based costing

Product	X	Y	Z	Total
Budgeted annual production (units)	20,000	16,000	22,000	
Batch size	500	800	400	
Number of batches (i.e. set ups)	**40**	**20**	**55**	**115**
Number of purchase orders per batch	4	5	4	
Total number of orders	**160**	**100**	**220**	**480**
Machine hours per unit	1.5	1.25	1.4	
Total machine hours	**30,000**	**20,000**	**30,800**	**80,800**

Cost driver rates:

Cost per machine set up	$280,000/115 = $2,434.78
Cost per order	$316,000/480 = $658.33
Cost per machine hour	($420,000 + $361,400)/80,800 = $9.67

Allocation of overheads to each product:

Product	X	Y	Z	Total
	$	$	$	
Machine set up costs	**97,391**	48,696	133,913	280,000
Material ordering costs	**105,333**	65,833	144,834	316,000
Machine running and facility costs	**290,100**	193,400	297,836	781,336
Total	**492,824**	307,929	576,583	1,377,336
Number of units produced	**20,000**	16,000	22,000	
Overhead cost per unit	**$24.64**	$19.25	$26.21	

3   B

Total cost per unit:	$ per unit	$ per unit	$ per unit
Direct materials	25	22	28
Direct labour	30	36	24
Overhead	24.64	19.25	26.21
ABC cost per unit	79.64	83.25	78.21

4   D

All statements are correct.

5   B

Statement (1) is not true. When activity based costing is used, the cost for product X is very similar to that cost calculated using full absorption costing. This means that the price for product X is likely to remain unchanged, because cost plus pricing is being used.

Statement (2) is correct. Demand for product X is relatively elastic but since no change in price is expected, sales volumes are likely to remain the same if ABC is introduced.

Statement (3) is correct. The cost for product Y is almost $10 per unit less using ABC. This means that the price of product Y will go down if cost plus pricing is used.

Statement (4) is incorrect. Given that demand for product Y is also elastic, like demand for product X, a reduced selling price is likely to give rise to increased sales volumes.

207   BECKLEY HILL (JUNE 2015)

1   C

	Procedure A	Procedure B
Total cost per procedure, as per question	$2,475.85	$4,735.85
Less: Surgical time and materials (direct cost)	($1,200)	($2,640)
Less: Anaesthesia time and materials (direct cost)	($800)	($1,620)
Overhead cost per procedure	$475.85	$475.85

2   A

$$\text{Administration cost per hour} = \frac{\text{Total admin cost}}{\text{Total number of admin hours}}$$

Administration cost per hour =

$$\frac{\$1,870,160}{(1 \text{ hour} \times 14,600 \text{ procedures 'A'}) + (1.5 \text{ hours} \times 22,400 \text{ procedures 'B'}}$$

Administration cost per hour = $38.80

3   D

Tutorial note

Make sure you use the number of patient hours, not admin hours, to answer this question.

$$\text{Nursing cost per hour} = \frac{\text{Total nursing cost}}{\text{Total number of patient hours}}$$

$$\text{Nursing cost per hour} = \frac{\$6,215,616}{(24 \text{ hours} \times 14,600) + (48 \text{ hours} \times 22,400)}$$

Nursing cost per hour = $4.36 per patient hour

4   A

Only statement (1) is correct. When activity-based costing (ABC) is used, the cost for Procedure A is approximately $2,297 as compared to the approximate $2,476 currently calculated by BH. For Procedure B, the cost using ABC is approximately $4,853 as compared to the approximate current cost of $4,736. Hence, the cost of Procedure A goes down using ABC and the cost of Procedure B goes up. This reflects the fact that the largest proportion of the overhead costs is the nursing and general facility costs. Both of these are driven by the number of patient hours for each procedure. Procedure B has twice as many patient hours as Procedure A.

5   C

Both statements are correct. ABC can be a lot of work to implement, and whilst the comparative costs are different, they are not significantly different. Given that ABC is costly to implement, it may be that a similar allocation in overheads can be achieved simply by using a fairer basis to absorb the costs. If patient hours are used as the basis of absorption instead of simply dividing the overheads by the number of procedures, the costs for Procedures A and B would be $2,296 and $4,853:

$17,606,352/1,425,600 hours = $12.35 per hour.

Therefore absorption cost for A = $1,200 + $800 + (24 × $12.35) = $2,296.

Same calculation for B but with 48 hours instead.

Hence, the same result can be achieved without going to all of the time and expense of using ABC. Therefore BH should not adopt ABC but use this more accurate basis of absorbing overheads instead.

208 BOWD

1   **The third and fourth statements are correct.**

Statement (1) is not correct: ABC provides a more accurate cost per unit. As a result, future pricing, sales strategy, performance management and decision making should be improved.

Statement (2) is not correct either; the benefits obtained from ABC might not justify the costs.

2   C

Tutorial note

Make sure you read through the technical article on ABC published on the ACCA website in the Performance Management (PM) section.

Both statements are correct. Statement (1) is correct: large cost savings are likely to be found in large cost elements and, with ABC, management's attention will start to focus on how this cost could be reduced.

Statement (2) is also correct. In traditional absorption costing, standard high-volume products receive a higher amount of overhead costs than with ABC. ABC allows for the unusually high costs of support activities for low-volume products (such as relatively higher set-up costs, order processing costs and so on).

3   **$98.25**

Purchase orders: cost per order = $142,500/475 = $300

So, cost for Else = 275 orders × $300 per order = $82,500

Set up costs: Cost per set up = $31,250/125 = $250

Cost for Else = $250 × 60 = $15,000

Other: Total labour hours 4 × 1,500 + 3 × 2,000 = 12,000 hours

Cost per hour $198,000/12,000 = $16.50

Cost for Else = 2,000 × 3 × $16.50 = $99,000

Overhead cost per unit of Else: ($99,000 + $82,500 + $15,000)/2,000 units of Else = $98.25

---

4   **$40/unit**

$142,500/475 orders in total = $300 per order

Dest has 200 orders × $300 = $60,000

$60,000/1,500 units of Dest = $40

5   **B**

Absorption costing =$371,750/12,000 hours = $30.98 per hour

Cost per unit of Dest = $30.98 × 4 = $123.92. Compared to $116.83, this is a decrease of $7.09.

Option A is not correct, as it compares the original system to current ($106.21 – $123.92). Option C is not correct as it compares the original system to ABC:

$106.21 – $116.83 = $10.62.

Option D uses Incorrect hours $30.98 × 3 = $92.94 giving $92.94 – $116.83 = $23.89

209   HELOT CO (SEPTEMBER 2016)

1   **D**

Target costing does encourage looking at customer requirements early on so that features valued by customers are included, so Statement 2 is correct. It will also force the company to closely assess the design and is likely to be successful if costs are designed out at this stage rather than later once production has started, so Statement 4 is correct.

Statement 1 explains a benefit of flow cost accounting. Statement 3 explains the concept of throughput accounting.

2   **A**

Target price is $45 and the profit margin is 35% which results in a target cost of $29.25. The current estimated cost is $31.30 which results in a cost gap of $2.05.

3   **NOT APPROPRIATE, APPROPRIATE, NOT APPROPRIATE, APPROPRIATE.**

	An appropriate way to close a cost gap	Not an appropriate way to close a cost gap
Buy cheaper, lower grade plastic for the game discs and cases.		
Using standard components wherever possible in production.	√	
Employ more trainee game designers on lower salaries.		
Use the company's own online gaming websites for marketing.	√	

Using more standardised components and using its own websites for marketing will reduce processing and marketing costs.

Using cheaper materials and trainee designers will reduce costs but could impact the quality and customer perception of the product which would impact the target price.

4   C

The change in the learning rate will increase the current estimated cost which will increase the cost gap.

The target cost will be unaffected as this is based on the target selling price and profit margin; neither of which are changing.

5   B

Services do use more labour relative to materials.

The other three statements are incorrect as uniformity is not a characteristic of services, there is no transfer of ownership and although it is difficult to standardise a service due to the human influence, target costing can still be used.

Tutorial note

The characteristics of target costing in service industries are frequently highlighted by the examining team as an absolute must-know. Make sure you learn them before attempting the exam.

210   CHEMICAL FREE CLEAN CO (DECEMBER 2015)

1   A

A product or service is developed which is perceived to be needed by customers and therefore will attract adequate sales volumes. A target price is then set based on the customers' perceived value of the product. This will therefore be a market based price. The required target operating profit per unit is then calculated. This may be based on either return on sales or return on investment. The target cost is derived by subtracting the target profit from the target price. If there is a cost gap, attempts will be made to close the gap.

2

Tutorial note

Make sure you remember the five characteristics of services that make target costing more difficult in service industries: intangibility, simultaneity (in Statement 2 here), heterogeneity, perishability (in statement 4 here) and no transfer of ownership.

The second and fourth statements are correct.

3   C

Both statements are correct.

4   The second and fourth statements are correct.

Statement (1) is not correct: a dominant company will find target costing less useful than a business faced with competitive pressures.

Statement (3) is not correct either: ignoring the market price in such a competitive market will only lead to C Co's erosion of market share.

5   C

Both statements are correct.

211 SHOE CO (JUNE 2016)

1 The third and fourth statements are correct.

2 **$6,960,000**

Total sales revenue		$34,300,000
Less costs:		
Development and design costs		($5,600,000)
Patent application costs (including $20K)		($500,000)
Patent renewal costs – 2 years		($400,000)
Total material costs	[(280,000 × $16) + (420,000 × $14)]	($10,360,000)
Total labour costs	[(280,000 × $8) + (420,000 × $7)]	($5,180,000)
Fixed production overheads		($3,800,000)
Selling and distribution costs		($1,500,000)
Profit		$6,960,000

3 The third and fourth statements are correct.

Statement (1) is not correct: identifying the costs of environment-related activities is difficult. Statement (2) is not correct either: EMA generates and analyses both financial and non-financial information in order to support internal environmental management processes.

4 **C**

Expected marketing cost in year 1: (0.2 × $2.2m) + (0.5 × $2.6m) + (0.3 × $2.9m) = $2.61m

Expected marketing cost year 2: (0.3 × $1.8m) + (0.4 × $2.1m) + (0.3 × $2.3m) = $2.07m

Total expected marketing cost = $4.68m

5 **D**

212 SWEET TREATS BAKERY (DECEMBER 2016)

Tutorial note

The Examiner has reported that performance was weaker in December 2016 on this scenario question, which tested throughput accounting in a situation where resources were scarce. It was interesting that this technique involved an understanding of limiting factor analysis. Understanding is particularly lacking in this area, so make sure you give it the time it deserves in your revision plan.

1   B

Process	Available minutes	Brownies	Muffins	Cupcakes	Total minutes required
Weighing	240	60	45	100	205
Mixing	180	80	48	60	188
Baking	1,440	480	330	600	1,410

The bottleneck is the mixing process as 188 minutes are required to meet maximum demand but there are only 180 minutes available.

Note: Four batches of brownies need to be made in order to have sufficient cakes to meet maximum demand as the cakes must be made in their batch sizes.

2   A

	Brownies	Muffins	Cupcakes
Throughput contribution ($)	50	37.5	35
Mixing minutes	20	16	12
Throughput per mixing minute ($)	2.50	2.34	2.91
Ranking	2	3	1

Optimal production plan:

Fulfil customer order	Number of cakes	Mixing minutes
1 batch of cupcakes	20	12
1 batch of brownies	40	20
1 batch of muffins	30	16
General production (based on ranking)		
4 batches of cupcakes	80	48
1 batch of brownies	40	20

Therefore the bakery should produce 80 brownies, 30 muffins and 100 cupcakes.

3   WILL NOT IMPROVE, WILL IMPROVE, WILL NOT IMPROVE, WILL IMPROVE.

	Will improve the TPAR	Will not improve the TPAR
The café customer will be given a loyalty discount		
A bulk discount on flour and sugar is available from suppliers	√	
There is additional demand for the cupcakes in the market.		
The rent of the premises has been reduced for the next year.	√	

Reduction in rent and discounts on materials will reduce costs and will improve the TPAR.

Giving a customer a loyalty discount will reduce sales revenue and as a result the TPAR. Demand for cupcakes can increase but it will not impact the TPAR as demand is not the restriction.

4   C

Each oven has a capacity of eight hours and each cupcake batch takes two hours, so four extra batches can be made. Extra throughput = four batches × $35 = **$140**.

Less the hire costs will result in an additional profit of $95.

5   A

As the TPAR exceeds 1, then the throughout contribution exceeds operating costs, so Statement 1 is false. Less idle time on a non-bottleneck process would not improve the TPAR, so Statement 2 is false.

Improving efficiency during the weighing process would improve the TPAR as any actions to improve throughput on a bottleneck will improve the TPAR, so Statement 3 is true.

DECISION-MAKING TECHNIQUES

213   SIP CO

1   Upholstery fabric = $85 × 20 + $7.50 × 20 = **$1,850**

Do not include the retainer as this is paid whether or not the refurbishment goes ahead.

Galley = $4,000 + 40 × $15 + 0.9 × 2,000 = **$6,400**

This is cheaper than the new galley of $6,500

2   A

If the teak in inventory is used, the relevant cost is sale proceeds lost plus the cost of sanding – $95 + $14 = $109. This is cheaper than buying new teak. The remaining 5m will need to be bought. All the teak needs staining and the machine resetting.

Relevant cost = 5 × $109 + 5 × $110 + $4.50 × 10 + $80 = $1,220

3   Skilled labour $2,640   Unskilled labour $648

The existing skilled labour can be used costing ($25 + $6) × 100 = $3,100

OR new labour can be hired and trained costing $25 × 100 + $14 × 10 = $2,640

Take the cheaper cost.

The unskilled workers are guaranteed work for $420/$12 = 35 hours.

They are currently working $372/$12 = 31 hours. Therefore there are 4 hours per week per worker spare capacity. There are 5 workers therefore 20 hours a week will have no cost, leaving 36 hours to be paid for at time and a half.

36 × $12 × 1.5 = $648

4   Committed, Notional, Committed

	Committed	Notional
Factory rates	√	
Depreciation		√
Interest	√	

5   The second and third statements are correct.

214 HARE EVENTS (DECEMBER 2016)

1   B

Total fixed costs = $385,000

Contribution per marathon entry ($55 – $18.20) = $36.80

BEP = 10,462

Margin of safety (20,000 – 10,462)/20,000 = 47.7%

2   C

Weighted average C/S ratio (2 × $36.80) + (1.4 × $18.00)/(2 × $55) + (1.4 × $30) = $98.80/$152 = 65% BER = $385,000/65% = $592,308

3   A

Weighted average C/S ratio = 65%

Revenue to achieve target profit = $885,000/65% = $1,361,538

Marathon ($110/$152) × $1,361,538 = $985,324/$55 = 17,915 entries

Half marathon ($42/$152) × $1,361,538 = $376,214/$30 = 12,540 entries

4   WILL NOT CHANGE, WILL CHANGE.

	Will change	Will not change
Breakeven volume		√
Breakeven revenue	√	

Current contribution = $12

Current BEP = $48,000/$12 = 4,000 units

Current BER = $48,000/($12/$20) = $80,000

Revised contribution (($20 × 1.1) – ($8 × 1.1) = $13.20

Revised fixed costs = $48,000 × 1.1 = $52,800

Revised BEP = $52,800/$13.20 = 4,000 units

Revised BER = $52,800/($13.20/$22) = $88,000

The BEP has not changed but the BER has increased by 10%.

5   C

CVP analysis assumes no movement in inventory and the C/S ratio can be used to indicate the relative profitability of different products, so Statements 1 and 2 are correct.

215 CARDIO CO (DECEMBER 2015)

1   A

Statements (1) and (2) are not valid: 'the elliptical trainers made a loss in 2015' and 'the elliptical trainers made a positive contribution in the year just passed' are sunk events.

Statement (5) is not valid either: businesses evolve and the fact that the business was founded to produce and sell elliptical trainers is irrelevant in this decision.

2   B

Statement (1) is not correct: fixed costs can be incremental to a decision, and in those circumstances would be relevant. Statement (2) is not correct either: notional costs are used to make cost estimates more realistic; however, they are not real cash flows and are not considered to be relevant.

3   B

	T	C	R
	$	$	$
Selling price	1,600	1,800	1,400
Material	(430)	(500)	(360)
Labour 40%	(88)	(96)	(76)
Variable overheads	(110)	($120)	(95)
Contribution	972	1,084	869
Sales units	420	400	380
Total contribution	$408,240	$433,600	$330,220

Total contribution achieved by all three products = $408,240 + $433,600 + $330,220 = $1,172,060

Margin of safety = budgeted sales – breakeven sales

Budgeted sales revenue = $1,924,000

Fixed labour costs = {(420 × $220) + (400 × $240) + (380 × $190)} × 0.6 = $156,360.

Therefore total fixed costs = $156,360 + $55,000 = $211,360.

$$\text{Breakeven sales revenue} = \frac{\text{Fixed costs}}{\text{Weighted average C/S ratio}}$$

$$\text{Breakeven sales revenue} = \frac{\$211,360}{60.92\%}$$

Breakeven sales revenue = $346,947.

Therefore margin of safety = $1,924,000 – $346,947 = $1,577,053.

4   A

If the more profitable products are sold first, this means that the company will cover its fixed costs more quickly. Consequently, the breakeven point will be reached earlier, i.e. fewer sales will need to be made in order to break even. So, the breakeven point will be lower.

5   B

The general fixed overheads should be excluded as they are not incremental, i.e. they are not arising specifically as a result of this order. They are not sunk as they are not past costs.

216 BEFT CO

1   The first and third statements are correct.

Statement (2) is not correct – it is usually the increase in extra contribution (not profit) that the shadow price represents. Statement (4) is not correct either: uncertainty does not feature in a limiting factor analysis.

2   **A**

	Square	Oval	Clover Leaf
	$	$	$
Selling price	39.00	56.50	68.00
Variable costs:			
– materials	6.00	8.00	10.00
– labour	11.00	23.00	22.00
Variable overheads	7.00	10.50	20.00
Contribution per unit	15.00	15.00	16.00
Number of hours of painting	0.5	1.5	2.0
Contribution per painting hour:	30.00	10.00	8.00
Ranking	1st	2nd	3rd

Production: 4,000 units of Square, using 2,000 hours of painting labour, leaving 5,250 hours.

5,250 hours of labour/1.5 = 3,500 units of Oval (less than maximum demand).

3   **3,400**

	Square	Oval	Clover Leaf
	$	$	$
Cost if painted in house	5.00	12.00	16.00
Cost in sub-contracted	7.00	15.00	22.00
Saving if painted in-house	2.00	3.00	6.00
Number of hours required if painted in house	0.5	1.5	2.0
Saving per labour hour	4.00	2.00	3.00
Ranking	1st	3rd	2nd
Paint in house	500	500	500
Hours used per unit	0.5	1.5	2.0
Total hours used	250	750	1,000

Therefore, 2,000 hours used, leaving 5,250 in house hours left.

Use these hours to make 3,500 square, using 1,750 hours and leaving 3,500 hours.

Use these to make the remaining 1,300 clover leaf, taking 2,600 hours and leaving 900 hours.

These 900 hours will make 600 ovals (900/1.5), which combined with the 500 already made above gives a total production in-house of 1,100 ovals.

Hence, 3,400 ovals should be sent to sub-contractor, being the market demand of 4,500 less those made in house of 1,100.

4   D

	Square	Oval
Metal	4.00kg	5.00kg
Paint	0.5L	0.75L
Hours – painting	0.5 hrs	1.5 hrs
Maximum demand	4,000	4,500
Remove Z Co	(500)	(500)
	3,500	**4,000**

Maximum metal required = 3,500 units × 4kg + 4,000 units × 5kg = 34,000 kgs – not binding.

Maximum paint required = 3,500 units × 0.5L + 4,000 units × 0.75L = 4,750 – binding condition.

Maximum painting labour required = 3,500 units × 0.5 hrs + 4,000 units × 1.5 hrs = 7,750 – still a binding condition.

5   C

217   ALG CO (JUNE 2015)

1   D

Tutorial note

Make sure you include variable overheads in the calculation of total variable costs per unit.

Variable cost per unit is $3.

Material cost = $2,400,000/200,000 = $12 per unit.

Labour cost = $1,200,000/200,000 = $6 per unit.

Therefore, total variable cost per unit = $21.

2   A

Fixed costs = $1,400,000 – (200,000 × $3) = $800,000

3   B

To find the optimum price, we need to find the demand function.

Demand function is P = a – bx, where P = price and x = quantity.

Therefore, we must find a value for 'a' and 'b' firstly.

b = ΔP/ΔQ = 2/2,000 = 0.001 (ignore the minus sign as it is already reflected in the formula P = a – bx.)

Therefore P = a – 0.001x

Find value for 'a' by substituting in the known price and demand relationship from the question, matching 'p' and 'x' accordingly.

60 = a – (0.001 × 250,000)   60 = a – 250 310 = a, therefore P = 310 – 0.001x.

Identify MC: MC = $21 calculated in (a)

State MR: MR = 310 – 0.002x

Equate MC and MR to find x 21 = 310 – 0.002 × 0.002x = 289 x = 144,500

Substitute x into demand function to find P P = 310 – (0.001 × 144,500)

P = $165.50

4   A

If certain conditions exist, the strategy could be a suitable one for ALG Co. The conditions are as follows: – Where a product is new and different, so that customers are prepared to pay high prices in order to gain the perceived status of owning the product early. All we know about ALG Co's product is that it is 'innovative', so it may well meet this condition.

Statement (3) is not correct: where products have a short life cycle this strategy is more likely to be used, because of the need to recover development costs and make a profit quickly. ALG Co's product does only have a three-year life cycle, which does make it fairly short.

Statement (4) is not correct: where barriers to entry exist, which deter other competitors from entering the market; as otherwise, they will be enticed by the high prices being charged. These might include prohibitively high investment costs, patent protection or unusually strong brand loyalty. According to the information we have been given, high development costs were involved in this case, which would be a barrier to entry.

5   C

Price skimming, complimentary product pricing and price discrimination would work. without brand loyalty or a long shelf life then a strategy of penetration is unlikely to work. Additionally the uniqueness of the product prevents low prices.

218   JEWEL CO (JUNE 2016)

1   **4 batches**

Tutorial note

The tabular approach to finding the optimum price Jewel Co should charge is required here. In this exam, pricing questions tend to test the algebraic method (MR=MC), cost-plus and pricing strategies – the tabular method appears less frequently. However, it is impossible to answer this question using the algebraic method, because of the changing fixed costs.

The other trap to avoid here is to calculate the profit per unit for each demand level. This is meaningless for comparison, as it's better to sell 2,000 units for a profit of $1.50 per unit than 1,000 units for a profit of $2 per unit.

Total profit = Total sales revenue – total variable costs – total fixed costs

Batches sold	Total revenue	Total variable costs	Total fixed costs per month	Total profit
		$	$	$
1	1,000 units × $20 = $20,000	1,000 units × $10 = $10,000	10,000	0
2	2,000 units × $18 = $36,000	2,000 units × $8.80 = $17,600	10,000	8,400
3	3,000 units × $16 = $48,000	3,000 units × $7.80 = $23,400	12,000	12,600
4	4,000 units × $13 = $52,000	4,000 units × $6.40 = $25,600	12,000	14,400
5	5,000 units × $12 = $60,000	5,000 units × $6.40 = $32,000	14,000	14,000

The highest total profit is achieved when 4 batches (4,000 units) are sold.

2   **C**

Statement (1) is correct. Jewel Co's fixed costs fit the stepped costs definition – a type of fixed cost that is only fixed within certain levels of activity. Once the upper limit of an activity level is reached then anew higher level of fixed cost becomes relevant.

Statement (2) is also correct. Working on the principle that large cost savings are likely to be found in large cost elements, management's attention should start to focus on how these set-up costs could be reduced. Is there any reason why the headphones units have to be produced in batches of only 1,000? A batch size of 2,000 units would dramatically reduce those set-up costs.

3   B

Statement (1) is not correct. It is the algebraic model that requires a consistent relationship between price (P) and demand (Q), so that a demand equation can be established, usually in the form P = a − bQ. Similarly, there must be a clear relationship between demand and marginal cost, usually satisfied by constant variable cost per unit and constant fixed costs.

Statement (2) is correct. The model is only suitable for companies operating in a monopoly, because any 'optimum' price might become irrelevant if competitors charge significantly lower prices and as Jewel Co is only setting up an online business, it is probably not a monopoly.

4   A

5 $25

When P= 0, demand (Q) = 72,000 units

When P = $5, demand (Q) = (72,000 units − 8,000 units) = 64,000 units.

So, demand (Q) = 72,000 − 5P, where 'P is the selling price in $ (because demand will drop by 8,000 units for every $5 increase in the selling price.)

If the optimum quantity Q = 32,000 units, P = 5/8,000 (72,000 units − 32,000 units) = $25.

219   GAM CO (JUNE 2014)

1   C

Price per unit $30			
Sales volume	Profit	Probability	EV of profit
120,000	$930,000	0.4	$372,000
110,000	$740,000	0.5	$370,000
140,000	$1,310,000	0.1	$131,000
		EV of profit	$873,000

2   C

Price per unit $35			
Sales volume	Profit	Probability	EV of profit
120,000	$1,172,000	0.3	$351,600
110,000	$880,000	0.3	$264,000
140,000	$742,000	0.4	$296,800
		EV of profit	$912,400

3   B

Under the maximin rule, the decision-maker selects the alternative which maximises the minimum payoff achievable.

4   B

Under this rule, the decision-maker selects the alternative which offers the most attractive worst outcome, i.e. the alternative which maximises the minimum profit. In the case of Gam Co, this would be the price of $35 as the lowest profit here is $742,000, as compared to a lowest profit of $740,000 at a price of $30.

5   **A**

The maximax rule involves selecting the alternative ($30 or $35 selling price) that maximises the maximum payoff available, which in this case is $1,310,000. Therefore, a price per unit of $30 should be selected.

BUDGETING AND CONTROL

220 MYLO (SEPTEMBER 2016)

1   **A**

The maximin rule selects the maximum of the minimum outcomes for each supply level. For Mylo the minimum outcomes are:

450 lunches – $1,170

620 lunches – $980

775 lunches – $810

960 lunches – $740

The maximum of these is at a supply level of 450 lunches.

2   **D**

The minimax regret rule selects the minimum of the maximum regrets.

Demand level	Supply level			
	450	620	775	960
	$	$	$	$
450		190	360	430
620	442	–	217	322
775	845	403	–	230
960	1,326	884	481	–
Max regret	1,326	884	481	430

The minimum of the maximum regrets is $430, so suggests a supply level of 960 lunches.

3   **B**

Expected values do not take into account the variability which could occur across a range of outcomes; a standard deviation would need to be calculated to assess that, so Statement 2 is correct.

Expected values are particularly useful for repeated decisions where the expected value will be the long-run average, so Statement 4 is correct.

Expected values are associated with risk-neutral decision-makers. A defensive or conservative decision-maker is risk averse, so Statement 1 is incorrect.

Expected values will take into account the likelihood of different outcomes occurring as this is part of the calculation, so Statement 3 is incorrect.

4   A

This requires the calculation of the value of perfect information (VOPI).

Expected value with perfect information = (0.15 × $1,170) + (0.30 × $1,612) + (0.40 × $2,015) + (0.15 × $2,496) = $1,839.50

Expected value without perfect information would be the highest of the expected values for the supply levels = $1,648.25 (at a supply level of 775 lunches).

The value of perfect information is the difference between the expected value with perfect information and the expected value without perfect information = $1,839.50 – $1,648.25 = $191.25, therefore $191 to nearest whole $.

5   D

The investment's sensitivity to fixed costs is 550% ((385/70) × 100), so Statement 3 is correct.

The margin of safety is 84.6%. Budgeted sales are 650 units and BEP sales are 100 units (70/0.7), therefore the margin of safety is 550 units which equates to 84.6% of the budgeted sales, so Statement 4 is therefore correct.

The investment is more sensitive to a change in sales price of 29.6%, so Statement 1 is incorrect.

If variable costs increased by 44%, it would still make a very small profit, so Statement 2 is incorrect.

221   LRA (JUNE 2015)

1   C

2   C

Statement (1) is not correct: At present, the LRA finds itself facing particularly difficult circumstances. The fires and the floods have meant that urgent expenditure is now needed on schools, roads and hospitals which would not have been required if these environmental problems had not occurred. Lesting is facing a crisis situation and the main question is therefore whether this is a good time to introduce anything new at the LRA when it already faces so many challenges.

Statement (2) is not correct: the introduction of ZBB in any organisation is difficult at any time because of the fact that the process requires far more skills than, for example, incremental budgeting. Managers would definitely need some specialist training as they simply will not have the skills which they would need in order to construct decision packages. This then would have further implications in terms of time and cost, and, at the moment, both of these are more limited than ever for the LRA.

Statement (3) is correct: with ZBB, the whole budgeting process becomes a lot more cumbersome as it has to be started from scratch. There is a lot of paperwork involved and the whole process of identifying decision packages and determining their costs and benefits is extremely time-consuming. There are often too many decision packages to evaluate and there is frequently insufficient information for them to be ranked. The LRA provides a wide range of services and it is therefore obvious that this would be a really lengthy and costly process to introduce. At the moment, some residents are homeless and several schools have been damaged by fire. How can one rank one as more important than the other when both are equally important for the community?

Statement (4) is correct: ZBB can cause conflict to arise as departments compete for the resources available. Since expenditure is urgently required for schools, roads and hospitals, it is likely that these would be ranked above expenditure on the recycling scheme. In fact, the final phase of the scheme may well be postponed. This is likely to cause conflict between departments as those staff and managers involved in the recycling scheme will be disappointed if the final phase has to be postponed.

3 **A**

4 **D**

ZBB will respond to changes in the economic environment since the budget starts from scratch each year and takes into account the environment at that time. This is particularly relevant this year after the fires and the floods. Without ZBB, adequate consideration may not be given to whether the waste management scheme should continue but, if ZBB is used, the scheme will probably be postponed as it is unlikely to rank as high as expenditure needed for schools, housing and hospitals. – If any of the activities or operations at LRA are wasteful, ZBB should be able to identify these and remove them. This is particularly important now when the LRA faces so many demands on its resources. – Managers may become more motivated as they have had a key role in putting the budget together. – It encourages a more questioning attitude rather than just accepting the status quo. – Overall, it leads to a more efficient allocation of resources. – All of the organisations activities and operations are reviewed in depth.

5 **B**

222 BOKCO (JUNE 2015)

1 **B**

Statement (2) is not true: a minor error in the design of the model at any point can affect the validity of data throughout the spreadsheet. Even if the spreadsheet is properly designed in the first place, it is very easy to corrupt a model by accidentally inputting data in the wrong place.

Statement (3) is not correct either: spreadsheets cannot take account of qualitative factors that are always, by definition, difficult to quantify.

2 **A**

Statement (3) is not correct: the operational variances do give a fair reflection of the actual results achieved in the actual conditions that existed. Statement (4) is not correct either: the analysis helps in the standard-setting learning process , which will hopefully result in more useful standards in the future.

3 **D**

Revised hours for actual production: Cumulative time per hour for 460 units is calculated by using the learning curve formula: $Y = ax^b$

$a = 7$

$x = 460$

$b = -0.1520$ Therefore $y = 7 \times 460^{-0.1520} = 2.7565054$

Therefore revised time for 460 units = 1,268 hours.

Labour efficiency planning variance (Standard hours for actual production – revised hours for actual production) × std rate = ([460 × 7] – 1,268) × \$12 = \$23,424F

4   C

Labour efficiency operational variance (Revised hours for actual production – actual hours for actual production) × std rate (1,268 – 1,860) × $12 = $7,104A

5   C

Option A is not correct: there **will** be unnecessary extra labour costs. Bokco will have hired too many temporary staff because of the fact that the new product can actually be produced more quickly than originally thought. Given that these staff are hired on three-month contracts, Bokco will presumably have to pay the staff for the full three months even if all of them are not needed.

Option B is therefore not correct either: since Bokco uses cost plus pricing for its products, the price for the product will have been set too high. This means that sales volumes may well have been lower than they otherwise might have been, leading to lost revenue for the company and maybe even failure of the new product launch altogether. This will continue to be the case for the next two months unless the price review is moved forward.

Option C is correct: since production is actually happening more quickly than anticipated, the company may well have run out of raw materials, leading to a stop in production. Idle time is a waste of resources and costs money. If there have been stockouts, the buying department may have incurred additional costs for expedited deliveries or may have been forced to use more expensive suppliers. This would have made the material price variance adverse and negatively affected the buying department's manager bonus.

Option D is not correct: the sales manager will be held responsible for the poorer sales of the product, which will probably be reflected in an adverse sales volume variance. This means that he may lose his bonus through no fault of his own.

223   CORFE CO (SEPTEMBER 2016)

1   D

An 80% activity level is 210,000 units.

Material and labour costs are both variable. Material is $4 per unit and labour is $5.50 per unit. Total variable costs = $9.50 × 210,000 units = $1,995,000

Fixed costs = $750,000

Supervision = $175,000 as five supervisors will be required for a production level of 210,000 units.

Total annual budgeted cost allowance = $1,995,000 + $750,000 + $175,000 = $2,920,000

2   B

Variable cost per hour ($850,000 – $450,000)/(5,000 hours – 1,800 hours) = $125 per hour Fixed cost ($850,000 – (5,000 hours × $125)) = $225,000

Number of machine hours required for production = 210 batches × 14 hours = 2,940 hours.

Total cost ($225,000 + (2,940 hours × $125)) = $592,500, therefore $593,000 to the nearest $000.

3   **C**

If the budget is flexed, then the effect on sales revenue of the difference between budgeted and actual sales volumes is removed and the variance which is left is the sales price variance.

4   **A**

Flexible budgeting can be time-consuming to produce as splitting out semi-variable costs could be problematic, so Statement 1 is correct.

Estimating how costs behave over different levels of activity can be difficult to predict, so Statement 2 is correct. A flexible budget will not encourage slack compared to a fixed budget, so Statement 3 is incorrect.

It is a zero-based budget, not a flexible budget, which assesses all activities for their value to the organisation, so Statement 4 is incorrect.

5   **C**

Spreadsheets can be used to change input variables and new versions of the budgets can be more quickly produced, so Statement 1 is correct.

Sensitivity analysis is also easier to do as variables are more easily changed and manipulated to assess their impact, so Statement 4 is correct.

A common problem of spreadsheets is that it is difficult to trace errors in a spreadsheet and data can be easily corrupted if a cell is changed or data is input in the wrong place, so Statement 2 is incorrect.

Spreadsheets do not show qualitative factors; they show predominantly quantitative data, so Statement 3 is incorrect.

224   OBC (DECEMBER 2015)

1   **A**

	Actual quantity used	Standard price	Total
White flour	408.50 Kgs	$1.80	$735.30
Wholegrain flour	152 kgs	$2.20	$334.40
Yeast	10 kgs	$20.00	$200.00
Actual quantity at standard price (AQ SP)			**$1,269.70**
Standard quantity at standard price (SQ SP)	950 loaves	$1.34	**$1,273**
Variance			**$3.3 F**

2   **C**

Ingredient	AQAM (kgs)	AQSM (kgs)	Difference (kgs)	Standard cost ($/kgs)	Variance ($)
White flour	408.50	420.86	12.36 F	1.80	22.25 F
Wholemeal flour	152	140.29	11.71 A	2.20	25.76 A
Yeast	10	9.35	0.65 A	20	13 A
	570.5	570.5			**16.51 A**

Tutorial note

These numbers in the 'Actual Quantity – Standard Mix (AQSM)' column are calculated by taking the actual input in total (that is, 570.5 kgs) from the previous column AQAM, and copying it across to the second column AQSM. Then, work it back in the standard proportions. For example, the standard proportion for 'white flour' is 450 grams out of 610; We take that (450/610) as a proportion and multiply it by the actual total of 570.5 kgs, giving us a standard proportion for white flour, on the actual weight, of (450/610) × 570.5 = 420.89 kgs.

3   D

Tutorial note

There are many ways in which to calculate a yield variance but the easiest is the 'total' method, presented here as the first alternative.

Method 1: the 'Total' method

Actual output (given)	950 loaves
Expected output from actual input	570,500 g/610 g per loaf = 935.25 loaves
Difference	14.75 loaves F
Standard cost per loaf	$1.34
Variance	**$19.77 F**

Method 2: the 'Individual' method:

Ingredient	SQSM (kgs)	AQSM (kgs)	Difference (kgs)	Standard cost ($/kg)	Variance ($)
White flour	427.50	420.86	6.64 F	1.80	11.95 F
Wholemeal flour	142.50	140.29	2.21 F	2.20	4.86 F
Yeast	9.50	9.35	0.15 F	20	3.00 F
	579.5 kgs (*)	570.5 kgs			**19.81 F**

(*) 610 g standard weight per loaf × 950 loaves = 579,500 g or 579.5 kgs

4   B

Statement (1) is not correct: if some mix was left behind, it is the efficiency of turning the inputs into outputs that would be diminished. Therefore, it would be the yield variance that is affected, not the mix variance.

5   C

Both statements are correct: Errors in the quality or proportions of ingredients will make the items sub-standard and therefore rejected by the quality inspector.

When baked at the wrong temperature and therefore be rejected by the quality inspector if they are burnt, or undercooked.

225 VARIANCES – SALES

1 **A**

"The difference between the sales quantity and **volume** variances is that the standard **mix** is considered in the former. The difference between standard and actual is **ignored**."

2

Profit per unit =	10,600 – (10,600/1.06) = $600
Actual market size =	(30,000/0.1) × 0.95 = 285,000
Sales expected	0.1 × 285,000 = 28,500 units
Actual sales	285,000 × 0.15 = 42,750
So:	
Market size variance	(30,000 – 28,500) × $600 = **$900,000** Adverse
Market share variance	(28,500 – 42,750) × $600 = **$8,550,000** Favourable

3 **$708,000 Adverse**

4 **$2,982,000 Adverse**

For questions 3 and 4:

	AQ and AM	SP	
Drastic	26,000	600	$41,040,000
Bomber	16,000	750	
Cracker	14,000	960	
	56,000		

$708,000 Adv

	AQ and SM	SP	
Drastic	25,200	600	$41,748,000
Bomber	14,000	750	
Cracker	16,800	960	
	56,000		

$2,982,000 Adv

	SQ and SM	SP	
Drastic	27,000	600	$44,730,000
Bomber	15,000	750	
Cracker	18,000	960	
	60,000		

5 **D**

226 ROMEO CO (DECEMBER 2016)

1   B

Dough 18.9 kg × ($7.60 – $6.50) = $20.79 favourable

Tomato sauce 6.6 kg × ($2.50 – $2.45) = $0.33 favourable

Cheese 14.5 kg × ($20.00 – $21.00) = $14.50 adverse

Herbs 2 kg × ($8.40 – $8.10) = $0.60 favourable

Total material price variance = $7.22 favourable

2   D

	AQSM	AQAM	Diff	Std	Variance
	kg	kg	kg	cost	$
Dough	20	18.9	1.1 F	7.60	8.36 F
Sauce	8	6.6	1.4 F	2.50	3.50 F
Cheese	12	14.5	2.5 A	20.00	50.00 A
Herbs	2	2		8.40	
	42	42			38.14 A

3   A

	SQSM	AQSM	Diff	Std	Variance
	kg	kg	kg	cost	$
Dough	22	21.43	0.57 F	7.60	4.33 F
Sauce	8.8	8.57	0.23 F	2.50	0.58 F
Cheese	13.2	12.86	0.34 F	20.00	6.80 F
Herbs	2.2	2.14	0.06 F	8.40	0.50 F
	46.2	45			12.21 F

4   A

A favourable mix variance indicates that a higher proportion of cheaper ingredients were used in production compared to the standard mix.

5   C

The actual cost per pizza will be lower than the standard cost per pizza because expensive cheese has been replaced with cheaper tomato sauce.

The usage variance equals the mix and yield variances. The yield variance will be zero as 100 pizzas used 42 kg, so the mix and usage variances will be the same.

Sales staff should not automatically lose their bonus as the reduced sales could be a result of the change in mix affecting the quality of the pizza and the new chef will only be responsible for the mix and yield variances as they have no control over the purchase costs of ingredients.

PERFORMANCE MEASUREMENT AND CONTROL

227 PIND CO

1   **31% and 2.625**

	25%	31%	2.625	1.625
Gearing ratio		√		
Interest cover			√	

Gearing: 190,000/610,000 = 31%   Interest cover 42,000/16,000 = 2.625

2   **B**

3   **B**

4   **26 days**

Quick ratio = 0.9.

We know payables is $50,000 and therefore, receivables + cash = $45,000.

As receivables : cash is 2 : 2.5, so receivables = $20,000 and hence receivable days are: (20,000/(42,000/0.15)) × 365 = 26 days

5   **C**

Current asset turnover = turnover/capital employed = (42,000/0.15)/610,000 = 0.459

Increase turnover by 20%: ((42,000/0.15) × 1.2)/610,000 = 0.551, which is an increase of 20%.

Section 6

ANSWERS TO CONSTRUCTED RESPONSE QUESTIONS – SECTION C

SPECIALIST COST AND MANAGEMENT ACCOUNTING TECHNIQUES

228 GADGET CO (DECEMBER 2010)

(a) **Cost per unit under full absorption costing**

Total annual overhead costs:	$
Machine set up costs	26,550
Machine running costs	66,400
Procurement costs	48,000
Delivery costs	54,320
	6,900
	_____
	195,270
	_____

Overhead absorption rate:

	A	B	C	Total
Production volumes	15,000	12,000	18,000	
Labour hours per unit	0.1	0.15	0.2	
Total labour hours	1,500	1,800	3,600	6,900

Therefore, overhead absorption rate = $195,270/6,900 = $28.30 per hour

Cost per unit

	A	B	C
	$	$	$
Raw materials ($1.20 × 2/3/4 kg)	2.4	3.6	4.8
Direct labour ($14.80 × 0.1/0.15/0.2 hrs)	1.48	2.22	2.96
Overhead ($28.30 × 0.1/0.15/0.2 hrs)	2.83	4.25	5.66
	_____	_____	_____
Full cost per unit	6.71	10.07	13.42
	_____	_____	_____

(b) Cost per unit using full absorption costing

Cost drivers:

Cost pools	$	Cost driver
Machine set up costs	26,550	36 production runs (16 + 12 + 8)
Machine running costs	66,400	32,100 machine hours (7,500 + 8,400 + 16,200)
Procurement costs	48,000	94 purchase orders (24 + 28 + 42)
Delivery costs	54,320	140 deliveries (48 + 30 + 62)
	195,270	

Cost per machine set up	$26,550/36 = $737.50
Cost per machine hour	$66,400/32,100 = $2.0685
Cost per order	$48,000/94 = $510.6383
Cost per delivery	$54,320/140 = $388

Allocation of overheads to each product:

	A	B	C	Total
	$	$	$	$
Machine set up costs	11,800	8,850	5,900	26,550
Machine running costs	15,514	17,375	33,510	66,400
Procurement costs	12,255	14,298	21,447	48,000
Delivery costs	18,624	11,640	24,056	54,320
	58,193	52,163	84,913	195,270
Number of units produced	15,000	12,000	18,000	
	$	$	$	
Overhead cost per unit	3.88	4.35	4.72	

Total cost per unit	A	B	C
Materials	2.4	3.6	4.8
Labour	1.48	2.22	2.96
Overheads	3.88	4.35	4.72
	7.76	10.17	12.48

(c) **Using activity-based costing**

When comparing the full unit costs for each of the products under absorption costing as compared to ABC, the following observations can be made:

Product A

The unit cost for product A is 16% higher under ABC as opposed to traditional absorption costing. Under ABC, it is $7.76 per unit compared to $6.71 under traditional costing. This is particularly significant given that the selling price for product A is $7.50 per unit. This means that when the activities that give rise to the overhead costs for product A are taken into account, product A is actually making a loss. If the company wants to improve profitability it should look to either increase the selling price of product A or somehow reduce the costs. Delivery costs are also high, with 48 deliveries a year being made for product A. Maybe the company could seek further efficiencies here. Also, machine set up costs are higher for product A than for any of the other products, due to the larger number of production runs. The reason for this needs to be identified and, if possible, the number of production runs needs to be reduced.

Product B

The difference between the activity based cost for B as opposed to the traditional cost is quite small, being only $0.10. Since the selling price for B is $12, product B is clearly profitable whichever method of overhead allocation is used. ABC does not really identify any areas for concern here.

Product C

The unit cost for C is 7% lower under ABC when compared to traditional costing. More importantly, while C looks like it is making a loss under traditional costing, ABS tells a different story. The selling price for C is $13 per unit and, under ABC, it costs $12.48 per unit. Under traditional absorption costing, C is making a loss of $0.42 per unit. Identifying the reason for the differences in C, it is apparent that the number of production runs required to produce C is relatively low compared to the volumes produced. This leads to a lower apportionment of the machine set up costs to C than would be given under traditional absorption costing. Similarly, the number of product tests carried out on C is low relative to its volume.

ABC is therefore very useful in identifying that C is actually more profitable than A, because of the reasons identified above. The company needs to look at the efficiency that seems to be achieved with C (low number of production runs less testing) and see whether any changes can be made to A, to bring it more in line with C. Of course, this may not be possible, in which case the company may consider whether it wishes to continue to produce A and whether it could sell higher volumes of C.

Marking scheme		Marks
(a)	Contribution per unit	
	Overhead absorption rate	2
	Cost for A	1
	Cost for B	1
	Cost for C	1
		___
	Maximum	**5**
		___
(b)	Cost under ABC	
	Correct cost driver rates	5
	Correct overhead unit cost for A	1
	Correct overhead unit cost for B	1
	Correct overhead unit cost for C	1
	Correct cost per unit under ABC	1
		___
	Maximum	**9**
		___
(c)	Using ABC to improve profitability	
	One mark per point about the Gadget Co	1
		___
	Maximum	**6**
		___
Total		**20**
		___

229 BRICK BY BRICK (JUNE 2010)

(a)   Costs and quoted prices for the GC and the EX using labour hours to absorb overheads:

		GC $	EX $
Materials		3,500	8,000
Labour	300 hrs × $15/hr	4,500	
	500 hrs × $15/hr		7,500
Overheads	300 hrs × $10/hr (W1)	3,000	
	500 hrs × $10/hr		5,000
		___	___
Total cost		11,000	20,500
		___	___
Quoted price		16,500	30,750
		___	___

Workings:

(W1) Overhead absorption rate is calculated as $400,000/40,000 hrs = $10/hr

(b) Costs and quoted prices for the GC and the EX using ABC to absorb overheads:

			GC $	EX $
Materials			3,500	8,000
Labour	300 hrs × $15/hr		4,500	
		500 hrs × $15/hr		7,500
Overheads				
– Supervisor	(W2)/(W3)		180	1,080
– Planers	(W2)/(W3)		280	1,400
– Property	(W2)/(W3)		1,800	3,000
Total cost			10,260	20,980
Quoted price			15,390	31,470

(W2)

	Costs	Number of drivers	Cost per driver
Supervisor	90,000	500	180
Planners	70,000	250	280
Property	240,000	40,000	6

(W3)

	Supervisor	Planner	Property
Cost per driver (W2)	$180	$280	$6
GC	180 × 1 = 180	280 × 1 = 280	6 × 300 = 1,800
EX	180 × 6 = 1,080	280 × 5 = 1,400	6 × 500 = 3,000

(c) The pricing policy is a matter for BBB to decide. They could elect to maintain the current 50% mark-up on cost and if they did the price of the GC would fall by around 7% in line with the costs. This should make them more competitive in the market.

They could also reduce the prices by a little less than 7% (say 5%) in order to increase internal margins a little.

It is possible that the issue lies elsewhere. If the quality of the work or the reputation and reliability of the builder is questionable then reducing prices is unlikely to improve sales. It is conceivable that BBB has a good reputation for EX but not for GC, but more likely that a poor reputation would affect all products. Equally poor service levels or lack of flexibility in meeting customer needs may be causing the poor sales performance. These too will not be 'corrected' by merely reducing prices.

It is also possible that the way salesmen discuss or sell their products for the GC is not adequate so that in some way customers are being put off placing the work with BBB.

BBB is in competition and it perhaps needs to reflect this in its pricing more (by 'going rate pricing') and not seek to merely add a mark-up to its costs.

BBB could try to penetrate the market by pricing some jobs cheaply to gain a foothold. Once this has been done the completed EX or GC could be used to market the business to new customers.

The price of the EX would also need consideration. There is no indication of problems in the selling of the EX and so BBB could consider pushing up their prices by around 2% in line with the cost increase. On the figures in my answer the price goes up for a typical extension to $31,470 from $30,750 a rise of $720. This does not seem that significant and so might not lose a significant number of sales.

The reliability and reputation of a builder is probably more important than the price that they charge for a job and so it is possible that the success rate on job quotes may not be that price sensitive.

(d) Marginal costs are those costs that are incurred as a consequence of the job being undertaken. In this case they would include only the materials and the labour. If overheads are included then this is known as total absorption costing.

Overheads are for many businesses fixed by nature and hence do not vary as the number of jobs changes. In a traditional sense any attempt to allocate costs to products (by way of labour hours for example) would be arbitrary with little true meaning being added to the end result. The overhead absorption rate (OAR) is merely an average of these costs (over labour hours) and is essentially meaningless. This switch (to marginal costing) would also avoid the problem of the uncertainty of budget volume. Budget volume is needed in order to calculate the fixed cost absorption rate.

The marginal cost (MC) is more understandable by managers and indeed customers and a switch away from total absorption cost (TAC) could have benefits in this way. Clearly if overheads are going to be excluded for the cost allocations then they would still have to be covered by way of a bigger margin added to the costs. In the end all costs have to be paid for and covered by the sales in order to show a profit.

A more modern viewpoint is that activity causes costs to exist. For example, it is the existence of the need for site visits that gives rise to the need for a supervisor and therefore, for his costs. If the activities that drive costs are identified, more costs can then be directly traced to products, hence eradicating the need for arbitrary apportionment of many overhead costs. This has the benefit of all costs being covered, rather than the potential shortfall that can arise if marginal cost plus pricing is used.

In the long run businesses have to cover all costs including fixed overheads in order to make a profit, whichever pricing strategy is adopted.

230 JOLA PUBLISHING CO (JUNE 2008)

Key answer tips

Candidates will be expected to understand why overhead allocation differs between activity based costing and traditional absorption costing. The examiner is unlikely to test only the numbers.

(a) The first thing to point out is that the overhead allocations to the two products have not changed by that much. For example the CB has absorbed only $0.05 more overhead. The reason for such a small change is that the overheads are dominated by property costs (75% of total overhead) and the 'driver' for these remains machine hours once the switch to ABC is made. Thus no difference will result from the switch to ABC in this regard.

The major effect on the cost will be for quality control. It is a major overhead (23% of total) and there is a big difference between the relative number of machine hours for each product and the number of inspections made (the ABC driver). The CB takes less time to produce than the TJ, due to the shortness of the book. It will therefore carry a smaller amount of overhead in this regard. However, given the high degree of government regulation, the CB is subject to 'frequent' inspections whereas the TJ is inspected only rarely. This will mean that under ABC the CB will carry a high proportion of the quality control cost and hence change the relative cost allocations.

The production set up costs are only a small proportion of total cost and would be, therefore, unlikely to cause much of a difference in the cost allocations between the two products. However this hides the very big difference in treatment. The CB is produced in four long production runs, whereas the TJ is produced monthly in 12 production runs. The relative proportions of overhead allocated under the two overhead treatments will be very different. In this case the TJ would carry much more overhead under ABC than under a machine hours basis for overhead absorption.

Tutorial note

Many candidates demonstrated an understanding of this area but failed to get enough depth to score a good mark. There are thirteen minutes available, which should be sufficient time to plan and write up a succinct and relevant answer. Rather than just discussing overheads in general, a good approach would be to review each of the three overhead costs in turn. It should be possible to get two marks for the discussion of each overhead. A general introduction and overall conclusion would gain another two marks.

(b)   Cost per unit calculation using machine hours for overhead absorption

	CB ($)		TJ ($)
Paper (400g at $2/kg)	0.80	(100g at $1/kg)	0.10
Printing (50 ml at $30/ltr)	1.50	(150 ml at $30/ltr)	4.50
Machine cost (6 mins at $12/hr)	1.20	(10 mins at $12/hr)	2.00
Overheads (6 mins at $24/hr) (W1)	2.40	(10 mins at $24/hr)	4.00
	———		———
Total cost	5.90		10.60
Sales price	9.30		14.00
	———		———
Margin	3.40		3.40
	———		———

Workings:

(W1) Workings for overheads:

Total overhead $2,880,000

Total machine hours (1,000,000 × 6 mins) + (120,000 × 10 mins) = 7,200,000 mins

= 120,000 hours

Cost per hour   = $2,880,000 ÷120,000

= $24 per hour

	CB ($)		TJ ($)
Paper (400g at $2/kg)	0.80	(100g at $1/kg)	0.10
Printing (50 ml at $30/ltr)	1.50	(150 ml at $30/ltr)	4.50
Machine cost (6 mins at $12/hr)	1.20	(10 mins at $12/hr)	2.00
Overheads (W2)	2.41	(W2)	3.88
Total cost	5.91		10.48
Sales price	9.30		14.00
Margin	3.39		3.52

(c) **Cost per unit calculations under ABC**

(W2) Working for ABC overheads — alternative approach

	Total $	CB $	TJ $	No of drivers	Cost/ driver	CB $	TJ $
Property costs	2,160,000	1,800,000	360,000	120,000	18/hr	1.80	3.00
Quality control	668,000	601,200	66,800	200	3340/ inspection	0.6012	0.56
Production set up	52,000	13,000	39,000	16	3250/ run	0.013	0.325
Total	2,880,000	2,414,200	465,800	Cost per unit		2.41	3.88
Production level		1,000,000	120,000				
Cost per unit		2.41	3.88				

The above overheads have been split on the basis of the following activity levels:

	Driver	CB	TJ
Property costs	Machine hours	100,000	20,000
Quality control	Inspections	180	20
Production set up	Set ups	4	12

A cost per driver approach is also acceptable.

Tutorial note

Ensure your answer is well laid out in a logical manner so you get follow- through marks, even if you make a silly error earlier on.

Note: The original question asked for implementation problems. The suggested solution is as follows:

There are many problems with ABC, which, despite its academic superiority, cause issues on its introduction.

- Lack of understanding: ABC is not fully understood by many managers and therefore is not fully accepted as a means of cost control.

- Difficulty in identifying cost drivers: In a practical context, there are frequently difficulties in identifying the appropriate drivers. For example, property costs are often significant and yet a single driver is difficult to find.

- Lack of appropriate accounting records: ABC needs a new set of accounting records, this is often not immediately available and therefore resistance to change is common. The setting up of new cost pools is needed which is time consuming.

	Marking scheme		
			Marks
(a)	Comment on rent and rates		2
	Comment on quality control		2
	Comment on production set up cost		2
	Comment on overall effect		1
		Maximum	**7**
(b)	Paper cost CB		½
	Paper cost TJ		½
	Printing ink cost CB		½
	Printing ink cost TJ		½
	Machine cost CB		½
	Machine cost TJ		½
	Overhead OAR		½
	Overhead cost CB		½
	Overhead cost TJ		½
	Margins		½
		Maximum	**5**
(c)	Split of rent and rates		2
	Split of quality control		2
	Split of production set up cost		2
	Overhead cost per unit CB		½
	Overhead cost per unit TJ		½
	Direct cost as above		1
		Maximum	**8**
Total			**20**

Examiner's comments (extract)

An activity based costing question. As is common with my questions I facilitated a commentary on some calculations already done (in part a) and then followed that up with a requirement to some calculations themselves parts (b) and (c).

In part (a) some candidates misread the requirement and gave text book explanations of the process involved in ABC. This gained very few marks. The old adage of 'answer the question' would have served well here. Vague references to 'activities' without referring to the specific activities in the question gained only a few marks. I wanted candidates to explain why these products costs had changed following the introduction of ABC.

Parts (b) and (c) were extremely well done by many.

Part (d) (i.e. the additional requirement) also produced some good answers. The requirement asked for implementation problems not merely "issues" and so marks were lost through poor focus.

---

231 ABKABER PLC

Key answer tips

Part (a) is a routine calculation of profit using ABC and traditional methods

Part (b) asks for a discussion of ABC for Abkaber. It is vital that you relate as many of your points as possible to the specific circumstances given.

(a)   (i)   Absorption costing using labour hour absorption rate

Total overhead cost	=	$2,400,000 + $6,000,000 + $3,600,000
	=	$12,000,000
Total labour hours	=	200,000 + 220,000 + 80,000
	=	500,000
Overhead absorption rate/labour hour	=	$12,000,000/500,000 = $24

	Sunshine	Roadster	Fireball
Units of production and sale	2,000	1,600	400
Direct labour hours	200,000	220,000	80,000
	$	$	$
Direct labour ($5/hour)	1,000,000	1,100,000	400,000
Materials (at $400/600/900)	800,000	960,000	360,000
Overheads ($24/direct labour hour)	4,800,000	5,280,000	1,920,000
	————	————	————
Total costs	6,600,000	7,340,000	2,680,000
	————	————	————

	Sunshine	Roadster	Fireball
	$	$	$
Cost per unit	3,300	4,587.5	6,700
Selling price	4,000	6,000.0	8,000
Profit/(loss) per unit	700	1,412.5	1,300
Total profit/(loss) per product	1,400,000	2,260,000	520,000

Total profit = $4,180,000

(ii) **Activity Based Costing**

Number of deliveries to retailers	100 + 80 + 70	=	250
Charge rate for deliveries	$2,400,000/250	=	$9,600
Number of set-ups	35 + 40 + 25	=	100
Charge rate for set-ups	$6,000,000/100	=	$60,000
Number of purchase orders	400 + 300 + 100	=	800
Charge rate for purchase orders	$3,600,000/800	=	$4,500

	Sunshine	Roadster	Fireball
Units of production and sale	2,000	1,600	400
	$	$	$
Direct labour (as above)	1,000,000	1,100,000	400,000
Materials (as above)	800,000	960,000	360,000
Overheads:			
Deliveries at $9,600 (100:80:70)	960,000	768,000	672,000
Set-ups at $60,000 (35:40:25)	2,100,000	2,400,000	1,500,000
Purchase orders at $4,500 (400:300:100)	1,800,000	1,350,000	450,000
Total costs	6,660,000	6,578,000	3,382,000

	Sunshine	Roadster	Fireball
	$	$	$
Cost per unit	3,330	4,111.25	8,455
Selling price	4,000	6,000.00	8,000
Profit/(loss) per unit	670	1,888.75	(455)
Total profit/(loss) per product	$1,340,000	$3,022,000	$(182,000)

Total profit = $4,180,000

(b) **The Finance Director**

Using the labour hours method of allocation, the Fireball makes an overall profit of $520,000 but using ABC it makes a loss of $182,000. There is a significant difference in the levels of cost allocated, and so in profitability, between the two methods.

The major reason for the difference appears to be that while labour hours are not all that significant for Fireball production, the low volumes of Fireball sales cause a relatively high amount of set-ups, deliveries and purchase processes, and this is recognised by ABC.

If the Fireball model is to continue, a review of the assembly and distribution systems may be needed in order to reduce costs.

The Marketing Director

The marketing director suggests that ABC may have a number of problems and its conclusions should not be believed unquestioningly. These problems include:

- For decisions such as the pricing of the new motorbike rental contract, what is really needed is the incremental cost to determine a break-even position. While ABC may be closer to this concept than a labour hours allocation basis, its accuracy depends upon identifying appropriate cost drivers.

- There may be interdependencies between both costs and revenues that ABC is unlikely to capture. Where costs are truly common to more than one product then this may be difficult to capture by any given single activity.

- As with labour hours allocations it is the future that matters. Any relationship between costs and activities based upon historic experience and observation may be unreliable as a guide to the future.

The Managing Director

- ABC normally assumes that the cost per activity is constant as the number of times the activity is repeated increases. In practice there may be a learning curve, such that costs per activity are non-linear. As a result, the marginal cost of increasing the number of activities is not the same as the average.

- Also in this case, fixed costs are included which would also mean that the marginal cost does not equal the average cost.

- The MD is correct in stating that some costs do not vary with either labour hours or any cost driver, and thus do not fall easily under ABC as a method of cost attribution as there is no cause and effect relationship. Depreciation on the factory building might be one example.

The Chairman

From a narrow perspective of reporting profit, it is true that the two methods give the same overall profit of $4,180,000, as is illustrated in answer (a). There are, however, a number of qualifications to this statement:

- If the company carried inventory then the method of cost allocation would, in the short term at least, affect inventory values and thus would influence profit.

- If the ABC information can be relied on as a method of identifying overhead costs that vary with activity, a decision might be taken to cease Fireball production, as it generates a negative profit of $182,000. This 'loss' was not apparent using traditional absorption costing and a direct labour hour absorption rate. Although we do not know the extent to which overheads would be reduced by ceasing production of fireball, ABC suggests that there is a possibility that closure would improve profitability, by up to $182,000 each year.

232 LIFECYCLE COSTING

(a) It is generally accepted that most products will have quite a distinct product life cycle, as illustrated below:

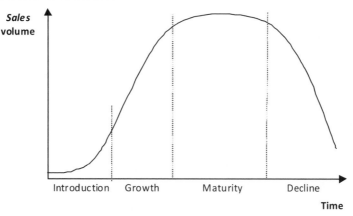

At the **introductory stage** the product is launched. It success depends upon awareness and trial of the product by consumers; this stage is likely to be accompanied by extensive marketing and promotion. A high level of set-up costs will already have been incurred by this stage, including research and development, product design and building of production facilities.

If the product is accepted, it will move into the **growth stage,** where sales volume increases dramatically; unit costs fall as fixed costs are recovered over greater volumes. Marketing and promotion will continue through this stage.

As market saturation is approached, with sales growth slowing, the product is entering its **maturity stage.** Initially profits will continue to increase, as initial set-up and fixed costs are recovered and marketing and distribution economies achieved. However, price competition and product differentiation will start to erode profitability as firms compete for the limited new customers remaining.

Eventually, in the **decline stage,** the product will move towards obsolescence as it is replaced by new and better alternatives. The product will be abandoned when profits fall to an unacceptable level, or when further capital commitment is required. Meanwhile, a replacement product will need to have been developed, incurring new levels of R&D and other product set-up costs.

In an advanced manufacturing environment, where products have low labour content, and are designed to make use of standard components and minimise wastage, rectification and warranty costs, the direct unit cost is relatively low. A very high proportion of the total costs over the product's life cycle will be in the form of initial development, design and production set-up costs, and ongoing fixed costs that are committed to at this stage.

In addition, in a globally competitive market, product life cycles are decreasing, making initial costs even more disproportionate in the early stages. The time scale between launch of one product and commencement of development of its successor can be very short, as can be seen in the modern car and computer industries. The recognition of product life cycles, with corresponding strategic planning of new development, marketing and finance, is of great importance for modern businesses.

(b) The commitment of a high proportion of a product's life cycle costs at the very early stages of the cycle has led to the need for accounting systems that compare the revenues from a product with all the costs incurred over the entire product life cycle.

Life cycle costing (LCC) is such a system, tracking and accumulating the actual costs and revenues attributable to each product from inception to abandonment. In this way, the final profitability of a given product is determined at the end of its life, whilst accumulated costs at any stage can be compared with life-cycle budgeted costs, product by product, for the purposes of planning and control.

Comparing this approach with the more traditional management accounting practices:

- Most accounting reporting systems are based upon periodic accounts, reporting product profitability in isolated calendar-based amounts, rather than focusing on the revenues and costs accumulated over the life cycle to date

- Recognition of the commitment needed over the entire life cycle of a product will generally lead to more effective resource allocation than the traditional annual budgeting system

- R&D, design, production set-up, marketing and customer service costs are traditionally reported on an aggregated basis for all products and recorded as a period expense. Life cycle costing traces these costs to individual products over their entire life cycles, to aid comparison with product revenues generated in later periods

- Relationships between early decisions re product design and production methods and ultimate costs can therefore be identified and used for subsequent planning.

(c) Activity Based Management (ABM) systems focus on the underlying causes of costs, the activities of the business. These would include design, production scheduling, set up, marketing and servicing. Costs are collected and reported by activity, through the use of cost drivers in Activity Based Costing (ABC).

The benefits arising from adoption of ABM include:

- better understanding of costs and their causes, leading to more effective cost management

- use of this information at the planning stage can lead to better use of resources

- highlights opportunities to reduce or eliminate non value-adding activities – e.g. by the introduction of quality control systems that will reduce product rectification work and handling of customer complaints etc

- the product value-analysis process that will often be part of ABM leads to improved product design, increased use of standard components, more efficient use of material and labour, which will all add to cost reductions

- identification of cost driver rates gives a measure of the cost efficiency of activities, which may be used in performance appraisal and comparison between similar activities in different areas of the business.

Note: Any TWO relevant benefits are acceptable

233 MANPAC

(a)   Life cycle costing

According to Bromwich and Bhimani, life cycle costing is the accumulation of costs for activities that occur over the entire life cycle of a product, from inception to abandonment.

If this were to apply to MANPAC then, from the moment the creators of the game thought about writing an interactive 3D game, any time and costs spent on the project should have been charged to the product. One would expect computer games products to incur very significant design and development costs. All design costs should be specifically charged to the MANPAC.

In order to maximise benefits over the life cycle of the MANPAC, life cycle costing advocates the following:

- Minimise time to the market: the MANPAC is the first of its kind to be launched. In order to gain dominance in the market it would be important to launch the product as far ahead of the competition as possible. It is easier to be a market leader if there is little or no competition.

- Maximise the length of the life cycle: this may be done by staggering the launch in different markets, segmenting the product in the future, selling accessories to the product, for example the MANPAC may be upgraded by superior software half way through its life.

- Design costs out of the product: 80 to 90% of a product's cost are committed at the design stage. In order to maximise benefit over the whole life cycle the product must be designed in a cost conscious manner with a view to the longer term impact on a product's costs.

Target costing

Currently SY Company uses cost-plus pricing. This is a push or bottom-up system starting with a forecast cost per unit, onto which a mark-up is added in order to calculate the selling price. Target costing is a pull system.

Target costing consists of several steps:

(i)   Start by understanding the market place. What sort of computer game might customers desire? And, importantly, how much are customers prepared to pay for the product?

(ii)   Once this target price has been determined, the required long-term profit margin must be established.

(iii)　In order to reach the target cost, simply deduct the profit margin from the target price.

(iv)　It is only once the target cost has been agreed that the design team can begin their work. The MANPAC must be designed within a pre-determined cost ceiling.

(v)　When designing the product it will be important to consider areas such as:

- Minimise the number of components

- Use common parts where possible. What existing products use components that can also be used on MANPAC?

- Consider extra features and accessories that may be included

- How will the product be packaged?

It is essential that during manufacturing the target cost is achieved at all times. Staff must accept the cost and then do everything within their power to ensure the cost is achieved. Staff must accept responsibility for achieving the cost.

(b)　When launching a brand new innovative product that is the first on the market, there are generally two strategies that may be employed:

Penetration pricing

This is where the product is launched at a very low price in order to gain rapid acceptance of the product.

Penetration pricing may be used for several reasons:

- To encourage customers to try a new and different product

- To discourage competition (profit margins are very low)

- If demand is very elastic, a low price generates a very high demand

- If there are significant economies of scale to be gained from high volume.

Market skimming

Here the product is launched at a very high price.

This policy may be successful in the following circumstances:

- If the new product is very different and ground-breaking, some customers are willing to pay a high price at the beginning of the product's life cycle

- If demand is totally unknown upon launch. If the skimming price is too high it can always be lowered

- If demand is very inelastic

- If the product has a relatively short life cycle. The manufacturers have very little time to recover the development costs and to generate a profit on the product.

It seems likely that the MANPAC should have launched at a market skimming (very high) price. There are several reasons for this:

- Development costs are huge

- Product life cycle is relatively short – two or three years perhaps

- Sales volumes are unlikely to be massive

- Hence, each unit sold is likely to be required to generate a reasonable profit in order to recover the design costs from a few units in a short space of time

- The product is innovative – it is a 3D interactive game – and some customers will be prepared to pay an extremely high price in the early stages in order to be one-up on their peers. If people are prepared to pay a high price, then perhaps SY Company should charge one.

(c) The product life cycle of the MANPAC is likely to be broken down into four stages.

(1)   Introduction

The product is introduced to the market. The product has been designed, developed and packaged. Several million pounds will have already have been spent on MANPAC up to this point.

Advertising and marketing: when the product is first launched on the market, demand is likely to be small. Lack of familiarity with the new product and its sources of availability will militate against large initial sales, and it will usually be necessary to spend heavily on advertising to bring the product to the attention of potential customers.

Pricing: as discussed previously MANPAC should perhaps have launched at a very high price.

A combination of relatively high unit costs, relatively low sales volume, and the potential problem of rejection by the market conspire to make this the riskiest stage in the life cycle.

(2)   Growth

Assuming the product successfully negotiates the perils of the introduction stage, it will enter the growth phase, where demand for the product increases steadily and average costs fall with the economies of scale that accompany the greater production volume. This stage should offer the greatest potential for profit to the producer, despite the fact that competitors will be prompted to enter the growing market.

Pricing decisions: as competition begins to increase in order to maintain market share, it is likely that the retail price of MANPAC will have to fall.

Advertising and marketing: SY Company should spend heavily on advertising and will try to increase brand awareness in the market place.

Cost reduction and control: as volumes increase and unit costs begin to fall, managers should avoid assuming that the product is cost efficient. The target cost (if used) should continually be reduced during this stage and staff should continue to develop new cost efficient production methods.

(3)   Maturity

By this stage the MANPAC will have reached the mass market and the increase in demand will begin to slow down. The sales curve will flatten out and eventually start to decline. Profitability will generally be at a lower level than in the growth phase.

Pricing: as competition is at its keenest in this stage, it is likely that the price of the game will be at its lowest.

Marketing and advertising: in order to maintain market share, managers must continue to spend on advertising. The emphasis may well be on increasing brand loyalty and developing a sense of prestige/quality associated with the MANPAC game.

Product development: in order to generate higher profits, SY Company may try to extend this phase in the product's life cycle. The product may be modified or improved, as a means of sustaining its demand. Managers may try to reach new market segments.

Cost reduction and control: the unit cost should be at its lowest during this phase. It remains important for the manufacturing process to remain lean and well managed.   A value analysis exercise may be undertaken on an ad-hoc basis.

(4)   Decline

The fall in sales accelerates when the market reaches saturation point. It is likely that new technology will mean that superior interactive games are being launched. Although it is still possible to make profits for a short period during this stage, it is only a matter of time before the rapidly dwindling sales volumes herald the onset of losses for all producers who remain in the market. The product has effectively reached the end of its life cycle and more profitable opportunities must be sought elsewhere.

The final decision that must be reached is when to withdraw the product from the market.

Note: Only ONE issue is required for each stage.

234 WARGRIN (DECEMBER 2008)

(a)   Lifecycle costing is a concept which traces all costs to a product over its complete lifecycle, from design through to cessation. It recognises that for many products there are significant costs to be incurred in the early stages of its lifecycle. This is probably very true for Wargrin Limited. The design and development of software is a long and complicated process and it is likely that the costs involved would be very significant.

The profitability of a product can then be assessed taking all costs in to consideration.

It is also likely that adopting lifecycle costing would improve decision-making and cost control. The early development costs would have to be seen in the context of the expected trading results therefore preventing a serious over spend at this stage or under pricing at the launch point.

Key answer tips

Easy marks were available for an explanation of this core costing technique. Common errors included candidates confusing lifecycle costing with the product life cycle and/ or a lack of discussion of lifecycle costing within the context of the scenario.

(b) **Budgeted results for game**

	Year 1 ($)	Year 2 ($)	Year 3 ($)	Total ($)
Sales	240,000	480,000	120,000	840,000
Variable cost (W1)	40,000	80,000	20,000	140,000
Fixed cost (W1)	80,000	120,000	80,000	280,000
Marketing cost	60,000	40,000		100,000
Profit	60,000	240,000	20,000	320,000

On the face of it the game will generate profits in each of its three years of life. Games only have a short lifecycle as the game players are likely to become bored of the game and move on to something new.

The pattern of sales follows a classic product lifecycle with poor levels of sales towards the end of the life of the game.

The stealth product has generated $320,000 of profit over its three year life measured on a traditional basis. This represents 40% of turnover – ahead of its target. Indeed it shows a positive net profit in each of its years on existence.

The contribution level is steady at around 83% indicating reasonable control and reliability of the production processes. This figure is better than the stated target.

Considering traditional performance management concepts, Wargrin Limited is likely to be relatively happy with the game's performance.

However, the initial design and development costs were incurred and were significant at $300,000 and are ignored in the annual profit calculations. Taking these into consideration the game only just broke even making a small $20,000 profit. Whether this is enough is debatable, it represents only 2.4% of sales for example. In order to properly assess the performance of a product the whole lifecycle needs to be considered.

Workings

(W1) Split of variable and fixed cost for Stealth

	Volume	Cost $
High	14,000 units	150,000
Low	10,000 units	130,000
Difference	4,000 units	20,000

Variable cost per unit = $20,000/4,000 unit = $5 per unit

Total cost = fixed cost + variable cost

$150,000 = fixed cost + (14,000 × $5)

$150,000 = fixed cost + $70,000

Fixed cost = $80,000 (and $120,000 if volume exceeds 15,000 units in a year.)

Key answer tips

Candidates must be comfortable with the high low method. The examiner is keen to test techniques such as this within the context of a longer calculation question. Good candidates ignored the design and development costs (a sunk cost).

Candidates needed to leave enough time to interpret the calculations and to discuss the expected performance of the game. Almost half of the marks were available for the written points.

(c)   Incremental budgeting is a process whereby this year's budget is set by reference to last year's actual results after an adjustment for inflation and other incremental factors. It is commonly used because:

- It is quick to do and a relatively simple process.

- The information is readily available, so very limited quantitative analysis is needed.

- It is appropriate in some circumstances. For example in a stable business the amount of stationery spent in one year is unlikely to be significantly different in the next year, so taking the actual spend in year one and adding a little for inflation should be a reasonable target for the spend in the next year.

There are problems involved with incremental budgeting:

- It builds on wasteful spending. If the actual figures for this year include overspends caused by some form of error then the budget for the next year would potentially include this overspend again.

- It encourages organisations to spend up to the maximum allowed in the knowledge that if they don't do this then they will not have as much to spend in the following year's budget.

- Assessing the amount of the increment can be difficult.

- It is not appropriate in a rapidly changing business.

- Can ignore the true (activity based) drivers of a cost leading to poor budgeting.

Key answer tips

Easy marks were available here. Candidates must be aware of all of the different approaches to budgeting together with their pros and cons.

Note: The original question also required a discussion of the setting of a meaningful standard. The suggested solution is shown below:

Design and development costs: Setting a standard cost for this classification of cost would be very difficult. Presumably each game would be different and present the program writers with different challenges and hence take a varying amount of time.

Variable production cost: A game will be produced on a CD or DVD in a fairly standard format. Each CD/DVD will be identical and as a result setting a standard cost would be possible. Allowance might need to be made for waste or faulty CDs produced. Some machine time will be likely and again this should be the same for all items and therefore setting a standard would be valid.

Fixed production cost: The standard fixed production cost of a game will be the product of the time taken to produce the game and the standard fixed overhead absorption rate for the business. This brings into question whether this is 'meaningful'. Allocating fixed costs to products in a standard way may not provide meaningful data. It can sometimes imply a variability (cost per unit) that is not the case and can therefore confuse non-accountants, causing poor decisions. The time per unit will be fairly standard.

Marketing costs: Games may have different target audiences and therefore require different marketing strategies. As such setting a standard may be difficult to do. It may be possible to set standards for each marketing media chosen. For example the rates for a page advert in a magazine could be set as a standard.

	Marking scheme		
			Marks
(a)	Performance assessment over whole life cycle		1.0
	Improved decision making/ cost control		1.0
	Relate to Wargrin		2.0
		Maximum	**4.0**
(b)	Sales		1.0
	Variable cost		1.0
	Fixed cost		2.0
	Marketing cost		1.0
	Comments on profit performance (against standard targets)		2.0
	Consideration of all lifecycle costs		2.0
		Maximum	**9.0**
(c)	Why incremental budgeting common – 1 mark per idea (max 3)		3.0
	Problems of incremental budgets – 1 mark per idea (max 4)		4.0
		Maximum	**7.0**
Total			**20**

Examiner's comments (extract)

Question 4 was partly based on lifecycle costing, which is not a topic that has been examined that often in other exams or indeed syllabi. This probably means a lack of good questions in the materials. As a result I did try and keep this question straightforward.

In part (a) a very large number of candidates confused life cycle costing with the product lifecycle. I was treated to large numbers of PLC diagrams and long winded explanations of the different stages of it. Most of which scored no marks at all. I did give credit if the PLC discussion stumbled into mentions of the costs.

The calculations in part (b) were quite well done by most. This was expected as it was far from difficult. The high low overhead calculation should have been a gift as this topic is fully examined at F2. A depressing number of candidates could not handle the stepped fixed cost aspect however. Part (b) also asked for an assessment of performance and I provided targets for net profit % and contribution %. The number of candidates that simply ignored these targets in the assessment of performance was staggering. Far too many simply provided a description of the figures (sales have gone up in the second year by x%, but then fall again in year 3). This is not an assessment of performance! Too many missed the point completely that the game's performance looked good until the initial development costs were included. This is the whole point behind lifecycle costing.

Part (c) should have been a gift of 6 marks and certainly for around 30% of candidates it was. This should have been nearer 70% of candidates. Some did not even know what incremental budgeting was, getting it confused with some form of rolling budget. I was amazed at this, as this is pure knowledge that some simply do not have.

Part (d) (i.e. the additional requirement) seemed to baffle almost all marginal and below candidates. This question asked is the standard "meaningful"? You can set standards for everything but not all would have meaning. For example the development time for a game could not really be standardised. Games would, presumably, be very different in their complexity and hence would take significantly different amounts of time to develop. This concept was not understood by the majority. Most also ignored my suggestion in the question to consider each of the cost classifications in turn, which is poor technique.

235 EDWARD CO (DECEMBER 2007) *Walk in the footsteps of a top tutor*

Key answer tips

This was an in-depth question on target costing that was done poorly by many students. The examiner has made it very clear that he will examine these themes again!

(a) Target costing process

Target costing begins by specifying a product an organisation wishes to sell. This will involve extensive customer analysis, considering which features customers value and which they do not. Ideally only those features valued by customers will be included in the product design.

The price at which the product can be sold at is then considered. This will take in to account the competitor products and the market conditions expected at the time that the product will be launched. Hence a heavy emphasis is placed on external analysis before any consideration is made of the internal cost of the product.

From the above price a desired margin is deducted. This can be a gross or a net margin. This leaves the cost target. An organisation will need to meet this target if their desired margin is to be met.

Costs for the product are then calculated and compared to the cost target mentioned above.

If it appears that this cost cannot be achieved then the difference (shortfall) is called a cost gap. This gap would have to be closed, by some form of cost reduction, if the desired margin is to be achieved.

Tutorial note

Easy marks were available here and a well prepared candidate should have been able to score full marks. Aim for at least three well explained points. Separate each point out using headings or a new paragraph. This will make it easier for the marker to review. The following headings could have been used:

(1) Estimate selling price

(2) Deduct required profit

(3) Calculate target cost

(4) Close Gap

(b)

Tutorial note

This section was more challenging and required the application of book knowledge. Brainstorm ideas first. This should focus attention on thinking of enough separate points and should help to give your answer a natural structure. This is the hard part done. It should then be fairly straightforward to write up the answer in the time remaining.

Benefits of adopting target costing

- The organisation will have an early external focus to its product development. Businesses have to compete with others (competitors) and an early consideration of this will tend to make them more successful. Traditional approaches (by calculating the cost and then adding a margin to get a selling price) are often far too internally driven.

- Only those features that are of value to customers will be included in the product design. Target costing at an early stage considers carefully the product that is intended. Features that are unlikely to be valued by the customer will be excluded. This is often insufficiently considered in cost plus methodologies.

- Cost control will begin much earlier in the process. If it is clear at the design stage that a cost gap exists then more can be done to close it by the design team. Traditionally, cost control takes place at the 'cost incurring' stage, which is often far too late to make a significant impact on a product that is too expensive to make.

- Costs per unit are often lower under a target costing environment. This enhances profitability. Target costing has been shown to reduce product cost by between 20% and 40% depending on product and market conditions. In traditional cost plus systems an organisation may not be fully aware of the constraints in the external environment until after the production has started. Cost reduction at this point is much more difficult as many of the costs are 'designed in' to the product.

- It is often argued that target costing reduces the time taken to get a product to market. Under traditional methodologies there are often lengthy delays whilst a team goes 'back to the drawing board'. Target costing, because it has an early external focus, tends to help get things right first time and this reduces the time to market.

(c) **Cost per unit and cost gap calculation**

	$ per unit
Component 1	
$(4.10 + \dfrac{\$2,400}{4,000\,\text{units}})$	4.70
Component 2	
$(\dfrac{25}{100} \times 0.5 \times \dfrac{100}{98})$	0.128
Material – other	8.10
Assembly labour	
$(\dfrac{30}{60} \times \$12.60/\text{hr} \times \dfrac{100}{90})$	7.00
Variable production overhead (W1)	
$(\dfrac{30}{60} \times \$20/\text{hr})$	10.00
Fixed production overhead (W1)	
$(\dfrac{30}{60} \times \$12/\text{hr})$	6.00
	———
Total cost	35.928
Desired cost ($44 × 0.8)	35.20
	———
Cost gap	0.728
	———

Working 1: Production overhead cost. Using a high low method

Extra overhead cost between month 1 and 2	$80,000
Extra assembly hours	4,000
Variable cost per hour	$20/hr
Monthly fixed production overhead	
$700,000 – (23,000 × $20/hr)	$240,000
Annual fixed production overhead ($240,000 × 12)	$2,880,000
FPO absorption rate $\dfrac{\$2,880,000}{240,000\ \text{hrs}} =$	$12/hr

Tutorial note

There is plenty of time to do this calculation (23 minutes) and so there is no need to panic or rush. Set out a cost card for the radio and then work through each of the costs mentioned in the question, including each cost as a separate line in the cost card. Clearly reference any workings back to the cost card. Remember to pick up the easy marks first -the more difficult hi-low and overhead absorption calculations were only worth four of the total marks. Even if these harder areas were ignored a good pass could still be obtained. Don't forget to identify the cost gap.

Note: The original question included a requirement to discuss closing the cost gap. The suggested solution to this requirement was as follows:

Steps to reduce a cost gap include:

Review radio features

Remove features from the radio that add to cost but do not significantly add value to the product when viewed by the customer. This should reduce cost but not the achievable selling price. This can be referred to as value engineering or value analysis.

Team approach

Cost reduction works best when a team approach is adopted. Edward Limited should bring together members of the marketing, design, assembly and distribution teams to allow discussion of methods to reduce costs. Open discussion and brainstorming are useful approaches here.

Review the whole supplier chain

Each step in the supply chain should be reviewed, possibly with the aid of staff questionnaires, to identify areas of likely cost savings. Areas which are identified by staff as being likely cost saving areas can then be focussed on by the team. For example, the questionnaire might ask 'are there more than five potential suppliers for this component?' Clearly a 'yes' response to this question will mean that there is the potential for tendering or price competition.

Components

Edward Limited should look at the significant costs involved in components. New suppliers could be sought or different materials could be used. Care would be needed not to damage the perceived value of the product. Efficiency improvements should also be possible by reducing waste or idle time that might exist. Avoid, where possible, non-standard parts in the design.

Assembly workers

Productivity gains may be possible by changing working practices or by de-skilling the process. Automation is increasingly common in assembly and manufacturing and Edward Limited should investigate what is possible here to reduce the costs. The learning curve may ultimately help to close the cost gap by reducing labour costs per unit.

Clearly reducing the percentage of idle time will reduce product costs. Better management, smoother work flow and staff incentives could all help here. Focusing on continuous improvement in production processes may help.

Overheads

Productivity increases would also help here by spreading fixed overheads over a greater number of units. Equally Edward Limited should consider an activity based costing approach to its overhead allocation, this may reveal more favourable cost allocations for the digital radio or ideas for reducing costs in the business.

<table>
<tr><td colspan="2" align="center">**Marking scheme**</td><td></td></tr>
<tr><td></td><td></td><td>*Marks*</td></tr>
<tr><td>(a)</td><td>Process description</td><td>1</td></tr>
<tr><td></td><td>Product specification</td><td>1</td></tr>
<tr><td></td><td>Selling price</td><td>1</td></tr>
<tr><td></td><td>Cost calculation</td><td>1</td></tr>
<tr><td></td><td align="right">**Maximum**</td><td>**3**</td></tr>
<tr><td>(b)</td><td>1 mark per benefit:</td><td>**4**</td></tr>
<tr><td>(c)</td><td>Cost calculation:</td><td></td></tr>
<tr><td></td><td>Component 1</td><td>2</td></tr>
<tr><td></td><td>Component 2</td><td>2</td></tr>
<tr><td></td><td>Material other</td><td>1</td></tr>
<tr><td></td><td>Assembly labour</td><td>2</td></tr>
<tr><td></td><td>Variable production overhead</td><td>1</td></tr>
<tr><td></td><td>High low calculation</td><td>2</td></tr>
<tr><td></td><td>Fixed production OAR calculation</td><td>1</td></tr>
<tr><td></td><td>Fixed production overhead</td><td>1</td></tr>
<tr><td></td><td>Cost gap identified</td><td>1</td></tr>
<tr><td></td><td align="right">**Maximum**</td><td>**13**</td></tr>
<tr><td>**Total**</td><td></td><td>**20**</td></tr>
</table>

Examiner's comments (extract)

The management accounting aspect of the syllabus is an important aspect.

Requirement (a) – most candidates gained at least half marks for describing the target costing process. However, I would have expected any well prepared candidate to pick up full marks for something that is after all simply 'knowledge' of a core topic. A substantial number of candidates had very little idea as to what target costing is, opting to guess in a large number of different ways. This suggests most candidates were not prepared for this.

Requirement (b) – the 'benefits' of target costing was less well done and this was expected. I am generally interested in why something is done as well as how it is done. This principle will be reflected again in future questions.

Requirement (c) – candidates scored good marks in Part (c); however all should revise high-low as I am disposed to use it again to provide overhead data within a question. High-low was poorly done by large numbers of candidates, which was a little disappointing given its simplicity and its existence in the F2 (and 1.2) syllabus. Allowances for waste and idle time were often incorrectly done. Any form of attempt scored something but this is an area that will be revisited and I would advise a look at the model answer and revise the correct method. Adding 10% to a cost (or time taken) is not the same as correctly adjusting by a factor of 100/90 (assuming a 10% loss for waste in this case).

Walk in the footsteps of a top tutor

The following answer was written to time to show what is achievable in the allocated time and how the answer can be structured to maximise marks.

(a)   Target costing in Edward Co should be carried out as follows:

(1)   Product specification

Target costing begins by specifying the product that the organisation wishes to sell. For Edward Co, the product is the new digital radio. The radio's features should fulfil the customer's needs.

(2)   Price

The price of the radio should be set next. Competitor's prices and market conditions must be considered.

(3)   Margin

Edward Co's required margin should then be deducted from the price. This will result in a target cost.

(b)   Benefits of early adoption of target costing include:

Early external focus

Edward Co will consider customer needs, competitors and market conditions, from the start of product development. This early external focus should increase the chance of success.

Customers' needs

Only features which will help to fulfil the needs of the customer will be included in the product. This should save time, money and increase the chance of success.

Early cost control

Steps can be taken to control costs right from the beginning of the development process.

Lower costs

Target costing has been shown to reduce product cost by 20–40% depending on the market conditions.

Note: For requirements (a) – (b) marks would be allocated for other relevant points.

(c)   Cost gap

Step 1: Calculate the target cost

Target selling price	=	$44.00
Target margin (20%)	=	($8.80)
		───────
Target cost	=	$35.20
		───────

Tutorial note

Work through each cost in turn and include as a separate line in a cost card. Set up separate, clearly referenced workings if necessary. Do not get stuck on the difficult areas but instead take a guess and move on. The key is to complete the cost card and to get most of it correct.

Step 2: Calculate the expected cost

	$
Component 1 – Board	4.10
– Delivery costs $2,000/4,000	0.60
Component 2 – 0.25m × $0.50/m × 100/98	0.128
Other material	8.10
Assembly labour	7.00
$12.60 per hour × 0.5 hours × 100/90	
Production overheads (W1) – variable	10.00
– fixed	6.00
	———
Total expected cost	35.928
	———

Workings

(W1) Production overheads

	Overheads ($)	Labour Hours
Hi	700,000	23,000
Low	620,000	19,000
	———	———
Difference	80,000	4,000
	———	———

Variable overhead per labour hour = $80,000/4,000 = $20 per hour
Variable overhead per unit = 0.5 hours × $20 per hour = $10

Total overhead of $700,000 = Fixed overhead + variable overhead of ($20 × 3,000 hours)

700,000 – $460,000 = Fixed overhead of $240,000 (This is the monthly amount)

Fixed OAR = Annual fixed overhead of ($240,000 × 12)/240,000 assembly hours = $12 per labour hour

Fixed overhead per unit = $12 per hour × 0.5 hours = $6

Step 3: Calculate the cost gap

Target cost = $35.20

Expected cost = $35.928

Cost gap = **Difference of $0.728**

236   YAM CO (JUNE 2009)

(a)   The output capacity for each process is as follows:

The total processing hours of the factory is given but can be proven as follows:

18 hours × 5 days × 50 weeks × 50 production lines = 225,000 hours.

Given this, the production capacity for pressing must be 225,000 hours/0.5 hours per metre = 450,000 metres. Using this method the production capacity for all processes is as follows:

	Product A	Product B	Product C
Pressing	450,000	450,000	562,500
Stretching	900,000	562,500	900,000
Rolling	562,500	900,000	900,000

The bottleneck is clearly the pressing process which has a lower capacity for each product. The other processes will probably be slowed to ensure smooth processing.

Tutorial note

*Clearly an alternative approach is simply to look at the original table for processing speed and pick out the slowest process. This is pressing. (full marks available for that **explained** observation). This would have been a much more straightforward approach in the exam.*

(b)   **TPAR for each product**

	Product A	Product B	Product C
Selling price	70.0	60.0	27.0
Raw materials	3.0	2.5	1.8
Throughput	67.0	57.5	25.2
Throughput per bottleneck hour*	134.0	115.0	63.0
Fixed costs per hour (W1)	90.0	90.0	90.0
TPAR	1.49	1.28	0.7
Working*	67/0.5 = 134	57.5/0.5 = 115	25.2/0.4 = 63

Workings

(W1)   The fixed cost per bottleneck hour can be calculated as follows:

Total fixed costs are $18,000,000 plus the labour cost. Labour costs $10 per hour for each of the 225,000 processing hours, a cost of $2,250,000.

Total fixed cost is therefore $18,000,000 + $2,250,000 = $20,250,000

Fixed cost per bottleneck hours is $20,250,000/225,000 = $90 per hour

Key answer tips

Calculate the TPAR in three stages:

- Firstly, calculate the throughput per bottleneck hour.
- Secondly, calculate the fixed cost per hour.
- Finally, calculate the TPAR.

Carry forward marks would be awarded if the incorrect bottleneck process was identified in requirement (a).

(c)   (i)   Yam could improve the TPAR of product C in various ways:

Speed up the bottleneck process. By increasing the speed of the bottleneck process the rate of throughput will also increase, generating a greater rate of income for Yam if the extra production can be sold. Automation might be used or a change in the detailed processes. Investment in new machinery can also help here but the cost of that would need to be taken into account.

Increase the selling prices. It can be difficult to increase selling prices in what we are told is a competitive market. Volume of sales could be lost leaving Yam with unsold stock or idle equipment. On the other hand, given the business appears to be selling all it can produce, then a price increase may be possible.

Reduce the material prices. Reducing material prices will increase the net throughput rate. Metal is available from many sources being far from a unique product. Given the industry is mature the suppliers of the raw material could be willing to negotiate on price; this could have volume or quality based conditions attached. Yam will have to be careful to protect its quality levels. Bulk buying increases stock levels and the cost of that would need to be considered.

Reduce the level of fixed costs. The fixed costs should be listed and targets for cost reduction be selected. ABC techniques can help to identify the cost drivers and with management these could be used to reduce activity levels and hence cost. Outsourcing, de-skilling or using alternative suppliers (for stationery for example) are all possible cost reduction methods.

(ii)   A TPAR of less than one indicates that the rate at which product C generates throughput (sales revenue less material cost) is less than the rate at which Yam incurs fixed cost. So on a simple level, producing a product which incurs fixed cost faster than it generates throughput does not seem to make commercial sense. Clearly the TPAR could be improved (using the methods above) before cessation is considered any further.

However, cessation decisions involve consideration of many wider issues (only three required).

Long-term expected net cash flows from the product allowing for the timing of those cash flows (NPV) are an important factor in cessation decisions

Customer perception could be negative in that they will see a reduction in choice

Lost related sales: if product C is lost will Yam lose customers that bought it along with another product?

What use could be made of the excess capacity that is created

Throughput assumes that all costs except raw materials are fixed; this may not necessarily be the case and only avoidable fixed costs need to be taken into account for a cessation decision. If few fixed costs can be avoided then product C is making a contribution that will be lost if the product ceased.

Tutorial note

Note that 11 of the 20 marks in this question are for the written requirements. This is typical of the examiner and therefore it is imperative to practice answering these written requirements.

				Marks
		Marking scheme		
(a)		Identification of bottleneck		1.0
		Explanation		2.0
			Maximum	**3.0**
(b)		Sales prices (per product)		0.5
		Raw material cost (per product)		0.5
		Throughput per bottleneck hour (per product)		0.5
		Fixed costs		1.5
		Fixed cost per hour		0.5
		TPAR (per product)		0.5
			Maximum	**8.0**
(c)	(i)	Increase speed of bottleneck		1.0
		Increase selling prices – difficult to do		1.0
		Reduce material prices		1.0
		Reduce level of fixed costs		1.0
			Maximum	**4.0**
	(ii)	Explain a TPAR		2.0
		Long-term cash flows		1.0
		Lost related sales		1.0
		Use of spare capacity		1.0
		Fixed costs		1.0
		Any other reasonable factor e.g. lost contribution		1.0
			Maximum	**5.0**
Total				**20**

Examiner's Comments (extract)

As is my usual style I tried to make the discursive elements of a question independent of the numbers. The idea here is to give all candidates a chance to demonstrate performance management skills regardless of any problems they may have had with the numbers.

It was clear that many candidates had poor knowledge of throughput accounting. Few could properly identify the bottleneck process. Many used total hours per product as their guide to a wrong answer.

In the throughput calculations many included labour in the calculation of contribution, whereas its exclusion is more normal. Labour is properly treated as a fixed cost and yet many did not include it in the overheads part of the calculations.

Most candidates could give some reasonable suggestions on how to improve a TPAR, however not enough scored the four easy marks on offer.

The final part of the question was least well done, as expected. It is an easy mistake to feel that an unprofitable product should cease to be made but the world is a more complicated place. Current profitability is a factor but the future is more relevant. The impact of the withdrawal on customers and staff and the effect on competition are all relevant. No detailed knowledge of future cash flows was expected at this stage of studies.

237 FLOPRO PLC

Key answer tips

This question draws on a range of basic management accounting techniques including product costing, contribution analysis and limiting factor analysis. The well prepared candidate will have a good background knowledge of these topics in addition to an understanding of the central syllabus topic of throughput accounting. Candidates should be able to demonstrate an understanding of the theory behind TA as well as being able to carry out a practical exercise.

(a) The net profit for each product is calculated as follows:

	Product A	Product B
	$	$
Direct material cost	2	40
Variable production overhead cost	28	4
Fixed production overhead $40 (W1) × hours	10	6
Total cost	40	50
Selling price	60	70
Net profit	20	20

Workings

(W1) Fixed production overhead is absorbed at an average rate per hour:

Total hours $(120,000 \times 0.25) + (45,000 \times 0.15) = 36,750$

Absorption rate per hour $= \$1,470,000/36,750 = \$40$

(b) **(i)** **Throughput return per bottleneck hour**

= (selling price – material cost)/bottleneck hours per unit

Product A $= (60 - 2)/0.02 = \$2,900$

Product B $= (70 - 40)/0.015 = \$2,000$

Flopro should sell product A up to its maximum demand and then product B using the remaining capacity

Maximum demand of product A $= 120,000 \times 120\% = 144,000$ units

Bottleneck hours required for A $= 144,000 \times 0.02 = 2,880$ hours

Bottleneck hours available for B $= 3,075 - 2,880 = 195$ hours

Output of product B which is possible $= 195/0.015 = 13,000$ units

The maximum net profit may be calculated as:

	$
Throughput return product A 144,000 × ($60 – 2)	8,352,000
Throughput return product B 13,000 × ($70 – 40)	390,000
Total throughput return	8,742,000
Less: Overhead cost	
shown as variable in (a) ((144,000 × $28) + (13,000 × $4))	(4,084,000)
Fixed	(1,470,000)
Net profit	3,188,000

(ii) Throughput return per bottleneck hour for product B (as calculated above)

$$= (70 - 40)/0.015 = \$2,000$$

Cost per bottleneck hour $\quad= (\$4,084,000 + \$1,470,000)/3,075$

$$= \$1,806.18$$

Throughput accounting ratio for product B $= \$2,000/\$1,806.18 = 1.11$

(iii) Where throughput accounting principles are applied, a product is worth producing and selling so long as its throughput return per bottleneck hour is greater than the production cost per throughput hour. This may be measured by the throughput accounting ratio. Where the ratio is greater than one, return exceeds cost and the focus should be on improving the size of the ratio.

Efforts may be made to improve the position for each product and in total by focusing on areas such as:

- Improved throughput ($) per unit by increasing selling price or reducing material cost per unit. Product B has a very high material element ($40 per unit)

- Improving the throughput ($) per unit by reducing the time required on the bottleneck resource. Reducing the time for product B from 0.015 hours to 0.01 hours through change methods would improve its ratio

- Improving the overall position by reducing the cost of spare capacity. This may be achieved by operational re-design aimed at reducing or eliminating the impact of any bottlenecks.

238 ENVIRONMENTAL MANAGEMENT ACCOUNTING

(a) (1) Waste disposal costs

FTX is likely to incur environmental costs associated with waste: for example, landfill taxes, or the costs of disposal of raw materials and chemicals not used in drug production, FTX may also be vulnerable to fines for compliance failures such as pollution.

Control measures could be implemented to identify how much material is wasted in production by using the 'mass balance' approach, whereby the weight of materials bought is compared to the product yield. From this process, potential cost savings may be identified. The cost of packaging lends itself particularly well to this analysis: by analysing how much packaging the drug uses and what percentage of that packaging is recyclable, FTX could also reduce its costs whilst being environmentally friendly.

(2) Water consumption costs

Like any other business, FTX will pay for water twice: first to buy it, and, secondly, to dispose of it. If FTX looks to reduce its water bill, it is important for the business to identify where water is used in the drug production process and how consumption can be decreased.

(3) Energy consumption costs

Like any other business or household, FTX should be able to reduce its energy costs significantly by switching production to night-time for example (when electricity is cheaper). Furthermore, environmental management accounts may help to identify inefficiencies and wasteful practices and therefore opportunities for cost savings.

(4) Transport and travel costs

Environmental Management Accounting can often help to identify savings in terms of business travel and transport of goods and materials. An obvious control measure, in this case, would be the replacement of FTX's vehicles by more fuel-efficient vans or cars.

(b) Environmental Management Accounting is a specialised part of the management accounts that focuses on things such as the cost of energy and water. EMA uses some standard accountancy techniques to identify, analyse, manage and hopefully reduce environmental costs in a way that provide mutual benefit to the company and the environment.

EMA techniques could include the following:

- **Input/outflow analysis**

  This technique records material inflows and balances this with outflows on the basis that, what comes in must go out. So, if 100 kg of materials have been bought and only 80 kg of materials have been produced, for example, then the 20 kg difference must be accounted for in some way. It may be, for example, that 10% of it has been sold as scrap and 10% of it is waste. By accounting for outputs in this way, both in terms of physical quantities and, at the end of the process, in monetary terms too, businesses are forced to focus on environmental costs.

- **Flow cost accounting**

  This technique uses not only material flows but also the organisational structure. It makes material flows transparent by looking at the physical quantities involved, their costs and their value. It divides the material flows into three categories: material, system and delivery and disposal. The values and costs of each of these three flows are then calculated. The aim of flow cost accounting is to reduce the quantity of materials which, as well as having a positive effect on the environment, should have a positive effect on a business' total costs in the long run.

- **Activity-based costing**

  ABC allocates internal costs to cost centres and cost drivers on the basis of the activities that give rise to the costs. In an environmental accounting context, it distinguishes between environment-related costs, which can be attributed to joint cost centres, and environment-driven costs, which tend to be hidden on general overheads.

- **Lifecycle costing**

  Within the context of environmental accounting, lifecycle costing is a technique which requires the full environmental consequences, and therefore costs, arising from production of a product to be taken account across its whole lifecycle, literally 'from cradle to grave'.

239 CHOCOLATES ARE FOREVER (CAF)

(a) The Breakeven point is that number if units produced and sold at which CAF will make no profit or no loss:

$$\text{Breakeven point} = \frac{\text{Fixed costs}}{\text{Contribution per unit}}; \ \text{Breakeven point} = \frac{\$20,000}{\$12 - 7}$$

Breakeven point = 4,000 units.

The margin of safety expresses the gap between budgeted sales and breakeven sales. It measures by how much CAF needs to fall short of budgeted sales before it starts making a loss:

$$\text{Margin of safety} = \frac{\text{Budgeted sales} - \text{Breakeven sales}}{\text{Budgeted sales}} \times 100\%$$

$$\text{Margin of safety} = \frac{6,000 \text{ units} - 4,000 \text{ units}}{6,000 \text{ units}} \times 100\%; \quad \text{Margin of safety} = 33.33\%$$

(b) A **breakeven chart** is a graphical representation of the data. It shows the breakeven point when the total cost line and the total revenue line intersect. The total cost line is a total variable cost line sitting on the fixed cost line. The Sales revenue line is also depicted and comes from the origin. (no sales, no revenue). The Margin of Safety can then be read off the chart on the horizontal axis – the difference between the budgeted output and the breakeven output.

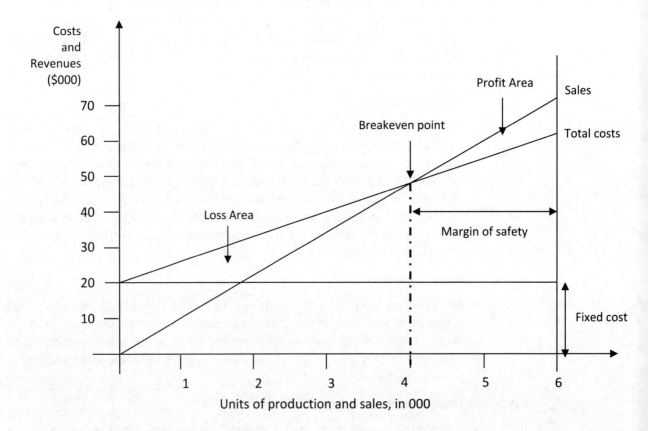

A contribution breakeven chart is based on the same principles as a basic breakeven chart, but it shows the variable cost line instead of the fixed cost line.

The same lines for total cost and sales revenue are shown so the breakeven point and profit can be read off in the same way as with a conventional chart. However, it is possible also to read the contribution for any level of activity.

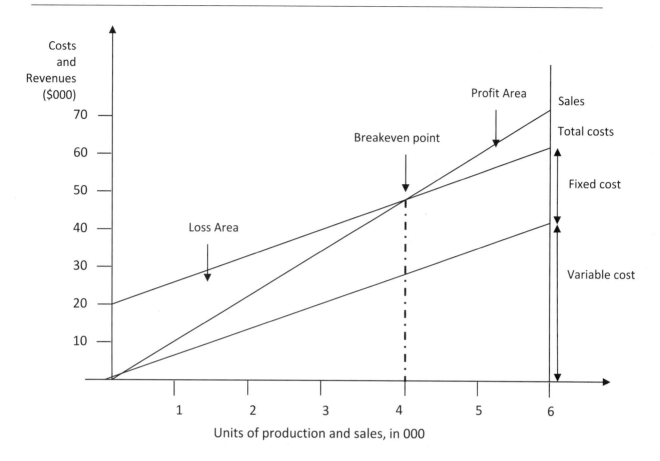

The Profit-Volume chart is an alternative chart, which is simpler, but gives a lot of the same information. By drawing a line between the fixed costs at zero output (where the amount of loss will equal the fixed costs) and the breakeven point – where the profit line crosses the x axis – the chart may be used to work out the expected profit at any level of output.

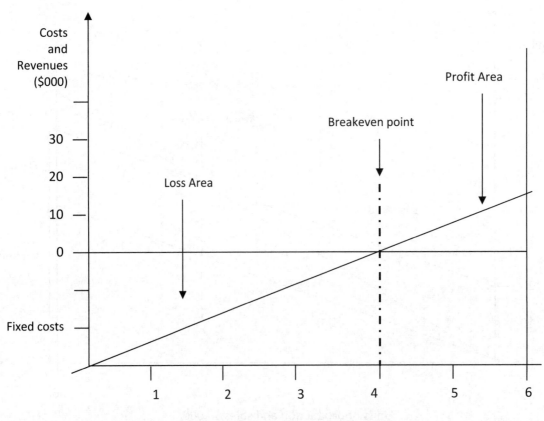

Units of production and sales, in 000

(c) Breakeven calculations and the graphs above involve a number of assumptions; the biggest criticism of CVP analysis is that these assumptions may not be observed in practice. For example:

- Costs behaviour is assumed to be linear, but costs may only be linear within a certain output range. The analysis and its results would change if the variable cost per unit were to change due to economies of scale (that would affect the material cost). Likewise, a learning curve effect could impact on the labour cost per unit.

- In practice, it can sometimes be difficult to separate variable and fixed costs, and the calculations will represent an approximation.

- Revenue is assumed to be linear but CAF, like many companies, may need to cut its unit price to sell more units and/or retain its market share.

- Breakeven analysis assumes that all units produced are sold, i.e. that no inventory is taken into account in calculations.

- Breakeven analysis ignores the effects of tax and inflation.

240 MANGO LEATHER

(a)

$$\text{Breakeven sales revenue} = \frac{\text{Fixed costs}}{\text{Weighted average contribution to sales ratio}}$$

$$\text{Breakeven sales revenue} = \frac{\$580,000}{0.35844 \text{ (W1)}}$$

Breakeven sales revenue = $1,618,123.

(b) Products first need to be ranked according to their contribution to sales ratio:

Products	Selling price (per unit)	Contribution per unit	C/S ratio	Rank
Bags	$400	$190	0.475	2
Belts	$125	$60	0.480	1
Shoes	$150	$55	0.367	3
Jackets	$300	$85	0.283	4

Secondly, cumulative sales and profits need to be established in preparation for the multi-product breakeven chart:

Sales	Cumulative revenue	Contribution (W1)	Cumulative profit or loss
None	$0	$0	$(580,000)
Belts	$250,000	$120,000	$(460,000)
Bags	$650,000	$190,000	$(270,000)
Shoes	$875,000	$82,500	$(187,500)
Jackets	$1,925,000	$297,500	$110,000

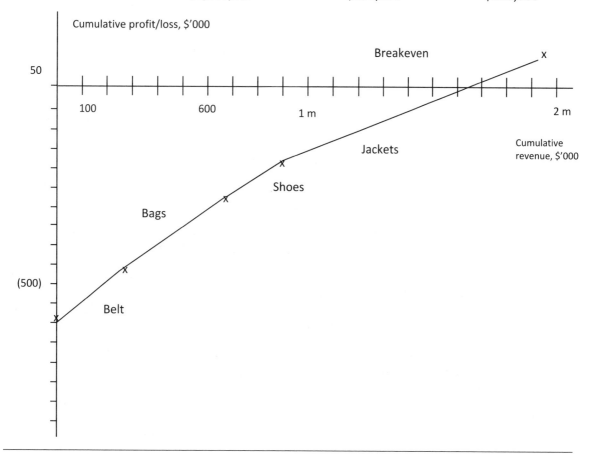

(c) Mango's production process is very dependent on leather. Leather is the only material and represents a third of total variable costs.

An increase of the cost of leather will severely impact on Mango. Any increase will erode contribution margins significantly. A higher material cost will affect contribution by making it lower. This will impact on the breakeven point, as the weighted average C/S ratio calculated in (a) will be lower (assuming that the selling prices, fixed costs and demand remain constant.)

Graphically, the breakeven revenue point will move to the right along the x-axis and the breakeven revenue will increase.

The unavailability of leather will severely disrupt the production process and will affect customer confidence in Mango, although it may encourage the company to look for substitutes and manage its dependency on its unique material a bit better.

(d) The major benefit of using breakeven analysis is that it indicates the lowest amount of activity necessary to prevent losses.

Breakeven analysis aids decision making as it explains the relationship between cost, production volume and returns. It can be extended to show how changes in fixed costs/variable costs relationships or in revenues will affect profit levels and breakeven points.

The following underlying assumptions will limit the precision and reliability of a given cost-volume-profit analysis.

(1) The behaviour of total cost and total revenue has been reliably determined and is linear over the relevant range.

(2) All costs can be divided into fixed and variable elements.

(3) Total fixed costs remain constant over the relevant volume range of the CVP analysis.

(4) Total variable costs are directly proportional to volume over the relevant range.

(5) Selling prices are to be unchanged.

(6) Prices of the factors of production are to be unchanged (for example, material, prices, wage rates).

(7) Efficiency and productivity are to be unchanged.

(8) The analysis either covers a single product or assumes that a given sales mix will be maintained as total volume changes.

(9) Revenue and costs are being compared on a single activity basis (for example, units produced and sold or sales value of production).

(10) Perhaps the most basic assumption of all is that volume is the only relevant factor affecting cost. Of course, other factors also affect costs and sales. Ordinary cost-volume-profit analysis is a crude oversimplification when these factors are unjustifiably ignored.

(11) The volume of production equals the volume of sales, or changes in beginning and ending inventory levels are insignificant in amount.

Working 1 – Weighted average contribution to sales ratio

Products	Sales units	Leather cost at @$60 per metre	Contribution per unit	Total sales	Total contribution
Bags	1,000	$60	$190	$400,000	$190,000
Belts	2,000	$15	$60	$250,000	$120,000
Shoes	1,500	$30	$55	$225,000	$82,500
Jackets	3,500	$90	$85	$1,050,000	$297,500
Total				**$1,925,000**	**$690,000**

$$\text{Weighted average contribution to sales ratio} = \frac{\text{Total contribution}}{\text{Total sales}}$$

$$\text{Weighted average contribution to sales ratio} = \frac{\$690,000}{\$1,925,000}$$

Weighted average contribution to sales ratio = 0.5844 or 35.84%

241 BREAKEVEN

(a) **p**   is the total sales revenue

q   Total cost (Fixed cost + variable cost)

r   Total variable cost

s   Fixed costs at the specific level of activity

t   Total loss at the specific level of activity

u   Total profit at that level of activity

v   Total contribution at the specific level of activity

w   Total contribution at a lower level of activity

x   Level of activity of output sales

y   monetary value of cost and revenue function for level of activity.

(b) At event 'm', the selling price per unit decreases, but it remains constant. P is a straight line, but with a lower gradient above 'm' compared to below 'm'.

At event 'n' there is an increase in fixed costs equal to the dotted line. This is probably due to an increase in capital expenditure in order to expand output beyond this point. Also, at this point, the variable cost per unit declines as reflected by the gradient of the variable cost line. This might be due to more efficient production methods associated with increased investment in capital equipment.

(c) Breakeven analysis is of limited use in a multi-product company, but the analysis can be a useful aid to management of a small single product company. The following are some of the main benefits:

- Breakeven analysis forces management to consider the functional relationship between costs, revenue and activity, and gives an insight to how costs and revenues vary with the level of activity.

- Breakeven analysis forces management to consider the fixed costs at various levels of activity and the selling price that will be required to achieve various levels of output.

242   EC LTD

(a)

$$\text{Breakeven revenue} = \frac{\text{Fixed costs \$1,212,000}}{\text{Average contribution to Sales ratio 50.5\% (W1)}}$$

Breakeven revenue = $2,400,000.

Working 1: Average Contribution to Sales Ratio (on a $100 total sales basis)

	Product X	Product Y	Total
Sales	$70	$30	$100
Contribution	$70 * 0.55 = $38.50	$30 * 0.4 = $12	$50.50

If $50.50 contribution is achieved for every $100 worth of sales,

$$\text{Average contribution to Sales ratio} = \frac{\$50.50}{\$100} = 0.505 \text{ or } 50.5\%$$

(b)

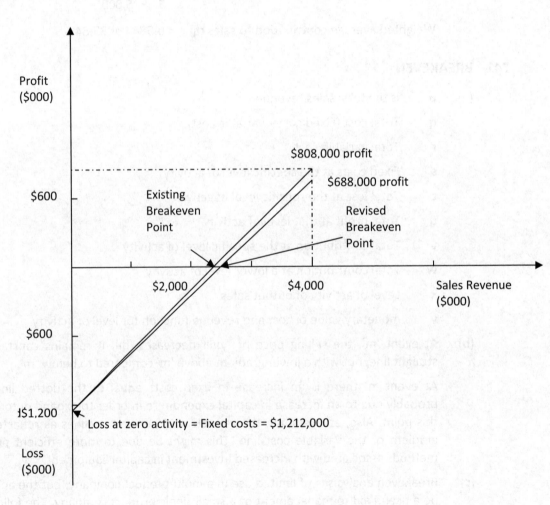

Effect of a change in the sales mix:

	Product X	Product Y	Total
Sales	$50	$50	$100
Contribution	$50 * 0.55 = $27.50	$50 * 0.4 = $20	$47.50

If $47.50 contribution is achieved for every $100 worth of sales,

Average contribution to Sales ratio = 47.50 % and

$$\text{Breakeven revenue} = \frac{\text{Fixed costs } \$1,212,000}{\text{Average contribution to Sales ratio 47.5\% (W1)}}$$

Breakeven revenue = $2,551,579.

(c)

$$\text{Sales revenue required} = \frac{\text{Attributable fixed costs } \$455,000 + \$700,000}{\text{X's contribution to Sales ratio 55\%}}$$

Sales revenue required = $2,100,000.

DECISION MAKING TECHNIQUES

243   B CHEMICALS

Key answer tips

With any linear programming question the key is to work through the different steps in a systematic manner.

(a)   Formulation of LP problem

Let x = the gallons of Super petrol produced;

         y = the gallons of Regular petrol produced each day; and

         C = the total contribution

The company needs to maximise an objective function $C = 0.25x + 0.1y$

Subject to constraints:

supply of heavy crude	$0.7x + 0.5y \leq 5,000$ (1)
supply of light crude	$0.5x + 0.7y \leq 6,000$ (2)
market conditions	$x \geq 2/3 \, (x + y)$
rearranging	$3x \geq 2x + 2y$
or x	$\geq 2y$ (3)
also x, y	≥ 0

(b)   Graph

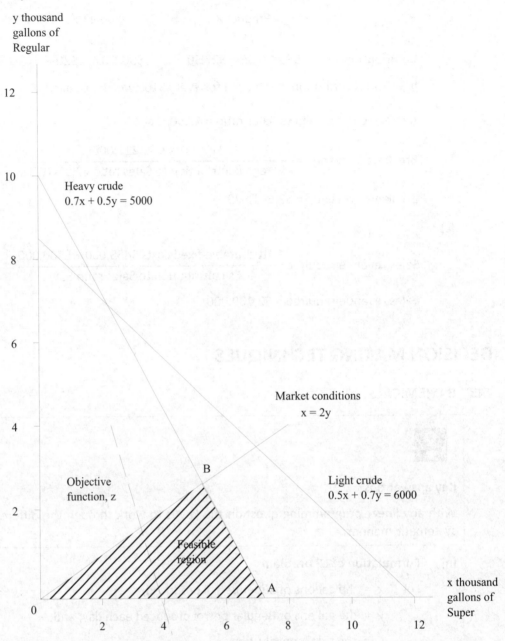

y thousand gallons of Regular (y-axis)

Heavy crude
0.7x + 0.5y = 5000

Market conditions
x = 2y

Objective function, z

Light crude
0.5x + 0.7y = 6000

Feasible region

x thousand gallons of Super (x-axis)

Note: the objective function is also shown.

(c)   Optimal policy and comment

From the graph, which also shows an objective function (z = 10,000 has been drawn), it is clear that the optimal solution lies at point A. This is the point where the line 0.7x + 0.5y = 5,000 cuts the horizontal axis, where y = 0 and x = 7,142.85.

The optimal production policy involves producing no Regular petrol and 7,142.85 gallons of Super petrol. The contribution that this generates is:

7,142.85 × $0.25 = $1,785.71 per day.

Comment

- Whilst the solution to the LP problem might involve no Regular petrol, a policy that abandons refining of one product may risk longer-term demand for that product

- The conclusion drawn is only as reliable as the underlying estimates whose accuracy should be checked

- It would only require a small change in estimates to move the optimal solution from A to B.

244 COSMETICS CO (DECEMBER 2010)

(a)   **Optimum production plan**

Define the variables

Let x = no. of jars of face cream to be produced

Let y = no. of bottles of body lotion to be produced

Let C = contribution

State the objective function

The objective is to maximise contribution, C

C = 9x + 8y

State the constraints

Silk powder	$3x + 2y \leq 5,000$
Silk amino acids	$1x + 0.5y \leq 1,600$
Skilled labour	$4x + 5y \leq 9,600$

Non-negativity constraints:

x, y ≥ 0

Sales constraint:

y ≤ 2,000

On the graph

Silk powder	$3x + 2y = 5,000$
Silk amino acids	$1x + 0.5y = 1,600$
Skilled labour	$4x + 5y = 9,600$

Solve using iso-contribution line

Using the iso-contribution line, the furthest vertex from the origin is point 'c', the intersection of the constraints for skilled labour and silk powder.

Solving the simultaneous equations for these constraints:

$4x + 5y = 9,600 \times 3$

$3x + 2y = 5,000 \times 4$

$12x + 15y = 28,800$ $12x + 8y = 20,000$

Subtract the second one from the first one $7y = 8,800$, therefore y = **1,257.14**.

If y = 1,257.14 and:

$4x + 5y = 9,600$

Then $5 \times 1,257.14 + 4x = 9,600$

Therefore x = 828.58

If C = 9x + 8y

C = $7,457.22 + $10,057.12 = $17,514.34

(b)   **Shadow prices and slack**

The shadow price for silk powder can be found by solving the two simultaneous equations intersecting at point c, whilst adding one more hour to the equation for silk powder.

$4x + 5y = 9,600 \times 3$

$3x + 2y = 5,001 \times 4$

$12x + 15y = 28,800$

$12x + 8y = 20,004$

Subtract the second one from the first one

$7y = 8,796$, therefore y = 1,256.57

$3x + (2 \times 1,256.57) = 5,001.$

Therefore x = 829.29

C = (9 × 829.29) + (8 × 1,256.57) = $17,516.17

Original contribution = $17,514.34

Therefore shadow price for silk powder is $1.83 per gram.

The slack for amino acids can be calculated as follows:

(828.58 × 1) + (0.5 × 1,257.14) = 1,457.15 grams used.

Available = 1,600 grams.

Therefore slack = 142.85 grams.

Marking scheme		Marks
(a)	Optimum production plan	
	Defining constraint for silk powder	1
	Defining constraint for amino acids	1
	Defining constraint for labour	1
	Non-negativity constraint	1
	Sales constraint: x	1
	Sales constraint: y	1
	Iso-contribution line worked out	1
	Optimum point identified	2
	Equations solved at optimum point	3
	Total contribution	2
		___
	Maximum	**14**
		___
(b)	Shadow prices and slack	
	Shadow price	4
	Slack	2
		___
	Maximum	**6**
		___
Total		**20**
		___

245 CUT AND STITCH (JUNE 2010)

(a) The optimal production mix can be found by solving the two equations given for F and T.

$7W + 5L = 3{,}500$

$2W + 2L = 1{,}200$

Multiplying the second equation by 2.5 produces:

$7W + 5L = 3{,}500$

$5W + 5L = 3{,}000$

$2W = 500$

$W = 250$

Substituting W = 250 in the fabric equation produces:

$2 \times 250 + 2L = 1{,}200$

$2L = 700$

$L = 350$

The optimal solution is when 250 work suits are produced and 350 lounge suits are produced. **The contribution gained is $26,000**:

$C = 48W + 40L$

$C = (48 \times 250) + (40 \times 350)$

$C = 26{,}000$

(b)   The shadow prices can be found by adding one unit to each constraint in turn.

Shadow price of T

$7W + 5L = 3,501$

$2W + 2L = 1,200$

Again multiplying the second equation by 2.5 produces:

$7W + 5L = 3,501$

$5W + 5L = 3,000$

$2W = 501$

$= 250.5$

Substituting W = 250.5 in the fabric equation produces:

$(2 \times 250.5) + 2L = 1,200$

$2L = 1,200 - 501$

$L = 349.5$

Contribution earned at this point would be = $(48 \times 250.5) + (40 \times 349.5) = 26,004$ which is an increase of $4.

Hence the shadow price of T is $4 per hour.

Shadow price of F

$7W + 5L = 3,500$

$2W + 2L = 1,201$

Again multiplying the second equation by 2.5 produces:

$7W + 5L = 3,500.0$

$5W + 5L = 3,002.5$

$2W = 497.5$

$W = 248.75$

Substituting W = 248.75 in the fabric equation produces:

$(2 \times 248.75) + 2L = 1,201$

$2L = 1,201 - 497.5$

$L = 351.75$

Contribution earned at this point would be = $(48 \times 248.75) + (40 \times 351.75) = 26,010$, which is an increase of $10. Hence the shadow price of F is $10 per metre.

(c)   The shadow price represents the maximum premium above the normal rate a business should be willing to pay for more of a scarce resource. It is equal to the increased contribution that can be gained from gaining that extra resource.

The shadow price of labour here is $4 per hour. The tailors have offered to work for $4.50 – a premium of $3.00 per hour. At first glance the offer seems to be acceptable.

However, many businesses pay overtime at the rate of time and a half and some negotiation should be possible to create a win/win situation. Equally some consideration should be given to the quality aspect here. If excessive extra hours are worked then tiredness can reduce the quality of the work produced.

(d)   If maximum demand for W falls to 200 units, the constraint for W will move left to 200 on the x axis of the graph. The new optimum point will then be at the intersection of:

W = 200 and

2W + 2L = 1,200

Solving these equations simultaneously, if:

W = 200, then (2 × 200) + 2L = 1,200

Therefore L = 400.

So, the new production plan will be to make 400L and 200W

Marking scheme		
		Marks
(a)	Optimal point calculation	3
	Contribution	1
		—
	Maximum	**4**
		—
(b)	For each shadow price	3
		—
	Maximum	**6**
		—
(c)	Rate discussion	3
	Other factors e.g. tiredness, negotiation	3
		—
	Maximum	**6**
		—
(d)	Find optimum point	1
	Solve 2 equations	2
	Conclusion	1
		—
	Maximum	**4**
		—
Total		**20**
		—

246   CSC CO (SEPTEMBER 2016)

Tutorial note

The first part of the question was a typical single limiting factor question, requiring candidates to formulate an optimal production plan and calculate maximum profit. Do not ignore the fact that the company had entered into a contract, and therefore these requirements should be produced first. Secondly there was a requirement to calculate the shortage of material – this was often omitted. Thirdly, many candidates used the dollar value of the limiting material to calculate their production plan, rather than the quantities. These errors didn't seem to come from a lack of understanding, more a lack of care. It's possible that candidates were running short of time by this point, meaning that the requirements and scenarios weren't read properly. This highlights the importance of good time management during the exam – ensuring that some of the more straightforward marks can be obtained.

(a)   **(Step 1) Calculate the shortage of Betta for the year**

Total requirements in grams:	
Cakes: grams used per cake	0.5
Expected demand	11,200
Total required:	5,600
Cookies: grams used per cookie	0.20
Expected demand	9,800
Total required:	1,960
Shakes: grams used per shake	1
Expected demand	7,500
Total required:	7,500
Overall total required:	**15,060**
Less available:	12,000
Shortage:	**3,060**

(Step 2) Contribution per gram of Betta and ranking

	Cakes	Cookies	Shakes	Shakes (contract)
	$	$	$	$
Contribution per unit	2.60	1.75	1.20	1.00
Grams of Betta per unit	0.5	0.2	1	1
	$	$	$	$
Contribution per gram	5.20	8.75	1.20	1.00
Rank	2	1	3	4

(Step 3) Optimum production plan

Product	Number to be produced	Grams per unit	Total grams per product	Cumulative grams	Contribution per unit	Total contribution
Shakes (contract)	5,000	1	5,000	5,000	1.00	5,000
Cookies	9,800	0.20	1,960	6,960	1.75	17,150
Cakes	10,080	0.5	5,040	12,000	2.60	26,208
						———
Total contribution						48,358
Less fixed costs						(3,000)
						———
Profit						45,358
						———

(b)

Tutorial note

The second part of this question was a discussion about whether the business should breach the contract they have to supply another business. You must not focus purely on the financial factors. Easy marks could be picked up here for realising that breaching a contract will have legal, reputational and ethical issues.

Breach of contract with Encompass Health (EH)

It would be bad for business if CSC Co becomes known as a supplier who cannot be relied on to stick to the terms of its agreements. This could make future potential customers reticent to deal with them.

Even more seriously, there could be legal consequences involved in breaching the contract with EH. This would be costly and also very damaging to CSC Co's reputation.

If CSC Co lets EH down and breaches the contract, EH may refuse to buy from them anymore and future sales revenue would therefore be lost. Just as importantly, these sales to EH are currently helping to increase the marketability of CSC Co's shakes. This will be lost if these sales are no longer made.

Therefore, taking these factors into account, it would not be advisable to breach the contract.

(c)

Tutorial note

You could attempt this part of the question before any other part of Section C – good examination technique especially when under time pressure. Although most candidates are comfortable with the steps involved in linear programming, there is a lack of in-depth understanding of how it works. For example, virtually all candidates could identify the iso-contribution line and feasible region when given on a graph, but few could explain what they meant. Many explained what they were for (finding the optimum point), but not that the iso-contribution line shows all points giving the same contribution, or that the feasible region shows all possible production plans that meet all of the constraints. Similarly, most could define slack in the context of scarce resources, but found it harder to identify slack variables from a completed graph.

(i) This line is what is called the 'iso-contribution line' and it is plotted by finding two corresponding x and y values for the 'objective function'. At any point along this line, the mix of cakes and cookies will provide the same total contribution, 'C'.

Since each cake provides a contribution of $2.60 and each cookie provides a contribution of $1.75, the objective function has been defined as 'C = 2.6x + 1.75y'. This means that the total contribution will be however many cakes are made (represented by 'x') at $2.60 each plus however many cookies are made (represented by 'y') at $1.75 each.

The area 0ABCD is called the 'feasible region'. Any point within this region could be selected and would show a feasible mix of production of cakes and cookies. However, in order to maximise profit, the optimum production mix will be at a point on the edge of the feasible region, not within it.

(ii) The further the iso-contribution line is moved away from the origin, 0, the greater the contribution generated will be. Therefore, a ruler will be laid along the line, making sure it stays at exactly the same angle as the line, and the ruler will then be moved outwards to the furthest vertex (intersection between two constraints) on the feasible region, as represented by either point A, B, C or D. In this case, the optimum point is 'C', the intersection of the 'labour' constraint and the 'demand for cakes' constraint.

(iii) A 'slack' value could arise either in relation to a resource or in relation to production of a product. It means that a resource is not being fully utilised or that there is unfulfilled demand of a product. Since the optimum point is the intersection of the labour and the demand for cakes lines, this means that there will be three slack values. First, there will be a slack value for cookies. This means that there will be unsatisfied demand for cookies since the optimum point does not reach as far as the 'demand for cookies' line on the graph. Also, there will be slack values for Betta and Singa, which means that both of these materials are not actually the binding constraints, such that there will be more material available than is needed

		Marking scheme		Marks
(a)		Calculating shortage of Betta		1.5
		Contribution per gram of Betta		1
		Ranking		0.5
		Optimum production plan		2
		Profit		1
			Maximum	**6**
(b)		Each valid point		1
			Maximum	**4**
(c)	(i)	Identification and explanation of the iso contribution line		2
		Identification and explanation of the feasible region		2
			Maximum	**4**
	(ii)	explaining how to use line for identification of optimum point		1.5
		Identification of optimum point		0.5
			Maximum	**2**
	(iii)	Explaining what slack values are		1
		Identifying Betta as slack		1
		Identifying Singa as slack		1
		Identifying slack demand for cookies		1
			Maximum	**4**
Total				**20**

247 BITS AND PIECES (JUNE 2009)

(a) The decision to open on Sundays is to be based on incremental revenue and incremental costs:

	Ref	$	$
Incremental revenue	(W1)		800,000
Incremental costs			
Cost of sales	(W2)	335,000	
Staff	(W3)	45,000	
Lighting	(W4)	9,000	
Heating	(W5)	9,000	
Manager's bonus	(W6)	8,000	
Total costs			(406,000)
Net incremental revenue			394,000

Conclusion

On the basis of the above it is clear that the incremental revenue exceeds the incremental costs and therefore it is financially justifiable.

Workings

(W1) Incremental revenue

Day	Sales	Gross profit	Gross profit	Cost of Sales
	$	%	$	$
Average	10,000	70%		
Sunday (+60% of average)	16,000	50%	8,000	8,000
Annually (50 days)	800,000		400,000	400,000
Current results (300 days)	3,000,000	70.0%	2,100,000	
New results	3,800,000	65.8%	2,500,000	

(W2) Purchasing and discount on purchasing

Extra purchasing from Sunday trading is $800,000 – $400,000 = $400,000

Current annual purchasing is $18,000 × 50 = $900,000

New annual purchasing is ($900,000 + $400,000) × 0.95 = $1,235,000

Incremental cost is $1,235,000 – $900,000 = $335,000 (a $65,000 discount)

(W3) Staff costs

Staff costs on a Sunday are 5 staff × 6 hours × $20 per hour × 1.5 = $900 per day Annual cost is $900 × 50 days = $45,000

(W4) Lighting costs

Lighting costs are 6 hours × $30 per hour × 50 days = $9,000

(W5) Heating costs

Heating cost in winter is 8 hours × $45 per hour × 25 days = $9,000

(W6) Manager's bonus

This is based on the incremental revenue $800,000 × 1% = $8,000 (or $160 per day)

Tutorial note

Only relevant cash flows should be taken into consideration when making this decision, i.e. the future incremental cash flows that occur as a result of Sunday opening. Prepare a summary of the relevant cash flows and reference in workings, where required.

(b) The manager's rewards can be summarised as follows:

Time off

This appears far from generous. The other staff are being paid time and a half and yet the manager does not appear to have this option and also is only being given time off in lieu (TOIL) at normal rates. Some managers may want their time back as TOIL so as to spend time with family or social friends; others may want the cash to spend. One would have thought some flexibility would have been sensible if the manager is to be motivated properly.

Bonus

The bonus can be calculated at $8,000 per annum (W6); on a day worked basis, this is $160 per day. This is less than that being paid to normal staff; at time and a half they earn 6 hours × $20 × 1.5 = $180 per day. It is very unlikely to be enough to keep the presumably better qualified manager happy. Indeed the bonus is dependent on the level of new sales and so there is an element of risk involved for the manager. Generally speaking higher risk for lower returns is far from motivating.

The level of sales could of course be much bigger than is currently predicted. However, given the uplift on normal average daily sales is already +60%, this is unlikely to be significant.

(c)   Discounts and promotion

When new products or in this case opening times are launched then some form of market stimulant is often necessary. B&P has chosen to offer substantial discounts and promotions. There are various issues here:

Changing buying patterns: It is possible that customers might delay a purchase a day or two in order to buy on a Sunday. This would cost the business since the margin earned on Sunday is predicted to be 20% points lower than on other days.

Complaints: Customers that have already bought an item on another day might complain when they see the same product on sale for much less when they come back in for something else on a Sunday. Businesses need to be strong in this regard in that they have to retain control over their pricing policy. Studies have shown that only a small proportion of people will actually complain in this situation. More might not, though, be caught out twice and hence will change the timing of purchases (as above).

Quality: The price of an item can say something about its quality. Low prices tend to suggest poor quality and vice versa. B&P should be careful so as not to suggest that

Marking scheme		
		Marks
(a)	Existing total sales	1.0
	New sales	1.0
	Incremental sales	1.0
	Existing purchasing	2.0
	Discount allowed for	1.0
	Incremental Sunday purchasing costs	1.0
	Staff cost	2.0
	Lighting cost	1.0
	Heating cost	1.0
	Manager's bonus	1.0
	Maximum	**12**
(b)	Time off at normal rate not time and a half	1.0
	Lack of flexibility	1.0
	Bonus per day worked calculation and comment	1.0
	Risk	1.0
	Maximum	**4**
(c)	Changing customer buying pattern	2.0
	Complaints risk	2.0
	Quality link	2.0
	Maximum	**4**
Total		**20**

Examiner's comments (extract)

This question (in the second two parts) required some common business sense. This is sadly lacking in many. The manager's pay deal offered him less money per hour than the staff (on current prediction of incremental sales) and time off on a one to one basis when the staff got time and a half. Most managers would be savvy enough to recognise a poor deal when they saw it. Equally a weekend day is for many a family day and a day off in the week is a poor substitute for that.

The offering of substantial discounts may well encourage sales (a mark earning point). However, surely it is likely that customers could switch from weekday shopping to weekend shopping to save money. Surprisingly few realised this.

Marks gained for part (a) were reasonable with incremental sales, staff costs, and lighting being done correctly by most candidates. For some reason the incremental heating cost was incorrectly calculated by many, with candidates electing to heat the stores all year as opposed to just the winter months as stated in the question.

There were two sunk costs to be excluded (rent and supervisor salary). It is always advisable for a candidate to indicate that the cost is to be excluded rather than simply not mention it at all.

Very few realised that the manager's pay deal was not overly generous both in terms of time off and the amount of cash on offer. Many candidates seemed to think that the mere existence of time off and the offer of money was enough to motivate. The amount of time off and cash was ignored. This is again naive, demonstrating a lack of understanding or experience.

248   STAY CLEAN (DECEMBER 2009)

(a)   The relevant costs of the decision to cease the manufacture of the TD are needed:

Cost or Revenue	Working reference	Amount ($)
Lost revenue	Note 1	(96,000)
Saved labour cost	Note 2	48,000
Lost contribution from other products	Note 3	(118,500)
Redundancy and recruitment costs	Note 4	(3,700)
Supplier payments saved	Note 5	88,500
Sublet income		12,000
Supervisor	Note 6	0
Net cash flow		(69,700)

Conclusion: It is not worthwhile ceasing to produce the TD now.

Note 1:   All sales of the TD will be lost for the next 12 months, this will lose revenue of 1,200 units × $80 = $96,000

Note 2:   All normal labour costs will be saved at 1,200 units × $40 = $48,000

Note 3:   Related product sales will be lost.

This will cost the business 5% × ((5,000u × $150) + (6,000u × $270)) = $118,500 in contribution (material costs are dealt with separately below)

Note 4: If TD is ceased now, then:

Redundancy cost	($6,000)
Retraining saved	$3,500
Recruitment cost	($1,200)
Total cost	($3,700)

Note 5: Supplier payments:

	DW ($)	WM ($)	TD ($)	Net cost ($)	Discount level	Gross cost ($)
Current buying cost	350,000	600,000	60,000	1,010,000	5%	1,063,158
Loss of TD			(60,000)	(60,000)	5%	(63,158)
Loss of related sales at cost	(17,500)	(30,000)		(47,500)	5%	(50,000)
New buying cost				921,500	3%	950,000
Difference in net cost				88,500		

Note 6: There will be no saving or cost here as the supervisor will continue to be fully employed.

An alternative approach is possible to the above problem:

Cash flow	Ref	Amount ($)
Lost contribution – TD	Note 7	12,000
Lost contribution – other products	Note 8	(71,000)
Redundancy and recruitment	Note 4 above	(3,700)
Lost discount	Note 9	(19,000)
Sublet income		12,000
Supervisor	Note 6 above	0
Net cash flow		(69,700)

Note 7: There will be a saving on the contribution lost on the TD of 1,200 units × $10 per unit = –$12,000

Note 8: The loss of sales of other products will cost a lost contribution of 5% ((5,000 × $80) + (6,000 × $170)) = $71,000

Note 9:

	DW	WM	TD	Total (net)	Discount	Total gross
Current buying cost	350,000	600,000	60,000	1,010,000	5%	1,063,158
Saved cost	(17,500)	(30,000)	(60,000)			
New buying cost	332,500	(570,000)	0	902,500	5%	950,000
				921,500	3%	950,000
Lost discount				(19,000)		

(b) **Complementary pricing**

Since the washing machine and the tumble dryer are products that tend to be used together, Stay Clean could link their sales with a complementary price. For example they could offer customers a discount on the second product bought, so if they buy (say) a TD for $80 then they can get a WM for (say) $320. Overall then Stay Clean make a positive contribution of $130 (320 + 80 – 180 – 90).

Product line pricing

All the products tend to be related to each other and used in the utility room or kitchen. Some sales will involve all three products if customers are upgrading their utility room or kitchen for example. A package price could be offered and as long as Stay Clean make a contribution on the overall deal then they will be better off.

(c) Outsourcing requires consideration of a number of issues (only 3 required):

- The cost of manufacture should be compared to cost of buying in from the outsourcer. If the outsourcer can provide the same products cheaper than it is perhaps preferable.

- The reliability of the outsourcer should be assessed. If products are delivered late then the ultimate customer could be disappointed. This could damage the goodwill or brand of the business.

- The quality of work that the outsourcer produces needs to be considered. Cheaper products can often be at the expense of poor quality of materials or assembly.

- The loss of control over the manufacturing process can reduce the flexibility that Stay Clean has over current production. If Stay Clean wanted, say, to change the colour of a product then at present it should be able to do that. Having contracted with an outsourcer this may be more difficult or involve penalties.

249 CHOICE OF CONTRACTS

	Note		North East		South Coast	
		$	$		$	$
Contract price			288,000			352,000
(1)	Material X: inventory	19,440				
(2)	Material X: firm orders	27,360				
(3)	Material X: not yet ordered	60,000				
(4)	Material Y				49,600	
(5)	Material Z				71,200	
(6)	Labour	86,000			110,000	
(8)	Staff accommodation and travel	6,800			5,600	
(9)	Penalty clause				28,000	
(10)	Loss of plant hire income				6,000	
			(199,600)			(270,400)
Profit			88,400			81,600

The company should undertake the North-east contract. It is better than the South coast contract by $6,800 ($88,400 – $81,600).

Notes:

(1)   Material X can be used in place of another material which the company uses. The value of material X for this purpose is 90% × $21,600 = $19,440. If the company undertakes the North-east contract it will not be able to obtain this saving. This is an opportunity cost.

(2)   Although the material has not been received yet the company is committed to the purchase. Its treatment is the same therefore as if it was already in inventory. The value is 90% × $30,400 = $27,360.

(3)   The future cost of material X not yet ordered is relevant.

(4)   The original cost of material Y is a sunk cost and is therefore not relevant. If the material was to be sold now its value would be 24,800 × 2 × 85% = $42,160, i.e. twice the purchase price less 15%, however, if the material is kept it can be used on other contracts, thus saving the company from future purchases. The second option is the better. The relevant cost of material Y is 2 × 24,800 = $49,600. If the company uses material Y on the South-coast contract, it will eventually have to buy an extra $49,600 of Y for use on other contracts.

(5)   The future cost of material Z is an incremental cost and is relevant.

(6)   As the labour is to be sub-contracted it is a variable cost and is relevant.

(7)   Site management is a fixed cost and will be incurred whichever contract is undertaken (and indeed if neither is undertaken), and is therefore not relevant.

(8)   It is assumed that the staff accommodation and travel is specific to the contracts and will only be incurred if the contracts are undertaken.

(9)   If the South-coast contract is undertaken the company has to pay a $28,000 penalty for withdrawing from the North-east contract. This is a relevant cost with regard to the South-coast contract.

(10) The depreciation on plant is not a cash flow. It is therefore not relevant. The opportunity cost of lost plant hire is relevant, however.

(11) It is assumed that the notional interest has no cash flow implications.

(12) It is assumed that the HQ costs are not specific to particular contracts.

250   HS EQUATION

(a) $p = a - bq$ where p is price and q is demand for product

When price = $1,350, demand = 8,000 units

When price = $1,400, demand = 7,000 units

So: (1) $1,350 = a - 8,000q$ and (2) $1,400 = a - 7,000q$

so subtracting equation (1) from equation (2), $50 = 1,000b$ and $b = 0.05$

and substituting in equation (2): $1,400 = a - 0.05 × 7,000$ so $a = 1,750$

so Price = $1,750 - 0.05q$ and marginal revenue = $1,750 - 0.1q$

To find variable production cost per unit, we need to separate fixed and variable costs from the historic cost data. Using the high-low method, dividing the difference in cost for the highest and lowest activity levels by the change in activity.

Variable production cost per unit $= \$(7{,}000 - 5{,}446) \times 1{,}000/(9{,}400 - 7{,}300)$

$= \$1{,}554 \times 1{,}000/2{,}100$

$= \$740$

Direct material cost $= \$270$

Total variable cost $= \$(270 + 740)$

$= \$1{,}010$

Price is maximised where marginal cost (= variable cost) = marginal revenue

$1{,}010 = 1{,}750 - 0.1q$

$q = 7{,}400$ units $\qquad$ and price $= 1{,}750 - 0.05 \times 7{,}400$

So optimum price $= \$1{,}380$

(b)

Tutorial note

*Note that the question only asks for **two** reasons.*

There are a number of reasons why it may be inappropriate for HS to use this model in practice:

- The model depends on the market structure being one in which there is:

  - Perfect competition (which is the closest situation to HS's market)

  - Monopolistic competition

  - Monopoly or

  - Oligopoly

  Whilst the market is highly competitive, it is unlikely that there is perfect competition (in which the action of one company cannot affect the market price).

- The model assumes that costs and demand follow a linear relationship and that there are no step changes in fixed costs. Again this may hold over a small range of volumes but is unlikely to be true for all possible volumes.

- This model can only be used if the company has detailed knowledge of demand and cost curves. It is unlikely that in practice HS would be able to derive accurate cost and demand curves.

251 MKL

(a) The selling price that should be charged for Product K is the one that maximises total contribution, i.e. a price of $75 for a demand of 1,400 units:

Selling price per unit	$100	$85	$80	$75
Variable cost	$38	$38	$38	$38
Unit contribution	$62	$47	$42	$37
Demand units	600 units	800 units	1200 units	1400 units
Total Weekly contribution	**$37,200**	**$37,600**	**$50,400**	**$51,800**

(b) 1,400 units of Product K will use up 1,400 standard hours; in order to utilise all of the spare capacity, we now need to use 600 hours for Product L, for the first 10 weeks.

$$\frac{600 \text{ hours}}{1.25 \text{ hours}} = 480 \text{ units will use all the spare capacity.}$$

To maximise profits, the optimum price P will be expressed as $P = a - bQ$.

Here, $a = \$100 + (\frac{1,000}{200} \times \$10)$

So $a = \$150$ and $b = \frac{\$10}{200} \, 0.05$

$P = \$150 - 0.05Q$

$P = \$150 - 0.05 \times 480$ units

$P = \$126$ for the first 10 weeks.

For the following 10 weeks when the extra capacity becomes available, the optimum price P will be expressed as $P = a - bQ$ and we need to equate MC = MR to maximise profits, with

$MR = a - 2bQ$.

Profit maximised when MC = MR, i.e. when $\$45 = a - 2bQ$

When $\$45 = \$150 - 0.10Q$ i.e. when $Q = 1,050$ units and $P = \$150 - 0.05 \times 1,050$

$P = \$97.50$

(c) **Skimming**

Given that the product is innovative and unlike any current products on the market, then a skimming strategy would seem a very good fit. As the product in new and exciting, charging a high early price would help target the early adopters in the introduction stage. This would also have the advantage of allowing product M to be produced in relatively low volumes, whilst still generating good cashflows to recoup the substantial R&D and launch costs traditionally linked to this kind of products.

Finally, as the market is untested for the product, it allows the firm to start with a high intro price and adjust downwards accordingly.

Penetration pricing

This tactic represents the alternative approach when launching a new product; it involves charging an initial low price to quickly gain market share. It offers the advantage of scaring off potential entrants to the market and may allow the firm to exploit economies of scale. However, given that our product M is differentiated and there will be little, if any, immediate competition, we think the company is right to adopt a skimming strategy for its pricing.

252 HAMMER (JUNE 2010)

(a) Price under existing policy

	$
Steel (0.4/0.95 × $4.00)	1.68
Other materials ($3.00 × 0.9 × 0.1)	0.27
Labour (0.25 × $10)	2.50
Variable overhead (0.25 × $15)	3.75
Delivery	0.50
Total variable cost	8.70
Mark-up 30%	2.61
Transfer price	11.31

(b) The only difference would be to add the fixed costs and adjust the mark-up %.

	$
Existing total variable cost	8.70
Extra fixed cost (0.25 × $15 × 0.8)	3.00
Total cost	11.70
Mark-up 10%	1.17
Transfer price	12.87

The price difference is therefore 12.87 − 11.31 = $1.56 per unit

(c) As far as the manufacturer is concerned, including fixed costs in the transfer price will have the advantage of covering all the costs incurred. In theory this should guarantee a profit for the division (assuming the fixed overhead absorption calculations are accurate). In essence the manufacturer is reducing the risk in his division.

The accounting for fixed costs is notoriously difficult with many approaches possible. Including fixed costs in the transfer price invites manipulation of overhead treatment.

One of the main problems with this strategy is that a fixed cost of the business is being turned into a variable cost in the hands of the seller (in our case the stores). This can lead to poor decision-making for the group since, although fixed costs would normally be ignored in a decision (as unavoidable), they would be relevant to the seller because they are part of their variable buy in price.

(d) **Degree of autonomy allowed to the stores in buying policy.**

If the stores are allowed too much freedom in buying policy Hammer could lose control of its business. Brand could be damaged if each store bought a different supplier's shears (or other products). On the other hand, flexibility is increased and profits could be made for the business by entrepreneurial store managers exploiting locally found bargains. However, the current market price for shears may only be temporary (sale or special offer) and therefore not really representative of their true market 'value'. If this is the case, then any long-term decision to allow retail stores to buy shears from external suppliers (rather than from Nail) would be wrong.

The question of comparability is also important. Products are rarely 'identical' and consequently, price differences are to be expected. The stores could buy a slightly inferior product (claiming it is comparable) in the hope of a better margin. This could seriously damage Hammer's brand.

Motivation is also a factor here, however. Individual managers like a little freedom within which to operate. If they are forced to buy what they see as an inferior product (internally) at high prices it is likely to de-motivate. Also with greater autonomy, the performance of the stores will be easier to assess as the store managers will have control over greater elements of their business.

Marking scheme			
			Marks
(a)	Steel		1
	Other material		1
	Labour		1
	Variable overhead		1
	Delivery		1
	Mark-up		1
			___
		Maximum	**6**
			___
(b)	Fixed cost		2
	Mark-up		2
			___
		Maximum	**4**
			___
(c)	Covers all cost		1
	Risk		1
	Fixed cost accounting		1
	Converts a FC to VC		2
			___
		Maximum	**4**
			___
(d)	Market price may be temporary		1
	Brand		1
	Profitability		1
	Flexibility		1
	Control		1
	Motivation		1
	Performance assessment		1
	Comparability		1
			___
		Maximum	**6**
Total			___
			20
			___

253 SNIFF CO (DECEMBER 2007)

Key answer tips

This is an in-depth question on relevant costing and the further processing decisions.

In part (a) the financial factors may seem obvious, i.e. process further if the profit will increase as a result. However, there are five marks available and so it is not enough to simply make this comment. Consider what will drive profit, e.g. future incremental sales and costs, sales volume. Each of these factors can then be explained briefly.

The main non-financial factor involves the health concerns surrounding the use of the hormones. Ethics is a key motivation of the examiner and so make sure issues such as this are discussed.

In part (b) it is vital that you apply the principles of relevant costing accurately. i.e. you should only include future incremental cash flows:

- Future – Exclude sunk costs such as the market research

- Incremental – The supervisor's salary and fixed costs should be ignored. On the other hand opportunity costs should be included for labour

(a) Sniff should consider the following factors when making a further processing decision:

Financial factors

- **Incremental revenue.** Sniff should only process the perfume further if the incremental revenues from the new product exceeds the incremental costs of processing the perfume.

- **Incremental costs.** A decision to further process can involve more materials and labour. Care must be taken to only include those costs that change as a result of the decision and therefore sunk costs should be ignored. Sunk costs would include, for example, fixed overheads that would already be incurred by the business before the further process decision was taken. The shortage of labour means that its 'true' cost will be higher and need to be included.

Also, Sniff should consider both the Direct costs and the indirect costs (although they may not all be easily identifiable) such as:

(1) The additional space required

(2) Branding costs

(3) Patent costs

(4) Supervisors' costs.

Other factors

- **Impact on overall sales volumes.** Sniff is selling a 'highly branded' product. Existing customers may well be happy with the existing product. If the further processing changes the existing product too much there could be an impact on sales and loyalty.

- **Impact on reputation.** As is mentioned in the question, adding hormones to a product is not universally popular. Many groups exist around the world that protest against the use of hormones in products. Sniff could be damaged by this association.

- **Potential legal cases** being brought regarding allergic reactions to hormones.

(b)

Tutorial note

There are 27 minutes to answer this requirement and therefore no need to panic. A logical, planned structure is essential. Start by calculating the contribution for 1,000 litres of standard perfume, working through each cost and sales item in turn. Once this is done, set up a separate working for the male and female versions. Calculate the extra costs and revenues of further processing. Take a guess if you are not sure of a particular area and move on. Don't forget to conclude, using the financial and non-financial factors.

Market research is a sunk cost and therefore should be ignored for the purpose of the calculation.

Production costs for 1,000 litres of the standard perfume

		$
Aromatic oils	10 ltrs × $18,000/ltr	180,000
Diluted alcohol	990 ltrs × $20/ltr	19,800
		———
Material cost		199,800
Labour	2,000 hrs × $15/hr	30,000
		———
Total		229,800
		———
Cost per litre		229.80
Sales price per litre		399.80

Lost contribution per hour of labour used on new products

($399,800 – $199,800) ÷ 2,000 hrs = $100/hr

Incremental costs

	Male version		Female version	
		$		$
Hormone	2 ltr × $7,750/ltr	15,500	8 ltr × $12,000/ltr	96,000
Supervisor	Sunk cost	0	Sunk cost	0
Labour	500 hrs × $100/hr	50,000	700 hrs × $100/hr	70,000
Fixed cost	Sunk cost	0	Sunk cost	0
Research	Sunk cost	0	Sunk cost	0
		———		———
Total		65,500		166,000
		———		———

Incremental revenues

	Male version		Female version	
		$		$
Standard	200 ltr × $399.80/ltr	79,960	800 ltr × $399.80	319,840
Hormone	202 ltr × $750/ltr	151,500	808 ltr × $595/ltr	480,760
		———		———
Inc. revenue		71,540		160,920
		———		———
Benefit/(cost)		6,040		(5,080)
		———		———

The Male version of the product is worth processing further in that the extra revenue exceeds the extra cost by $6,040.

The Female version of the product is not worth processing further in that the extra cost exceeds the extra revenue by $5,080.

In both cases the numbers appear small. Indeed, the benefit of $6,040 may not be enough to persuade management to take the risk of damaging the brand and the reputation of the business. To put this figure into context: the normal output generates a contribution of $170 per litre and on normal output of about 10,000 litres this represents a monthly contribution of around $1.7m (after allowing for labour costs).

Future production decisions are a different matter. If the product proves popular, however, Sniff might expect a significant increase in overall volumes. If Sniff could exploit this and resolve its current shortage of labour then more contribution could be created. It is worth noting that resolving its labour shortage would substantially reduce the labour cost allocated to the hormone added project. Equally, the prices charged for a one off experimental promotion might be different to the prices that can be secured in the long run.

Note: The original question had parts (c) and (d) as well. The answers to these requirements are as follows:

(c)   The selling price charged would have to cover the incremental costs of $166,000. For 808 litres that would mean the price would have to be

$$\frac{(\$166,000 + \$319,840)}{808 ltrs} = \$601.29/ltr$$

or about $60.13 per 100 ml.

This represents an increase of only 1.05% on the price given and so clearly there may be scope for further consideration of this proposal.

(d)   Outsourcing involves consideration of many factors, the main ones being:

Cost. Outsourcing often involves a reduction in the costs of a business. Cost savings can be made if the outsourcer has a lower cost base than, in this case, Sniff. Labour savings are common when outsourcing takes place.

Quality. Sniff would need to be sure that the quality of the perfume would not reduce. The fragrance must not change at all given the product is branded. Equally Sniff should be concerned about the health and safety of its customers since its perfume is 'worn' by its customers

Confidentiality. We are told that the blend of aromatic oils used in the production process is 'secret. This may not remain so if an outsourcer is employed. Strict confidentiality should be maintained and be made a contractual obligation.

Reliability of supply. Sniff should consider the implications of late delivery on its customers.

Primary Function. Sniff is apparently considering outsourcing its primary function. This is not always advisable as it removes Sniff's reason for existence. It is more common to outsource a secondary function, like payroll processing for example.

Access to expertise. Sniff may find the outsourcer has considerable skills in fragrance manufacturing and hence could benefit from that.

Marking scheme		Marks
(a)	Per factor outlined	1
		—
	Maximum	5
		—
(b)	Hormone costs	2
	Supervisor excluded	1
	Direct labour	3
	Fixed cost allocation excluded	1
	Market research	1
	Incremental revenue	3
	Net benefit	2
	Concluding comment	2
		—
	Maximum	15
		—
Total		20
		—

Examiner's comments (extract)

Part (a) was fairly well done with most mentioning incremental costs and health concerns. Rather fewer mentioned incremental revenue, which was rather worrying.

Part (b) was very mixed with poor layout undermining many efforts. The numbers, including blatantly non relevant costs, was disappointing. This was a decision-making question, so existing fixed costs; the existing supervisor cost and the market research were all correctly excluded as sunk cost. I would prefer in future that sunk costs that are correctly omitted from calculations be mentioned as sunk rather than simply ignored. The marking team will then be able to tell whether the sunk cost treatment has been understood or merely forgotten.

254 FURNIVAL

Key answer tips

Approach the question one step at a time, applying fundamental decision-making principles

(a)　Identify incremental revenues and incremental costs including opportunity costs.

(b)　Ignore fixed costs.

(c)　Ignore costs incurred prior to the split off point.

(i)　Process R further if incremental revenues are greater than incremental costs.

Incremental revenues

	$
Selling price at split off point (per gallon)	1.50
Selling price after mixing	10.00
	———
Increase per gallon	8.50
∴ Total for 500 gallons $8.50 × 500	$4,250

Incremental costs

Variable costs + Opportunity costs

	$
90% of process costs 0.90 × $3,000	2,700
Other separable costs	500
	———
Total	3,200

Opportunity costs

Mixing hours are limited and scarce. If R is not produced, the 'other work' could earn a contribution – this is foregone by processing R further.

Contribution = Profit + Fixed costs

Product R requires 10 hours work.

	$
Therefore, total profit from other work = $200 × 10 hours =	2,000
Fixed cost element 10% of $3,000 ($30 per hour × 10 hours) =	300
Total contribution	2,300
∴ Total incremental costs $3,200 + $2,300	5,500

Therefore do not process further. R should be sold at the split off point.

Tutorial note

The joint process costs are ignored as they are incurred prior to the separation point.

(ii)

Tutorial note

R is sold at the split off point and production remains at 500 gallons. Therefore, R is not relevant to the decision at hand and it may be ignored.

Consider new output from the distillation plant.

P :	700 gallons
Q :	800 gallons
R :	500 gallons
Production of P falls by (1,000 – 700)	300 gallons
Production of Q increases by (800 – 500)	300 gallons

Joint process costs will not change as total production remains at 2,000 gallons. Relevant costs only arise in the mixing plant.

		Product P		Product Q
Revenue per gallon		$12.50		$20.00
Variable costs:				
Process costs	$\dfrac{\$2,700}{1,000g}$	($2.70)	$\dfrac{\$2,700}{500g}$	($5.40)
Other	$\dfrac{\$2,000}{1,000g}$	($2.00)	$\dfrac{\$500}{500g}$	($1.00)
Contribution per gallon		$7.80		$13.60

Loss in contribution from P = 300 × $7.80 =	($2,340)
Gain in contribution from Q = 300 × $13.60 =	$4,080
Net gain	$1,740
Extra cost of Q = 300 × $1 =	($300)
Total	$1,440

However, this change in output will require additional machine hours:

Production of P: Hours used falls by $\dfrac{10}{1,000} \times 300 = 3$ hours

Production of Q: Hours used rise by $\dfrac{10}{500} \times 300 = 6$ hours

Therefore, additional hours required 3 hours

Thus 3 hours' contribution from 'other work' is forgone.

Contribution per hour from other work = $230 (see earlier).

Lost contribution with new plan = $230 × 3 hours = $690

Overall effect of new plan = $1,440 − $690 = $750 gain

Recommendations – Produce P : Q : R ratio of 7 : 8 : 5 and sell R at the split off point.

255 MAN CO (JUNE 2016)

(a) Maximising group profit

Division L has enough capacity to supply both Division M and its external customers with component L. Therefore, incremental cost of Division M buying externally is as follows:

Cost per unit of component L when bought from external supplier: $37 Cost per unit for Division L of making component L: $20.

Therefore incremental cost to group of each unit of component L being bought in by Division M rather than transferred internally: $17 ($37 − 20).

From the group's point of view, the most profitable course of action is therefore that all 120,000 units of component L should be transferred internally.

(b) **Calculating total group profit**

Total group profits will be as follows:

Division L:

Contribution earned per transferred component = $40 – $20 = $20 Profit earned per component sold externally = $40 – $24 = $16

	$
120,000 × $20	2,400,000
160,000 × $16	2,560,000
	4,960,000
Less fixed costs	(500,000)
Profit	4,460,000

Division M:

Profit earned per component sold externally = $27 – $1 = $26

	$
120,000 × $26	3,120,000
Less fixed costs	(200,000)
Profit	2,920,000
Total profit	7,380,000

(c) **Problems with current transfer price and suggested alternative**

The problem is that the current transfer price of $40 per unit is now too high. Whilst this has not been a problem before since external suppliers were charging $42 per unit, it is a problem now that Division M has been offered component L for $37 per unit. If Division M now acts in its own interests rather than the interests of the group as a whole, it will buy component L from the external supplier rather than from Division L. This will mean that the profits of the group will fall substantially and Division L will have significant unused capacity.

Consequently, Division L needs to reduce its price. The current price does not reflect the fact that there are no selling and distribution costs associated with transferring internally, i.e. the cost of selling internally is $4 less for Division L than selling externally. So, it could reduce the price to $36 and still make the same profit on these sales as on its external sales. This would therefore be the suggested transfer price so that Division M is still saving $1 per unit compared to the external price. A transfer price of $37 would also presumably be acceptable to Division M since this is the same as the external supplier is offering.

	Marking scheme		Marks
(a)	Maximising group profits		
	Calculating incremental cost per unit		2
	Recommendation		1
		Maximum	3
(b)	Profit		
	Profit of L		3
	Profit of M		2
	Total profit		1
		Maximum	6
(c)	Discussion		
	Transfer price is too high		2
	Division M will not buy		1
	Profits for group will fall		1
	S/D costs should mean lower TP anyway		2
	Suggested transfer price		1
		Maximum	6
Total			15

256 RECYC

(a) Payoff table

		Level of waste		
		High	Medium	Low
Advance	High	962.5	636.5	397.5
order of	Medium	912.5	655.5	442.5
chemical	Low	837.5	617.5	457.5

Workings

(W1)

Advance order of chemical X	Level of waste	Prob.	Contrib. (excl. X) (W2) $000	Chemical X cost (W3) $000	Net contribution $000
High	High	0.30	1,462.5	500	962.5
	Medium	0.50	1,111.5	475	636.5
	Low	0.20	877.5	480	397.5
Medium	High	0.30	1,462.5	550	912.5
	Medium	0.50	1,111.5	456	655.5
	Low	0.20	877.5	435	442.5
Low	High	0.30	1,462.5	625	837.5
	Medium	0.50	1,111.5	494	617.5
	Low	0.20	877.5	420	457.5

(W2) Waste available

	High	Medium	Low
Aluminium extracted (000 kg)	7,500	5,700	4,500
	$000	$000	$000
Sales revenue (at $0.65 per kg)	4,875.0	3,705.0	2,925.0
Variable cost (at 70%)	3,412.5	2,593.5	2,047.5
Contribution	1,462.5	1,111.5	877.5

(W3) Examples of workings for chemical X cost

- High advance level of order for chemical X and low actual requirement: The price of $1.00 is subject to a penalty of $0.60 per kg. The cost of chemical X is, therefore, 300,000 kg × $1.60 = $480,000

- Low advance level of order for chemical X and medium actual requirement: The price is subject to a discount of $0.10 per kg. The cost of chemical X is, therefore, 380,000 × $1.30 = $494,000.

(b) Maximax suggests that the decision maker should look for the largest possible profit from all the outcomes. In this case this is a high advance order of chemical X where there is a possibility of a contribution of $962,500. This indicates a risk seeking preference by management. Although it offers the possibility of the highest contribution, there is also a 20% likelihood that the worst outcome of $397,500 will occur.

Maximin suggests that the decision maker should look for the strategy which maximises the minimum possible contribution. In this case this is a low advance order of chemical X where the lowest contribution is $457,500. This is better than the worst possible outcomes from high or medium advance orders of chemical X. This indicates a risk-averse management posture.

257 TICKET AGENT *Walk in the footsteps of a top tutor*

Key answer tips

It would be easy to get absorbed in the detail of this question and to spend too much time trying to perfect the calculations. However, to pass the exam, focus on the easy marks. If mistakes are made in earlier calculations, carry forward marks will be available.

(a) The question specifies that a long-run perspective is being taken so decisions can be made by reference to expected values.

Expected sales demand

An easy 3 marks are available here.

	Probability	Demand	EV
Popular artistes	0.45	500	225
Lesser known artistes	0.30	350	105
Unknown artistes	0.25	200	50
			380

Expected demand = 380 tickets per concert

Maximising profit

This part is harder but there are 20 minutes available for this requirement and therefore enough time to understand the scenario and to set out clear workings.

To determine the best decision, the expected profits for each possible order level need to be calculated.

- Payoff table showing profit (W1, W2)

There are 12 calculations to complete. Show the workings for at least one, so that the marker can follow the approach

		Actual sales demand		
		200	350	500
	200	1,200	1,200	1,200
Purchase	300	(570)	2,250	2,250
Level	400	(2,040)	2,190	3,600
	500	(2,460)	1,770	6,000

- Expected values

		EV
200 tickets	1,200 × 1	1,200
300 tickets	(570) × 0.25 + 2,250 × 0.75	1,545
400 tickets	(2,040) × 0.25 + 2,190 × 0.3 + 3,600 × 0.45	1,767
500 tickets	(2,460) × 0.25 + 1,770 × 0.3 + 6,000 × 0.45	2,616

Don't forget to conclude. Another easy mark available.

The optimum purchase level is 500 tickets per concert, which will give an expected profit of $2,616 per concert.

Workings

(W1) The gross profit made per ticket is the discount received on the selling price of $30.

Purchase level	Discount			Profit per ticket sold
200	20%	20% × $30	=	$6.00
300	25%	25% × $30	=	$7.50
400	30%	30% × $30	=	$9.00
500	40%	40% × $30	=	$12.00

(W2) Each net profit calculation consists of up to three elements:

1. the profit on the units sold;

2. the cost of the units which are unsold and returned;

3. the value of the returns

EV of returns = $30.00 × 60% × 10% = $1.80 per return.

Example calculation:

Buy 300 tickets but can only sell 200 $\Rightarrow$ Sell 200 tickets and return 100 tickets

	$
Sales 200 tickets × 7.50 (W1)	1,500
EV of returns 100 tickets × $1.80	180
	———
	1,680
Cost of returns 100 tickets × $22.50 (25% discount)	(2,250)
	———
	(570)
	———

This part is relatively easy.

This part is harder. Take a guess if unsure and move on.

(b) **Maximax**

An easy 2 marks .

The agent should order 500 tickets as this gives a maximum possible gain of $6,000 per concert

Maximin

The agent should buy 200 tickets to maximise the minimum possible pay-off ($1,200).

Minimax regret

A regret table is found by comparing the actual profit with what could have been made given the level of demand that occurred:

This is harder. Even if you can't do the calculation, explain what minimax regret is. This will gain 1 easy mark.

		Actual sales demand		
		200	350	500
	200	0	1,050	4,800
Purchase	300	1,770	0	3,750
Level	400	3,240	60	2,400
	500	3,660	480	0

The agent would thus order 400 tickets as this limits the maximum regret to $3,240.

This level of order would give an average profit of $1,767 per concert.

(c) The advice depends on the risk perspective of the agent

More easy marks available. The advice should be linked back to parts (a) and (b). Points should be separate and succinct.

- If he is willing to take a long term perspective and accept short-term uncertainty, then the expected value calculations in part (a) should be adopted, giving an order of 500 tickets

- If he is an optimist, then the maximax criteria would suggest ordering 500 tickets

- If he is a pessimist, then the maximin criteria would suggest ordering 200 tickets

- If he is a sore loser, then the minimax regret approach would suggest buying 400 tickets.

In reality the agent may be best advised to insist on knowing who the artists are before having to place an order.

258 SHIFTERS HAULAGE (DECEMBER 2008)

(a) Maximax stands for maximising the maximum return an investor might expect. An investor that subscribes to the maximax philosophy would generally select the strategy that could give him the best possible return. He will ignore all other possible returns and only focus on the biggest, hence this type of investor is often accused of being an optimist or a risk-taker.

Maximin stands for maximising the minimum return an investor might expect. This type of investor will focus only on the potential minimum returns and seek to select the strategy that will give the best worst case result. This type of investor could be said to be being cautious or pessimistic in his outlook and a risk-avoider.

Expected value averages all possible returns in a weighted average calculation.

For example if an investor could expect $100 with a 0.3 probability and $300 with a 0.7 probability then on average the return would be:

$(0.3 \times \$100) + (0.7 \times \$300) = \$240$

This figure would then be used as a basis of the investment decision. The principle here is that if this decision was repeated again and again then the investor would get the EV as a return. Its use is more questionable for use on one-off decisions.

Key answer tips

Easy marks were available here. This is a core knowledge area and no application of knowledge was required. There will be easy marks for knowledge in each exam.

(b) **Profit calculations**

	Small Van	Medium Van	Large Van
Capacity	100	150	200
Low Demand (120)	300 (W1)	468 (W3)	368 (W5)
High Demand (190)	300 (W2)	500 (W4)	816 (W6)

Workings	(W1)	(W2)	(W3)	(W4)	(W5)	(W6)
Sales	1,000	1,000	1,200	1,500	1,200	1,900
VC	(400)	(400)	(480)	(600)	(480)	(760)
Goodwill	(100)	(100)		(100)		
VC adjustment			48		48	76
Depreciation	(200)	(200)	(300)	(300)	(400)	(400)
Profit	300	300	468	500	368	816

Tutorial note

Some candidates were confused about which level of demand should be used. The only levels of demand mentioned were 120 and 190 units and therefore these should have been used. Other candidates were confused about the appropriate adjustments that should have been made for variable costs, goodwill and depreciation.

Profit tables are a key part of risk and uncertainty. The approach to preparing them will always be similar and therefore candidates should practice a number of questions before sitting the exam.

(c)   Which type of van to buy?

This depends on the risk attitude of the investor. If they are optimistic about the future then the maximax criteria would suggest that they choose the large van as this has the potentially greatest profit.

If they are more pessimistic then they would focus on the minimum expected returns and choose the medium van as the worst possible result is $468, which is better than the other options. We are also told that the business managers are becoming more cautious and so a maximin criterion may be preferred by them.

Expected values could be calculated thus:

Small van	$300
Medium van ($468 × 0.4) + ($500 × 0.6) =	$487
Large van ($368 × 0.4) + ($816 × 0.6) =	$637

Given SH is considering replacing a number of vans you could argue that an EV approach has merit (not being a one-off decision – assuming individual booking sizes are independent of each other).

The final decision lies with the managers, but given what we know about their cautiousness a medium sized van would seem the logical choice. The small van could never be the correct choice.

Key answer tips

Good candidates discussed the results for the small, medium and large van in turn. Candidates linked their discussion back to the information provided in the scenario and expanded on the points made in part (a) of the answer.

Note: The original question asked for a discussion of three methods that could be used to analyse and assess the risk in decision making. The suggested answer is given below:

Market research: This can be desk-based (secondary) or field-based (primary). Desk-based is cheap but can lack focus. Field-based research is better in that you can target your customers and your product area but can be time consuming and expensive. The internet is bringing down the cost and speeding up this type of research, email is being used to gather information quickly on the promise of free gifts etc.

Simulation: Computer models can be built to simulate real life scenarios. The model will predict what range of returns an investor could expect from a given decision without having risked any actual cash. The models use random number tables to generate possible values for the uncertainty the business is subject to. Again computer technology is assisting in bringing down the cost of such risk analysis.

Sensitivity analysis: This can be used to assess the range of values that would still give the investor a positive return. The uncertainty may still be there but the affect that it has on the investor's returns will be better understood. Sensitivity calculates the % change required in individual values before a change of decision results. If only a (say) 2% change is required in selling price before losses result an investor may think twice before proceeding. Risk is therefore better understood.

Calculation of worst and best case figures: An investor will often be interested in range. It enables a better understanding of risk. An accountant could calculate the worst case scenario, including poor demand and high costs whilst being sensible about it. He could also calculate best case scenarios including good sales and minimum running costs. This analysis can often reassure an investor. The production of a probability distribution to show an investor the range of possible results is also useful to explain risks involved. A calculation of standard deviation is also possible.

	Marking scheme		
			Marks
(a)	Maximax explanation		2.0
	Maximin explanation		2.0
	Expected value explanation		2.0
		Maximum	**5.0**
(b)	Small van sales		0.5
	Small van VC		0.5
	Small van goodwill or VC adjustment		1.0
	Small van depreciation		1.0
	Medium van – as above for small van		3.0
	Large van as above for small van		3.0
		Maximum	**9.0**
(c)	Optimist view		2.0
	Pessimist view		2.0
	Expected value calculation		1.0
	Expected value discussion		1.0
		Maximum	**6.0**
Total			**20**

Examiner's comments (extract)

Part (a) was well done by most. The biggest issue was that some did not mention risk attitudes at all (an optimist would naturally favour maximax for example) this omission meant that 0.5 less marks were scored each time by failing to collect the allocated mark.

Part (b) was also reasonably done by many. There were problems here though:

- A surprising number of candidates did not seem to understand that if the capacity of a van is 150 and demand is 190 then sales must be restricted to 150. A large number of candidates still put down sales at the 190 level. This indicates a lack of understanding of the question (I assume that they do not read it properly).

- Many candidates did not include the goodwill adjustment in the profit calculation. This was not entirely unexpected. More than half marks were still available even if this adjustment were ignored.

- A common mistake was to try and calculate expected sales first and then work out some sort of answer accordingly.

Part (c) was more mixed. I expected that each potential risk attitude be taken in turn and applied to the figures. Where this was done good marks were earned. A surprising number failed to apply themselves to this. Some clearly knew what maximax, maximin and expected value were but could not then apply this knowledge to the question. The step up from F2 is significant and surely an element of application is part of that step.

Part (d) (i.e. the additional requirement) was poorly done by many. Those that had revised the area of risk in decision making did well and scored good marks. Many clearly did not have the knowledge required. Minimax regret was not a valid answer despite what about 50% of candidates thought. Sensitivity, simulation and market research comments all scored good marks.

259   RY DECISION TREE

(a) and (b)

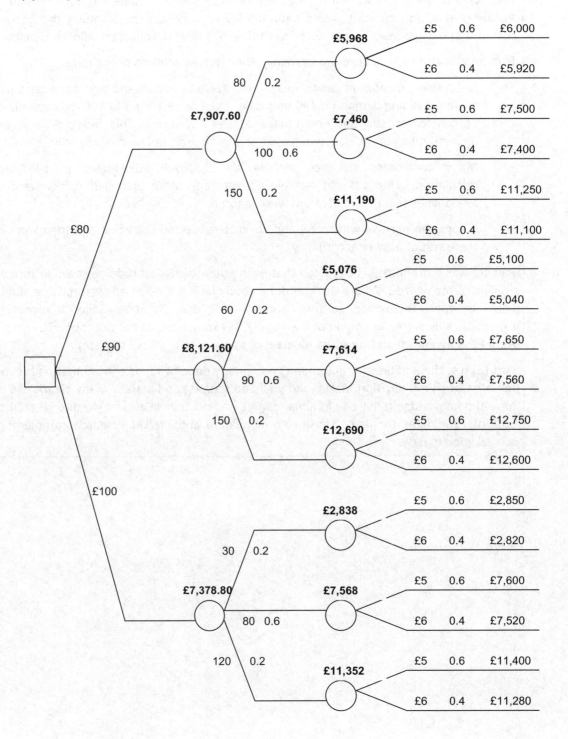

(b) continued

The optimum price to set is £90. The answer can be calculated from the decision tree (see diagram).

Alternative working:

Expected variable cost per customer; $(£5 × 0.6) + (£6 × 0.4) = £5.40$

Price	Contribution per customer	Expected demand	Total contribution
£80	£74.60	106 (W1)	£7,907.60
£90	£84.60	96 (W2)	£8,121.60
£100	£94.60	78	£7,378.80

(W1) $(80 × 0.2) + (100 × 0.6) + (150 × 0.2) = 106$

(W2) $(60 × 0.2) + (90 × 0.6) + (150 × 0.2) = 96$

(c) Consider the expected contribution for each price alternative if demand is pessimistic;

At £80, expected contribution (for pessimistic market) is £5,968

At £90, expected contribution (for pessimistic market) is £5,076

At £100, expected contribution (for pessimistic market) is £2,838.

Note: These figures have been extracted from the decision tree. They could have been calculated without the use of the tree.

Hence a price of £80 should be set

260 AMELIE

(a) In order to decide whether or not to hire the consultant, expected valued for decision alternatives are calculated, starting on the right hand side of the tree and moving leftwards (backtracking).

At node D:

EV(I) = $(0.9 × \$30,000) – (0.1 × \$10,000) = \$26,000$

EV(J) = $(0.9 × \$60,000) – (0.1 × \$40,000) = \$50,000$

EV(K) = $(0.9 × \$0) – (0.1 × \$0) = \$0$

So, the decision at Node D should be to go for a large shop, as the EV of outcome J is the highest of the three possible decisions I, J and K.

At node E:

EV(L) = $(0.12 × \$30,000) – (0.88 × \$10,000) = (\$5,200)$

EV(M) = $(0.12 × \$60,000) – (0.88 × \$40,000) = (\$28,000)$

EV(N) = $(0.12 × \$0) – (0.88 × \$0) = \$0$

So, the decision at Node E should be not to go for any shop at all, as the EV of outcome N is the only non-loss making option.

At node C:

EV(F) = (0.5 × $30,000) – (0.5 × $10,000) = $10,000

EV(G) = (0.5 × $60,000) – (0.5 × $40,000) = $10,000

EV(H) = (0.5 × $0) – (0.5 × $0) = $0

So, the decision at Node C should be to go for either a small or a large shop, as both offer the same positive EV of a profit.

To decide between hiring a consultant at $5,000 and not hiring a consultant, we need to calculate the EV of profits at node B :

EV(B) = (0.6 × $50,000) + (0.4 × $0) = $30,000

Therefore, profits if a consultant is hired are expected to reach

$30,000 – cost of research $5,000 = $25,000

EV(C) = $10,000, if no market research is undertaken. The expected value of profits is higher if market research is undertaken, therefore Amelie should hire the consultant.

(b) We first need to calculate what the expected value of profits with perfect information would be. If the second consultant predicts a favourable cheese market (0.6 probability), we should opt for a large shop and obtain $60,000 profit. If the consultant predicts an unfavourable market, we should not go for no shop at all (and profits will be nil.)

Therefore EV of profits with perfect information   = 0.6 × $60,000 + (0 × $0)

                                                          = $36,000

Expected profit with imperfect market research information from first consultant

                                                          = $25,000

Value of perfect information   **= $11,000**

BUDGETING AND CONTROL

261 STATIC CO (DECEMBER 2016)

(a)   Workings

From budgeted figures: need to work out what the compound growth rate is and the distribution costs as a percentage of revenue.

Compound sales growth: $13,694/13,425 or $13,967/13,694 = 2% Distribution costs: $671/$13,425 = 5%

From actual figures: GPM = $5,356/14,096 = 38%

Distribution costs: $705/14,096 = still 5%.

Starting point for revenue now $14,096 but compound growth rate still 2%.

Rolling budget for the 12 months ending 30 November 20X7

	Q2	Q3	Q4	Q1
	$000	$000	$000	$000
Revenue	14,378	14,666	14,959	15,258
Cost of sales	(8,914)	(9,093)	(9,275)	(9,460)
Gross profit	5,464	5,573	5,684	5,798
Distribution costs	(719)	(733)	(748)	(763)
Administration costs	(2,020)	(2,020)	(2,020)	(2,020)
Operating profit	2,725	2,820	2,916	3,015

Tutorial note

The question made it clear that the assumptions of the original budget were accurate but incorrect prices had been used in the first place. This meant that, before the rolling budget could be prepared, the actual gross profit margin (GPM) from the quarter that had just ended needed to be calculated and this percentage then needed to be applied when calculating the cost of sales and gross profit figures for the rolling budget. If you simply calculate the GPM from the original budget and ignore the actual quarter 1 figures, the cost of sales and gross profit figures will be incorrect in their rolling budget.

Another mistake to avoid would be to start the rolling budget with the actual quarter 1 figures that had been given in the question and then only produce three further quarters. This would show a lack of understanding of how rolling budgets work.

(b)   Problems

The use of fixed budgeting has caused serious problems at Static Co. The fact they were using inaccurate sales forecast figures led them to invest in a production line which was not actually needed, even though they knew they were inaccurate. This unnecessary investment cost them $6m and caused the return on investment to halve. Had rolling budgets been used at the time, and used properly, the sales forecasts for the remaining quarters would have been adjusted to reflect a fall in demand and the investment would not have been made.

Presumably, inaccurate sales forecasts would have led the business to get their staffing levels and materials purchases wrong as well. This too will have cost the business money. They were forced to heavily discount their goods in order to try to reach their targets at the end of the year, which was simply unrealistic. It can often be difficult to put prices back up again once they have been discounted. However, the actual results from the first quarter suggest that prices have increased again, which is fortunate.

Improvements

The use of rolling budgets should mean that a downturn in demand is adjusted for in future quarters, rather than sales simply being pushed into the last quarter, which is not a realistic adjustment. Management is forced to reassess the budget regularly and produce up to date information. This means that accurate management decisions can then be made and mistakes like investing in a new production line which is not needed should not happen again. Planning and control will be more accurate.

Tutorial note

Do not make the mistake to simply copy out parts of the scenario without adding any value to them. For example, it was not enough to say that a problem of the previous system was that many product lines had to be heavily discounted in the last quarter. Answers needed to go on and say that this discounting was a problem because it led to reduced sales revenues for the company and made it difficult to subsequently increase prices to their original level in later quarters.

(c)   **Problems trying to implement new budgeting system**

The first problem may be trying to obtain the right information needed to update the budget. The FD has been sacked and two other key finance personnel are off work due to stress. This could make it very difficult to obtain information if the department is understaffed and lacking the direction given by the FD. Staff in the finance department may not have the skills to update the budget and roll it forward, having never done it before. Similarly, the sales department is without a SD and he would usually have played a key part in reviewing figures for the sales forecasts. Hence, it may be difficult to obtain reliable sales data.

Even without this staffing issue, obtaining the correct information could be difficult as actually preparing rolling budgets is new for Static Co. Staff will need training. They are only used to preparing fixed budgets, although these have often been revised in the past to move sales into later periods. Staff are not familiar with the process of updating all of their financial information again: reviewing sales demand to realistically reforecast, updating costs, etc. This process takes time and staff may feel resentful about having to do this again so soon after the annual budgeting process which would recently have been undertaken.

The new MD is new to this industry and therefore lacks experience of how it works. Whilst he is confident that the assumptions of the original fixed budget still stand true, he is not in a good position to know that this is in fact the case. They may be wrong and, if they are, the new rolling budget will be unreliable.

Tutorial note

Make double sure that you read the requirement carefully. On the whole, the problems of implementing rolling budgeting are different from the problems of using rolling budgets on an ongoing basis, apart from the fact that both implementation and ongoing use of rolling budgets are time consuming and therefore expensive. Please carefully review this suggested answer for this part of the question, because answers on exam day were fairly weak here and many opportunities to gain marks were lost.

	Marking scheme		
			Marks
(a)	Growth rate		1
	Actual distribution cost %		0.5
	Actual GPM %		0.5
	Use of Q1 actuals		1
	Rolling budget: sales		1
	COS		1
	GPM		0.5
	Distribution costs		1
	Administration costs		1
	Operating profit		0.5
			───
		Maximum	8
			───
(b)	Problems and improvements		6
			───
(c)	Implementation problems		6
			───
Total			20
			───

262 EFFECTIVE BUDGETING

(a) Effective budgeting involves devising optimum sales/production/resource usage plans, and the setting of appropriate standards and targets that will encourage their achievement.

Plans must be devised based upon the current and expected future business and economic environments, with the organisation's reactions to known opportunities and threats built in. Alternative short- and medium-term strategies must be considered, and standards must be set taking account of expected variations from past data.

(b) Whilst much of the data required to make budgeting decisions can be collected, computed and analysed from various software packages, many decisions must be made by the managers themselves. Indeed, the managers will initially have to decide the relevant data that the computer should be given to work on.

The impact of alternative strategies on profits, cash flow, resource availability etc. can be calculated by the computer, but the choice of the optimum strategy, probably incorporating multiple objectives with varying priorities, is down to management.

Certainly the budget number-crunching can now be a routine, automatic process, but the use of the numbers produced in decision making by management will determine the effectiveness of the budgeting system itself.

(c) **A periodic budget** is one that is drawn up for a full budget period, such as one year. A new budget will not be introduced until the start of the next budget period, although the existing budget may be revised if circumstances deviate markedly from those assumed during the budget preparation period.

A **continuous, or rolling budget** is one that is revised at regular intervals by adding a new budget period to the full budget as each budget period expires. A budget for one year, for example, could have a new quarter added to it as each quarter expires. In this way, the budget will continue to look one year forward. Cash budgets are often prepared on a continuous basis.

The advantages of periodic budgeting are that it involves less time, money and effort than continuous budgeting. For example, frequent revisions of standards could be avoided and the budget-setting process would require managerial attention only on an annual basis.

A major advantage of continuous budgeting is that the budget remains both relevant and up to date. As it takes account of significant changes in economic activity and other key elements of the organisation's environment, it will be a realistic budget and hence is likely to be more motivating to responsible staff. Another major advantage is that there will always be a budget available that shows the expected financial performance for several future budget periods.

It has been suggested that if a periodic budget is updated whenever significant change is expected, a continuous budget would not be necessary. Continuous budgeting could be used where regular change is expected, or where forward planning and control are essential, such as in a cash budget.

(d) **Budget bias (budgetary slack)** occurs when managers aim to give themselves easier budget targets by understating budgeted sales revenue or overstating budgeted costs.

Cost control using budgets is achieved by comparing actual costs for a budget period with budgeted or planned costs. Significant differences between planned and actual costs can then be investigated and corrective action taken where appropriate.

Budget bias will lead to more favourable results when actual and budgeted costs are compared. Corrective action may not be taken in cases where costs could have been reduced and in consequence inefficiency will be perpetuated and overall profitability reduced.

Managers may incur unnecessary expenditure in order to protect existing budget bias with the aim of making their jobs easier in future periods, since if the bias were detected and removed, future budget targets would be more difficult to achieve. Unnecessary costs will reduce the effectiveness of cost control in supporting the achievement of financial objectives such as value for money or profitability.

Where budget bias exists, managers will be less motivated to look for ways of reducing costs and inefficiency in those parts of the organisation for which they bear responsibility. The organisation's costs will consequently be higher than necessary for the level of performance being budgeted for.

263 NN

(a) **The adoption of zero-based budgeting within NN Ltd**

During recent years the management of NN Ltd has used the traditional approach to incremental budgeting. The approach entails the use of the previous year's budget being rolled forward into the next year's budget purely budget.

Zero-based budgeting was developed to overcome the shortcomings of the technique of incremental budgeting. The implementation of a zero-based budgeting would require each manager within NN Ltd to effectively start with a blank sheet of paper and a budget allowance of zero. The managers would be required to defend their budget levels at the beginning of each and every year.

The implementation of a system of zero-based budgeting will require a consideration of the following:

- The need for major input by management

- The fact that it will prove extremely time consuming

- The need for a very high level of data capture and processing

- The subjective judgement inherent in its application

- The fact that it might be perceived as a threat by staff

- Whether its adoption may encourage a greater focus upon the short-term to the detriment of longer-term planning.

(b) The implementation of zero-based budgeting will require a major planning effort by our personnel. It is through the planning process that important guidelines and directions are provided for the development and ranking of the decision packages. Also, the planning process will enable managers to prepare for the uncertainty of the future. Long-range planning allows managers to consider the potential consequences of current decisions over an extended timeframe.

Zero-based budgeting addresses and supports comprehensive planning, shared decision-making, the development and application of strategies and allocation of resources as a way of achieving established goals and objectives. In addition, zero-based budgeting supports the added processes of monitoring and evaluation.

Zero-based budgeting, when properly implemented, has the potential to assist the personnel of an organisation to plan and make decisions about the most efficient and effective ways to use their available resources to achieve their defined mission, goals and objectives.

There is no doubt that the process of zero-based budgeting will consume a great deal more management time than the current system of budgeting does. This will certainly be the case in implementation of the system because managers will need to learn what is required of them. Managers may object that it is too time-consuming to introduce zero-based budgeting, however, it could be introduced on a piece-meal basis. As regards the imposition upon management time, managers may object that they simply do not have the necessary time in order to undertake an in-depth examination of every activity each year. However, if this proves to be the case then we could consider the establishment of a review cycle aimed at ensuring that each activity is reviewed on at least one occasion during every two or three years.

I propose that we hold a series of training seminars for our management to help in the transition to a system of zero-based budgeting. We must also ensure that we 'sell the benefits' that would arise from a successful implementation. A zero-based budgeting system would assist our managers to:

- Develop and/or modify the organisation's mission and goals

- Establish broad policies based on the mission and goals

- Efficiently identify the most desirable programs to be placed in operation

- Allocate the appropriate level of resources to each program

- Monitor and evaluate each program during and at the end of its operation and report the effectiveness of each program.

Thus, as a consequence of the adoption of zero-based budgeting our managers should be able to make decisions on the basis of an improved reporting system.

It is quite possible that zero-based budgeting would help identify and eliminate any budget bias or 'budget slack' that may be present. Budgetary slack is 'a universal behavioural problem' which involves deliberately overstating cost budgets and/or understating revenue budgets to allow some leeway in actual performance. We must acknowledge that in organisations such as ours where reward structures are based on comparisons of actual with budget results, bias can help to influence the amount paid to managers under incentive schemes. However, we should emphasise that if managers are to earn incentives as a consequence of incentive schemes that are based upon a comparison of actual outcomes with budgeted outcomes, then a zero-based budget would provide a fair yardstick for comparison.

It is important to provide reassurance to our managers that we do not intend to operate a system of zero-based budgeting against the backdrop of a blame-culture. This will help to gain their most positive acceptance of the change from a long established work practice that they may perceive afforded them a degree of 'insurance'.

(c) The finance director is probably aware that the application of zero-based budgeting within NN Ltd might prove most fruitful in the management of discretionary costs where it is difficult to establish standards of efficiency and where such costs can increase rapidly due to the absence of such standards. A large proportion of the total costs incurred by NN Ltd will comprise direct production and service costs where the existence of input: output relationships that can be measured render them more appropriate to traditional budgeting methods utilising standard costs. Since the predominant costs incurred by a not for profit health organisation will be of a discretionary nature, one might conclude that the application of zero-based budgeting techniques is more appropriate for service organisations such as the not for profit health organisation than for a profit-seeking manufacturer of electronic office equipment. A further difference lies in the fact that the ranking of decision packages is likely to prove less problematic within an organisation such as NN Ltd which is only involved in the manufacture and marketing of electronic office equipment. By way of contrast, there is likely to be a much greater number of decision packages of a disparate nature, competing for an allocation of available resources within a not for profit health organisation.

264 ZERO BASED BUDGETING (DECEMBER 2010)

(a) Difficulties in the public sector

In the public sector, the objectives of the organisation are more difficult to define in a quantifiable way than the objectives of a private company. For example, a private company's objectives may be to maximise profit. The meeting of this objective can then be set out in the budget by aiming for a percentage increase in sales and perhaps the cutting of various costs. If, on the other hand, the public sector organisation is a hospital, for example, then the objectives may be largely qualitative, such as ensuring that all outpatients are given an appointment within eight weeks of being referred to the hospital. This is difficult to define in a quantifiable way, and how it is actually achieved is even more difficult to define.

This leads onto the next reason why budgeting is so difficult in public sector organisations. Just as objectives are difficult to define quantifiably, so too are the organisation's outputs. In a private company the output can be measured in terms of sales revenue.

There is a direct relationship between the expenditure that needs to be incurred i.e. needs to be input in order to achieve the desired level of output. In a hospital, on the other hand, it is difficult to define a quantifiable relationship between inputs and outputs. What is more easy to compare is the relationship between how much cash is available for a particular area and how much cash is actually needed. Therefore, budgeting naturally focuses on inputs alone, rather than the relationship between inputs and outputs.

Finally, public sector organisations are always under pressure to show that they are offering good value for money, i.e. providing a service that is economical, efficient and effective. Therefore, they must achieve the desired results with the minimum use of resources. This, in itself, makes the budgeting process more difficult.

(b)   Incremental and zero-based budgeting

'Incremental budgeting' is the term used to describe the process whereby a budget is prepared using a previous period's budget or actual performance as a base, with incremental amounts then being added for the new budget period.

'Zero-based budgeting', on the other hand, refers to a budgeting process which starts from a base of zero, with no reference being made to the prior period's budget or performance. Every department function is reviewed comprehensively, with all expenditure requiring approval, rather than just the incremental expenditure requiring approval.

(c)   Stages in zero-based budgeting

Zero-based budgeting involves three main stages:

(1)   Activities are identified by managers. These activities are then described in what is called a 'decision package'. This decision package is prepared at the base level, representing the minimum level of service or support needed to achieve the organisation's objectives. Further incremental packages may then be prepared to reflect a higher level of service or support.

(2)   Management will then rank all the packages in the order of decreasing benefits to the organisation. This will help management decide what to spend and where to spend it.

(3)   The resources are then allocated based on order of priority up to the spending level.

(d)   No longer a place for incremental budgeting

The view that there is no longer a place for incremental budgeting in any organisation is a rather extreme view. It is known for encouraging slack and wasteful spending, hence the comment that it is particularly unsuitable for public sector organisations, where cash cutbacks are being made. However, to say that there is no place for it at all is to ignore the drawbacks of zero-based budgeting. These should not be ignored as they can make ZBB implausible in some organisations or departments. They are as follows:

•   Departmental managers will not have the skills necessary to construct decision packages. They will need training for this and training takes time and money.

•   In a large organisation, the number of activities will be so large that the amount of paperwork generated from ZBB will be unmanageable.

•   Ranking the packages can be difficult, since many activities cannot be compared on the basis of purely quantitative measures. Qualitative factors need to be incorporated but this is difficult.

- The process of identifying decision packages, determining their purpose, costs and benefits is massively time consuming and therefore costly.

- Since decisions are made at budget time, managers may feel unable to react to changes that occur during the year. This could have a detrimental effect on the business if it fails to react to emerging opportunities and threats.

It could be argued that ZBB is more suitable for public sector than for private sector organisations. This is because, firstly, it is far easier to put activities into decision packages in organisations which undertake set definable activities. Local government, for example, have set activities including the provision of housing, schools and local transport. Secondly, it is far more suited to costs that are discretionary in nature or for support activities. Such costs can be found mostly in not for profit organisations or the public sector, or in the service department of commercial operations.

Since ZBB requires all costs to be justified, it would seem inappropriate to use it for the entire budgeting process in a commercial organisation. Why take so much time and resources justifying costs that must be incurred in order to meet basic production needs? It makes no sense to use such a long-winded process for costs where no discretion can be exercised anyway. Incremental budgeting is, by its nature, quick and easy to do and easily understood. These factors should not be ignored.

In conclusion, whilst ZBB is more suited to public sector organisations, and is more likely to make cost savings in hard times such as these, its drawbacks should not be overlooked.

Marking scheme		Marks
(a)	Explanation	
	Difficulty setting objectives quantifiably	2
	Difficulty in saying how to achieve them	1
	Outputs difficult to measure	2
	No relationship between inputs and outputs	2
	Value for money issue	2
		—
	Maximum	5
		—
(b)	Incremental and zero-based budgeting	
	Explaining 'incremental budgeting'	2
	Explaining 'zero-based budgeting'	2
		—
	Maximum	4
		—
(c)	Stages involved in zero-based budgeting	
	Each stage	1
		—
	Maximum	3
		—
(d)	Discussion	
	Any disadvantage of inc. that supports statement (max. 3)	1
	Incremental budgeting is quick and easy	1
	Any disadvantage of ZBB that refutes statement (max. 3)	1
	Easier to define decision packages in public sector	2
	more appropriate for discretionary costs	2
	Conclusion	1
		—
	Maximum	8
		—
Total		20
		—

265 BIG CHEESE CHAIRS (DECEMBER 2009)

(a) The average cost of the first 128 chairs is as follows:

		$
Frame and massage mechanism		51.00
Leather	2 metres × $10/mtr × 100/80	25.00
Labour	(W1)	20.95
Total		96.95

Target selling price is $120.

Target cost of the chair is therefore $120 × 80% = $96

The cost gap is $96.95 – $96.00 = $0.95 per chair

Workings

(W1) The cost of the labour can be calculated using learning curve principles. The formula can be used or a tabular approach would also give the average cost of 128 chairs. Both methods are acceptable and shown here.

Tabulation:

Cumulative output (units)	Average time per unit (hrs)	Total time (hrs)	Average cost per chair at $15 per hour
1	2		
2	1.9		
4	1.805		
8	1.71475		
16	1.6290125		
32	1.54756188		
64	1.47018378		
128	1.39667459	178.77	20.95

Formula:

$Y = ax^b$

$Y = 2 \times 128^{-0.074000581}$

$Y = 1.396674592$

The average cost per chair is $1.396674592 \times \$15 = \$20.95$

(b) To reduce the cost gap various methods are possible (only four are needed for full marks)

- Re-design the chair to remove unnecessary features and hence cost

- Negotiate with the frame supplier for a better cost. This may be easier as the volume of sales improve as suppliers often are willing to give discounts for bulk buying. Alternatively a different frame supplier could be found that offers a better price. Care would be needed here to maintain the required quality

- Leather can be bought from different suppliers or at a better price also. Reducing the level of waste would save on cost. Even a small reduction in waste rates would remove much of the cost gap that exists

- Improve the rate of learning by better training and supervision

- Employ cheaper labour by reducing the skill level expected. Care would also be needed here not to sacrifice quality or push up waste rates.

(c) The cost of the 128th chair will be:

		$
Frame and massage mechanism		51.00
Leather	2 metres × $10/mtr × 100/80	25.00
Labour	1.29 hours × $15 per hour (W2)	19.35
		——
Total		95.35
		——

Against a target cost of $96 the production manager is correct in his assertion that the required return is now being achieved.

(W2) Using the formula, we need to calculate the cost of the first 127 chairs and deduct that cost from the cost of the first 128 chairs.

$$Y = ax^b$$

$$Y = 2 \times 127^{-0.074000581}$$

$$Y = 1.39748546$$

Total time is $127 \times 1.39748546 = 177.48$ hours

Time for the 128th chair is $178.77 - 177.48 = 1.29$ hours

<table>
<tr><th colspan="3" align="center">Marking scheme</th></tr>
<tr><td></td><td></td><td>Marks</td></tr>
<tr><td>(a)</td><td>Frame cost</td><td>1.0</td></tr>
<tr><td></td><td>Leather cost</td><td>2.0</td></tr>
<tr><td></td><td>Labour average time for 128 units</td><td>1.0</td></tr>
<tr><td></td><td>Labour total time for 128 units</td><td>1.0</td></tr>
<tr><td></td><td>Average cost per chair</td><td>1.0</td></tr>
<tr><td></td><td>Target cost</td><td>1.0</td></tr>
<tr><td></td><td>Cost gap</td><td>1.0</td></tr>
<tr><td></td><td align="right">Maximum</td><td>8.0</td></tr>
<tr><td>(b)</td><td>Per suggestion</td><td>1.5</td></tr>
<tr><td></td><td align="right">Maximum</td><td>6.0</td></tr>
<tr><td>(c)</td><td>Frame</td><td>0.5</td></tr>
<tr><td></td><td>Leather</td><td>0.5</td></tr>
<tr><td></td><td>Average time per unit</td><td>2.0</td></tr>
<tr><td></td><td>Total time</td><td>1.0</td></tr>
<tr><td></td><td>Time for 128th chair</td><td>1.0</td></tr>
<tr><td></td><td>Conclusion</td><td>1.0</td></tr>
<tr><td></td><td align="right">Maximum</td><td>6.0</td></tr>
<tr><td>Total</td><td></td><td>20</td></tr>
</table>

266 HENRY COMPANY (DECEMBER 2008)

(a) There are various issues that HC should consider in making the bid. (Only five are required for two marks each.)

Contingency allowance. HC should consider the extent to which its estimates are accurate and hence the degree of uncertainty it is subjected to. It may be sensible to allow for these uncertainties by adding a contingency to the bid.

Competition. HC must consider which other businesses are likely to bid and recognise that the builder may be able to choose between suppliers. Moreover HC has not worked for this builder before and so they will probably find the competition stiff and the lack of reputation a problem.

Inclusion of fixed overhead. In the long run fixed overhead must be covered by sales revenue in order to make a profit. In the short run it is often correctly argued that the level of fixed cost in a business may not be affected by a new contract and therefore could be ignored in bid calculation. HC needs to consider to what extent the fixed costs of its business will change if it wins this new contract. It is these incremental fixed costs that are relevant to a bid calculation.

Materials and loose tools. No allowance has been made for the use of tools and the various fixings (screws etc) that will be needed to assemble and fit the kitchens. It is possible that most fixings would be provided with the kitchen units but HC should at least consider this.

Supervision of labour. The time given in the question is 24 hours to 'fit' the first kitchen. There seems no allowance for supervision of the labour force. It could of course be included within the overhead figures but no detail is shown.

Idle time. It is common for building works to be delayed by lack of materials for example. The labour time figure needs to reflect this.

Likelihood of repeat business. Some businesses consider it worthwhile to accept a low price for a new contract if it establishes a reputation with a new buyer. HC could offer to do this work cheaper in the hope of more profitable work later on.

The risk of non-payment. HC may decide not to bid at all if it feels that the builder may struggle to pay.

Opportunity costs of alternative work.

Possibility of working in overtime.

Key answer tips

Easy marks were available here for discussing any sensible and relevant factors that should be taken into account. Good candidates related their discussion back to the information provided in the scenario and used short paragraphs to explain each factor, with the aim of scoring one mark for each of the factors explained.

(b) Bid calculations for HC to use as a basis for the apartment contract.

Cost	Hours	Rate per hour	Total
			$
Labour	9,247 (W1)	$15	138,705
Variable overhead	9,247	$8 (W2)	73,976
Fixed overhead	9,247	$4 (W2)	36,988
			_____
Total cost			249,669
			_____

Workings

(W1) Need to calculate the time for the 200th kitchen by taking the total time for the 199 kitchens from the total time for 200 kitchens.

For the 199 Kitchens

Using

$y = ax^b$ OR $y = ax^b$

$y = 24 \times 199^{-0.074}$ $y = (24 \times 15) \times 199^{-0.074}$

$y = 16.22169061$ hours $y = 243.32536$

Total time = 16.22169061 × 199   Total cost = $48,421.75

Total time = 3,228.12 hours

For the 200 Kitchens

$y = ax^b$ OR $y = ax^b$

$y = 24 \times 200^{-0.074}$ $y = (24 \times 15) \times 200^{-0.074}$

$y = 16.21567465$ hours   Total cost = $48,647.02

Total time = 16.21567465 × 200 200th cost = $225.27

Total time = 3,243.13 hours

The 200th Kitchen took 3,243.13 − 3,228.12 = 15.01 hours

Total time is therefore:

For first 200	3,243.13 hours
For next 400 (15.01 hours × 400)	6,004.00 hours
Total	9,247.13 hours (9,247 hours)

(W2) The overheads need to be analysed between variable and fixed cost elements.

Taking the highest and lowest figures from the information given:

	Hours	Cost $
Highest	9,600	116,800
Lowest	9,200	113,600
Difference	400	3,200

Variable cost per hours is $3,200/400 hours = $8 per hour

Total cost = variable cost + fixed cost

116,800 = 9,600 × 8 + fixed cost

Fixed cost = $40,000 per month

Annual fixed cost = $40,000 × 12 = $480,000

Fixed absorption rate is $480,000/120,000 hours = $4 per hour

---

Key answer tips

Requirements (b)and (c) Involved learning curve calculations. This is a core knowledge area and candidates who had practised learning curve calculations will have scored well.

(c) A table is useful to show how the learning rate has been calculated.

Number of Kitchens	Time for Kitchen (hours)	Cumulative time (hours)	Average time (hours)
1	24.00	24.00	24.00
2	21.60	45.60	22.80

The learning rate is calculated by measuring the reduction in the average time per kitchen as cumulative production doubles (in this case from 1 to 2).

The learning rate is therefore 22.80/24.00 or 95%

Marking scheme		
		Marks
(a)	1 mark for each description **Maximum**	5.0
(b)	Average time for the 199th kitchen	1.0
	Total time for 199 kitchens	1.0
	Average time for the 200th kitchen	1.0
	Total time for 200 kitchens	1.0
	200th kitchen time	1.0
	Cost for the first 200	1.0
	Cost for the next 400	1.0
	Variable cost per hour	2.0
	Fixed cost per month	1.0
	Fixed cost per hour	1.0
	Cost for variable overhead	1.0
	Cost for fixed overhead	1.0
	Maximum	13
(c)	Average time per unit and explanation	2
Total		20

Examiner's comments (extract)

Part (a) was not done well by many. All that was required was sensible ideas about figures that might have to be included in the bid (without calculations). The marking scheme was generously applied and marks were given if candidates included factors relating whether or not to bid instead of factors concerning the amount of the bid. Some marks were also given for a more theoretical approach (opportunity costs should be allowed for...). Despite this the average mark struggled to reach half marks. Perhaps candidates were looking for something more difficult than is there or grasping at the text book hoping for a text book answer to fit.

Part (b) was well done by many candidates despite it being a fairly demanding aspect of learning curves (the steady state).

Part (c) was reasonably attempted by most.

267 TR CO (SEPTEMBER/DECEMBER 2017)

(a)   **Step 1: Establish the demand function**

Tutorial note

This is a fairly technical part (a).

The first skill tested here is the choice of the right pricing method. As students are given information about how changes in price will affect demand, it is the MR = MC method (as opposed to the tabular method) that must be picked.

Students are expected to recognise that information about the learning effect must be taken into account to calculate labour costs and, in turn, establish the 'Marginal Cost' component of their pricing calculations.

Armed with this a sound knowledge of cost behaviour (fixed costs remain fixed!), the step-by-step approach to calculating the optimum price is the perfect example of a tool from the examiner's metaphorical 'toolbox' approach.

b = change in price/change in quantity

b = $2/5,000 units = 0.0004

The maximum demand for Parapain is 1,000,000 units, so where P = 0, Q = 1,000,000, so 'a' is established by substituting these values for P and Q into the demand function:

0 = a − (0.0004 × 1,000,000)

0 = a − 400

Therefore a = 400 and the demand function is therefore: $P = 400 - 0.0004Q$

Step 2: Establish the marginal cost

		Total in $
Material Z	500 g × $010	50
Material Y	300 g × $0.50	150
Labour	Working 1	6.6039
Machine running cost	(20/60) × $6.00	2
Total marginal cost per batch		208.6039

Note: Fixed overheads have been ignored as they are not part of the marginal cost.

The marginal cost will now be rounded down to $208.60 per batch.

Working 1: Labour

The labour cost of the 1,000th unit needs to be calculated as follows as this is the basis TR Co will determine the price for Parapain:

Learning curve formula: $Y = aX^b$

'a' is the cost for the first batch: 5 hours × $18 = $90

If X = 1,000 batches and b = –0.321928, then $Y = 90 \times 1,000^{-0.321928} = 9.7377411$

Total cost for 1,000 batches = $9,737.7411

If X = 999 batches, then $Y = 90 \times 999^{-0.321928} = 9.7408781$

Total cost for 999 batches = $9,731.1372

Therefore the cost of the 1,000 batches ($9,737.7411 – $9,731.1372) = $6.6039

Step 3: Establish the marginal revenue function: MR = a – 2bQ

Equate MC and MR and insert the values for 'a' and 'b' from the demand function in step 1.

208.60 = 400 – (2 × 0.0004 × Q)

Step 4: Solve the MR function to determine optimum quantity, Q

208.60 = 400 – 0.0008Q

0.0008Q = 191.4

Q = 239,250 batches

Step 5: Insert the value of Q from step 4 into the demand function determined in step 1 and calculate the optimum price

P = 400 – (0.0004 × 239,250)

P = $304.30

Step 6: Calculate profit

	Total in $
Revenue (239,250 batches × $304.30)	72,803,775
Variable cost (239,250 batches × $208.60)	(49,907,550)
Fixed costs (250,000 batches × $2)	(500,000)
Profit	22,396,225

(b)   Market penetration pricing

Tutorial note

Requirement (b) asked discussions and recommendations; for students wondering where to start, pros and cons of different strategies are a good point to make initially. It is interesting to notice that even if all information pointed towards skimming as the strategy of choice, students would have not maximised marks unless market penetration was mentioned, too.

With penetration pricing, a low price would initially be charged for the anti-malaria drug. The ideology behind this is that the price will make the product accessible to a larger number of buyers and therefore the high sales will compensate for the lower prices being charged. The anti-malaria drug would rapidly become accepted as the only drug worth buying, i.e. it would gain rapid acceptance in the marketplace.

The circumstances which would favour a penetration pricing policy are:

–   Highly elastic demand for the anti-malaria drug, i.e. the lower the price, the higher the demand. There is no evidence that this is the case.

–   If significant economies of scale could be achieved by TR Co so that higher sales volumes would result in sizeable reductions in costs. It cannot be determined if this is the case here.

–   If TR Co was actively trying to discourage new entrants into the market, however in this case, new entrants cannot enter the market anyway due to the patent.

–   If TR Co wished to shorten the initial period of the drug's life-cycle so as to enter the growth and maturity stages quickly but there is no evidence the company wish to do this.

Market skimming pricing

With market skimming, high charges would initially be charged for the anti-malaria drug rather than low prices. This would enable TR Co to take advantage of the unique nature of the product. The most suitable conditions for this strategy are:

–   The product has a short life cycle and high development costs which need to be recovered. There is no information about the drug's life cycle but development costs have been high.

–   Since high prices attract competitors, there needs to be barriers to entry if competitors are to be deterred. In TR Co's case it has a patent for the drug and also the high development costs could act as a barrier.

–   Where high prices in the early stages of a product's life cycle are expected to generate high initial cash flows, this will help TR Co recover the high development costs it has incurred.

Recommendation

Given the unique nature of the drug and the barriers to entry, a market skimming pricing strategy would appear to be the far more suitable pricing strategy. Also, whilst there is demand curve data, it is unknown how reliable this data is, in which case a skimming strategy may be the safer option.

	Marking scheme		
			Marks
(a)	Demand function		1.5
	Marginal cost/batch		2.5
	Labour 1,000th batch		3.5
	Establishing MR function		0.5
	Solve MR to find Q		1.0
	Use demand function and Q to find P		1.0
	Contribution based on P and Q		1.0
	Deduction of fixed costs		0.5
	Profit		0.5
			———
		Maximum	12
			———
(b)	Penetration pricing		3
	Skimming pricing		3
	Other relevant comments/recommendation		2
			———
		Maximum	8
Total			20

268 PERSEUS CO – REVISION OF BASIC VARIANCES

Key answer tips

It is unlikely that a question in the PM exam will just include variances covered in the 'Management Accounting' (MA) paper. The purpose of this question is to allow you to revise these 'basic variances'.

(a) **Workings**

Standard variable cost per unit		$
Materials:		
007	6 kilos at $12.25 per kilo	73.50
XL90	3 kilos at $3.20 per kilo	9.60
		———
		83.10
Labour	4.5 hours at $8.40 per hour	37.80
		———
		120.90
		———

Standard usages:

Material 007	15,400 units should use (× 6)	92,400 kilos
Material XL90	15,400 units should use (× 3)	46,200 kilos
Labour	15,400 units should take (× 4.5)	69,300 hours

15,400 units of production and sale

	Actual		Standard	
	$	$	$	$
Sales	(at $138.25)	2,129,050	(at $140)	2,156,000
		————		————
Costs				
Materials				
007		1,256,640	(15,400 × $73.50)	1,131,900
XL90		132,979	(15,400 × $9.60)	147,840
Labour		612,766	(15,400 × $37.80)	582,120
Fixed overheads		96,840		86,400
		————		————
Total costs		2,099,225		1,948,260
		————		————
Profit		29,825		207,740
		————		————

(b) Reconciliation

Workings

Sales price	$	
15,400 units should sell for	2,156,000	
They did sell for	2,129,050	
	————	
Sales price variance	26,950	(A)
	————	

Materials 007	kg	
15,400 units should use	92,400	
They did use	98,560	
	————	
Material 007 usage variance (kg)	6,160	(A)
	————	

Standard price/kg	$12.25	
Usage variance in $	$75,460	(A)

Materials 007	$	
98,560 kg should cost (× $12.25)	1,207,360	
They did cost	1,256,640	
	————	
Material price variance	49,280	(A)
	————	

Materials XL90	kg	
15,400 units should use	46,200	
They did use	42,350	
Material 007 usage variance (kg)	3,850	(F)

Standard price/kg	$3	
	20	
Usage variance in $	$12,320	(F)

Materials XL90	$	
42,350 kg should cost (× $3.20)	135,520	
They did cost	132,979	
Material price variance	2,541	(F)

Actual hours worked = $612,766 ÷ $8.65 = 70,840 hours

Labour efficiency	Hours	
15,400 units should take	69,300	
They did take	70,840	
Labour efficiency variance (hrs)	1,540	(A)

Standard rate/hour	$8.40	
Efficiency variance in $	$12,396	(A)

Labour rate	$	
70,840 hours should cost		
(× $8.40)	595,056	
They did cost	612,766	
Material price variance	17,710	(A)

	$	
Fixed overhead expenditure		
Budgeted fixed overhead costs	86,400	
Actual fixed overhead costs	96,840	
Expenditure variance	10,440	(A)

Reconciliation

	Fav	Adverse	$
Standard profit on 15,400 units of sale, on previous page			207,740
	$	$	
Variances:			
Sales price		26,950	
Materials 007 usage		75,460	
Materials XL90 usage	12,320		
Materials 007 price		49,280	
Materials XL90 price	2,541		
Labour efficiency		12,936	
Labour rate		17,710	
Fixed overhead expenditure variance		10,440	
	14,861	192,776	
Total variances			177,915 A
Actual profit			29,825

(c) The causes of variances might be inter-related, and the reason why one variance is favourable could also help explain why another variance is adverse.

Using poor quality materials could result in a favourable price variance because of paying a lower price. The poor quality material could be the cause of both an adverse material usage variance and an adverse labour efficiency variance, because cheaper materials might be more difficult to work with, resulting in more rejects/spoilt work, or more waste.

If a higher grade of labour was used, compared with that which was planned, there would most certainly be an adverse labour rate variance. The higher skill level employed could well be the reason for a favourable labour efficiency variance and a favourable material usage variance, for example due to a lower number of rejects and less waste of materials.

(d) Possible causes of an adverse labour rate variance include the following:

- The standard labour rate per hour may have been set too low.

- Employees may have been of a higher grade than standard, with a consequent increase in the hourly rate paid.

- There may have been an unexpected increase in the prevailing market rate of pay for employees with appropriate skills.

- Where bonuses are included as a part of direct labour costs, increased bonus payments may have been made, above the standard level expected.

- There may have been a change in the composition of the work force, which resulted in an increase in the average rate of pay.

Note: Only TWO possible causes are required.

269   VALET CO (JUNE 2014)

(a)   **Variances**

(i)   **The sales mix contribution variance**

Calculated as (actual sales quantity – actual sales quantity in budgeted proportions) × standard contribution per unit.

Standard contributions per valet:

Full = $50 × 44.6% = $22.30 per valet

Mini = $30 × 55% = $16.50 per valet

Actual sales quantity in budgeted proportions (ASQBP):

Full: 7,980 × (3,600/5,600) = 5,130

Mini: 7,980 × (2,000/5,600) = 2,850

Valet type	AQAM	AQBM	Difference	Standard contribution	Variance
				$	$
Full	4,000	5,130	(1,130)	22.30	25,199 A
Mini	3,980	2,850	1,130	16.50	18,645 F
					6,554 A

(ii)   **The sales quantity contribution variance**

Calculated as (actual sales quantity in budgeted proportions – budgeted sales quantity) × standard contribution per unit.

Valet type	AQBM	BQBM	Difference	Standard contribution	Variance
				$	$
Full	5,130	3,600	1,530	22.30	34,119 F
Mini	2,850	2,000	850	16.50	14,025 F
					48,144 F

(b)   **Description**

The sales mix contribution variance This variance measures the effect on profit of changing the mix of actual sales from the standard mix. The sales quantity contribution variance This variance measures the effect on profit of selling a different total quantity from the budgeted total quantity.

(c)   Sales performance of the business The sales performance of the business has been very good over the last year, as shown by the favourable sales quantity variance of $48,144. Overall, total sales revenue is 33% higher than budgeted (($319,400 – $240,000)/$240,000). This is because of a higher total number of valets being performed. When you look at where the difference in sales quantity actually is, you can see from the data provided in the question that it is the number of mini valets which is substantially higher. This number is 99% ((3,980 – 2,000)/2,000) higher than budgeted, whereas the number of full valets is only 11% ((4,000 – 3,600)/3,600) higher. Even 11% is still positive, however.

The fact that the number of mini valets is so much higher combined with the fact that they generate a lower contribution per unit than the full valet led to an adverse sales mix variance of $6,554 in the year. This cannot be looked at in isolation as a sign of poor performance; it is simply reflective of the changes which have occurred in Strappia. We are told that disposable incomes in Strappia have decreased by 30% over the last year.

This means that people have less money to spend on nonessential expenditure such as car valeting. Consequently, they are opting for the cheaper mini valet rather than the more expensive full valet. At the same time, we are also told that people are keeping their cars for an average of five years now as opposed to three years. This may be leading them to take more care of them and get them valeted regularly because they know that the car has to be kept for a longer period. Thus, the total quantity of valets is higher than budgeted, particularly the mini valets. Also, there is now one less competitor for Valet Co than there was a year ago, so Valet Co may have gained some of the old competitor's business. Together, all of these factors would explain the higher number of total valets being performed and in particular, of the less expensive type of valet.

Note: Other valid points will be given full credit

270   THE SCHOOL UNIFORM COMPANY (MARCH/JUNE 2017)

Tutorial note

The first requirement is to "Calculate the material variances in as much detail as the information allows for the month of February." It is clear then, that we need to know material variances. The question is not specific however, and we don't know which variances are required – this is one of the key skills that are being tested. There are several variances we might be able to calculate here – the "basic" price and usage variances and the more advanced planning and operational variances or mix and yield.

Reading the scenario very carefully, and being on the lookout for information about both standard and actual usage and prices for material, will help. The second paragraph provides information – firstly that the design has changed, and now requires more material than previously – the standard cost card will need to be revised to allow for this, and any usage variance should be analysed between the planning variance caused by the change in design, and the operational variance which we can use to assess the production manager. Secondly, a new material is being used, which is cheaper than the previous material. It is worth noting here that the new material was chosen by GPST – a customer of SU, therefore this decision was not made by the production manager. This is crucial for two reasons – firstly this cannot be used to assess the production manager's performance for part (c) and secondly an uncontrollable change from the original standard means that we should split our materials price variance into planning and operational components – the 5% reduction in price constitutes the planning variance.

In answering parts (a) and (b), it's obviously essential to know the variances calculations. Most students do, but the main reason for low scores is that only the basic variances are calculated. Avoid the pitfall in the exam: there are 12 marks available in total – for 6 variances – materials price (planning and operational), materials usage (planning and operational) and labour efficiency (planning and operational). Calculating just the 3 basic variances would not score a passing mark.

(a)   SP (standard price per metre: $2.85/0.95) $3.00

SQ (standard quantity per dress: 2.2 metres/1.1)   2 metres

From scenario the revised price per metre (RP) is $2.85, the actual price per metre (AP) is $2.85 and the revised quantity per dress (RQ) is 2.2 metres.

SQAP (standard quantity for actual production: 2 metres × 24,000) 48,000 metres
RQAP (revised quantity for actual production: 2.2 metres × 24,000) 52,800 metres

From the scenario the actual production level (AP) is 24,000 dresses and actual quantity of material bought and used (AQ) is 54,560 metres.

Material price variances

Planning variance (SP – RP) × AQ: ($3.00 – $2.85) × 54,560	8,184F
Operational variance (RP – AP) × AQ: ($2.85 – $2.85) × 54,560	0
Total price variance	8,184 F

Material usage variances

Planning variance (SQAP – RQAP) × SP: (48,000 – 52,800) × $3.00	14,400 A
Operational variance (RQAP – AQ) × SP: (52,800 – 54,560) × $3.00	5,280 A
Total usage variance	19,680 A
Total material variance	11,496 A

Tutorial note: *The most common error when calculating variances of this type is to use budgeted production to calculate standard usage. For example, taking the basic materials usage variance –many candidates write this as the difference between the actual quantity of material at the standard price, and the standard quantity of material at the standard price. It is the SQ that causes the problems – it means the standard (expected) quantity of material to make ACTUAL production.*

So in our case, actual production was 24,000 units – the original standard amount per unit was 2m, so SQ would be 2m*24,000 = 48,000m. Similarly, the revised standard quantity would be 2.2*24,000 = 52,800m. You would never use the budgeted quantity to calculate standard usage, as you're comparing it to the actual quantity of material used to make ACTUAL production.

Tutorial note: *These variances could have been calculated using the alternative approach as below:*

Material price variances

Planning variance

(AP × RQ) × (SP – RP): 24,000 × 2.2 metres × ($3.00 – $2.85)   *7,920 F*

Operational variance

(RP – AP) × AQ: 54,560 metres × ($2.85 – $2.85)

Material usage variances

Planning variance

(SQ – RQ) × AP × SP: 24,000 × (2 metres – 2.2 metres) × $3.00	14,400 A

Operational variance

((AP × RQ) – AQ) × RP: 24,000 × 2.2 metres – 54,560 × $2.85	5,016 A
Total material variance	11,496 A

(b)

AH (actual hours worked and paid): 24 × 160 hours	3,840 hours
SHAP (standard hours for actual production): (24,000 × 8)/60	3,200 hours RHAP
(revised hours for actual production): (24,000 × 10)/60	4,000 hours

From the scenario the standard rate per hour (SR) is $12, the standard time per dress is eight minutes and the revised time per dress is 10 minutes.

Labour efficiency variances

Planning variance (SHAP – RHAP) × SR: (3,200 – 4,000) × $12	9,600 A
Operational variance (RHAP – AH) × SR: (4,000 – 3,840) × $12	1,920 F
Total labour efficiency variance	7,680 A

Tutorial note: *We know we will need details about labour time to calculate our efficiency variance. Again, the change in design has had an effect on time taken – the new design will take 2 minutes longer to make. Again, this will cause a planning variance – the original standard will need to be revised to allow for this extra time, as the production manager should not be criticised for the change in design, which was not their decision. We are also told that there was no idle time, ruling out any idle time variances.*

Next we are given budgeted and actual production. Actual production levels are essential in working out variances, as they compare actual figures to the flexed budget (based on actual production). The budgeted production figure is less important here, although it could be noted that actual production was 20% under budget, which may have a knock-on effect on profits.

(c)

Tutorial note: *In the final paragraph, we are told that the production manager is responsible for purchasing and production issues. This means that they can be have some control over the materials price variance, as well as materials usage and labour efficiency variances, so we can use these to assess their performance.*

The production manager did not have any control over the change in the design of the dress as this change was requested by the client. Similarly, it was not his fault that the company accountant responsible for updating standard costs was off sick and therefore unable to update the standards. Therefore, the production manager should be judged only by those variances over which he has control, which are the operational variances.

Materials

No operational variance arose in relation to materials price, since the actual price paid was the same as the revised price. A planning variance of $8,184F does arise but the production manager cannot take the credit for this, as the material chosen by GPST for the new dresses just happens to be cheaper. As regards usage, an adverse variance of $5,280 arose. This suggests that, even with the revised quantity of material being taken into account, staff still used more than 2.2 metres on average to produce each dress. This is probably because they had to learn a new sewing technique and they probably made some mistakes, resulting in some wastage. The manager is responsible for this as it may have been caused by insufficient training. However, the labour efficiency variances below shed some more light on this.

Tutorial note

It was much easier to score well on part (c) if you had already determined what was controllable and what was not. Easy marks could be gained here for explaining that the materials usage was due to the change in design, and therefore not controllable, and the materials price planning variance was due to GPST's decision to change the material – again, not controllable. You could then look at the operational variances and, based on whether they were adverse or favourable, decide whether the production manager had performed well or not.

Labour

Tutorial note

Easy marks could be gained here for explaining that labour efficiency planning variances were due to the change in design, and therefore not controllable, You could then look at the operational variances and, based on whether they were adverse or favourable, decide whether the production manager had performed well or not.

Remember that in many cases the variances have some interconnectivity. For example here, the operational labour efficiency variance was favourable, showing that the workers worked faster than expected. However the operational material usage variance was adverse, meaning that more material was used to make the actual production of 24,000 dresses than expected. This could have been because the workers were rushing, and therefore more material was wasted. Identifying possible cause and effect relationships like this will lead to a lot of credit being given.

The labour efficiency operational variance was favourable, which suggests good performance by the production manager. Staff took less than the expected revised 10 minutes per dress. However, when looked at in combination with the material usage operational variance above, it could be inferred that staff may have rushed a little and consequently used more material than necessary.

Tutorial note

When assessing performance it is also useful to give a conclusion. This should be in line with your previous findings – using total operational variance here would be a useful yardstick.

When both of the operational variances are looked at together, the adverse materials usage $5,280 far outweighs the favourable labour efficiency variance of $1,920. Consequently, it could be concluded that, overall, the manager's performance was somewhat disappointing.

Marking scheme		
		Marks
(a)	Standard price	1
	Standard quantity	0.5
	SQAP	0.5
	RQAP	0.5
	Price planning variance	1.5
	Usage planning variance	1.5
	Usage op variance	1.5
	Maximum	**7**
(b)	Actual hours	1
	SHAP	0.5
	RHAP	0.5
	Planning variance	1.5
	Operating variance	1.5
	Maximum	**5**
(c)	Controllability	1
	Variances/performance	6
	Other/conclusion	1
	Maximum	**8**
Total		**20**

271 GLOVE CO (JUNE 2016)

(a) Basic variances

Tutorial note

A fundamental mistake to avoid here is to use the labour rate per unit ($42) rather than the labour rate per hour ($42 per unit/3 hours per unit = $14 per labour hour). Using $42 by mistake would lead to very large labour variances and ring alarm bells for the candidate.

Labour rate variance

Standard cost of labour per hour = $42/3 = $14 per hour.

Labour rate variance = (actual hours paid × actual rate) – (actual hours paid × std rate)

Actual hours paid × actual rate = $531,930.

Actual hours paid × std rate = 37,000 × $14 = $518,000.

Therefore rate variance = $531,930 – $518,000 = $13,930 A

Labour efficiency variance

Labour efficiency variance = (actual production in std hours – actual hours worked) × std rate [(12,600 × 3) – 37,000] × $14 = $11,200 F

(b) Planning and operational variances

Labour rate planning variance

(Revised rate – std rate) × actual hours paid = [$14.00 – ($14.00 × 1.02)] × 37,000 = $10,360 A.

Labour rate operational variance

Revised rate × actual hours paid = $14.28 × 37,000 = $528,360. Actual cost = $531,930.

Variance = $3,570 A.

Labour efficiency planning variance

(Standard hours for actual production – revised hours for actual production) × std rate Revised hours for each pair of gloves = 3.25 hours.

[37,800 – (12,600 × 3.25)] × $14 = $44,100 A.

Labour efficiency operational variance

(Revised hours for actual production – actual hours for actual production) × std rate (40,950 – 37,000) × $14 = $55,300 F.

(c)   Analysis of performance

Tutorial note

Most students are aware that uncontrollable factors are not to be used to assess performance, and will score marks in the exam for saying so. But in order to bag even more marks, identifying WHY things happened, and what they mean, is essential. A good understanding of the variances helps here. For example, if we have an adverse operational labour rate variance, what does this mean? It means that our hourly rate was higher than expected, after adjusting for the uncontrollable factors. Why would this be – look for help in the scenario. An overtime rate is mentioned – this would explain a higher hourly rate. Explaining reasons for variances or movements will score many more marks than bland comments such as 'the variance is adverse which is bad.' This doesn't assess the performance of the production manager.

At a first glance, performance looks mixed because the total labour rate variance is adverse and the total labour efficiency variance is favourable. However, the operational and planning variances provide a lot more detail on how these variances have occurred.

The production manager should only be held accountable for variances which he can control. This means that he should only be held accountable for the operational variances. When these operational variances are looked at it can be seen that the labour rate operational variance is $3,570 A. This means that the production manager did have to pay for some overtime in order to meet demand but the majority of the total labour rate variance is driven by the failure to update the standard for the pay rise that was applied at the start of the last quarter. The overtime rate would also have been impacted by that pay increase.

Then, when the labour efficiency operational variance is looked at, it is actually $55,300 F. This shows that the production manager has managed his department well with workers completing production more quickly than would have been expected when the new design change is taken into account. The total operating variances are therefore $51,730 F and so overall performance is good.

The adverse planning variances of $10,360 and $44,100 do not reflect on the performance of the production manager and can therefore be ignored here.

Marking scheme			
			Marks
(a)	Basic variances		
	Each variance		1
		Maximum	**2**
(b)	Operational and planning variance		
	Labour rate planning		1.5
	Labour rate operational		1.5
	Labour efficiency planning		1.5
	Labour efficiency operational		1.5
		Maximum	**6**
(c)	Performance		
	Only operational variances		1
	Adverse op. variance		2
	Failure to update the standard		1
	Overtime rate impacted		1
	Favourable efficiency variance		2
	Good overall		1
		Maximum	**7**
Total			**15**

272 SAFE SOAP CO (DECEMBER 2014)

(a) Variance calculations

Mix variance

Total kg of materials per standard batch = 0.25 + 0.6 + 0.5 = 1.35 kg

Therefore standard quantity to produce 136,000 batches = 136,000 × 1.35 kg = 183,600 kg

Actual total kg of materials used to produce 136,000 batches = 34,080 + 83,232 + 64,200 = 181,512 kg

Material	Actual quantity standard mix in kgs	Actual quantity actual mix in kgs	Variance in kgs	Standard cost per kg in $	Variance $
Lye	181,512 × 0.25/1.35 = 33,613.33	34,080	(466.67)	10	(4,666.70)
Coconut oil	181,512 × 0.6/1.35 = 80,672	83,232	(2,560)	4	(10,240)
Shea butter	181,512 × 0.5/1.35 = 67,226.67	64,200	3,026.67	3	9,080.01
	181,512	181,512			(5,826.69)A

Yield variance

Material	Standard quantity standard mix in kgs	Actual quantity standard mix in kgs	Variance in kgs	Standard cost per kg in $	Variance $
Lye	0.25 × 136,000 = 34,000	33,613.33	386.67	10	3,866.70
Coconut oil	0.6 × 136,000 = 81,000	80,672	928	4	3,712
Shea butter	0.5 × 136,000 = 68,000	67,226.67	773.33	3	2,319.99
	183,600	181,512			9,898.69 F

(b) **(i)** A materials mix variance will occur when the actual mix of materials used in production is different from the standard mix. So, it is inputs which are being considered. Since the total mix variance is adverse for the Safe Soap Co, this means that the actual mix used in September and October was more expensive than the standard mix.

A material yield variance arises because the output which was achieved is different from the output which would have been expected from the inputs. So, whereas the mix variance focuses on inputs, the yield variance focuses on outputs. In both September and October, the yield variance was favourable, meaning that the inputs produced a higher level of output than one would have expected.

(ii) Whilst the mix and yield variances provide Safe Soap Co with a certain level of information, they do not necessarily explain any quality issues which arise because of the change in mix. The consequences of the change may well have an impact on sales volumes. In Safe Soap Co's case, the sales volume variance is adverse, meaning that sales volumes have fallen in October. It is not known whether they also fell in September but it would be usual for the effects on sales of the change in mix to be slightly delayed, in this case by one month, given that it is only once the customers start receiving the slightly altered soap that they may start expressing their dissatisfaction with the product.

There may also be other reasons for the adverse sales volume variance but given the customer complaints which have been received, the sales manager's views should be taken on board.

(c) The **theory of motivation** suggests that having a clearly defined target results in better performance than having no target at all, that targets need to be accepted by the staff involved, and that more demanding targets increase motivation provided they remain accepted. It is against this background that basic, ideal, current and attainable standards can be discussed.

A **basic standard** is one that remains unchanged for several years and is used to show trends over time. Basic standards may become increasingly easy to achieve as time passes and hence, being undemanding, may have a negative impact on motivation. Standards that are easy to achieve will give employees little to aim at.

Ideal standards represent the outcome that can be achieved under perfect operating conditions, with no wastage, inefficiency or machine breakdowns. Since perfect operating conditions are unlikely to occur for any significant period, ideal standards will be very demanding and are unlikely to be accepted as targets by the staff involved as they are unlikely to be achieved. Using ideal standards as targets is therefore likely to have a negative effect on employee motivation.

Current standards are based on current operating conditions and incorporate current levels of wastage, inefficiency and machine breakdown. If used as targets, current standards will not improve performance beyond its current level and their impact on motivation will be a neutral one or a negative one since employees may feel unmotivated due to the lack of challenge.

Attainable standards are those that can be achieved if operating conditions conform to the best that can be practically achieved in terms of material use, efficiency and machine performance. Attainable standards are likely to be more demanding than current standards and so will have a positive effect on employee motivation, provided that employees accept them as achievable.

PERFORMANCE MEASUREMENT AND CONTROL

273 B5 CARS EIS

Key answer tips

This question tests your knowledge of sources of information and the operation of an executive information system (EIS).

In answering the question you need to recognise the costs and benefits associated with information with particular reference to the distinction between internally produced information and that gathered from external sources.

(a) One of the main reasons why B5 Cars' EIS is becoming expensive to operate is the amount of data which has been, and is being, accumulated. For an EIS to be effective there is a requirement for large amounts of information to be easily accessible – the data should be on-line and as up-to-date as possible. This has disc storage implications which increase over time as the volume of information increases.

The increased costs do not end with disk storage, however. As the system is required to handle larger volumes of data, there are numerous knock-on costs. The larger the database the more processing power required to conduct straightforward operations. Therefore, another increased expense may be a requirement to invest in hardware as the original processor proves inadequate to handle the volume of information within acceptable response times.

Data is obtained from various different external sources; this may be causing a requirement for extra disk storage in excess of the amount required as a result of the normal growth of the databank.

The information requirements of the executives using an EIS may change over time. This means that, however carefully the system was set up originally, there will be costs involved in making changes to the way in which the system is set up. The degree with which maintenance and support costs increase will be dependent to some extent on the original design of the programs and database and to what extent the information requirements alter.

Another area where costs may increase is the network service. As the volume of data increases, particularly if appropriate hardware investment is not made, it is likely that it will take longer to extract the required information. This will result in greater costs of actually using the line. The rental of the line may also have increased.

The EIS uses data collated from various sources. There are potential costs associated with the capture of this data; large amounts of data may need to be manually keyed in which has implications on staffing costs or the cost of hiring an agency to do the work.

(b) Management's decision to concentrate on internally-produced information will have serious implications.

Market information

It is important for companies to be aware of the activities of their competitors. By collecting only internally-produced information the management are getting a restricted picture of what is really taking place. Management need to know how their products measure up to those of their competitors in terms of quality, design etc.

Without external information the information system can hardly be described as an EIS, but would be providing information at an operational level. It is important for organisations to establish their own indicators as a means of measuring their performance, but it is at least as important to set these in context. For example, if a production unit is performing well against its own measures but is failing to perform well in relation to its competitors, management needs to be aware of this and take action to recover the situation.

Without competitor information B5 Cars may find that they are out of line with the rest of the industry. They may find that their competitors are offering free finance, as an example, whereas B5 Cars are offering 'cheap' finance at 7% APR; their main competitors may offer free finance for the first year after purchase. This information is invaluable to B5 Cars to ensure that they remain competitive.

Customer information

One of the sources of information which will be lost will be that relating to customers. This loss will have a damaging impact on the firm; any organisation needs to know about its market, both existing and potential, to survive and grow. Even if an organisation currently enjoys a strong position in its sector of the market it would be short-sighted to assume that this situation would remain without consideration of the ever-changing market. Predicting market behaviour is challenging enough with access to wide-ranging information from external sources; without these tools the task becomes virtually impossible.

The industry

There are many sources of information on specific industries, in this case the motor vehicle industry, which will be lost. Societies established for manufacturers in a particular industry can provide useful information and comparisons about all manufacturers within an industry.

The effect on the company's information system

An EIS needs to afford access to information which is up-to-date and relevant for managers to manage the organisation. The loss of access as described above will, in a very short time, produce the effect that the information available via the EIS is inadequate for effective decision-making. The decisions taken will be short-term and reactive.

The system will cease to be an EIS but will, instead, provide a control mechanism. The kind of information the system will provide will be at an operational level (how many man hours was taken to produce a particular car; how many hours of overtime etc.) rather than providing information to support management decisions.

The effect on the company's products

Without access to external information, B5 Cars will be unaware of technological innovations; as a result their products will lag behind the rest of the industry and their own innovations may not take full advantage of new technological breakthroughs. There is the danger of 'reinventing the wheel' which will leave them behind in terms of technological advances and incur unnecessary research and development costs.

External market information would assist B5 Cars to identify trends in the motor industry, from which they could attempt to create marketing opportunities. Without this information marketing opportunities will be forgone.

The dearth of market information will mean that the organisation cannot accurately position their products in terms of pricing which in turn will affect their profitability. With accurate market information a producer is in a better position to optimise profits by pricing their product at a price low enough to sell, but high enough to ensure maximum profits. The effects on the products identified above will adversely affect the customer's perception thereof.

The Board's decision appears to be misguided which, in the longer-term, may affect the organisation's profitability and future market share.

274 PRINTING COMPANY

Key answer tips

Although this question is framed from the viewpoint of MIS, it is really an examination of your knowledge of the requirements of a divisionalised company.

Unitary to divisionalised structure

- Each division will now require its own accounts.

- There is now a need to assess the financial and non-financial performance of every division.

- Internal and external income will have to be identified – a cross charging/transfer pricing system will have to be devised that ensures corporate goal congruence.

- Information concerning the various external markets is required to permit the performance of a manager to be distinguished from the performance of the business unit managed.

Central direction to empowerment

- There may be a need to separate the transmission of strategic and operational information. The empowered team leaders will not require strategic information, but principally, data concerned with the day-to-day management of the business. Whereas the senior management may now be able to dispense with information concerned with operational details.

- This may also require the development of new reporting formats that are understandable to the team leaders. They may need even more detailed information at more frequent intervals than was available previously.

- New control systems will be required to meet the needs of the newly empowered team leaders and the senior management. The shift from a few to many decision makers will necessitate control systems to ensure standardisation and consistency throughout the company.

The shift to outsourcing

- New information systems will be needed to facilitate access to the external providers of services e.g. approved contractor lists.

- Authorisation/approval systems need to be developed to ensure procedures are being adhered to.

- Systems to monitor the price and quality of work undertaken by contractors will be needed.

- Financial appraisal systems may be installed to compare the 'life' costs of alternative suppliers in comparison with internal resourcing. If internal suppliers are permitted to bid for work and compete against contractors, then there is a need for the costing systems to clearly identify the activities driving costs.

Expansion in part-time and temporary employees

- The traditional personnel systems will need to adapt to the new situation.

- The employment of part-time staff to replace full timers will result in greater numbers of employees, perhaps by a factor of two or three times. Can the existing system cope? Is there sufficient storage and memory capacity?

- Part-timers and temporary staff tend to stay in jobs for shorter periods and hence creating more activity within the personnel department. Once again can the system cope with the additional workload?

- Long serving full-time employees will have more opportunity, and perhaps more incentive to understand and use effectively a complex MIS. On the other hand, part-timers and temporary staff will have less opportunity to 'come to grips' with a complex system, therefore it may be necessary to modify/simplify the systems to suit the new staffing situation.

Customers adopting JIT systems

- The company could previously operate with low or zero stocks, and therefore a small/simple stock holding system might suffice. The advent of JIT for customers puts the onus on the company to replenish stocks immediately. This will necessitate the installation of a larger, accurate and responsive inventory system. The system adopted will need to provide information concerning minimum stock levels, re-order cycles and Economic Order Quantities. None of this information may have been required previously because stock levels were not so business critical.

Long print runs to high value low volume

- The new customers will have more complex, individualistic and diverse requirements. The established ordering and printing systems will need to be modified to manage the heterogeneous business activity.

- High value business normally permits lower margins of error and deficiencies in quality standards. This may entail close monitoring and low tolerance control systems being installed.

    Note: This list of issues is not exhaustive and therefore other considerations mentioned by the candidates should be credited. The crucial requirement is to assess whether the examinees are thinking coherently about the consequences on the organisation of the change in the business environment.

275   REES INVESTMENTS

Tutorial note:

Where possible points should be illustrated using examples relevant to the organisation described in the question.

(a)   Decision support systems are software solutions designed to support managers making semi-structured or unstructured decisions. Such systems are best suited to situations where part of the problem is well understood, and hence can be automated, but part is not well understood and the manager will have to use judgement to come to a final decision. Many managers develop simple decision support systems using spreadsheets to provide them with an understanding of the data relevant data.

Decision support systems will usually consist of:

- A large database of information usually drawn from both internal and external sources.

- Problem exploration facilities which allow users to explore different scenarios using what-if and sensitivity analysis.

- Goal seeking and optimisation functions to allow users to determine the values of variables required to achieve a pre-determined or optimal solution.

- Graphical tools to display statistical data.

- In-built statistical, simulation and financial functions to allow users to develop relevant models quickly.

A decision support system could be useful at Rees Investments because the investment decisions are essentially semi-structured or unstructured. Hence a significant part of the problem can be understood from an analysis of data. However, Mark Rees will still be reliant upon his analysts correctly interpreting the information and making appropriate judgements. The decision support system is more likely to be successful if the current investment problems are caused by poor analysis of data rather than by poor judgement or by difficulties due to the worsening economic climate.

(b) An expert system is a software model of the knowledge, facts and reasoning of an acknowledged human expert. The expert system software usually represents knowledge as a set of inter-connected rules. These rules have usually been derived from discussions with experts as well as from observing and recording their decision making behaviour. Experts systems are usually perceived as a specialised form of a decision support system where reasoning is more important than computation. Such systems are particularly appropriate for handling situations where decisions have to be taken on incomplete information.

An expert system usually consists of:

- a knowledge base where the rules and facts are stored

- an inference engine which stores problem solving procedures to perform the reasoning

- a knowledge acquisition facility to allow the expert to enter knowledge and facts

- a knowledge presentation and explanation function to allow users to interrogate the expert system and to have the expert system's decision explained to them.

In the Rees Investments example, it would be possible to use expert system software to build an expert system of the knowledge and expertise of Mark Rees. In this way, less accomplished analysts could use his expertise to help them make their own investment decisions.

This may be particularly attractive to Mark Rees because:

- the company was successful when he used his approach

- he would be reasonably confident that analysts would be using a standard proven approach.

However, it has to be hoped that his approach is still valid in the changed economic environment and that the early success of the company was largely due to his expertise and not the favourable economic climate prevailing at that time.

276 CDE

Key answer tips

There are many types of information system that are available to firms like CDE. It is worth thinking about both parts of (a) together, since you will obviously need to ensure that your recommended system for part (ii) is one that you outline in part (i). Note that there are only 10 marks available in part (a) so this is not an opportunity to write all you know about every system!

In making your recommendation in part (a)(ii) it is critical that you recommend a system that meets the needs of CDE, so your answer should refer to points made in the scenario when justifying your recommendation.

Part (b) of the question commences with a statement about the business environment and the desire to reduce the cost of accounting. These points should be borne in mind throughout your answer, particularly when you come to recommendations in part (ii). You will need to review the scenario again to find precise examples of the current management accounting system (simply look for anything that you will have studied in your earlier management accounting exams!), and then go onto to evaluate these elements.

(a) **(i)** The following types of information system are available to manufacturing firms like CDE:

A **transaction processing system** (TPS) serves the operational level of the organisation. The system records all of the daily routine transactions that take place within the organisation, relating to each particular aspect of operational activities.

Data from the TPS is fed into a **management information system** (MIS). An MIS takes the bulk of data from the TPS and develops it into something useful to management in support of its decision-making responsibility. The MIS is usually computer-based, making use of spreadsheets where 'what if?' analysis can be carried out.

An **enterprise resource planning** (ERP) system is a sophisticated MIS system that covers the whole range of the organisation's activities. It promises the 'seamless integration of all the information flowing through the company'. ERP can be thought of as a development of the MRP II system used currently by CDE. A data warehouse is maintained of inputs from the TPS and MIS systems, from which any required customised report can be produced.

A **strategic enterprise management** (SEM) system assists management in making high-level strategic decisions. Tools such as activity-based management (ABM) and the balanced scorecard are applied to the data in the data warehouse to enable the strategic goals of the organisation to be worked towards.

An **executive information system** (EIS) or **executive support system** (ESS) gives management access to both internal and external data. Managers can access information to monitor the operations of the organisation and to scan general business conditions. The data for an EIS is online and updated in real time to ensure its integrity for decision making at a senior management level.

(ii) CDE is a substantially sized company, listed on the stock exchange, and operating in a highly competitive and fast-moving business. It currently uses an MRP II system to control production scheduling and labour and machine utilisation. This is satisfactory as far as controlling day-to-day operational requirements, but there is an absence of information being collected and presented to management for strategic and decision support purposes.

I recommend that CDE moves towards establishing an EIS system. This will enable managers to integrate the data from the current MRP II system with the known data about customer requirements and available suppliers. Then managers will be able to see an overview of the business as a whole, and can drill down if they wish to see more detail on the contents of any particular figure.

Tutorial note

Other systems could be recommended here and marks will be awarded if reasons are provided. An ERP system would be highly effective at meeting the need for integrated information, the lack of which was mentioned a couple of times in the scenario. Or a SEM system would suit a business such as this in a fast moving, competitive, modern manufacturing environment.

(b) **(i)** The current management accounting system provides:

- a detailed annual budgeting exercise

- standard costing for labour and materials

- production overhead recovery on the basis of machine hours.

Labour and material costs are analysed from operator and machine timesheets, and variances from standard costs are calculated and investigated.

CDE is therefore carrying out traditional old-fashioned management accounting, whose relevance can be questioned in a fast-moving business environment such as the manufacture of automotive components.

An annual budget is currently drawn up at the beginning of each year and then used for feedforward (planning) and feedback (control) purposes. However, with an uncertain sales mix and in a competitive sales environment, it will be very difficult to draw up an accurate budget. The objective of accuracy may be frustrated, anyway, by managers submitting sales targets that are very low and easy to achieve so that they will not be under any pressure to achieve the budgeted amounts.

Overhead allocation will be difficult to achieve accurately when so many different components are being offered for sale, in both large and small batches. Allocating such overhead on the basis of machine hours is a convenient, but essentially arbitrary, method.

Standard costing is currently carried out for labour and for materials. A standard cost card will be drawn up for each product, suggesting the 'standard' amount of cost of labour and materials that is appropriate. Variances are then calculated between actual amounts and standard amounts. Such traditional standard costing is appropriate in a mass production scenario where competitive advantage is sought by obtaining a low unit cost of production by producing very large production runs. It is much less appropriate in a JIT environment such as at CDE.

In conclusion, the current management accounting system is not altogether relevant to the JIT operations of CDE in the competitive environment in which it operates.

(ii) The management accounting system should be improved by:

- introducing rolling budgets rather than fixed budgets

- replacing the current detailed standard costing system with a 'lean' management accounting system focused on eliminating waste rather than on building up inventories to reduce the unit cost of production

- moving to an ABC method of overhead allocation rather than recovery on the basis of machine hours worked. This should enable accurate costing and pricing decisions to be taken, which is essential in the price sensitive market in which CDE operates.

CDE currently operates a management accounting system dominated by the costings of its MRP II system. As described in part (a), the move to an EIS system should enable a more holistic view of decision taking by management, concentrating on adding value and satisfying customers rather than on the pursuit of accounting-based cost control.

277 THE MG ORGANISATION

Key answer tips

Part (a) is a straightforward section, requiring you to look at the benefits of two system types over a TPS. Try to include reference to the situation of MG where possible in your answer.

There is a lot to talk about for only 5 marks in part (b) so plan your answer first and ensure that you make the best points only.

(a)   Explanations of system types

A transaction processing system is designed primarily for processing transactions, often within a stand-alone system for a job-specific application. Management reports are produced from such systems, but these are essentially a summary of the transactions that have been processed or provide an analysis of data on the computer master files. The information produced by transaction processing systems is therefore of operational or tactical value, but not strategic value, and it is used to prepare reports for the line management responsible for the particular area of operations.

An ERPS is a commercial software package that integrates information from a variety of sources, both internal and external. The information is both financial and non-financial. An ERP system might capture transaction data from a number of different transaction systems, as well as information from external sources (such as suppliers). This information can then be used to prepare specially-designed reports for management covering a range of different activities, and of strategic as well as tactical value.

Benefits of an ERP system

ERP systems can be used to provide performance data for multi-functional activities, rather than specific transactions, and so can be valuable for activity-based costing, balanced scorecard performance analysis and supply chain management.

ERP systems can provide benefits in excess of transaction processing systems because they provide better-quality strategic management information for senior management. The actual value of any particular ERPS obviously depends on the circumstances of each case, but as a general rule, an information system is beneficial if the expected improvements in management decision-making exceed the cost of providing the system.

Benefits of an EIS

Executive information systems (EIS) as their name suggests, provide information to senior executives within an organisation, from information sources both inside and outside the organisation. They allow executives to monitor the performance of the organisation and scan general business conditions at any time and in 'real time'. They allow executives to obtain summary performance information, and 'drill down' into further detail if required. They can also be used to make 'one-off' file interrogations to obtain information. Crucially, they are easy to use, and an executive does not have to be an IT expert or systems expert to benefit from using an EIS.

An EIS allows senior management to obtain performance information in 'real time' and should therefore help management to improve their control over the organisation. This is a benefit that transaction processing systems are unable to provide.

(b)   Budgetary allocations

Budget allocations for IT in the past have been made using an inefficient system. The system has been to allow a 5% to 10% increase in the budget allocation each year to allow for inflation and system upgrades. This approach to budgeting inevitably builds 'slack' into the budget and encourages wasteful spending.

The system is also weak because it appears to be based on the view that the existing IT systems are more or less satisfactory, and will simply need improving or changing with upgrades from time to time. The budgeting process does not appear to consider whether the IT systems remain adequate for the information needs of the organisation.

The appropriate approach should be to consider the information requirements of the organisation and its management, and the benefits that would be obtained from the information. Costs of providing information should be compared with the potential benefits. New IT system developments should also be considered, in terms of costs and benefits. Instead of following an incremental budgeting approach, an activity-based budgeting approach or a zero-based budgeting approach would probably be more effective in constructing a better budget.

Tutorial note

Although you did not have to use terms like zero-based budgeting, it is good to bring in topics from your earlier studies in this exam.

Evaluation of benefits

The benefits of an ERPS or EIS are difficult to measure quantitatively. They should provide better management information, and it is important that any new system should be capable of providing the information that management need.

To estimate the benefits of a system, it would be appropriate to consider the improvements in management information that the system would provide (more information, more up-to-date information, more accurate information, and so on) and how this should improve the quality of decision-making within the organisation. If an estimate can be made of how decision-making might improve, it should be possible to make a rough estimate of the potential benefits, for example in terms of revenues, cost savings or profits.

278 JUMP PERFORMANCE APPRAISAL (JUNE 2010)

(a) Bonus calculation:

	Qtr to 30 June 2009	Qtr to 30 September 2009	Qtr to 31 December 2009	Qtr to 31 March 2010	Bonus; hits'
Staff on time?					
On-time %	430/450 = 95.5%	452/480 = 94.2%	442/470 = 94.0%	460/480 = 95.8%	
Bonus earned?	Yes	No	No	Yes	2
Members visits					
Target visits					
	60% × 3,000 × 12 = 21,600	60% × 3,200 × 12 = 23,040	60% × 3,300 × 12 = 23,760	60% × 3,400 × 12 = 24,480	
Actual visits	20,000	24,000	26,000	24,000	
Bonus earned?	No	Yes	Yes	No	2
Personal training					
Target	10% × 3,000 = 300	10% × 3,200 = 320	10% × 3,300 = 330	10% × 3,400 = 340	
Actual sessions	310	325	310	339	
Bonus earned	Yes	Yes	No	No	2
Total					6

The bonus earned by the manager would be 6 × $400 = $2,400, which is 50% of the total bonus available.

(b) An important principle of any target based bonus system is that the targets must be based on controllable aspects of the manager's role.

Staff on time

The way in which a manager manages staff can have a big bearing on whether or not an individual staff member is keen to work and arrive on time. We are told that the local manager has the power to vary employment contracts so he should be able to agree acceptable shift patterns with staff and reward them for compliance. In this respect the lateness of staff is controllable by the manager.

On the other hand an individual staff member may be subject to home pressures or problems with public or other transport meaning that even they cannot control the time of arrival at work on some days. The manager cannot control these events either. If this problem became regular for a member of staff then the local manager could vary the contract of employment accordingly.

Overall, lateness to work is controllable by the local manager.

Member use of facilities

The local manager controls the staff and hence the level of customer service. Good quality customer services would probably encourage members to use the facilities more often. Equally, by maintaining the club to a high standard then the local manager can remove another potential reason for a member not to use the facilities regularly.

On the other hand customers are influenced by many factors outside of the club. Their state of health or their own work pressures can prevent members being able to come to the club.

Overall, the local manager can only partly control the number of member visits.

Personal training sessions

Again, the local manager controls the level of customer service and the standard of maintenance in the personal training department. He also has control over prices so, if the bookings fall, he is able to reduce price or make special offers to encourage use of the facilities.

On the other hand, personal training sessions may be seen as a luxury by customers and in times of financial difficulty they are expendable by them. Personal training sessions are often available from other sources and competition can force down the sales of the club. The manager can respond to that by improving services. He cannot, however, make significant investment in improving the facilities without board approval.

Overall, the local manager can only partly control the number of personal training sessions booked.

(c) There are a variety of methods that the performance data can be manipulated:

Cut off

The unethical manager could record visits in a different period than was actually the case. For example in quarter three the target for personal training sessions was not met by 20 sessions. This was probably obvious to the manager in the last few days of that quarter. He could have therefore recorded some sessions as having taken place in the next quarter. Indeed, only one session would have to be moved in this way in order for the manager to meet the target in the final quarter and gain another $400 of bonus.

Reduce prices to below economic levels to encourage use

The targets that the manager is subject to are mainly volume driven. A reduction in prices would harm profitability but would not damage the manager's bonus potential. More sessions are bound to follow if the price is set low enough.

(Other ideas would be acceptable including advising staff to take the day off if they were going to be late. This would damage service levels admittedly, but would potentially gain a bonus for lateness.)

Marking scheme			
			Marks
(a)	Per target		2
			—
		Maximum	6
			—
(b)	For each target – supporting controllability		1.5
	For each target – denying controllability		1.5
			—
	Target		**9**
(c)	For each idea of manipulation up to		2.5
			—
		Maximum	5
			—
Total			20
			—

279 ACCOUNTANCY TEACHING CO (DECEMBER 2010)

Turnover has decreased from $72.025 million in 2009 to $66.028 million in 2010, a fall of 8.3%. However, this must be assessed by taking into account the change in market conditions, since there has been a 20% decline in demand for accountancy training. Given this 20% decline in the market place, AT Co's turnover would have been expected to fall to $57.62m if it had kept in line with market conditions. Comparing AT Co's actual turnover to this, it's actual turnover is 14.6% higher than expected. As such, AT Co has performed fairly well, given market conditions.

It can also be seen from the non-financial performance indicators that 20% of students in 2010 are students who have transferred over from alternative training providers. It is likely that they have transferred over because they have heard about the improved service that AT Co is providing. Hence, they are most likely the reason for the increased market share that AT Co has managed to secure in 2010.

Cost of sales

Cost of sales has decreased by 19.2% in 2010. This must be considered in relation to the decrease in turnover as well. In 2009, cost of sales represented 72.3% of turnover and in 2010 this figure was 63.7%. This is quite a substantial decrease. The reasons for it can be ascertained by, firstly, looking at the freelance staff costs.

In 2009, the freelance costs were $14.582m. Given that a minimum 10% reduction in fees had been requested to freelance lecturers and the number of courses run by them was the same year on year, the expected cost for freelance lecturers in 2010 was $13.124m. The actual costs were $12.394m. These show that a fee reduction of 15% was actually achieved. This can be seen as a successful reduction in costs.

The expected cost of sales for 2010 before any cost cuts, was $47.738m assuming a consistent ratio of cost of sales to turnover. The actual cost of sales was only $42.056m, $5.682m lower. Since freelance lecturer costs fell by $2.188m, this means that other costs of sale fell by the remaining $3.494m. Staff costs are a substantial amount of this balance but since there was a pay freeze and the average number of employees hardly changed from year to year, the decreased costs are unlikely to be related to staff costs. The decrease is therefore most probably attributable to the introduction of online marking. AT Co expected the online marking system to cut costs by $4m, but it is probable that the online marking did not save as much as possible, hence the $3.494m fall. Alternatively, the saved marking costs may have been partially counteracted by an increase in some other cost included in cost of sales.

Gross profit

As a result of the above, the gross profit margin has increased in 2010 from 27.7% to 36.3%. This is a big increase and reflects very well on management.

Indirect expenses

- Marketing costs: These have increased by 42.1% in 2010. Although this is quite significant, given all the improvements that AT Co has made to the service it is providing, it is very important that potential students are made aware of exactly what the company now offers. The increase in marketing costs has been rewarded with higher student numbers relative to the competition in 2010 and these will hopefully continue increasing next year, since many of the benefits of marketing won't be felt until the next year anyway. The increase should therefore be viewed as essential expenditure rather than a cost that needs to be reduced.

- Property costs: These have largely stayed the same in both years.

- Staff training: These costs have increased dramatically by over $2 million, a 163.9% increase. However, AT Co had identified that it had a problem with staff retention, which was leading to a lower quality service being provided to students. Also, due to the introduction of the interactive website, the electronic enrolment system and the online marking system, staff would have needed training on these areas. If AT Co had not spent this money on essential training, the quality of service would have deteriorated further and more staff would have left as they became increasingly dissatisfied with their jobs. Again, therefore, this should be seen as essential expenditure.

- Given that the number of student complaints has fallen dramatically in 2010 to 84 from 315, the staff training appears to have improved the quality of service being provided to students.

- Interactive website and the student helpline: These costs are all new this year and result from an attempt to improve the quality of service being provided and, presumably, improve pass rates. Therefore, given the increase in the pass rate for first time passes from 48% to 66% it can be said that these developments have probably contributed to this. Also, they have probably played a part in attracting new students, hence improving turnover.

- Enrolment costs have fallen dramatically by 80.9%. This huge reduction is a result of the new electronic system being introduced. This system can certainly be seen as a success, as not only has it dramatically reduced costs but it has also reduced the number of late enrolments from 297 to 106.

Net operating profit

This has fallen from $3.635m to $2.106m. On the face of it, this looks disappointing but it has to be remembered that AT Co has been operating in a difficult market in 2010. It could easily have been looking at a large loss. Going forward, staff training costs will hopefully decrease. Also, market share may increase further as word of mouth spreads about improved results and service at AT Co. This may, in turn, lead to a need for less advertising and therefore lower marketing costs.

It is also apparent that AT Co has provided the student website free of charge when really, it should have been charging a fee for this. The costs of running it are too high for the service to be provided free of charge and this has had a negative impact on net operating profit.

Note: Students would not have been expected to write all this in the time available.

Workings (Note: All workings are in $000)

(1) Turnover

Decrease in turnover = $72,025 – $66,028/$72,025 = 8.3%

Expected 2010 turnover given 20% decline in market = $72,025 × 80% = $57,620
Actual 2010 turnover CF expected = $66,028 – $57,620/$57,620 = 14.6% higher

(2) Cost of sales

Decrease in cost of sales = $42,056 – $52,078/$52,078 = 19.2%

Cost of sales as percentage of turnover: 2009 = $52,078/$72,025 = 72.3% 2010 = $42,056/$66,028 = 63.7%

Freelance staff costs: in 2009 = $41,663 × 35% = $14,582 Expected cost for 2010 = $14,582 × 90% = $13,124 Actual 2010 cost = $12,394

$12,394 − $14,582 = $2,188 decrease $2,188/$14,582 = 15% decrease in freelancer costs

Expected cost of sales for 2010, before costs cuts, = $66,028 × 72.3% = $47,738.

Actual cost of sales = $42,056.

Difference = $5,682, of which $2,188 relates to freelancer savings and $3,494 relates to other savings.

(3) **Gross profit margin**

2009: $19,947/$72,025 = 27.7%

2010: $23,972/$66,028 = 36.3%

(4) Increase in marketing costs = $4,678 − $3,291/$3,291 = 42.1%

(5) Increase in staff training costs = $3,396 − $1,287/$1,287 = 163.9%

(6) Decrease in enrolment costs = $960 − 5,032/5,032 = 80.9%

(7) Net operating profit

Decreased from $3,635 to $2,106. This is fall of 1,529/3,635 = 42.1%

Marking scheme		
		Marks
Turnover		
8.3% decrease		0.5
Actual t/o 14.6% higher		0.5
Performed well CF market conditions		1
Transfer of students		1
		___
	Max. turnover	**3**
		___
Cost of sales		
19.2% decrease		0.5
63.7% of turnover		0.5
15% fee reduction from freelance staff		2
Other costs of sale fell by $3.555m		2
Online marking did not save as much as planned		1
		___
	Max. COS	**5**
		___
Gross profit – numbers and comment		1
Indirect expenses:		
Marketing costs		
42.1% increase		0.5
Increase necessary to reap benefits of developments		1
Benefits may take more than one year to be felt		0.5
Property costs – stayed the same		0.5
Staff training		
163.9% increase		0.5
Necessary for staff retention		1
Necessary to train staff on new website etc		1
Without training, staff would have left		1
Less student complaints		1
Interactive website and student helpline		
Attracted new students		1

Increase in pass rate	1
Enrolment costs	
Fall of 80.9%	0.5
Result of electronic system being introduced	1
Reduced number of late enrolments	1
Max. Indirect expenses	**9**
Net operating profit	
Fallen to $2.106	0.5
Difficult market	1
Staff training costs should decrease in future	1
Future increase in market share	1
Lower advertising cost in future	1
Charge for website	1
Max. net operating profit	**3**
Total	**20**

280   LENS CO (DECEMBER 2016)

(a)   **Return on investment**

Controllable profit

	Division P	Division O
	$000	$000
Revenue	14,000	18,800
Direct labour	(2,400)	(3,500)
Direct materials	(4,800)	(6,500)
Divisional overheads excl. uncontrollable depreciation	(3,480)	(4,740)
Exchange gain/(loss)	(200)	460
Net divisional profit	3,120	4,520

Net assets controlled by the divisions

	Division P	Division O
	$000	$000
Non-current assets controlled by division	15,400	20,700
Inventories	1,800	3,900
Trade receivables	6,200	8,900
Overdraft	(500)	–
Trade payables	(5,100)	(7,200)
Net controllable assets	17,800	26,300

ROI for Division P

Controllable profit/controllable assets

= $3,120/$17,800

= 17.53%.

ROI for Division O

$4,520/$26,300 = 17.19%

Tutorial note

'A basis ... suitable for measuring the divisional managers' performance' means that calculations should have been based on controllable profit. Whilst most items affecting profit were either clearly controllable or uncontrollable, the exchange rate gain/loss could have been argued either way, provided that the explanation in part (b) was sufficient. Similarly, the assets figure used for the calculation should have only included <u>controllable</u> assets.

(b) The ROIs in part (a) have been calculated by applying the principle of 'controllability'. This principle states that managers should only be held accountable for areas which they can control. This means that, when calculating 'profit' for the purposes of calculating ROI, the only revenues and costs included should be controllable by the manager. Similarly, when calculating 'net assets' for the ROI calculation, only assets which the divisional managers can control should be included.

Applying the principles of controllability, treatment of certain costs is explained below:

Gain on sale of equipment

This has been excluded from the profit figure as the decision to dispose of a large amount of equipment in division P was taken by Head Office. The divisional manager had no control over this decision.

Divisional overheads

The depreciation on HO controlled assets has been excluded when calculating profit for ROI purposes. Again, this is because divisional managers do not control some of the assets.

Exchange gains/losses

These have been left in when arriving at a profit figure for ROI purposes. This is because the scenario states that the divisions choose to give the overseas customers 60 days' credit and it is this delay between the point of sale and the point of payment which gives rise to the exchange gain or loss. The managers make the choice to deal with these customers so they have control here.

Exceptional cost of factory closure

The effect of this has been removed from the 'profit' calculation as this decision was made by Head Office, not the manager of division O. It was therefore beyond his control and its effect should be excluded.

Allocated Head Office costs

These have been excluded when calculating profit as the divisional managers have no control over these and should not be held accountable for them.

Non-current assets controlled by Head Office

These have been excluded from the 'net assets' calculation as these assets are not under the control of the divisional managers.

Tutorial note

Given the use of the verb 'explain' and the fact that this part was worth 8 marks, many of the items needed more explanation than simply saying that they were 'controllable' or 'uncontrollable'. It needed to be explained why they were controllable or uncontrollable. Do not lose easy marks with answers that are repetitive and too brief. You must always be careful to interpret the instruction and be guided by the marks available in determining how much they need to write.

(c) **Investment centres**

An investment centre is a type of responsibility centre in which managers have responsibility for not only sales prices, volume and costs but also for investment in working capital and non-current assets. Both divisions do have responsibility for working capital; that is clear from the scenario. However, they only have responsibility over some of the assets. In the circumstances, it could be argued that it is correct to treat them as investment centres provided that appropriate adjustments are made when using ROI to assess their performance.

On the other hand, however, managers are only able to sign off $15,000 of capital expenditure, which is a relatively small amount, suggesting that treatment as an investment centre is not appropriate. Bringing the divisions under Head Office control may even be beneficial as then exchange rate risk can be managed more closely.

Tutorial note

In order to answer a requirement of this nature, it is necessary to state what an investment centre is and then very briefly discuss whether this seems to be the case for the divisions in question.

(d) **Problems of using ROI**

The main disadvantage of using ROI is that the percentage increases as assets get older. This is because the net book value of the assets decreases as a result of higher accumulated depreciation, hence capital employed falls. This, in turn, can lead managers to hold onto ageing assets rather than replace them, especially where their bonuses are linked to ROI. It may be that division P's manager would not have made the same decision which Head Office made to invest in the more advanced technology for this reason.

Another disadvantage is that ROI is based on accounting profits, which are subjective, rather than cash flows. It is therefore open to manipulation.

Additionally, it does not take into account the cost of capital. It merely looks at profits relative to capital employed without taking into account the cost of the capital which has been invested. It is therefore not consistent with maximising returns to investors.

Tutorial note

The trap to avoid here is spending too long discussing the problems of using residual income, which was not asked for. This wasted time and therefore their potential to earn marks elsewhere.

	Marking scheme		Marks
(a)	Calculation of controllable profit		2
	Calculation of controllable assets		2
	ROI		2
		Maximum	6
(b)	Explanation about controllability		2
	Inclusion/exclusion explanations		6
		Maximum	8
(c)	Description of investment centre		1
	Application to Lens Co		1
		Maximum	2
(d)	Problems with using ROI		4
Total			20

281 CIM (DECEMBER 2015)

(a) **(i)** **Division F**

Controllable profit = $2,645k.

Total assets less trade payables = $9,760k + $2,480k – $2,960k = $9,280k.

ROI = 28.5%.

Division N

Controllable profit = $1,970k.

Total assets less trade payables = $14,980k + $3,260k – $1,400k = $16,840k.

ROI = 11.7%.

In both calculations controllable profit has been used to reflect profit, rather than net profit. This is because the managers do not have any control over the Head Office costs and responsibility accounting deems that managers should only be held responsible for costs which they control. The same principle is being applied in the choice of assets figures being used. The current assets and current liabilities figures have been taken into account in the calculation because of the fact that the managers have full control over both of these.

(ii)   Bonus

Bonus to be paid for each percentage point = $120,000 × 2% = $2,400.

Maximum bonus = $120,000 × 0.3 = $36,000.

Division F: ROI = 28.5% = 18 whole percentage points above minimum ROI of 10%.

18 × $2,400 = $43,200.

Therefore manager will be paid the maximum bonus of $36,000.

Division N: ROI = 11.7% = 1 whole percentage point above minimum.

Therefore bonus = $2,400.

(b)   Discussion

The manager of Division N will be paid a far smaller bonus than the manager of Division F. This is because of the large asset base on which the ROI figure has been calculated. Total assets of Division N are almost double the total assets of Division F. This is largely attributable to the fact that Division N invested $6.8m in new equipment during the year. If this investment had not been made, net assets would have been only $10.04m and the ROI for Division N would have been 19.62%. This would have led to the payment of a $21,600 bonus (9 × $2,400) rather than the $2,400 bonus. Consequently, Division N's manager is being penalised for making decisions which are in the best interests of his division. It is very surprising that he did decide to invest, given that he knew that he would receive a lower bonus as a result. He has acted totally in the best interests of the company. Division F's manager, on the other hand, has benefitted from the fact that he has made no investment even though it is badly needed. This is an example of sub-optimal decision making.

Division F's trade payables figure is much higher than Division N's. This also plays a part in reducing the net assets figure on which the ROI has been based. Division F's trade payables are over double those of Division N. In part, one would expect this because sales are over 50% higher (no purchases figure is given). However, it is clear that it is also because of low cash levels at Division F. The fact that the manager of Division F is then being rewarded for this, even though relationships with suppliers may be adversely affected, is again an example of sub-optimal decision making.

If the controllable profit margin is calculated, it is 18.24% for Division F and 22.64% for Division N. Therefore, if capital employed is ignored, it can be seen that Division N is performing better. ROI is simply making the division's performance look worse because of its investment in assets. Division N's manager is likely to feel extremely demotivated by his comparatively small bonus and, in the future, he may choose to postpone investment in order to increase his bonus. Managers not investing in new equipment and technology will mean that the company will not keep up with industry changes and affect its overall future competitiveness.

To summarise, the use of ROI is leading to sub-optimal decision making and a lack of goal congruence, as what is good for the managers is not good for the company and vice versa. Luckily, the manager at Division N still appears to be acting for the benefit of the company but the other manager is not. The fact that one manager is receiving a much bigger bonus than the other is totally unfair here and may lead to conflict in the long run. This is not good for the company, particularly if there comes a time when the divisions need to work together.

(c) ROI is expressed as a percentage and is more easily understood by non-financial managers.

ROI can be used to compare performance between different sized divisions or companies.

It is not necessary to know the cost of capital in order to calculate ROI.

ROI may lead to dysfunctional decisions. For instance, if a division has a very high ROI of say, 40%, and is considering a project with an ROI of 30%, which is still well above the cost of capital of say 10%, then the project should be accepted as it provides a return well in excess of the cost of capital. The division may quite possibly reject the project, however, as when added to its existing operations it will reduce the ROI from 40%.

Using residual income as a performance measure should ensure that divisions make decisions which are in the best interests of the group as a whole and should eliminate the problem outlined in the previous paragraph.

Different divisions can use different rates to reflect different risk when calculating residual income.

Residual income is not useful for comparing divisions of different sizes.

Both residual income and ROI improve as the age of the assets increase and both provide an incentive to hang onto aged possibly inefficient machines.

Other methods of assessment that could be used in addition to ROI or RI include:

- expected value added is similar to residual income except that, instead of using book values for profit and capital employed, the figures are adjusted to reflect the true economic value of the profit and of the capital employed

- the Balanced Scorecard, which still looks at financial performance, perhaps using residual income or ROI, but also encompasses three other perspectives: the customer perspective, the internal business process perspective, and the learning and innovation perspective.

282 SPORTS CO (SEPTEMBER/DECEMBER 2017)

Tutorial note

The concepts of Return On Investment (ROI), Residual Income (RI) and their limitations are fundamental areas of knowledge for the 'Performance Management' candidate. Likewise, controllability and associated concepts are key.

With this 'Sports Co' question, the Examiner eases the candidates in by splitting the 20-marker requirement into manageable chunks. Furthermore, both requirements (a) and (b) are themselves split into 2 sub-requirements, making the planning element of exam technique as smooth as possible.

(a) **(i)**

Tutorial note

In (a) (i), calculating the ROI should have been very straightforward indeed for the well prepared candidate. The areas to watch out for, or pitfalls to avoid, centred around the controllability of some of the fixed costs. The skill tested here is the ability to adjust profit calculations by discarding uncontrollable fixed costs.

Return on investment = controllable profit/average divisional net assets

Controllable profit

	C	E
	$'000	$'000
Net profit	1,455	3,950
Add back depreciation on non-controllable assets	49.5	138
Add back Head Office costs	620	700
Controllable profit	2,124.50	4,788

Average divisional net assets

	$'000	$'000
Opening assets	13,000	24,000
Closing assets	9,000	30,000
Average assets	11,000	27,000
ROI	19.3%	17.7%

(ii)

Tutorial note

The discursive aspects of questions very often drive candidates to focus on the irrelevant or the unnecessary. In here, once the ROI difference between the divisions had been established, time should be spent establishing the impact of that difference as part of the discussion.

Other narrative marks worth harvesting centred around behavioural considerations such as how a demotivated manager would be tempted to try and manipulate figures by not investing and thereby improving ROI artificially.

Whilst Division C has exceeded the target ROI, Division E has not. If controllable profit in relation to revenue is considered, Division C's margin is 56% compared to Division E's margin of 57%, so Division E is actually performing slightly better.

However, Division E has a larger asset base than Division C too, hence the fact that Division C has a higher ROI.

Since Division E appears to be a much larger division and is involved in sports equipment manufacturing, then it could be expected to have more assets. Division

E's assets have gone up partly because it made substantial additions to plant and machinery. This means that as well as increasing the average assets figure, the additions will have been depreciated during the year, thus leading to lower profits. This may potentially have had a large impact on profits since Division E uses the reducing balance method of depreciation, meaning that more depreciation is charged in the early years.

Based on the ROI results, the manager of Division C will get a bonus and the manager of Division E will not. This will have a negative impact on the motivation level of the manager of Division E and may discourage him from making future investments, unless a change in the performance measure used is adopted.

(b)   (i)

	C	E
	$'000	$'000
Controllable profit	2,124.50	4,788
Less: imputed charge on assets at 12%	(1,320)	(3,240)
Residual income	804.50	1,548

From the residual income results, it can clearly be seen that both divisions have performed well, with healthy RI figures of between $0.8m and $1.55m. The cost of capital of Sports Co is significantly lower than the target return on investment which the company seeks, making the residual income figure show a more positive position.

(ii)

Tutorial note

Don't simply state the pros and cons of the RI measure - explain in as much detail as necessary. A tip to candidates: the use of the word 'because' often helps to grasp the last remaining marks. For example, simply stating that 'RI reduces dysfunctional decision making' is not enough; explaining that 'RI reduces dysfunctional decision making because it uses the whole company's cost of capital, so positive RI projects for the company would also be accepted by the division' is more likely to maximise marks.

Advantages

The use of RI should encourage managers to make new investments, if the investment adds to the RI figure. A new investment can add to RI but reduce ROI and in such a situation measuring performance with RI would not result in the dysfunctional behaviour which has already been seen at Sports Co. Instead, RI will lead to decisions which are in the best interests of the company as a whole being made.

RI reduces dysfunctional decision making <u>because</u> it uses the whole company's cost of capital, so positive RI projects for the company would also be accepted by the division.

Since an imputed interest charge is deducted from profits when measuring the performance of the division, managers are made more aware of the cost of assets under their control. This is a benefit as it can discourage wasteful spending.

Alternative costs of capital can be applied to divisions and investments to account for different levels of risk. This can allow more informed decision-making.

Disadvantages

RI does not facilitate comparisons between divisions since the RI is driven by the size of divisions and their investments. This can clearly be seen in Sports Co where the RI of Division E is almost twice that of Division C, which will be related to Division E being a much larger division.

RI is also based on accounting measures of profit and capital employed which may be subject to manipulation so as, for example, to obtain a bonus payment. In this way it suffers from the same problems as ROI.

Marking scheme				Marks
(a)	(i)	Net profit		1
		Add back depreciation		1
		Add back HO costs		1
		Controllable profits		1
		Average assets		1
		ROI		1
			Maximum	6
	(ii)	Discussion		6
(b)	(i)	Controllable profit		1
		Imputed interest		1
		RI		1
		Comment		1
			Maximum	4
	(ii)		Maximum	4
Total				20

283 ROTECH (JUNE 2014)

(a) **Ratios**

(i) **ROCE = operating profit/capital employed × 100%**

		$000	ROCE
W Co	Design Division	6,000/23,540	25.49%
	Gearbox division	3,875/32,320	11.99%
C Co		7,010/82,975	8.45%

(ii) **Asset turnover = sales/capital employed × 100%**

		$000	Asset turnover
W Co	Design Division	14,300/23,540	0.61
	Gearbox division	25,535/32,320	0.79
C Co		15,560/82,975	0.19

(iii) **Operating profit margin = operating profit/sales × 100%**

		$000	Operating profit
W Co	Design Division	6,000/14,300	41.96%
	Gearbox division	3,875/25,535	15.18%
C Co		7,010/15,560	45.05%

Both companies and both divisions within W Co are clearly profitable. In terms of what the different ratios tell us, ROCE tells us the return which a company is making from its capital.

The Design division of W Co is making the highest return at over 25%, more than twice that of the Gearbox division and nearly three times that of C Co. This is because the nature of a design business is such that profits are largely derived from the people making the designs rather than from the assets. Certain assets will obviously be necessary in order to produce the designs but it is the employees who are mostly responsible for generating profit.

The Gearbox division and C Co's ROCE are fairly similar compared to the Design division, although when comparing the two in isolation, the Gearbox division's ROCE is actually over three percentage points higher than C Co's (11.99% compared to 8.45%).

This is because C Co has a substantially larger asset base than the Gearbox division. From the asset turnover ratio, it can be seen that the Gearbox division's assets generate a very high proportion of sales per $ of assets (79%) compared to C Co (19%).

This is partly because the Gearbox division buys its components in from C Co and therefore does not need to have the large asset base which C Co has in order to make the components. When the unit profitability of those sales is considered by looking at the operating profit margin, C Co's unit profitability is much higher than the Gearbox division (45% operating profit margin as compared to 15%).

The Design division, like the Gearbox division, is also using its assets well to generate sales (asset turnover of 61%) but then, like C Co, its unit profitability is high too (42% operating profit margin.) This is why, when the two ratios (operating profit margin and asset turnover) are combined to make ROCE, the Design division comes out top overall – because it has both high unit profitability and generates sales at a high level compared to its asset base.

It should be noted that any comparisons between such different types of business are of limited use. It would be more useful to have prior year figures for comparison and/or industry averages for similar businesses. This would make performance review much more meaningful.

(b) **Transfer prices**

From C Co's perspective

C Co transfers components to the Gearbox division at the same price as it sells components to the external market. However, if C Co were not making internal sales then, given that it already satisfies 60% of external demand, it would not be able to sell all of its current production to the external market.

External sales are $8,010,000, therefore unsatisfied external demand is ([$8,010,000/0.6] – $8,010,000) = $5,340,000. From C Co's perspective, of the current internal sales of $7,550,000, $5,340,000 could be sold externally if they were not sold to the Gearbox division.

Therefore, in order for C Co not to be any worse off from selling internally, these sales should be made at the current price of $5,340,000, less any reduction in costs which C Co saves from not having to sell outside the group (perhaps lower administrative and distribution costs). As regards the remaining internal sales of $2,210,000 ($7,550,000 – $5,340,000), C Co effectively has spare capacity to meet these sales.

Therefore, the minimum transfer price should be the marginal cost of producing these goods. Given that variable costs represent 40% of revenue, this means that the marginal cost for these sales is $884,000. This is therefore the minimum price which C Co should charge for these sales. In total, therefore, C Co will want to charge at least $6,224,000 for its sales to the Gearbox division.

From the Gearbox division's perspective

The Gearbox division will not want to pay more for the components than it could purchase them for externally. Given that it can purchase them all for 95% of the current price, this means a maximum purchase price of $7,172,500.

Overall

Taking into account all of the above, the transfer price for the sales should be somewhere between $6,224,000 and $7,172,500.

284 CTD

(a) The current transfer price is ($40 + $20)) × 1.1 = $66.

		FD		TM	
		$000	$000	$000	$000
Internal sales	15,000 × $66		990		
External sales	5,000 × $80		400		
	15,000 × $500				7,500
			———		———
			1,390		7,500
Production – variable costs	20,000 × $40	(800)			
	15,000 × $366			(5,490)	
Selling/distribution – variable costs	5,000 × $4	(20)			
	15,000 × $25			(375)	
		———		———	
			(820)		(5,865)
			———		———
			570		1,635
Production overheads	20,000 × $20	(400)			
	15,000 × $60			(900)	
Administration overheads	20,000 × $4	(80)			
	15,000 × $25			(375)	
		———		———	
Net profit			90		360
Interest charge	$750,000\$1,500,000 × 12%		(90)		(180)
			———		———
Residual income (RI)			0		180
			———		———
Target RI			85		105
Bonus	$180,000 × 5%		0		9

Implications of the current reward system

While the TM manager has received a bonus and presumably will be pleased about it, the FD manager has received nothing. This will not be very motivating and may lead to problems within the division as a whole, such as inefficiency, staff turnover and unreliability. Since the TM division relies so completely on the FD division, this situation is clearly unacceptable.

Key answer tips

The calculations involved in this question are very straightforward, but don't be deceived – the real thrust of this question is to make sure that you both understand the principles of different transfer pricing methods, and can apply them to a situation.

(b) **(i)** In order to achieve a 5% bonus, the manager of TM division will be willing to accept a decrease in residual income of $(180,000 – 105,000) = $75,000. This is an increase in transfer price of the 15,000 units transferred of $75,000/15,000 = $5. Thus the transfer price would rise to $66 + $5 = $71.

(ii) In order to achieve a 5% bonus, the manager of FD division will want an increase in residual income of $85,000. This is an increase in transfer price of the 15,000 units transferred of $85,000/15,000 = $5.67. Thus the transfer price would have to rise to $66 + $5.67 = $71.67.

285 DIVISION A

Key answer tips

This is a demanding question linking transfer prices to performance targets. As with all transfer pricing questions the key aspects of discussion are linking transfer prices to managerial performance.

(a) **(i)** Profit required by division A to meet RI target:

	$
Cost of capital $3.2m @ 12%	384,000
Target RI	180,000
Target profit	564,000
Add fixed costs	1,080,000
Target contribution	1,644,000
Contribution earned from external sales 90,000 @ ($35 – $22)	1,170,000
Contribution required from internal sales	474,000
Contribution per bit on internal sales ($474,000/60,000)	$7.90
Transfer price to division C $22.00 + $7.90	$29.90

(ii) The two transfer prices based on opportunity costs:

40,000 units (150,000 – 110,000) at the marginal cost of $22.00

20,000 units (110,000 – 90,000) at the external selling price of $35.00

(b) Where divisional managers are given total autonomy to purchase units at the cheapest price and where divisional performance is assessed on a measure based on profit, sub-optimal behaviour could occur i.e. divisional managers could make decisions that may not be in the overall interests of the group.

Impact of group's current transfer pricing policy

Division C's objective is to maximise its RI in order to achieve its target RI. It will therefore endeavour to find the cheapest source of supply for Bits. As C requires 60,000 Bits and X is willing to supply them at $28 each, C would prefer to buy them from X rather than division A. However this will not benefit the group, as division A will be unable to utilise its spare capacity of 40,000 Bits. The effect on the group's profit will be as follows:

	$
Additional payment by division C 60,000 Bits@ ($28 – $22)	(360,000)
Gain in contribution by Division A 20,000 Bits @ $13	260,000
Net loss to group	(100,000)

Impact of group's proposed transfer pricing policy

If division A were to set transfer prices based on opportunity costs the effect on its divisional profit would be as follows:

	$
Reduction in profit 40,000 Bits @ ($29.90 – $22.00)	(316,000)
Increase in profit 20,000 Bits @ ($35 – $29.90)	102,000
Net loss to division	(214,000)

Division C has the following two purchase options:

	$
Purchase from division A 40,000 Bits @ $22	880,000
Purchase from Z 20,000 Bits @ $33	660,000
Total cost of Bits	1,540,000
Or: Purchase 60,000 from X 60,000 Bits @ $28	1,680,000

As division C will opt to source the Bits from the cheapest supplier(s) it will choose to purchase 40,000 Bits from division A at $22 per Bit and the remaining 20,000 Bits from Z at $33 per Bit. This also benefits the group, as there is no opportunity cost to division A on the 40,000 units transferred to division C.

When marginal cost is used as the transfer price division C will make the correct decision and the group will maximise profits. However division A would suffer. This can be overcome by changing the way it measures the performance of its divisions – rather than using a single profit-based measure it needs to introduce a variety of quantitative and qualitative measures.

(c) **Purchase of 60,000 Bits from division A**

	Contribution $	Taxation $	Net effect $
A – external sales 90,000 Bits @ ($35 – $22)	1,170,000		
– internal sales 60,000 Bits @ ($30 – $22)	480,000		
Total contribution from A	1,650,000		
Taxation @ 55%		(907,500)	
C – purchases 60,000 Bits @ $30	(1,800,000)		
Taxation @ 25%		450,000	
Net effect	(150,000)	(457,500)	(607,500)

Purchase of 60,000 Bits from X

	Contribution $	Taxation $	Net effect $
A – external sales 110,000 Bits @ ($35 – $22)	1,430,000		
Taxation @ 55%		(786,500)	
C – purchases 60,000 Bits @ $28	(1,680,000)		
Taxation @ 25%		420,000	
Net effect	(250,000)	(366,500)	(616,500)

The group will maximise its profits if division C purchased the Bits from division A.

286 JUNGLE CO (SEPTEMBER 2016)

Tutorial note

The key with these questions is to identify 'cause and effect' relationships. Marks will be awarded for explaining WHY something has changed, along with how it might affect other aspects of the business. The most common mistake made by candidates was not applying the above. Most candidates were comfortable calculating percentage movement, but added no value to their calculations. Points such as "Cost of sales have decreased by 18%. This is a good performance." were common, but apart from the calculation scored no marks. Answers which looked into why cost of sales might have decreased, or what impact that might have had, scored many more marks. In this case, the decrease in cost of sales could partly be put down to a fall in revenue, but the main point is that the scenario explains how the company changed to a cheaper supplier – this would have a direct effect on their cost of sales. Even better answers would discuss how the rise in customer complaints may have been caused by the poor quality of these supplies. Another common error was to offer the business advice. The requirement clearly stated "discuss the performance," and marks could not be given for advice. It is really important to read the requirement carefully and answer the question being asked.

Sales volumes

Since prices have remained stable year on year, it can be assumed that changes to revenue are as a result of increases or decreases in sales volumes. Overall, revenue has increased by 15%, which is a substantial increase. In order to understand what has happened in the business, it is necessary to consider sales by looking at each of the different categories.

Household goods

Although this was the largest category of sales for Jungle Co last year, this year it has decreased by 5% and has now been overtaken by electronic goods. The company changed suppliers for many of its household goods during the year, buying them instead from a country where labour was cheap. It may be that this has affected the quality of the goods, thus leading to decreased demand.

Electronic goods

Unlike household goods, demand for electronic goods from Jungle Co has increased dramatically by 28%. This is now Jungle Co's leading revenue generator. This is partly due to the fact that the electronic goods market has grown by 20% worldwide. However, Jungle Co has even outperformed this, meaning that it has secured a larger segment of the market.

Cloud computing service

This area of Jungle Co's business is growing rapidly, with the company seeing a 90% increase in this revenue stream in the last year. Once again, the company has outperformed the market, where the average growth rate is only 50%, suggesting that the investment in the cloud technology was worthwhile.

Gold membership fees

This area of the business is relatively small but has shrunk further, with a decrease in revenue of 30%. This may be because customers are dissatisfied with the service that they are receiving. The number of late deliveries for Gold members has increased from 2% to 14% since Jungle Co began using its own logistics company. This has probably been at least partly responsible for the massive increase in the number of customer complaints.

Gross profit margins

Overall, the company's gross profit margin (GPM) has increased from 37% to 42%. Whilst the GPM for electronic goods has only increased by 1 percentage point, the margin for household goods has increased by 10 percentage points. This is therefore largely responsible for the increase in overall GPM. This has presumably occurred because Jungle Co is now sourcing these products from new, cheaper suppliers.

Gold membership fees constitute only a small part of Jungle Co's income, so their 2 percentage point fall in GPM has had little impact on the overall increase in GPM. Cloud computing services, on the other hand, now make up over $12m of Jungle Co's sales revenue. For some reason, the GPM on these sales has fallen from 76% to 66%. This is now 14 percentage points less than the market average gross profit margin of 80%. More information is needed to establish why this has happened. It has prevented the overall increase in GPM being higher than it otherwise would have been.

Administration expenses/customer complaints

Tutorial note

When it comes to the discussion, use the calculations to guide you to the key areas to focus on. If administrative expenses have increased by 0.2%, don't waste any time worrying about why – it's not significant.

Administration expenses have increased by 60% from $1.72m to $2.76m. This is a substantial increase. The costs of the customer service department are in here.

Given the number of late deliveries increase from 2% to 14%, and the corresponding increase in customer complaints from 5% to 20% of customers, the number of complaints has actually increased by 338% in absolute terms. Therefore, it is not surprising that the administration costs have increased. As well as being concerned about the impact on profit of this increase of over $1m, Jungle Co should be extremely worried about the effect on its reputation. Bad publicity about reliable delivery could affect future business.

Distribution costs

Despite an increase in sales volumes of 15%, distribution expenses have increased by less than 2 percentage points. They have gone down from $0.16 to $0.14 per $ of revenue. Although this means that Jungle Co has been successful in terms of saving costs, as discussed above, the damage which late deliveries are doing to the business cannot be ignored. The company needs to urgently address the issue of late deliveries.

Net profit margin

This has increased from 19% to 25%. This means that, all in all, Jungle Co has had a successful year, with net profit having increased from $15.6m to $23.8m. However, the business must address its delivery issues if its success is to continue.

Gross profit margins	31 August 20X6	31 August 20X5
Household goods	40.00%	30.00%
Electronic goods	36.00%	35.00%
Cloud computing services	65.81%	75.77%
Gold membership fees	92.86%	95.00%
Overall	42.39%	37.19%
Net profit margin	25.15%	18.95%

Increase/decrease in revenue

Household goods	−5.27%
Electronic goods	28.28%
Cloud computing services	90.18%
Gold membership fees	−30.00%
Total revenue increase	14.99%

Increase/decrease in cost of sales

Household goods	−18.80%
Electronic goods	26.31%
Cloud computing services	168.35%
Gold membership fees	0.00%
Total cost of sales increase	5.46%

Increase in administration expenses	60.47%
Increase in distribution expenses	1.82%
Increase in other operating expenses	27.27%
Increase in costs of customer service department	120.93%

([$1,900,000 – $860,000]/$860,000)

	31 August 20X6	*31 August 20X5*
Customer complaints as % customers	19.72%	4.92%
Delivery cost per $ of revenue	$0.14	$0.16

Marking scheme	
	Marks
Sales volumes (up to 2 marks per revenue stream)	8
COS and gross margins	5
Administration expenses/customer complaints	3
Distribution costs/late deliveries	2
Net profit margin	2
Total	**20**

287 OLIVER'S SALON (JUNE 2009)

(a) The average price for hairdressing per client is as follows:

2008: Female clients paid $200,000 for 8,000 visits. This is an average price per visit of $200,000/8,000 = $25.

In 2009 the female hairdressing prices did not increase and the mix of sales did not change so of the total revenue $170,000 (6,800 × $25) was from female clients. This means that the balance of $68,500 ($238,500 – $170,000) was from male clients at an average price of $20 per visit ($68,500/3,425).

(b) **Financial performance assessment**

Hairdressing sales growth: Oliver's Salon has grown significantly during the two years, with an increase of 19.25% (W1). This is impressive in a mature industry like hairdressing.

The increase has come from the launch of the new male hairdressing with a significant contraction in the core female business – down 15% (W1).

Hairdressing gross margin: Oliver's hairdressing overall gross margin has reduced significantly, down from 53% to 47.2% in 2009 (W2).

There has been an increase in staff numbers for the female part of the business and this, combined with the fall in the volume of sales from female clients, has significantly damaged margins from that customer type, with a fall from 53% to 40.5% (W2).

The margins from male clients in 2009 are 63.5% which is better than that achieved in 2008 from the female clients. This is probably mainly due to faster throughput, so that despite the lower average prices charged the overall margin was still quite good.

Staff costs: The staffing levels have had to increase to accommodate the new male market and the extra levels of business. The new hairdresser for the male clients is being paid slightly more than the previously employed staff (W3). This might encourage dissatisfaction. The addition of a junior will clearly reduce the overall average wage bill but increases costs overall whilst the volume of female clients is shrinking.

Advertising spend: This has increased by 150% in the year (W4). This is probably nothing to worry about as it is likely that the launching of the new product range (males!) will have required advertising. Indeed, given the increase in sales of male hair services it is fair to say that the money was well spent.

Rent is clearly a fixed cost and administrative expenses have gone up a mere 5.5%; these costs appear under control given the overall volume of clients is well up on 2008.

Electricity costs have jumped 14.3% which seems a lot but is probably a cost which Oliver would find hard to control. Energy companies are often very large organisations where competition is rarely significant. Small businesses have little choice but to pay the going rate for energy.

Net profit: Overall net profit has worsened to 33.5% from 39% (W8). This is primarily due to the weakening gross margin and extra costs incurred for advertising. The advertising cost may not recur and so the net margin might improve next year.

Overall it is understandable that Oliver is disappointed with the financial results. With a 19.25% increase in overall sales he might have expected more net profit.

(c) **Non-financial performance**

Quality: The number of complaints is up by 283% (W5) and is proportionately more frequent. This seems to be due to two main reasons. Firstly the switch away from a single gender salon has upset the existing customer base. It is possible that by trying to appeal to more customer types Oliver is failing to meet the needs of at least one group. It may be that the quality of hair services has not worsened but that the complaints are regarding the change towards a multi-gender business.

Secondly the wage rates paid to the new junior staff seem to be well below the wage rates of the existing staff (W3). This implies that they are in training and could be of poorer quality. It is stated that they are in a supporting role but if not properly supervised then mistakes could occur. This can easily lead to customer complaints.

Resource utilisation: The main resources that Oliver has are the staff and the rented property. As far as the property is concerned the asset is being used to a much higher degree with 27.8% more clients being serviced in the year (W6). However, as the overall margins are lower one might argue that just focusing solely on volume misses the point on asset utilisation.

As far as the staff usage is concerned it is a mixed scene. The female specialists are producing less per member of staff than in 2008 after the recruitment of one more staff member and a fall in volume of female clients. Each specialist served 2,000 female clients in 2008 and only 1,360 in 2009 (W9). Oliver may have been concerned with the complaints coming in and decided to do something about service levels by increasing resources for the female clients.

The specialist dealing with male clients has produced far more treatments than those serving the females. This is probably not unusual; we are told that the male customer requires only a simple service. Without comparative data we cannot say whether 3,425 customers per year is good. We also cannot say that this specialist is doing 'better' than the others. Cutting men's hair is quicker, so more output is inevitable.

Workings:

(W1) Sales growth overall is $238,500/$200,000 or +19.25%. The female hairdressing sales has though fallen by 15% ($200,000 − $170,000)/$200,000. This is entirely reflected in volume as there was no price increase in 2009 for female clients.

(W2) Gross margin overall is $106,000/$200,000 or 53% in 2008 and $112,500/ 238,500 or 47.2% in 2009. This can be analysed between the female and male clients:

	2008		2009	
	Female $	$	Female $	Male $
Sales	200,000		170,000	68,500
Less cost of sales:				
Hairdressing staff costs (W3)	(65,000)		(74,000)	(17,000)
Hair products – female	(29,000)		(27,000)	
Hair products – male				(8,000)
Gross profit	106,000		69,000	43,500
GP%	53%		40.5%	63.5%

(W3) Staff cost growth is $91,000/$65,000 or +40%. In absolute terms average staff costs were $65,000/4 = $16,250 in 2008.

Additional staff cost $26,000 ($91,000 − $65,000) in total for two people. The junior was paid $9,000 and so the new specialist for the male customers must have been paid $17,000

(W4) Advertising increased by $5,000/$2,000 or 150%

(W5) Number of complaints up by 46/12 or 283%. Complaints per customer visit up from 12/8,000 or 0.15% to 46/10,225 or 0.44%

(W6) Client growth is 10,225/8,000 or 27.8%

(W7) Number of female clients per specialist is 8,000/4 or 2,000 in 2008 and 6,800/5 or 1,360 in 2009. Number of male clients per specialist is 3,425 in 2009.

(W8) Net profit is $78,000/200,000 or 39% in 2008 and $80,000/238,500 or 33.5% in 2009.

			Marks
Marking scheme			
(a)	Average price for female customers		1.0
	Average price for male customers		2.0
		Maximum	**3.0**
(b)	Sales growth		2.0
	Gross margin		2.0
	Rent		1.0
	Advertising spend		2.0
	Staff costs		2.0
	Electricity		1.0
	Overall comment		1.0
		Maximum	**11**
(c)	Quality – single gender		1.5
	Quality – wage levels		1.5
	Quality – other		1.5
	Resource utilisation – property		1.0
	Resource utilisation – staff		2.0
	Resource utilisation – other		1.5
		Maximum	**6.0**
Total			**20**

Examiner's comments

This was a pure performance management question and the core of the exam. Candidates were presented with two years of income based financial results. The last part of the question involved the use of non-financial indicators of success.

Astonishingly a significant number of candidates could not calculate the prices for female and male clients in the two years in question. An average price for the two client types was often the fall back. Basic numeracy is not an unreasonable expectation for accountants.

In part (b) there was some improvement in candidate's ability to assess performance. There were problems however:

Mathematical descriptions are not performance assessments. For example Sales are up 19%, but costs are up by 29% and so profits are only up by 3%.

Simply stating the % increases in numbers is not enough.

Indicating the absolute change in a cost is rarely that useful.

Too narrow a range of figures considered, virtually all the numbers in the question carry marks.

Surprisingly some were so desperate to calculate ROCE that they made up figures for assets values. Not surprisingly there were no marks for this.

I have written many times on this topic suggesting approaches that could be used. Without wishing to repeat myself too often candidates need to calculate a ratio (0.5 marks), make a qualitative statement (1 mark) and suggest a cause or some other comment (1 mark).

The non-financial indicators candidates were asked to consider were surrounding quality and resource utilisation.

Answers on quality dealt with the complaints issue well, but very few talked about the new members of staff and how their performance might be suspect. The lack of a pay rise can be de-motivating and so quality might suffer, this too was rarely picked up.

On resource utilisation candidates had a mixed result. The male throughput per specialist was very high but this was perhaps due to the fact that male hair tends to be easier (quicker) to cut. The female situation was different, with fewer clients for more staff. Many candidates recognised this. Very few talked about the property utilisation at all.

288 TIES ONLY (DECEMBER 2007)

Key answer tips

This is an in-depth question on performance appraisal where the key is to be able to discuss figures given or calculated. It is also an excellent example of how the examiner wants you to be able to discuss both financial and non-financial data. Non-financial performance is one of the examiner's key motivations. The examiner has stated that 'organisations seem obsessed with financial performance measures, but the future is determined more by non-financial performance. Both are important'.

In part (a) the simplest approach is to aim for eight points and try to use the key lines of table one as headings, e.g. sales, gross profit, website development. It is more meaningful to do some straightforward numerical analysis, e.g. calculate the percentage change in gross profit, than to just include the $ figure. Ensure a comment is made about each of the key figures included. Use the information in the scenario together with any other relevant knowledge.

In part (b) aim for four separate points and try to give a balanced answer pointing out the causes for concern, e.g. a falling gross profit percentage, in addition to the positive points.

In part (c) use each line of table two as a key heading. If you have time, include some straightforward calculations, e.g. calculate the percentage change between quarter 1 and 2 and compare to the industry average. This will make the data more meaningful and will make it easier to comment.

(a)   **Financial performance of Ties Only Limited**

   Sales growth

   Ties Only Limited has had an excellent start to their business. From a standing start they have made $420,000 of sales and then grown that figure by over 61% to $680,000 in the following quarter. This is impressive particularly given that we know that the clothing industry is very competitive. Equally it is often the case that new businesses make slow starts, this does not look to be the case here.

   Gross profit

   The gross profit for the business is 52% for quarter 1 and 50% for quarter 2. We have no comparable industry data provided so no absolute comment can be made. However, we can see the gross profit has reduced by two points in one quarter. This is potentially serious and should not be allowed to continue.

The cause of this fall is unclear, price pressure from competitors is possible, who may be responding to the good start made by the business. If Ties Only Limited is reducing its prices, this would reflect on the gross profit margin produced.

It could also be that the supply side cost figures are rising disproportionately. As the business has grown so quickly, it may have had to resort to sourcing extra new supplies at short notice incurring higher purchase or shipping costs. These could all reduce gross margins achieved.

Website development

Website costs are being written off as incurred to the management accounting profit and loss account. They should be seen as an investment in the future and unlikely to continue in the long term. Website development has been made with the future in mind; we can assume that the future website costs will be lower than at present. Taking this into consideration the loss made by the business does not look as serious as it first appears.

Administration costs

These are 23.9% of sales in quarter 1 and only 22.1% of sales in quarter 2. This could be good cost control, impressive given the youth and inexperience of the management team.

Also any fixed costs included in the cost (directors' salaries are included) will be spread over greater volume. This would also reduce the percentage of cost against sales figure. This is an example of a business gaining critical mass. The bigger it gets the more it is able to absorb costs. Ties Only Limited may have some way to go in this regard, gaining a much greater size than at present.

Distribution costs

This is a relatively minor cost that again appears under control. Distribution costs are likely to be mainly variable (postage) and indeed the proportion of this cost to sales is constant at 4.9%.

Launch marketing

Another cost that although in this profit and loss account is unlikely to continue at this level. Once the 'launch' is complete this cost will be replaced by more general marketing of the website. Launch marketing will be more expensive than general marketing and so the profits of the business will improve over time. This is another good sign that the results of the first two quarters are not as bad as they seem.

Other costs

Another cost that appears under control in that it seems to have simply varied with volume.

(b) Although the business has lost over $188,000 in the first two quarters of its life, this is not as disastrous as it looks. The reasons for this view are:

- New businesses rarely breakeven within six months of launch

- The profits are after charging the whole of the website development costs, these costs will not be incurred in the future

- Launch marketing is also deducted from the profits. This cost will not continue at such a high level in the future

The major threat concerns the fall in gross profit percentage which should be investigated.

The owners should be relatively pleased with the start that they have made. They are moving in the right direction and without website development and launch marketing they made a profit of $47,137 in quarter 1 and $75,360 in quarter 2.

If sales continue to grow at the rate seen thus far, then the business (given its ability to control costs) is well placed to return significant profits in the future.

The current profit (or loss) of a business does not always indicate a business's future performance.

(c) **Non-financial indicators of success**

Website hits

This is a very impressive start. A new business can often find it difficult to make an impression in the market. Growth in hits is 25% between the two quarters. If this continued over a year the final quarter hits would be over 1.3m hits. The internet enables new businesses to impact the market quickly.

Number of ties sold

The conversion rates are 4% for quarter 1 and 4.5% for quarter 2. Both these figures may seem low but are ahead of the industry average data. (Industry acquired data must be carefully applied, although in this case the data seems consistent). It appears that the business has a product that the market is interested in. Ties Only Limited are indeed looking competitive.

We can use this statistic to calculate average price achieved for the ties.

Quarter 1

$$\frac{\$420,000}{27,631} = \$15.20 \text{ per tie}$$

Quarter 2

$$\frac{\$680,000}{38,857} = \$17.50 \text{ per tie}$$

This suggests that the fall in gross profit has little to do with the sales price for the ties. The problem of the falling gross profit must lie elsewhere.

On time delivery

Clearly the business is beginning to struggle with delivery. As it expands, its systems and resources will become stretched. Customers' expectations will be governed by the terms on the website, but if expectations are not met then customers may not return. More attention will have to be placed on the delivery problem.

Sales returns

Returns are clearly common in this industry. Presumably, ties have to be seen and indeed worn before they are accepted as suitable by customers. The concern here is that the business's return rate has jumped up in quarter 2 and is now well above the average for the industry. In other words, performance is worsening and below that of the competitors. If the business is under pressure on delivery (as shown by the lateness of delivery) it could be that errors are being made. If wrong goods are sent out then they will be returned by disappointed customers.

The alternative view is that the quality of the product is not what is suggested by the website. If the quality is poor then the products could well be returned by unhappy customers.

This is clearly concerning and an investigation is needed.

System down time

System down time is to be avoided by internet based sellers as much as possible. If the system is down then customers cannot access the site. This could easily lead to lost sales at that time and cause customers not to try again at later dates. Downtime could be caused by insufficient investment at the development stage (we are told that the server was built to a high specification) or when the site is under pressure due to peaking volumes. This second explanation is more likely in this case.

The down time percentage has risen alarmingly and this is concerning. Ideally, we would need figures for the average percentage down time achieved by comparable systems to be able to comment further.

The owners are likely to be disappointed given the level of initial investment they have already made. A discussion with the website developers may well be warranted.

Summary

This new business is doing well. It is growing rapidly and ignoring non-recurring costs is profitable. It needs to focus on delivery accuracy, speed and quality of product. It also needs to focus on a remedy for the falling gross profit margin.

Workings

(W1) Gross profit

Quarter 1:   Quarter 2:

$$\frac{218,400}{420,000} = 52\% \qquad \frac{339,320}{680,000} = 50\%$$

(W2) Website conversion rates

Quarter 1:   Quarter 2:

$$\frac{27,631}{690,789} = 4\% \qquad \frac{38,857}{863,492} = 4.5\%$$

(W3) Website hits growth

Between quarter 1 and quarter 2 the growth in website hits has been:.

$$\frac{863,492}{690,789} = 1.25 = 25\%$$

Marking scheme			
			Marks
(a)	Sales		2
	Gross profit		3
	Website development		2
	Administration		2
	Distribution		1
	Launch marketing		2
	Overall comment		2
			—
		Maximum	**8**
			—
(b)	Future profits comment		**4**
			—
(c)	Website hits		2
	Number of tie sales		1
	Tie price calculation		2
	On time delivery		2
	Returns		2
	System down time		1
	Summary comment		1
			—
		Maximum	**8**
			—
Total			**20**
			—

Examiner's comments (extract)

I wanted some attempt at a qualitative assessment of the financial in part (a) and non-financial performance in part (c). Calculating a ratio without real comment did not gain full marks. For example in part (a) the sales were up 61% from quarter 1 to quarter 2. This calculation gained a half mark only. Saying that this growth was 'impressive' scored a mark! Saying that growth rates such as this are hard to maintain or that market share was probably increasing impressed the markers for more marks. Far too often candidates did little more than calculate a ratio. This is not good enough to pass.

Part (b) was done reasonably with most scoring at least 2 marks. Of the failing candidates it was clear that a deeper understanding of what simple financial data tells you was not present. If this business continued to grow, maintained the same gross profit and controlled its administration and other costs then it would make profit. It would also benefit from the inevitable reduction in 'launch' marketing and website 'development'. These last two short sentences would have scored full marks.

The problem was not as acute in part (c) where candidates seemed more willing to give a qualitative assessment of the non-financial data. Linking the problems of poor delivery times and the rapid growth of the business was not uncommon and gained good credit. However, failing candidates did little more than repeat the data I had given them or calculated a % change in them without any qualitative comment at all.

For the record, increasing sales returns proportion is not a good thing, as a substantial minority thought.

The qualitative comments required were not too difficult. For example I gave data suggesting that the web system was down more often in quarter 2 than in quarter 1. Marks were awarded for comments such as:

- the website was a critical aspect of the business

- the increased amount of time was significant

- sales could be lost

- that it was disappointing, given the high level of investment.

Markers were given flexibility in this area to give credit for any reasonable comments.

It might be worth pointing out here that I did not ask for suggestions as to what should be done by the business to correct the apparent problem (e.g. raise more finance for the rapid growth) and so these type of comments did not earn marks.

289   JAMAIR (DECEMBER 2014)

(a) **Arguments in favour of using the profit measure** in evaluating the performance of a business

- Profit (however calculated) is a generally accepted measure to evaluate a business both internally and externally. Internal users of financial information identify profit as the reward for the skills of being a successful entrepreneur. This measure is still a major determinant of the reward systems of managers of decentralised units. If they meet certain quantified performance targets they obtain the financial rewards that recognise their entrepreneurial skills.

- External users of accounts recognise profit as a measure for identifying the success or failure of the policies of the directors who, as stewards of the assets, are entrusted with the task of increasing the wealth of shareholders. Why do an investors invest? Generally to improve their financial position over time. How do investors improve their financial position over time? Hopefully the stock market's system of intelligence identifies the important factors in the performance of a business and this is reflected in the share price. How do market analysts identify performance? Certainly the measure of 'earnings' is a major determinant in the influential commentaries that can influence investor behaviour.

- The concept of profit is intuitive. A street trader buys inventory at $100 and sells it at the end of the day for $500. He makes a gain of $400 out of which he replenishes his inventory, pays his living expenses and has a surplus to demonstrate that his wealth has increased after meeting all necessary expenditure.

- 'Profit' is the maximum amount that the company can distribute during the year and still expect to be as well off at the end of the year as at the beginning. Consequently profit-based measures such as return on capital employed and earnings per share recognise this all-encompassing need to measure how wealth (or capital) grows or is maintained.

(b) The four perspectives are:

Financial perspective: this perspective is concerned with how a company looks to its shareholders. How can it create value for them? Kaplan and Norton identified three core financial themes which will drive the business strategy: revenue growth and mix, cost reduction and asset utilisation.

Customer perspective – this considers how the organisation appears to customers. The organisation should ask itself: 'to achieve our vision, how should we appear to our customers?' The customer perspective should identify the customer and market segments in which the business will compete. There is a strong link between the customer perspective and the revenue objectives in the financial perspective. If customer objectives are achieved, revenue objectives should be too.

Internal perspective – this requires the organisation to ask itself: 'what must we excel at to achieve our financial and customer objectives?' It must identify the internal business processes which are critical to the implementation of the organisation's strategy. These will include the innovation process, the operations process and the post-sales process.

Learning and growth perspective – this requires the organisation to ask itself whether it can continue to improve and create value. The organisation must continue to invest in its infrastructure – i.e. people, systems and organisational procedures – in order to improve the capabilities which will help the other three perspectives to be achieved.

(c) **Goals and measures**

Tutorial note

Only one goal and measure were required for each perspective. In order to gain full marks, answers had to be specific to Jamair as stated in the requirements.

Financial perspective	
Goal	**Performance measure**
To use fewer planes to transport customers	Lease costs of plane per customer
Explanation – operating efficiency will be driven by getting more customers on fewer planes. This goal and measure cover the cost side of this.	

Financial perspective	
Goal	**Performance measure**
To increase seat revenue per plane	Revenue per available passenger mile
Explanation – this covers the first part of achieving operating efficiency – by having fewer empty seats on planes.	

Customer perspective	
Goal	**Performance measure**
To ensure that flights are on time	'On time arrival' ranking from the aviation authority
Explanation – Jamair is currently number 7 in the rankings. If it becomes known as a particularly reliable airline, customers are more likely to use it, which will ultimately increase revenue.	

Customer perspective	
Goal	**Performance measure**
To reduce the number of flights cancelled	The number of flights cancelled
Explanation – again, if flights are seen to be cancelled frequently by Jamair, customers will not want to use it. It needs to be perceived as reliable by its customers.	

Internal perspective	
Goal	**Performance measure**
To improve turnaround time on the ground	'On the ground' time
Explanation – Less time spent on the ground means fewer planes are needed, which will reduce plane leasing costs. However, it is important not to compromise the quality of cleaning or make errors in refuelling as a consequence of reducing on the ground time.	

Internal perspective	
Goal	**Performance measure**
To improve the cleanliness of Jamair's planes	The percentage of customers happy with the standard of the planes, as reported in the customer satisfaction surveys
Explanation – at present, only 85% of customers are happy with the standard of cleanliness on Jamair's planes. This could be causing loss of revenue.	

Internal perspective	
Goal	**Performance measure**
To develop the online booking system	Percentage downtime
Explanation – since the company relies entirely on the booking system for customer booking of flights and check-in, it is critical that it can deal with the growing number of customers.	

Learning perspective	
Goal	**Performance measure**
To reduce the employee absentee rate	The number of days absent per employee
Explanation – it is critical to Jamair that its workforce is reliable as, at worse, absent staff lead to cancelled flights.	

Learning perspective	
Goal	**Performance measure**
To increase ground crew training on cleaning refuelling procedures	and Number of days' training per ground crew member
Explanation – if ground crew are better trained, they can reduce the number of minutes that the plane stays on the ground, which will result in fewer planes being required and therefore lower costs. Also, if their cleaning is better, customer satisfaction and retention will increase.	

290 THE PEOPLE'S BANK (MARCH/JUNE 2017)

(a)

Tutorial note

Part (a) asks why the balanced scorecard would be more useful to the People's Bank than using solely financial performance measures. Although there are only four marks available, it highlights some candidates' weakness in not being able to use the information in the scenario to help them answer the question.

It is easy to identify the generic point that the balanced scorecard gives a more rounded view by looking at a wider range of performance measures (financial and non-financial) as well as internal and external factors. However, the scenario gives us more help and shows us how important these non-financial factors are to the bank – the 3 values given highlight this. If their performance was assessed purely on profit they would never strive to meet those values, or looking at it another way they might be judged to have failed by spending money on improving customer accessibility or simplifying their processes.

The balanced scorecard approach looks not only at the financial performance but also non-financial performance. In order to maintain a competitive edge, organisations have to be very aware of the changing needs of their customers.

In the case of The People's Bank, this has involved identifying specific categories of customers which have particular needs, like SMEs in a commercial context, or like the disabled or visually impaired in a non-commercial context. This permits these needs to be addressed. The People's Bank has a vision and strategy which goes far beyond just making money. They want to help the community and disadvantaged people and give something back to customers also. Hence, by using the balanced scorecard, performance measures which address whether the Bank is being successful in pursuing their vision can be incorporated.

In addition, from a purely business perspective, if employees and customers are valued and internal processes are efficient, an organisation should have more chance of achieving long-term success anyway. So, even putting aside the social objectives The People's Bank has, the balanced scorecard can be useful to The People's Bank to measure these other aspects of future success too.

(b)

Tutorial note

Part (b) was a more traditional performance assessment question. Exam technique was crucial here. The note in the requirement says to use each of the four headings of the balanced scorecard to structure your answer. Ignoring this makes it much harder to score well on this question, as it would be harder to see how their points corresponded to the perspectives of the balanced scorecard. Use the headings suggested (which were given in the scenario). Similarly, the requirement specifically asked candidates to use the bank's vision and values to assess performance. Therefore, a sensible approach would be to take each perspective, use the performance measures given and details in the scenario to see how they link to the bank's vision and values.

The performance of the bank will be considered under each of the headings used in the balanced scorecard:

Financial perspective

The People's Bank has had a year of mixed success when looking at the extent to which it has met its financial targets. Its return on capital employed (ROCE) shows how efficiently it has used its assets to generate profit for the business. The target for the year was 12% but it has only achieved an 11% return. The People's Bank's interest income, however, was in fact $0.5m higher than its target, which is good. This may have been achieved by offering slightly better interest rates to customers than competing banks, as the interest margin The People's Bank achieved is slightly lower than target. The most likely reason for the under target ROCE is therefore probably the investment which The People's Bank has made in IT security and facilities for the disabled and visually impaired. Whilst this may have reduced ROCE, this investment is essentially a good idea as it helps The People's Bank pursue its vision and will keep customers happy. It will also, in the case of the IT security investment, prevent the bank and its customers from losing money from fraud in the future.

The other performance measure, the amount of new lending to SMEs, is a little bit disappointing, given The People's Bank's stated value of making a difference to communities. The failure to meet this target may well be linked to the fact that an insufficient number of staff were trained to provide advice to SMEs and consequently, fewer of them may have been successful in securing additional finance.

Tutorial note

The other key skill in these questions is to identify linkages between measures – cause and effect relationships. For example on the Financial perspective we can see that new lending to SMEs was significantly (10%) down on target. The first point you should make is that this is not in line with the bank's third value – to support SMEs. This alone will be given credit, and similar points should be made for each heading, however even more credit can be given if you go on to say that the drop in new lending to SMEs is due to the fact that fewer colleagues have been trained to provide advice to SMEs (under learning and growth.

Customer perspective

With regard to its customers, The People's Bank has performed well in the year. It has exceeded its target to provide mortgages to new homeowners by 6,000. This is helping The People's Bank pursue its vision of helping new homeowners. It has also managed to beat the target for customer complaints such that there are only 1.5 complaints for every 1,000 customers, well below the target of 2. This may be as a result of improved processes at the bank or improved security. It is not clear what the precise reason is but it is definitely good for The People's Bank's reputation.

The bank has also exceeded both of its targets to help the disabled and visually impaired, which is good for its reputation and its stated value of making services more accessible.

Internal processes

The number of processes simplified within the bank has exceeded the target, which is good, and the success of which may well be reflected in the lower customer complaints levels. Similarly, the investment to improve IT systems has been a success, with only three incidences of fraud per 1,000 customers compared to the target of 10. However, perhaps because of the focus on this part of the business, only two new services have been made available via mobile banking, instead of the target of five, which is disappointing. Similarly, it is possible that some of the new systems have prevented the business from keeping its CO_2 emissions to their target level.

Learning and growth

The People's Bank has succeeded in helping the community, exceeding both of its targets relating to hours of paid volunteer work and number of community organisations supported by volunteers or funding. These additional costs could have contributed to the fact that the bank did not quite meet its target for ROCE. However, the bank has not quite met its targets for helping small businesses and helping the disadvantaged.

As mentioned earlier, the shortfall in training of employees to give advice to SMEs may have had an impact on The People's Bank's failure to meet its target lending to SMEs. As regards the percentage of trainee positions, the target was only just missed and this may well have been because the number of candidates applying from these areas was not as high as planned and the bank has no control over this.

Tutorial note

Finally, a long discussion question like this should finish with a brief, overall conclusion. This should be in line with your findings – sometimes it will be very clear that performance has been good or bad, otherwise you might have to say something like "with the exception of the financial perspective, The People's Bank has performed well in meeting its vision."

Overall, the bank has had a fairly successful year, meeting many of its targets. However, it still has some work to do in order to meet its stated values and continue to pursue its vision.

291 PUBLIC SECTOR ORGANISATION

Budget preparation

It would be in line with the principles of modern management if the department manager was encouraged to participate more in setting the budget. In this way, he would be more likely to show commitment to the organisational goals in general and the budget in particular. He is closer to the activity for which the budget is prepared, and so the relevance and accuracy of the budget should be improved. This involvement should extend also to discussion of the form and frequency of the reporting which is to take place for his/her department.

Activity volume

The volume of visits undertaken is 20% greater than that budgeted. It is inappropriate to compare the actual costs of visiting 12,000 clients with a budget for 10,000 clients. Costs such as wages, travel expenses and consumables would be expected to be higher than the fixed budget in these circumstances.

One way to deal with this is to adjust, or flex, the budget to acknowledge the cost implications of the higher number of visits, or to be aware of it when making any comparison. If a factor of 1.20 is applied to the overall wages budget for permanent and casual staff (i.e. on the assumption that it is a variable cost), the flexed budget $5,040 ($4,200 × 1.2) is greater than the actual cost of $4,900. Taking a similar approach to travel expenses and consumables expenses:

- actual travel expenses are exactly in line with the flexed budget (1,500 × 1.20), but

- the consumables costs seem to be highly overspent compared to the flexed budget (4,000 × 1.2).

To circulate a report as originally constructed seems to highlight and publicise some invalid comparisons from which inappropriate conclusions may be drawn. It is recommended that for cost control purposes, a report is prepared which compares actual spending with a flexed budget based on the actual activity. This would require an estimate of the variable, fixed and semi-variable nature of the cost items.

Controllability

It is possible to question whether all the costs shown need to feature in the report. For example, the allocated administrative costs and equipment depreciation are book entries that do not directly affect the department and are not likely to be controllable by employees of the department. There are, therefore, adverse variances on the report contributing to the overall overspend that are not the responsibility of the departmental manager. The difference between actual and budgeted cost of administration serves no useful purpose in this report, because the manager can take no action to influence this directly. The only justification to include this is if the manager can bring about some pressure to reduce this spending by someone else.

It may be unwise to adopt the guide of a 5% deviation to judge variances. The key is whether a cost is out of control and can be corrected by managerial action. Also, 5% of some values can be significant whilst on others 5% of the total cost might be of little consequence.

Funding allocation

The Director is correct in pointing out that 'the department must live within its funding allocation'. However, it is not like a commercial organisation where more output can result in more revenue and hence more money to spend. Increased funding will only be achieved if this organisation and the department is allocated more funds as a result of national or local government decisions to support an increase in services.

It would be appropriate for the funding allocation to be compared with the flexible budget (based on actual activity) to encourage the managers to be aware of and live within the budget allocation. Ways can always be found to spend more money, and so authority structures must be in place to ensure that requests to spend have been budgeted and appropriately funded. Hence the organisational arrangements which authorised the increased visits would be examined.

The nature of the activity for which the budget is being developed should not be lost sight of. It is more complex to deal with budget decisions related to the welfare needs of society than those for a typical manufacturing firm. There are no clear input-output relationships in the former, and hence it is difficult to judge what is justifiable spending for the department compared with other departments and public sector organisations.

Other aspects

One possible outcome from discussion over the appropriate form of report would be the use of non-financial measures. The total staff hours worked, client satisfaction and size of the potential client population are all examples of extensions to the reporting procedure which would help to place the results in context.

The style of the approach adopted by the Director may show some lack of behavioural insight. The despatch of a memo to deal with a prototype report may result in lower staff morale and increased tension in the Homecare department. This may lead to inappropriate future decisions on spending and budget 'game playing' within the department. It may, of course, be a conscious decision of the Director to place the manager in the position of having to reduce spending to the allocated level.

Although this is the first month's report, in the future it may be helpful to use an additional column of the report to show the year-to-date figures. This would help to identify trends and assist discussion of whether costs are being controlled over the longer term. To show future results for only one month may be insufficient; for example, the repairs to equipment may not follow a regular pattern and this would be revealed if cumulative data existed.

292 WOODSIDE CHARITY (JUNE 2007)

(a) **Discussion of performance of Woodside Charity**

In a year which saw fundraising fall $80,000 short of the target level, costs were over budget in all areas of activity except overnight shelter provision. The budget provided for a surplus of $98,750, but the actual figures for the year show a shortfall of $16,980.

Free meals provision cost $12,750 (14%) more than budgeted. Most of the variance (69%) was due to providing 1,750 more meals than budgeted, although $4,000 of it was due to an increase of 20p in the average cost per meal.

Variable cost of overnight shelter provision was $26,620 (11%) less than budgeted. $31,000 was saved because usage of the service was 1,240 bed-nights below budget, but an adverse variance of $4,380 arose because of an increase of 50p in the average unit cost of provision.

Variable advice centre costs were $16,600 (37%) above budget. This was due to increased usage of the service, which was 17% up on budget from 3,000 to 3,500 sessions, and to an increase in the average cost of provision, which rose by 17% from $15 to $17.60 per session.

Fixed costs of administration and centre maintenance were $18,000 (28%) above budget and the costs of campaigning and advertising were $15,000 (10%) above budget.

While investigation of some of the variances in the reconciliation statement below may be useful in controlling further cost increases, the Woodside charity appears to have more than achieved its objectives in terms of providing free meals and advice. The lower usage of overnight shelter could lead to transfer of resources from this area in the next budget to the services that are more in demand. The reasons for the lower usage of overnight shelter are not known, but the relationship between the provision of effective advice and the usage of overnight shelter could be investigated.

Operating statement

	$	$	$
Budgeted surplus (W1)			98,750
Funding shortfall (W3)			(80,000)
			———
			18,750
	Favourable	*Adverse*	
Free meals (W4)			
Price variance		4,000	
Usage variance		8,750	
Overnight shelter (W5)			
Price variance		4,380	
Usage variance	31,000		
Advice centre (W6)			
Price variance		9,100	
Usage variance		7,500	
Campaigning and advertising (W7)			
Expenditure variance		15,000	
Fixed cost (W8)			
Expenditure variance		18,000	
	———	———	
	31,000	66,730	(35,730)
			———
Actual shortfall (W2)			(16,980)
			———

Workings

(W1) Budgeted figures

	$	
Free meals provision	91,250	(18,250 meals at $5 per meal)
Overnight shelter (variable)	250,000	(10,000 bed-nights at $30 – $5 per night)
Advice centre (variable)	45,000	(3,000 sessions at $20 – $5 per session)
Fixed costs	65,000	(10,000 × $5) + (3,000 × $5)
Campaigning and advertising	150,000	
	601,250	
Surplus for unexpected costs	98,750	
Fundraising target	700,000	

(W2) Actual figures

	$	
Free meals provision	104,000	(20,000 meals at $5.20 per meal)
Overnight shelter	223,380	(8,760 bed-nights $25.50 per night)
Advice centre	61,600	(3,500 sessions at $17.60 per session)
Fixed costs	83,000	
Campaigning and advertising	165,000	
	636,980	
Shortfall	16,980	
Funds raised	620,000	

(W3) Funding shortfall – 700,000 – 620,000 = $80,000 (A)

(W4) Free meals price variance = (5.00 – 5.20) × 20,000 = $4,000 (A)

Free meals usage variance = (18,250 – 20,000) × 5.00 = $8,750 (A)

(W5) Overnight shelter price variance = (25.00 – 25.50) × 8,760 = $4,380 (A)

Overnight shelter usage variance – (10,000 – 8,760) × 25 = $31,000 (F)

(W6) Advice centre price variance = (17.60 – 15.00) × 3,500 = $9,100 (A)

Advice centre usage variance = (3,000 – 3,500) × 15.00 = $7,500 (A)

(W7) Campaigning and advertising expenditure variance = 150,000 – 165,000 = $15,000 (A)

(W8) Fixed cost expenditure variance = 65,000 – 83,000 = $18,000 (A)

(b) Financial management and control in a not-for-profit organisation (NFPO) such as the Woodside charity must recognise that the primary objectives of these organisations are essentially non-financial. Here, these objectives relate to helping the homeless and because the charity has no profit-related objective, financial management and control must focus on providing value for money. This means that resources must be found economically in order to keep input costs as low as possible; that these resources must be used as efficiently as possible in providing the services offered by the charity; and that the charity must devise and use effective methods to meet its objectives. Financial objectives could relate to the need to obtain funding for offered services and to the need to control costs in providing these services.

Preparing budgets

The nature of the activities of a NFPO can make it difficult to forecast levels of activity. In the case of the Woodside charity, homeless people seeking free meals would be given them, and more food would be prepared if necessary, regardless of the budgeted provision for a given week or month. The level of activity is driven here by the needs of the homeless, and although financial planning may produce weekly or monthly budgets that consider seasonal trends, a high degree of flexibility may be needed to respond to unpredictable demand. This was recognised by the charity by budgeting for a fundraising surplus for unexpected costs.

It is likely that forecasting cost per unit of service in a NFPO can be done with more precision if the unit of service is small and the service is repetitive or routine, and this is true for the Woodside charity. It is unlikely, though, that a detailed analysis of costs has been carried out along these lines, and more likely that an incremental budget approach has been used on a total basis for each service provided. It depends on the financial skills and knowledge available to the charity from its three full-time staff and team of volunteers.

Controlling costs

Because of the need for economy and efficiency, this is a key area of financial management and control for a NFPO. The costs of some inputs can be minimised at the point of buying, for example the Woodside charity can be economical when buying food, drink, crockery, blankets, cleaning materials and so on. The costs of other inputs can be minimised at the point of use, for example the Woodside charity can encourage economy in the use of heating, lighting, water consumption, telephone usage and postage. In an organisation staffed mainly by volunteers with an unpredictable clientele, cost control is going to depend to a large extent on the way in which responsibility and authority are delegated.

Collecting information

Cost control is not possible without collecting regularly information on costs incurred, as well as storing and processing this information. In the Woodside charity, provision has been made in the budget for fixed administration costs and the administration duties must hopefully relate in part to this collecting of costing information. Without it, budgeting and financial reporting would not be possible. Annual accounts would be needed in order to retain charitable status and to show providers of funds that their donations were being used to their best effect.

Meeting objectives

A NFPO organisation must be able to determine and demonstrate whether it is meeting its declared objectives and so needs to develop measures to do this. This can be far from easy. The analysis of the performance of the Woodside charity over the last year shows that it may be possible to measure objective attainment quantitatively, i.e. in terms of number of free meals served, number of bed-nights used and number of advice sessions given. Presumably, objectives are being met to a greater extent if more units of service are being provided, and so the adverse usage variances for free meals and advice sessions can in fact be used to show that the charity is meeting a growing need.

The meaning of quantitative measures of service provision may not be clear, however. For example, the lower usage of bed-nights could be attributed to the effective provision of advice to the homeless on finding housing and financial aid, and so may also be seen as a success. It could also be due to dissatisfaction amongst the homeless with the accommodation offered by the shelter. In a similar vein, the higher than budget number of advice sessions may be due to repeat visits by homeless people who were not given adequate advice on their first visit, rather than to an increase in the number of people needing advice. Qualitative measures of objective attainment will therefore be needed in addition to, or to supplement, quantitative ones.

Section 7

SPECIMEN EXAM QUESTIONS

Exam Summary

Time allowed: This specimen exam is not timed.

This exam is divided into three sections:

Section A

- 15 objective test (OT) questions, each worth 2 marks.
- 30 marks in total.

Section B

- Three OT cases, each containing a scenario which relates to five OT questions, each worth 2 marks.
- 30 marks in total.

Section C

- Two constructed response questions, each containing a scenario which relates to one or more requirement(s).
- Each constructed response question is worth 20 marks in total.
- 40 marks in total.

Please note that the live exam is worth a total of 110 marks, 10 marks of which are for questions that do not count towards your final result and are included for quality assurance purposes. This specimen exam is worth a total of 100 marks, reflecting the element of the live exam on which your result will be based.

All questions are compulsory.

Section A

This section of the exam contains **15 objective test (OT) questions**.

Each question is worth **2 marks** and is compulsory.

This exam section is worth **30 marks** in total.

Select **Next** to continue.

Q1

A company manufactures two products, C and D, for which the following information is available:

	Product C	Product D	Total
Budgeted production (units)	1,000	4,000	5,000
Labour hours per unit / in total	8	10	48,000
Number of production runs required	13	15	28
Number of inspections during production	5	3	8

Total production set up costs	$140,000
Total inspection costs	$80,000
Other overhead costs	$96,000

Other overhead costs are absorbed on a labour hour basis.

Using activity-based costing, what is the budgeted overhead cost per unit of product D?

- $43.84
- $46.25
- $131.00
- $140.64

Q2

The selling price of product X is set at $550 for each unit and sales for the coming year are expected to be 800 units.

A return of 30% on the investment of $500,000 in product X will be required in the coming year.

What is the target cost for each unit of product X (to two decimal places)?

$ _____

Q3

P Co makes two products, P1 and P2. The budgeted details for each product are as follows:

	P1 ($)	P2 ($)
Selling price	10.00	8.00
Cost per unit:		
Direct materials	3.50	4.00
Direct labour	1.50	1.00
Variable overhead	0.60	0.40
Fixed overhead	1.20	1.00
Profit per unit	**3.20**	**1.60**

Budgeted production and sales for the year ended 30 November 20X5 are:

Product P1	10,000 units
Product P2	12,500 units

The fixed overhead costs included in P1 relate to apportionment of general overhead costs only. However, P2 also included specific fixed overheads totalling $2,500.

If only product P1 were to be made, how many units would need to be sold in order to achieve a profit of $60,000 each year (to the nearest whole unit)?

| | units

Q4

Which TWO of the following statements, regarding environmental cost accounting, are true?

☐ The majority of environmental costs are already captured within a typical organisation's accounting system. The difficulty lies in identifying them

☐ Input/output analysis divides material flows within an organisation into three categories: material flows; system flows; and delivery and disposal flows

☐ One of the cost categories used in environmental activity-based costing is environment-driven costs which is used for costs which can be directly traced to a cost centre

☐ Environmental life-cycle costing enables environmental costs from the design stage of the product right through to decommissioning at the end of its life to be considered

Q5

To produce 19 litres of product X, a standard input mix of 8 litres of chemical A and 12 litres of chemical B is required.

Chemical A has a standard cost of $20 per litre and chemical B has a standard cost of $25 per litre.

During September, the actual results showed that 1,850 litres of product X were produced, using a total input of 900 litres of chemical A and 1,100 litres of chemical B.

The actual costs of chemicals A and B were at the standard cost of $20 and $25 per litre respectively.

Based on the above information, which of the following statements is true?

Select... ▼
Select...
Both variances were adverse
Both variances were favourable
The total mix variance was adverse and the total yield variance was favourable
The total mix variance was favourable and the total yield variance was adverse

Q6

A budget is a quantified plan of action for a forthcoming period. Budgets can be prepared using a variety of different approaches.

Match each of the following statements to the correct budgeting process.

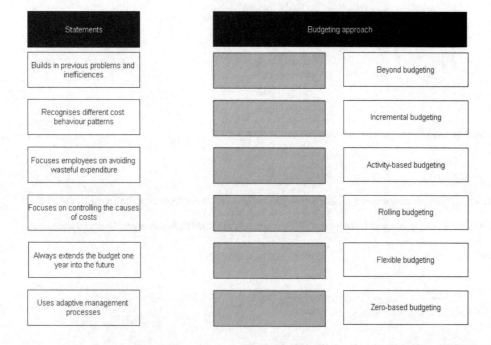

Statements		Budgeting approach
Builds in previous problems and inefficiences		Beyond budgeting
Recognises different cost behaviour patterns		Incremental budgeting
Focuses employees on avoiding wasteful expenditure		Activity-based budgeting
Focuses on controlling the causes of costs		Rolling budgeting
Always extends the budget one year into the future		Flexible budgeting
Uses adaptive management processes		Zero-based budgeting

Q7

A leisure company owns a number of large health and fitness resorts, but one is suffering from declining sales and is predicted to make a loss in the next year. As a result management have identified a number of possible actions:

(1) Shut down the resort and sell off the assets
(2) Undertake a major upgrade to facilities costing $4.5m
(3) Undertake a minor upgrade to facilities costing $2m

The upgrades are predicted to have variable results and the probability of good results after a major upgrade is 0.8, whereas the probability of good results after a minor upgrade is 0.7.

The company is risk neutral and has prepared the following decision tree.

Using the information below, identify, by clicking on the relevant branch of the decision tree, which action the company should take.

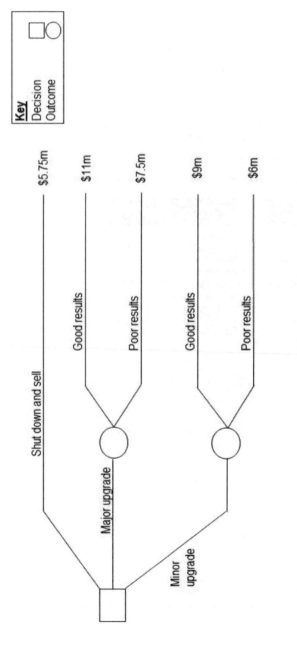

Q8

A company has the following production planned for the next four weeks. The figures reflect the full capacity level of operations. Planned output is equal to the maximum demand per product.

Product	A ($ per unit)	B ($ per unit)	C ($ per unit)	D ($ per unit)
Selling price	160	214	100	140
Raw material cost	24	56	22	40
Direct labour cost	66	88	33	22
Variable overhead cost	24	18	24	18
Fixed overhead cost	16	10	8	12
Profit	30	42	13	48
Planned output	300	125	240	400
Direct labour hours per unit	6	8	3	2

It has now been identified that labour hours available in the next four weeks will be limited to 4,000 hours.

Rank the products in the order they should be manufactured, assuming that the company wants to maximise profits in the next four weeks.

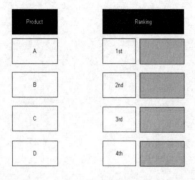

Q9

Def Co provides accounting services to government departments. On average, each staff member works six chargeable hours per day, with the rest of their working day being spent on non-chargeable administrative work. One of the company's main objectives is to produce a high level of quality and customer satisfaction.

Def Co has set its targets for the next year.

Match the correct value for money performance category to each of the following targets for Def Co.

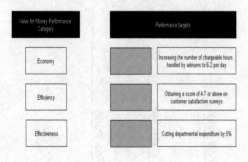

Q10

Different types of information systems provide the information which organisations need for strategic planning, management and operational control.

Match the following characteristics to the relevant information systems.

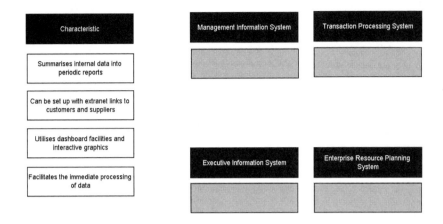

Q11

Which TWO of the following are examples of direct data capture costs?

☐ Use of bar coding and scanners

☐ Completion of timesheets by employees

☐ Payroll department processing time of personnel costs

☐ Input of data into the production system

☐ Emails sent to staff on matters that do not relate to them

Q12

Which TWO of the following statements regarding life-cycle costing are correct?

☐ It can be applied not only to products but also to an organisation's customers

☐ Often between 70% to 90% of costs are determined early in the product life-cycle

☐ It includes any opportunity costs associated with production

☐ The maturity phase is characterised by a rapid build up in demand

Q13

A company manufactures a product which requires four hours per unit of machine time. Machine time is a bottleneck resource as there are only ten machines which are available for 12 hours per day, five days per week. The product has a selling price of $130 per unit, direct material costs of $50 per unit, labour costs of $40 per unit and factory overhead costs of $20 per unit. These costs are based on weekly production and sales of 150 units.

What is the throughput accounting ratio?

 1.33

2.00

0.75

0.31

Q14

Ox Co has two divisions, A and B. Division A makes a component for air conditioning units which it can only sell to division B. It has no other outlet for sales.

Current information relating to division A is as follows:

Marginal cost per unit	$100
Transfer price of the component	$165
Total production and sales of the component each year (units)	2,200
Specific fixed costs of division A per year	$10,000

Cold Co has offered to sell the component to division B for $140 per unit. If division B accepts this offer, division A will be closed.

If division B accepts Cold Co's offer, what will be the impact on profits per year for the group as a whole?

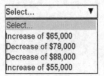

Select...
Increase of $65,000
Decrease of $78,000
Decrease of $88,000
Increase of $55,000

Q15

Identify, by clicking on the relevant box in the table below, whether each of the statements regarding Fitzgerald and Moon's Building Blocks model is true or false.

The determinants of performance are quality, innovation, resource utilisation and competitiveness	TRUE	FALSE
Standards are targets for performance and should be fair, achievable and controllable	TRUE	FALSE
Rewards encourage staff to work towards the standards and should be clear, motivating and controllable	TRUE	FALSE
It is a performance measurement framework suitable for service organisations	TRUE	FALSE

Section B

This section of the exam contains **three OT cases**.

Each OT case contains a scenario which relates to **five OT questions**.

Each question is worth **2 marks** and is compulsory.

This exam section is worth **30 marks** in total.

Select **Next** to continue.

Glam Co is a hairdressing salon which provides both 'cuts' and 'treatments' to clients. All cuts and treatments at the salon are carried out by one of the salon's three senior stylists. The salon also has two salon assistants and two junior stylists.

Every client attending the salon is seen first by a salon assistant, who washes their hair; next, by a senior stylist, who cuts or treats their hair depending on which service the client wants; then finally, a junior stylist who dries their hair. The average length of time spent with each member of staff is as follows:

	Cut (Hours)	Treatment (Hours)
Assistant	0.1	0.3
Senior stylist	1.0	1.5
Junior stylist	0.6	0.5

The salon is open for eight hours each day for six days per week. It is only closed for two weeks each year. Staff salaries are $40,000 each year for each senior stylist, $28,000 each year for each junior stylist and $12,000 each year for each of the assistants. The cost of cleaning products applied when washing clients' hair is $1.50 per client. The cost of all additional products applied during a 'treatment' is $7.40 per client. Other salon costs (excluding labour and raw materials) amount to $106,400 each year.

Glam Co charges $60 for each cut and $110 for each treatment.

The senior stylists' time has been correctly identified as the bottleneck activity.

Q16

What is the annual capacity of the bottleneck activity?

- ○ 2,400 cuts or 1,600 treatments
- ○ 4,800 cuts or 4,800 treatments
- ○ 7,200 cuts or 4,800 treatments
- ○ 9,600 cuts or 9,600 treatments

Q17

The salon has calculated the cost per hour to be $42.56.

Calculate the throughput accounting ratio (TPAR) for both services (to two decimal places).

Cuts   [   ]

Treatments   [   ]

Q18

Which THREE of the following activities could the salon use to improve the TPAR?

☐ Identify ways to reduce the material costs for the services

☐ Increase the time spent by the bottleneck activity on each service

☐ Improve the control of the salon's total operating expenses

☐ Increase the level of inventory to prevent stockouts

☐ Increase the productivity of the stage prior to the bottleneck

☐ Apply an increase to the selling price of the services

Q19

What would be the effect on the bottleneck if the salon employed another senior stylist?

◉ The senior stylists' time will be a bottleneck for cuts only

◉ The senior stylists' time will be a bottleneck for treatments only

◉ The senior stylists' time will remain the bottleneck for both cuts and treatments

◉ There will no longer be a bottleneck

Q20

Which of the following statements regarding the theory of constraints are correct?

(1) It focuses on identifying stages of congestion in a process when production arrives more quickly than the next stage can handle

(2) It is based on the concept that organisations manage three key factors - throughput, operating expenses and inventory

(3) It uses a sequence of focusing steps to overcome a single bottleneck, at which point the improvement process is complete

(4) It can be applied to the management of all limiting factors, both internal and external, which can affect an organisation

◉ 1 and 2 only

◉ 1, 2 and 3

◉ 2, 3 and 4

◉ 1, 3 and 4

Chair Co has several new products in development. Information relating to two of these products is as follows:

Luxury car seat
The estimated labour time for the first unit is 12 hours but a learning curve of 75% is expected to apply for the first eight units produced. The cost of labour is $15 per hour.

The cost of materials and other variable overheads is expected to total $230 per unit. Chair Co plans on pricing the seat by adding a 50% mark-up to the total variable cost per seat, with the labour cost being based on the incremental time taken to produce the eighth unit.

High chair
Another product which Chair Co has in development is a new design of high chair for feeding young children. Based on previous experience of producing similar products, Chair Co had assumed that a learning rate of 85% would apply to the manufacture of this new design but after the first phase of production had been completed, management realised that a learning rate of 80% had been achieved.

Chair Co uses cost-plus pricing when setting prices for its products.

Q21

In relation to the luxury car seat, what is the labour cost of the eighth unit?

◯ $45.65

◯ $75.94

◯ $4.32

◯ $3.04

Q22

The first phase of production has now been completed for the new car seat. The first unit actually took 12.5 hours to make and the total time for the first eight units was 34.3 hours, at which point the learning effect came to an end. Chair Co are planning on adjusting the price to reflect the actual time it took to complete the eighth unit.

What was the actual rate of learning which occurred (to two decimal places)?

[   ] %

Q23

In relation to the new design of high chair, which THREE of the following statements could explain why the actual rate of learning differed from the rate which was expected?

☐ Staffing levels were stable during the first manufacturing phase

☐ There were machine breakdowns during production

☐ Assembly of the chairs was manual and very repetitive

☐ There was high staff turnover during this period

☐ There were minimal stoppages in the production process

☐ The design of the chair was changed several times at this early phase

Q24

Identify, by clicking on the table below, whether each of the statements regarding cost-plus pricing strategies is true or false.

Marginal cost-plus pricing is easier where there is a readily identifiable variable cost	TRUE	FALSE
Full cost-plus pricing requires the budgeted level of output to be determined at the outset	TRUE	FALSE
Cost-plus pricing is a strategically focused approach as it accounts for external factors	TRUE	FALSE
Cost-plus pricing requires that the profit mark-up applied by an organisation is fixed	TRUE	FALSE

Q25

Chair Co has also developed a new type of office chair and management is trying to formulate a budget for this product. They have decided to match the production level to demand, however, demand for this chair is uncertain.

Management have collected the following information:

	Demand (units)	Probability
Worst possible outcome	10,000	0.3
Most likely outcome	22,000	0.5
Best possible outcome	35,000	0.2

The selling price per unit is $25. The variable cost per unit is $8 for any production level up to 25,000 units. If the production level is higher than 25,000 units then the variable cost per unit will decrease by 10% and this reduction will apply to all the units produced at that level.

Total fixed costs are estimated to be $75,000.

Using probabilistic budgeting, what is the expected budgeted contribution of this product (to the nearest whole $)?

$ [   ]

The Hi Life Co makes sofas. It has recently received a request from a customer to provide a one-off order of sofas, in excess of normal budgeted production. The order would need to be completed within two weeks.

The following cost estimate has already been prepared:

		$
Direct materials:		
Fabric	200 m² at $17 per m²	3,400
Wood	50 m² at $8.20 per m²	410
Direct labour:		
Skilled	200 hours at $16 per hour	3,200
Semi-skilled	300 hours at $12 per hour	3,600
Factory overheads	500 hours at $3 per hour	1,500
Total production cost		**12,110**
General fixed overheads at 10% of total production cost		1,211
Total cost		**13,321**

A quotation now needs to be prepared on a relevant cost basis so that Hi Life Co can offer as competitive a price as possible for the order.

Q26

The fabric is regularly used by Hi Life Co. There are currently 300 m^2 in inventory, which cost $17 per m^2. The current purchase price of the fabric is $17.50 per m^2.

The wood is regularly used by Hi Life Co and usually costs $8.20 per m^2. However, the company's current supplier's earliest delivery time for the wood is in three weeks' time. An alternative supplier could deliver immediately but they would charge $8.50 per m^2. Hi Life Co already has 500 m^2 in inventory but 480 m^2 of this is needed to complete other existing orders in the next two weeks. The remaining 20 m^2 is not going to be needed until four weeks' time.

What is the cost of the fabric and the wood which should be included in the quotation (to the nearest whole $)?

Fabric $ [   ]

Wood $ [   ]

Q27

The skilled labour force is employed under permanent contracts of employment under which they must be paid for 40 hours per week's labour, even if their time is idle due to absence of orders. Their rate of pay is $16 per hour, although any overtime is paid at time and a half. In the next two weeks there is spare capacity of 150 labour hours.

There is no spare capacity for semi-skilled workers. They are currently paid $12 per hour or time and a half for overtime. However, a local agency can provide additional semi-skilled workers for $14 per hour.

What cost should be included in the quotation for skilled labour and semi-skilled labour (to the nearest $)?

Skilled $ [   ]

Semi-skilled $ [   ]

Q28

Of the $3 per hour factory overheads costs, $1.50 per hour reflects the electricity costs of running the cutting machine which will be used to cut the fabric and wood for the sofas. The other $1.50 per hour reflects the cost of the factory supervisor's salary. The supervisor is paid an annual salary and is also paid $15 per hour for any overtime he works. The supervisor will need to work 20 hours' overtime if this order is accepted.

What is the cost which should be included in the quotation for factory overheads (to the nearest $)?

$ [   ]

Q29

Which statement correctly describes the treatment of the general fixed overheads when preparing the quotation?

○ The overheads should be excluded because they are a sunk cost

○ The overheads should be excluded because they are not incremental costs

○ The overheads should be included because they relate to production costs

○ The overheads should be included because all expenses should be recovered

Q30

Which FOUR of the following statements about relevant costing are true?

☐ An opportunity cost will always be a relevant cost even if it is a past cost

☐ Fixed costs are always general in nature and are therefore never relevant

☐ Committed costs are never considered to be relevant costs

☐ An opportunity cost represents the cost of the best alternative forgone

☐ Notional costs are always relevant as they make the estimate more realistic

☐ Avoidable costs would be saved if an activity did not happen and so are relevant

☐ Common costs are only relevant if the viability of the whole process is being assessed

☐ Differential costs in a make or buy decision are not considered to be relevant

Section C

This section of the exam contains **two constructed response questions**.

Each question contains a scenario which relates to one or more requirement(s) which may be split over multiple question screens.

Each question is worth **20 marks** and is compulsory.

This exam section is worth **40 marks** in total.

Important: In your live exam please show all notes/workings that you want the marker to see within the spreadsheet or word processing answer areas. Remember, any notes/workings made on the Scratch Pad or on your workings paper will not be marked.

Select **Next** to continue.

Q31

Carad Co is an electronics company which makes two types of television - plasma screen TVs and LCD TVs. It operates within a highly competitive market and is constantly under pressure to reduce prices. Carad Co operates a standard costing system and performs a detailed variance analysis of both products on a monthly basis. Extracts from the management information for the month of November are shown below:

		Note
Total number of units made and sold	1,400	1
Material price variance	$28,000 A	2
Total labour variance	$6,050 A	3

Notes:

(1) The budgeted total sales volume for TVs was 1,180 units, consisting of an equal mix of plasma screen TVs and LCD screen TVs. Actual sales volume was 750 plasma TVs and 650 LCD TVs. Standard sales prices are $350 per unit for the plasma TVs and $300 per unit for the LCD TVs. The actual sales prices achieved during November were $330 per unit for plasma TV and $290 per unit for LCD TVs. The standard contributions for plasma TVs and LCD TVs are $190 and $180 per unit respectively.

(2) The sole reason for this variance was an increase in the purchase price of one of its key components, X. Each plasma TV made and each LCD TV made requires one unit of component X, for which Carad Co's standard cost is $60 per unit. Due to a shortage of components in the market place, the market price for November went up to $85 per unit for X. Carad Co actually paid $80 per unit for it.

(3) Each plasma TV uses 2 standard hours of labour and each LCD TV uses 1.5 standard hours of labour. The standard cost for labour is $14 per hour and this also reflects the actual cost per labour hour for the company's permanent staff in November. However, because of the increase in sales and production volumes in November, the company also had to use temporary labour at the higher cost of $18 per hour. The total capacity of Carad Co's permanent workforce is 2,200 hours production per month, assuming full efficiency. In the month of November, the workforce were wholly efficient, taking exactly 2 hours to complete each plasma TV and exactly 1.5 hours to produce each LCD TV. The total labour variance therefore relates solely to the temporary workers, who took twice as long as the permanent workers to complete their production.

(a) Calculate the following for the month of November, showing all workings clearly:

(i) The sales price variance and sales volume contribution variance;

(4 marks)

(ii) The material price planning variance and material price operational variance;

(2 marks)

(iii) The labour rate variance and the labour efficiency variance.

(5 marks)

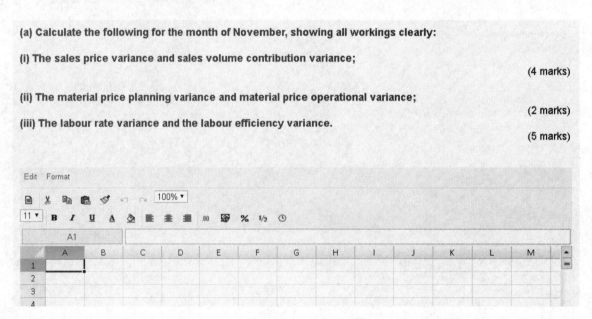

(b) Explain the reasons why Carad Co would be interested in the material price planning variance and the material price operational variance.

(9 marks)

(20 marks)

Q32

Thatcher International Park (TIP) is a theme park and has for many years been a successful business, which has traded profitably. About three years ago the directors decided to capitalise on their success and reduced the expenditure made on new thrill rides, reduced routine maintenance where possible (deciding instead to repair equipment when it broke down) and made a commitment to regularly increase admission prices. Once an admission price is paid customers can use any of the facilities and rides for free.

These steps increased profits considerably, enabling good dividends to be paid to the owners and bonuses to the directors. The last two years of financial results are shown below.

	20X4	20X5
	$	$
Sales	5,250,000	5,320,000
Less expenses:		
Wages	2,500,000	2,200,000
Maintenance - routine	80,000	70,000
Repairs	260,000	320,000
Directors' salaries	150,000	160,000
Directors' bonuses	15,000	18,000
Other costs (including depreciation)	1,200,000	1,180,000
Net profit	**1,045,000**	**1,372,000**
Book value of assets at start of year	13,000,000	12,000,000
Dividend paid	500,000	650,000
Number of visitors	150,000	140,000

TIP operates in a country where the average rate of inflation is around 1% per annum.

(a) Assess the financial performance of TIP using the information given above.

(14 marks)

During the early part of 20X4 TIP employed a newly qualified management accountant. He quickly became concerned about the potential performance of TIP and to investigate his concerns, he started to gather data to measure some non-financial measures of success. The data he has gathered is shown below:

Table 1		
	20X4	**20X5**
Hours lost due to breakdown of rides (Note 1)	9,000 hours	32,000 hours
Average waiting time per ride	20 minutes	30 minutes

Note 1:
TIP has 50 rides of different types. It is open 360 days of the year for ten hours each day.

(b) Assess the QUALITY of the service which TIP provides to its customers using Table 1 and any other relevant data and indicate the RISKS it is likely to face if it continues with its current policies.

(6 marks)

(20 marks)

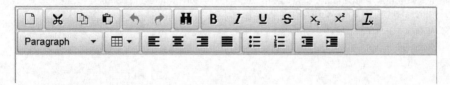

Section 8

ANSWERS TO SPECIMEN EXAM QUESTIONS

SECTION A

Q1 $46.25

Set-up costs per production run = $140,000/28 = $5,000
Cost per inspection = $80,000/8 = $10,000
Other overhead costs per labour hour = $96,000/48,000 = $2

Overhead costs of product D:

	$
Set-up costs (15 x $5,000)	75,000
Inspection costs (3 x $10,000)	30,000
Other overheads (40,000 x $2)	80,000
	185,000

Overhead cost per unit = $185,000/4,000 units = $46.25

Q2 $362.50

Return: $500,000 x 30% = $150,000
Total sales revenue = $550 x 800 = $440,000
Therefore total cost = $440,000 - $150,000 = $290,000
Unit cost = $290,000/800 = $362.50

Q3   18,636 units

The number of units required to make a target profit = (fixed costs + target profit)/contribution per unit of P1.
Fixed costs = ($1.20 x 10,000) + ($1.00 x 12,500) - $2,500 = $22,000
Contribution per unit of P1 = $3.20 + $1.20 = $4.40
($22,000 + $60,000)/$4.40 = 18,636 units

Q3   18,636 units

The number of units required to make a target profit = (fixed costs + target profit)/contribution per unit of P1.

Fixed costs = ($1.20 x 10,000) + ($1.00 x 12,500) - $2,500 = $22,000
Contribution per unit of P1 = $3.20 + $1.20 = $4.40
($22,000 + $60,000)/$4.40 = 18,636 units

Q4   Statements (1) and (4) are correct.

Most organisations do collect data about environmental costs but find it difficult to split them out and categorise them effectively.

Life-cycle costing does allow the organisation to collect information about a product's environmental costs throughout its lifecycle.

The technique which divides material flows into three categories is material flow cost accounting, not input/output analysis

ABC does categorise some costs as environment-driven costs, however, these are costs which are normally hidden within total overheads in a conventional costing system. It is environment-related costs which can be allocated directly to a cost centre.

Q5

Mix variance:

Material	AQSM	AQAM	Difference (litres)	Standard cost ($/litre)	Variance ($)
A	800	900	100 A	20	2,000 A
B	1,200	1,100	100 F	25	2,500 F
	2,000	2,000			500 F

Yield variance:

Material	SQSM	AQSM	Difference (litres)	Standard cost ($/litre)	Variance ($)
A	779	800	21 A	20	420 A
B	1168	1,200	32 A	25	800 A
	(W1)1,947	2,000			1,220 A

Q6

Beyond budgeting attempts to move away from conforming to a rigid annual budget and uses adaptive management processes to encourage management to be responsive to current situations.

An incremental budget builds from the previous year's figures and so any inefficiencies will be carried forward.

Activity-based budgeting is based on the principles of activity-based costing and will attempt to identify the drivers of costs in order to formulate a budget.

Rolling budgeting are budgets which are continuously updated throughout the year by adding a new budget period once the most recent budget period has ended. This means that the budget is always extended one year into the future and so forces managers to reassess plans more regularly.

Flexible budgets are designed to show the changes in financial figures based on different activity levels and so will recognise different cost behaviour patterns.

Zero-based budgeting starts from scratch with each item justified for its inclusion in the budget and so should encourage the identification of waste and non-value adding activities.

Q7

EV for major upgrade = (0.80 x $11m) + (0.2 x $7.5m) = $10.3m
EV for minor upgrade = (0.70 x $9m) + (0.3 x $6m) = $8.1m

Decision

Shutdown and sell	$5.75m
Major upgrade (10.3m - 4.5m)	$5.8m
Minor upgrade ($8.1m - $2m)	$6.1m

As the minor upgrade has the highest expected return that should be the option chosen.

Q8

In a single limiting factor situation products should be ranked based on their contribution per unit of limiting factor, which in this case is labour hours.

Product	A	B	C	D
Contribution per unit ($)	46	52	21	60
Number of labour hours required per unit	6	8	3	2
Contribution per labour hour ($)	7.67	6.50	7.00	30.00
Ranking	2nd	4th	3rd	1st

Q9

Target 1 is measuring the rate of work handled by staff which is an efficiency measure.

Target 2 is assessing output, so is a measure of effectiveness.

Target 3 is a financial measure and so assesses economy factors.

Q10

Transaction processing systems facilitate the immediate processing of data.

Management information systems summarise data from TPS into periodic reports for management to use for decision-making.

Executive information systems draw data from the MIS and support senior managers to make strategic decisions. They usually have dashboard and interactive graphics so that the big picture can be seen.

Enterprise resource planning systems are software packages that integrate all the key processes in an organisation and so this permits data to be shared more easily between departments. It can also have extranet links set up with customers and suppliers.

Q11

Direct data capture is a type of data input in which there is no data entry but instead it is captured for a specific purpose. Therefore the use of bar coding and scanners and the completion of timesheets are examples of direct data capture costs.

Time spent by the payroll department processing personnel costs and the input of data into the production system are examples of process costs.

The sending of emails to staff regarding matters that are not pertinent to them is classed as an inefficient use of information cost.

Q12

Customer life-cycle costing can be used by organisations.

It has been reported that the majority of a products costs are determined early on, i.e. at the design phase.

Life-cycle costing does not include any opportunity costs associated with production.

The growth phase is characterised by a rapid increase in demand.

Q13

Return per factory hour = ($130 – $50)/4 hours = $20
Factory costs per hour = ($20/4) + ($40/4) = $15
TPAR = $20/$15 = 1.33

Q14

Increase in variable costs per unit from buying in ($140 - $100) =$40
Therefore total increase in variable costs (2,200 units x $40) = $88,000
Less the specific fixed costs saved if A is shut down = ($10,000)
Decrease in profit = $78,000

Q15

The determinants of performance are quality, innovation, resource utilisation and flexibility. Competitiveness is a result of the determinants.

Standards should be fair, achievable and staff should have ownership of them. Controllability is a feature of the rewards block.

Rewards should be clear, motivating and controllable.

It is a framework designed to attempt to overcome the problems associated with performance management in service companies.

Q16

Total salon hours = 8 x 6 x 50 = 2,400 each year.

There are three senior stylists, therefore total hours available = 7,200.

Based on the time taken for each activity, they can perform 7,200 cuts (7,200 hours/1 hour per cut) or 4,800 treatments(7,200 hours/1·5 hours per treatment).

Q17

Cuts
Return per hour = (Selling price - materials)/time taken on the bottleneck = (60 - 1.50)/1 = 58.50
TPAR = Return per hour/cost per hour = 58.50/42.56 = 1.37(to 2 decimal places)

Treatments
Return per hour = (Selling price - materials)/time taken on the bottleneck = (110 - 8.90)/1.5 = 67.40
TPAR = Return per hour/cost per hour = 67.40/42.56 = 1.58(to 2 decimal places)

Q18

The factors that are included in the TPAR are selling price, material costs, operating expenses and bottleneck time. Increasing the selling price and reducing costs will improve the TPAR.

Increasing the time which each service takes on the bottleneck (the senior stylists' time) will only reduce the number of services they can provide, so this will not improve throughput.

Throughput accounting does not advocate the building of inventory as it is often used in a just-in-time environment and there is no point increasing the activity prior to the bottleneck as it will just create a build-up of work-in-progress. Neither of these will improve the rate of throughput through the process.

Q19

The existing capacity for each activity is:

	Cut	Treatment
Assistants	48,000	16,000
Senior stylists	7,200	4,800
Junior stylists	8,000	9,600

If another senior stylist is employed, this will mean that their available hours will be (4 x 2,400) = 9,600.
This will give them capacity to now do 9,600 cuts (9,600 hours/1 hour per cut) and 6,400 treatments (9,600 hours/1.5 hours per treatment).

As a result, the senior stylists will still be the bottleneck activity for treatments but for cuts the bottleneck will now be the junior stylists as they can only do 8,000 cuts compared to the senior stylists of 9,600.

Q20

The theory of constraints is focused on identifying restrictions in a process and how to manage that restriction (commonly termed a bottleneck).

It is based on the concept of managing throughput, operating expenses and inventory.

It does use a series of focusing steps but it is not complete once the bottleneck has been overcome. In fact it is an ongoing process of improvement, as once the bottleneck has been elevated it is probable that another bottleneck will appear and the process will continue.

It cannot be applied to all limiting factors as some, particularly those external to the organisation, may be out of the organisation's control.

Q21

Learning curve formula = $y = ax^b$
Cumulative average time per unit for 8 units: $Y = 12 \times 8^{-.415} = 5.0628948$ hours.
Therefore cumulative total time for 8 units = 40.503158 hours.
Cumulative average time per unit for 7 units: $Y = 12 \times 7^{-.415} = 5.3513771$ hours.
Therefore cumulative total time for 7 units = 37.45964 hours.
Therefore incremental time for 8th unit = 40.503158 hours − 37.45964 hours = 3.043518 hours.
Total labour cost for 8th unit = 3.043518 × \$15 = \$45.65277

Q22

Actual learning rate:

Cumulative number of seats produced	Cumulative total hours	Cumulative average hours per unit
1	12.5	12.5
2	?	12.5 x r
4	?	12.5 x r^2
8	34.3	12.5 x r^3

Using algebra: $34 \cdot 3 = 8 \times (12 \cdot 5 \times r^3)$

$4 \cdot 2875 = (12 \cdot 5 \times r^3)$

$0 \cdot 343 = r^3$

$r = 0 \cdot 70$

Therefore the learning rate was 70%

Q23

An 80% learning rate means that the learning was faster than expected.

Factors which are present for a learning curve to take effect are a highly manual and repetitive process (so staff can become quicker the more they perform the same series of tasks), no stoppages to production (so the learning rate will not be lost whilst staff are idle) and a stable workforce (so the learning process does not have to keep restarting).

If there is high staff turnover, stoppages in production and continual design changes, then the learning rate will not be effective and should be slower.

Q24

As marginal costing is based on variable costs it is easier when a readily identifiable variable cost has been established.

The budgeted volume of output does need to be determined for full cost-plus pricing as it would be used to calculate the overhead absorption rate for the calculation of the full cost per unit.

Cost-plus pricing is internally focused and a drawback of the technique is that it fails to consider external influences, like competitor pricing strategies.

The mark-up percentage does not have to be fixed; it can vary and be adjusted to reflect market conditions.

Q25

As the variable cost per unit is changing depending on the production level, contribution for each level needs to be calculated and then the probabilities applied to the outcomes.

Demand (units	Contribution (per unit)	Total contribution	Probability	Expected budgeted contribution
10,000	17.00	170,000	0.3	51,000
22,000	17.00	374,000	0.5	187,000
35,000	17.80	623,000	0.2	124,600
				362,600

Q26

Fabric is in regular use, so the replacement cost is the relevant cost $(200m^2 \times \$17.50) = \$3,500$.

$30m^2$ of wood will have to be ordered in from the alternative supplier but the remaining $20m^2$ which is in inventory and not needed for other work can be used and then replaced by an order from the usual supplier $(30m^2 \times \$8.50) + (20m^2 \times \$8.20) = \$419$.

Q27

Skilled labour:

There is no cost for the first 150 hours as there is spare capacity. The remaining 50 hours required will be paid at time and a half, which is $16 x 1.5 = $24.

50 hours x $24 = $1,200

Semi-skilled labour:

There is no spare capacity so the company will either need to pay overtime or hire in additional staff. The cost of paying overtime would be $18 per hour so it would be cheaper to hire in the additional staff for $14 per hour

300 hours x $14 = $4,200

Q28

The electricity costs are incremental as the machine will be used more to produce the new order (500 hours x $1.50) = $750.

The supervisor's salary is not relevant as it is paid anyway; however, the overtime is relevant (20 hours x $15) = $300.

Q29

The general fixed overheads should be excluded as they are not incremental, i.e. they are not arising specifically as a result of this order.

They are not sunk as they are not past costs. This is a common misconception.

Q30

An opportunity cost does represent the cost of the best alternative forgone, however, if it is an historic (past) cost, it would not be relevant.

Fixed costs can be incremental to a decision and in those circumstances would be relevant.

Committed costs are costs the organisation has already agreed to and can no longer influence and so are not relevant.

Notional costs are used to make cost estimates more realistic; however, they are not real cash flows and are not considered to be relevant.

Avoidable costs are saved if an activity is not undertaken and if this occurs as a result of the decision, then they are relevant.

Common costs are relevant if the whole process is being evaluated; however, they aren't relevant to a further processing decision.

Differential costs are relevant in a make or buy decision as the organisation is trying to choose between two options.

Q31

(i) Sales price variance and sales volume variance

Sales price variance = (actual price − standard price) x actual volume

	Actual price	Standard price	Difference	Actual volume	Sales price variance
	$	$	$		$
Plasma TVs	330	350	−20	750	15,000 A
LCD TVs	290	300	−10	650	6,500 A
					21,500 A

Sales volume contribution variance = (actual sales volume − budgeted sales volume) x standard margin

	Actual sales volume	Budgeted sales volume	Difference	Standard margin	Sales volume variance
				$	$
Plasma TVs	750	590	160	190	30,400 F
LCD TVs	650	590	60	180	10,800 F
	1,400	1,180			41,200 F

(ii) Material price planning and purchasing operational variances

Material planning variance = (original target price − general market price at time of purchase) x quantity purchased
($60 − $85) x 1,400 = $35,000 A

Material price operational variance = (general market price at time of purchase − actual price paid) x quantity purchased
($85 − $80) x 1,400 = $7,000 F

(iii) Labour rate and labour efficiency variances

Labour rate variance = (standard labour rate per hour − actual labour rate per hour) x actual hours worked

Actual hours worked by temporary workers:
Total hours needed if staff were fully efficient = (750 x 2) + (650 x 1·5) = 2,475.
Permanent staff provide 2,200 hours, therefore excess = 2,475 − 2,200 = 275.
However, temporary workers take twice as long, therefore hours worked = 275 x 2 = 550.

Labour rate variance relates solely to temporary workers; therefore ignore permanent staff in the calculation.
Labour rate variance = ($14 − $18) x 550 = $2,200 A

Labour efficiency variance = (standard labour hours for actual production – actual labour hours worked) x standard rate
(275 – 550) x $14 = $3,850 A

Marking scheme

Part	Sub Part		Maximum marks	Marks awarded
a	i	SP var - Plasma	1	
		SP var - LCD	1	
		SV var - Plasma	1	
		SV var - LCD	1	
a	ii	MP planning var	1	
		MP operating var	1	
a	iii	Actual hrs worked	3	
		Labour rate var	1	
		Labour eff var	1	

(b) Explanation of planning and operational variances

Before the material price planning and operational variances were calculated, the only information available as regards material purchasing was that there was an adverse material price variance of $28,000. The purchasing department will be assessed on the basis of this variance, yet, on its own, it is not a reliable indicator of the purchasing department's efficiency. The reason it is not a reliable indicator is because market conditions can change, leading to an increase in price, and this change in market conditions is not within the control of the purchasing department.

By analysing the materials price variance further and breaking it down into its two components – planning and operational – the variance actually becomes a more useful assessment tool. The planning variance represents the uncontrollable element and the operational variance represents the controllable element.

The planning variance is really useful for providing feedback on just how skilled management is in estimating future prices. This can be very easy in some businesses and very difficult in others. Giving this detail could help to improve planning and standard setting in the future, as management will be increasingly aware of factors which could create volatility in their forecasts.

The operational variance is more meaningful in that it measures the purchasing department's efficiency given the market conditions which prevailed at the time. As can be seen in Carad, the material price operational variance is favourable which demonstrates that the purchasing department managed to acquire the component which was in short supply at a better price than expected. Without this breakdown in the variance, the purchasing department could have been held accountable for the overall adverse variance which was not indicative of their actual performance. This is then a fairer method of assessing performance and will, in turn, stop staff from becoming demotivated.

Marking scheme

Part		Maximum marks	Marks awarded
b	Controllability	2	
	MP planning	3	
	MP operating	3	
	Other – plan/oper	1	

Q32

(a) TIP's financial performance can be assessed in a number of ways:

Sales growth

Sales are up about 1·3% (W1) which is a little above the rate of inflation and therefore a move in the right direction. However, with average admission prices jumping about 8·6% (W2) and numbers of visitors falling, there are clearly problems. Large increases in admission prices reduce the value proposition for the customer, it is unlikely that the rate of increase is sustainable or even justifiable. Indeed with volumes falling (down by 6·7% (W6)), it appears that some customers are being put off and price could be one of the reasons.

Maintenance and repairs

There appears to be a continuing drift away from routine maintenance with management preferring to repair equipment as required. This does not appear to be saving any money as the combined cost of maintenance and repair is higher in 20X5 than in 20X4 (possible risks are dealt with in part (b)).

Directors' pay

Absolute salary levels are up 6·7% (W3), well above the modest inflation rate. It appears that the shareholders are happy with the financial performance of the business and are prepared to reward the directors accordingly. Bonus levels are also well up. It may be that the directors have some form of profit related pay scheme and are being rewarded for the improved profit performance. The directors are likely to be very pleased with the increases to pay.

Wages

Wages are down by 12% (W5). This may partly reflect the loss of customers (down by 6·7% (W6)) if it is assumed that at least part of the wages cost is variable. It could also be that the directors are reducing staff levels beyond the fall in the level of customers to enhance short-term profit and personal bonus. Customer service and indeed safety could be compromised here.

Net profit

Net profit is up a huge 31·3% (W7) and most shareholders would be pleased with that. Net profit is a very traditional measure of performance and most would say this was a sign of good performance.

Return on assets

The profitability can be measured relative to the asset base which is being used to generate it. This is sometimes referred to as ROI or return on investment. The return on assets is up considerably to 11·4% from 8% (W8). This is partly due to the significant rise in profit and partly due to the fall in asset value. We are told that TIP has cut back on new development, so the fall in asset value is probably due to depreciation being charged with little being spent during the year on assets. In this regard it is inevitable that return on assets is up but it is more questionable whether this is a good performance. A theme park (and thrill rides in particular) must be updated to keep customers coming back. The directors of TIP are risking the future of the park.

Workings:

(W1) Sales growth is $5,320,000/$5,250,000 = 1·01333 or 1·3%.

(W2) Average admission prices were:
20X4: $5,250,000/150,000 = $35 per person
20X5: $5,320,000/140,000 = $38 per person
An increase of $38/$35 = 1·0857 or 8·57%.

(W3) Directors' pay up by $160,000/$150,000 = 1·0667 or 6·7%.

(W4) Directors' bonuses levels up from $15,000/$150,000 or 10% to $18,000/$160,000 or 12·5% of turnover. This is an increase of 3/15 or 20%.

(W5) Wages are down by (1 – $2,200,000/$2,500,000) or 12%.

(W6) Loss of customers is (1 – 140,000/150,000) or 6·7%.

(W7) Profits up by $1,372,000/$1,045,000 = 1·3129 or 31·3%.

(W8) Return on assets:
20X4: $1,045,000/$13,000,000 = 1·0803 or 8·03%
20X5: $1,372,000/$12,000,000 = 1·114 or 11·4%

Marking scheme

Part		Maximum marks	Marks awarded
a	Sales growth	3	
	Maintenance	3	
	Directors' pay	2	
	Wages	2	
	Net profit	2	
	Return on assets	2	

(b) Quality provision

Reliability of the rides
The hours lost has increased significantly. Equally the percentage of capacity lost due to breakdowns is now approaching 17·8% (W9). This would appear to be a very high number of hours lost. This would surely increase the risk that customers are disappointed being unable to ride. Given the fixed admission price system, this is bound to irritate some customers as they have effectively already paid to ride.

Average queuing time
Queuing will be seen by customers as dead time. They may see some waiting as inevitable and hence acceptable. However, TIP should be careful to maintain waiting times at a minimum. An increase of 10 minutes (or 50%) is likely to be noticeable by customers and is unlikely to enhance the quality of the TIP experience for them. The increase in waiting times is probably due to the high number of hours lost due to breakdown with customers being forced to queue for a fewer number of ride options.

Safety
The clear reduction in maintenance could easily damage the safety record of the park and is an obvious quality issue.

Risks
If TIP continues with current policies, then they will expose themselves to the following risks:

– The lack of routine maintenance could easily lead to an accident or injury to a customer. This could lead to compensation being paid or reputational damage.

– Increased competition. The continuous raising of admission prices increases the likelihood of a new competitor entering the market (although there are significant barriers to entry in this market, e.g. capital cost, land and so on).

– Loss of customers. The value for money which customers see when coming to TIP is clearly reducing (higher prices, less reliability of rides and longer queues). Regardless of the existence of competition, customers could simply choose not to come, substituting another leisure activity instead.

– Profit fall. In the end if customers' numbers fall, then so will profit. The shareholders, although well rewarded at the moment, could suffer a loss of dividend. Directors' job security could then be threatened.

Workings:

(W9) Capacity of rides in hours is 360 days x 50 rides x 10 hours per day = 180,000.
20X4 lost capacity is 9,000/180,000 = 0.05 or 5%.
20X5 lost capacity is 32,000/180,000 = 0.177 or 17.8%.

Marking scheme

Part		Maximum marks	Marks awarded
b	Reliability of rides	2	
	Av queuing time	2	
	Risks	2	